Against Leviathan
Government Power and a Free Society

Against Leviathan

Government Power and a Free Society

Robert Higgs

The **INDEPENDENT**
INSTITUTE

Oakland, California

The Independent Institute
100 Swan Way, Oakland, CA 94621-1428
Telephone: 510-632-1366 • Fax: 510-568-6040
Email: info@independent.org
Website: www.independent.org

Library of Congress Cataloging-in-Publication Data
Higgs, Robert.
Against Leviathan : Government Power and a Free Society / Robert Higgs.
    p. cm.
Articles chiefly published previously beginning in 1981.
Includes bibliographical references and index.
ISBN 0-945999-95-X (hardcover : alk. paper)
ISBN 0-945999-96-8 (pbk. : alk. paper)
1. United States—Economic policy. 2. Power (Social sciences)—United
States. 3. United States—Politics and government—20th century. 4. United
States—Politics and government—2001–   I. Title.
HC106.8.H55 2004
330.973–dc22
                                        2004010052

10 9 8 7 6 5 4 3 2 1

Contents

Acknowledgments

The author and publisher wish to thank the following who have kindly given permission for the use of copyright material.

Critical Review for "Coercion is Not a Societal Constant," *Critical Review* 9 (summer 1995): 431–36; "Origins of the Corporate Liberal State," *Critical Review* 5 (fall 1991): 475–95.

The Foundation for Economic Education for "The Welfare State: Promising Protection in an Age of Anxiety," *Freeman* 46 (May 1996): 260–66; "Nineteen Neglected Consequences of Income Redistribution," *Freeman* 44 (December 1994): 652–57; "The Mythology of Roosevelt and the New Deal," *Freeman* 48 (September 1998): 557–61; "To Deal with a Crisis: Government Program or Free Market?" *Freeman* 36 (September 1986): 331–35.

James D. Gwartney and Richard Wagner for "Can the Constitution Protect Private Property Rights during National Emergencies?" *Public Choice and Constitutional Economics,* ed. James D. Gwartney and Richard Wagner (Greenwich, Conn.: JAI Press, 1988), pp. 369–86.

The Independent Institute for "Public Choice and Political Leadership," *The Independent Review* 1 (winter 1997): 465–67; "Bolingbroke, Nixon, and the Rest of Them," *The Independent Review* 2 (summer 1997): 465–67; "What Professor Stiglitz Learned in Washington," *The Independent Review* 3 (fall 1998): 301–02; "Regulatory Harmonization: A Sweet-Sounding, Dangerous Development," *The Independent Review* 4, (winter 2000): 467–74; "Puritanism, Paternalism, and Power," *The Independent Review* 2 (winter 1998): 469–74; "We're All Sick, and Government Must Heal Us," *The Independent Review* 3 (spring 1999): 623–27; "Lock 'em Up!" *The Independent Review* 4 (fall 1999): 309–13; "Government Protects Us?" *The Independent Review* 7 (fall 2002): 309–13; "Official Economic Statistics: The Emperor's Clothes Are Dirty," *The Independent Review* 3 (summer 1998): 147–53; "A Tale of Two Labor Markets," *The Independent Review* 2 (spring 1998): 625–30; "Death and Taxes," *The Independent Review* 2 (fall 1997): 325–28; "A Carnival of Taxation," *The Independent*

Review 3 (winter 1999): 433–38; "Unmitigated Mercantilism," *The Independent Review* 5 (winter 2001): 469–72; "Results of a Fifty-Year Experiment in Political Economy," *The Independent Review* 5 (spring 2000), 153; "Results of Another Fifty-Year Experiment in Political Economy," *The Independent Review* 5 (spring 2001): 625; "Pity the Poor Japanese," *The Independent Review* 7 (summer 2002): 149–51; "The Cold Was Is Over, but U.S. Preparation for It Continues," *The Independent Review* 6 (fall 2001): 287–305; "Escaping Leviathan?" *The Independent Review* 4 (summer 1999): 153–58; "The So-Called Third Way," *The Independent Review* 4 (spring 2000): 625–30.

Intercollegiate Studies Institute for "Is More Economic Equality Better?" *Intercollegiate Review* 16 (spring–summer 1981): 99–102; "When Ideological Worlds Collide: Reflections on Kraditor's *Radical Persuasion*," *Continuity* (fall 1983): 99–112.

Kluwer Academic Publishers for "On Ackerman's Justification of Irregular Constitutional Change: Is Any Vice You Get Away With a Virtue?" *Constitutional Political Economy* 10 (November 1999): 375–83; "Thank God for the Nation State?" *Review of Austrian Economics* 14 (2001): 355–62.

Liberty Magazine for "The Myth of War Prosperity," *Liberty* 4 (March 1991): 23–26, 30; "Leviathan at Bay?" *Liberty* 5 (November 1991): 64–70; "The Bloody Hinge of American History," *Liberty* 10 (May 1997): 51–57.

The Ludwig von Mises Institute for "Great Presidents?" *The Free Market* (March 1997): 1–3; "War and Leviathan in Twentieth-Century America: Conscription as the Keystone," in *The Costs of War: America's Pyhrric Victories*, ed. John V. Denson (New Brunswick, N.J.: Transaction Publishers, 1997), pp. 309–22; "Defending the Homeland," *The Free Market* (February 2002): 1–2.

Reason Magazine (www.reason.com) for "In the Name of Emergency," *Reason* (July 1987): 36–40; "Beware the Pork-Hawk: In Pursuit of Reelection Congress Sells Out the Nation's Defense," *Reason* 21 (June 1989): 28–34.

The World & I for "Crisis and Quasi-Corporatist Policymaking: The U.S. Case in Historical Perspective," *The World & I* (November 1988): 551–73; "The Rise of Big Business in America," *The World & I* 3 (March 1988): 404–09.

For Elizabeth, who made it possible.

"Love" and "Pontchartrain" don't rhyme. Too bad.

None are more hopelessly enslaved than those who falsely believe they are free.

—Johann Wolfgang von Goethe

Introduction

What should we call the vast hodgepodge of statutes, regulations, court rulings, government bureaus, police departments, law courts, military organizations, and assorted authoritative busybodies under whose weight we Americans are now suffocating? Following Thomas Hobbes, I have settled on the term *Leviathan.* Unlike Hobbes, however, I do not recommend the beast. Instead, I have come, not lightly but in the course of some forty years of studying how it operates, to oppose it root and branch. Finding it to be for the most part wasteful, destructive, and vicious—an insult to every genuinely humane sentiment and ideal—I have concluded that Edmund Burke was right: the thing itself is the abuse. The essays collected in this volume present some of the reasons why I have come to this conclusion.

If I had to use a single word to describe what is fundamentally wrong with government today, I would use the word *fraud.* Certainly nowadays—perhaps in every age—government is not what it claims to be (competent, protective, and just), and it *is* what it claims *not* to be (bungling, menacing, and unjust). In actuality, it is a vast web of deceit and humbug, and not for a good purpose, either. Indeed, its true purposes are as reprehensible as its noble claims are false. Its stock in trade is pretense. The velvet glove of its countless claims of benevolence scarcely conceals its iron fist of violence and threats of more violence. It wants to be loved, but it will settle for being feared. The one thing it will not do is simply leave us alone.

Consider, for example, its vaunted welfare state, the hydra-headed legal and bureaucratic monstrosity with which it pretends to protect the people from every common adversity of life, while taking from the (always guilty) rich in order to give to the (always innocent) poor. As I show in the first three chapters here, this gigantic undertaking fails every moral and practical test imaginable, but it certainly has substantial effects, including the unfortunate ones I describe in chapter 3, "Nineteen Neglected Consequences of Income Redistribution." Nor do these consequences just take their toll once and for all. Far worse, they eat away at the moral, social, and economic foundations of what was once a considerably more honest and self-reliant culture. Societies that have embraced the welfare state have embarked on a course of self-destruction, and we Americans are already well along on that ruinous journey.

As the national government has risen to its imperial heights during the past century, we have been blessed with a succession of glorious leaders. Chief among them, of course, looms the sainted Franklin Delano Roosevelt, now beloved by politicians of both major parties as the kind of strong, compassionate, charismatic leader that all aspirants to the presidency dream of becoming. The received understanding of FDR, however, is sheer bunk, as I show in chapter 4, "The Mythology of Roosevelt and the New Deal." FDR was a wily and successful politician, one must admit; but intelligent, knowledgeable, compassionate, or responsible he was not. That so many came to love this wretched politico testifies sadly to the condition into which the once-proud American people had fallen in the depths of the Great Depression—a tragedy that, notwithstanding the court historians' claims to the contrary, his New Deal policies only worsened and prolonged.

Later presidents, aping the great FDR, fell short of his enduring mass popularity but came close to equaling his duplicity and mendacity, as I suggest in chapter 6, "Bolingbroke, Nixon, and the Rest of Them." If Americans could only hear what the great politicians say in the privacy of their inner sanctums— as the public did when Nixon's secret oval-office tapes became public—they would have a far different impression of their leaders. They might even decide to come after those clown princes with pitchforks.

Adulation of "great presidents" epitomizes the prevailing misunderstanding of the nature of politics and government, as I argue in chapter 5, "Public Choice and Political Leadership." Why, one wonders, is this point so difficult to grasp? People do not expect to find chastity in a whorehouse. Why, then, do they expect to find honesty and humanity in government, a congeries of institutions whose modus operandi consists of lying, cheating, stealing and, if need be, murdering those who resist? The public persists in supposing that good leaders can be found to replace the currently ruling brutes, but ferocious prizefighters do not tend to be replaced by pacifistic Milquetoasts, and in the event that the latter happened to gain office, they would be quickly ousted by the former.

These days the gap between government's pretense of protecting the people and the reality of its harming them is perhaps nowhere greater than in relation to the Food and Drug Administration (FDA), a power-grabbing agency that maintains a tight regulatory grip on goods that account for some 25 percent of the consumer budget. Far from saving lives, as it claims, this organization excels only in public relations, where one must admit it has been fabulously successful. The real outcome of its operations, however, must be counted in terms of hundreds of thousands of premature deaths and unimaginable amounts of human suffering, not to mention its suppression of liberty in the most intimate areas of human life. If people really crave being treated as docile and stupid children, then the FDA is just what they need. Sad to say, as I show in chapter 10, "Regulatory Harmonization: A Sweet-Sounding, Dangerous Development," the kind of despotism practiced by the FDA is presently spreading throughout the world, as governments join forces to crush individual choice and to confine their duped populations in an iron cage of paternalistic tyranny from which they will never escape because any place to which they might flee will be equally bad.

Not content with this faux protective "soft" despotism, the U.S. government has exercised a steel-hard variety in its never-ending "war on drugs." In large part in the performance of this assault on basic liberties, U.S. governments at all levels have now jammed more than 2 million persons into jails and prisons, and subjected more than 4 million others to probation, parole, or some other form of "correctional supervision," as I show in chapter 13, "Lock 'Em Up!" Welcome to the land of the free. Just remember: your body belongs to the state.

Proceeding hand in hand with this quintessential yahoo-Christian crusade we find an advancing secular therapeutic ethos in which every human misstep represents a "disease" from which only a government-imposed treatment can save us, as I discuss in chapter 12, "We're All Sick, and Government Must Heal Us." Thus, a cultural development that might otherwise have been dismissed as merely misguided or silly has greased the skids for ever more intrusive government actions that now penetrate homes, schools, courtrooms, prisons, and a variety of other venues in a quest to save people from their insufficient self-esteem and the manifold maladies to which that insufficiency supposedly gives rise—all of them working under threat of government violence, of course (can't let the inmates run the prison, now can we?).

For the greater part of the past century, the U.S. government—in common with many other, equally presumptuous governments—has undertaken to manage the economy, ostensibly in the public interest. Its doing so presupposes that it knows what to do and that it has an incentive to take the proper actions, but all such presuppositions are complete tomfoolery. The U.S. government no more knows how to manage the economy than I know how to build a perpetual-motion machine, and even if it did know how, it wouldn't do so because there'd be no payoff for the political pirates who preside over the beastly Leviathan. As I show in the essays placed under the rubric of "Economic Disgraces," the government is good at just one thing: stripping the populace of trillions of dollars in the form of taxes, fees, confiscations, and other rip-offs.

Ours is not, of course, the only government capable of such outrages, and in certain respects other governments—including some among the presumably civilized nations—are even worse offenders, as I show in chapter 17, "A Tale of Two Labor Markets" (which pertains to western Europe), and chapter 23, "Pity the Poor Japanese." In chapters 21 and 22, my illustrations of the extremes of government mismanagement, as demonstrated by the economic devastation the central planners wreaked in North Korea and the People's Republic of China, come close to being cases in which the facts really do speak for themselves. Fortunately, in these cases we have excellent natural experiments to confirm our suspicions.

If governments have come to wield vast economic powers, they have done so in large part as a result of the policies and practices they first adopted during great national emergencies, especially during the two world wars. Those wars provided plausible occasions for the adoption of multiple government economic-management schemes—everything from interference in labor-management relations to wage-price controls to central allocations of raw materials. Of all such endeavors, the absolute worst was the conscription of men to serve in the armed forces: in the United States, nearly 3 million during World War I, some 10 million during World War II, and additional millions during the Cold War through 1972, many of the latter serving as cheap cannon fodder in Korea and Vietnam. By this draft, the government proved that it would indeed, as Jack Kennedy promised, pay any price, so long as that price consisted of the lives and liberty of hapless young men. (I propose that the U.S. Congress adopt as its official slogan, "Better you than me, pal.")

Strange to say, the government has always bragged about its plunging the nation into the Big One because, according to the orthodox interpretation, it thereby "got the economy out of the Great Depression." (Why, wouldn't you be willing to sacrifice a few hundred thousand young men's lives in order to get everybody into a regular job?) This experience has been understood ever since in terms of primitive Keynesian macroeconomics; indeed, it did much to fasten that unsound economic theory on the economics profession and the general public in the first place. There's just one problem: no "wartime prosperity" occurred, as I show in chapter 27, "The Myth of War Prosperity." People went to work, all right, those who were not forced into the armed forces, but civilian consumption and investment declined after 1941, and genuine economic recovery did not occur until the demobilization and reconversion of 1945–47. The economy produced plenty of guns and ammo during the war, to be sure, but such production is scarcely the stuff of true prosperity.

The wartime government actions left a multitude of legacies—some institutional, as when emergency laws remained on the statute books or emergency agencies continued to function, and some ideological, as when the people came to accept as normal a variety of government actions they had previously regarded as unconstitutional or beyond the moral or practical pale. Without the government's World War I program, the New Deal would have been well-nigh unthinkable, and without the World War I program and the New Deal, the government never could have achieved the monstrous size and scope of its World War II program. Such contingencies illustrate the notion of "path dependency"—the idea that what is likely to happen next depends to some extent on what has happened in the past. In a social, economic, and political world sub-ject to path dependency, extraordinary occurrences are never just aberrations or statistical "outliers"; they are causal factors in the ongoing stream of events. After World War II ended, the U.S. government quickly launched into fighting the Cold War. It must be admitted that for the major players of the military-industrial-congressional complex (MICC), this was a mighty good deal, as I show in chapter 25, "Crisis and Quasi-corporatist Policymaking," and chapter 29, "Beware the Pork Hawk." Indeed, the deal was so good that when the Cold War ended, the movers and shakers of the MICC decided to keep plowing ahead as if nothing had changed—same force structure, same kinds of weapons, same chronic waste, abuse, and mismanagement. Hey, why give up a good deal if you don't have to! (See chapter 30, "The Cold War Is Over, but U.S. Preparation for It Continues.") The attacks of September 11, 2001, ought to have revealed this military house of cards for the sham that it is, but, of course, when government runs the show, cause and effect don't work normally. No heads rolled; nobody was punished for failing to protect the American peo-ple. Instead, the MICC is now being *rewarded* by the biggest run-up of mili-tary spending in a generation. (For the national-security apparatus, I propose the official slogan, "No failure goes unrewarded.")

Speaking of things that have not been rolled back, I also have something to say here about the oft-encountered idea that the world has entered a new era in which government is in retreat. In some commentators' view, modern technol-ogy has tipped the balance decisively in favor of the public prey, as against the government predator. The Internet, the global capital market, the competition among nation-states for mobile resources—such are the clubs people are now wielding to whack Leviathan away, or so it is argued. I find these arguments greatly exaggerated, as I explain in chapters 31–33 under the interrogatory heading "Retreat of the State?"

In my view, the U.S. government is growing stronger, not weaker, all things considered. Perhaps the most important reason for this ongoing growth of gov-ernment is ideological; it is that so few people in the United States today really give a damn about living as free men and women. After a century of fighting a losing battle against their own governments, the American people have finally accepted that the best course open to them is simply to label their servitude as freedom and to concentrate on enjoying the creature comforts that the govern-ment still permits them to possess. They may be slaves, but they are affluent slaves, and that condition is good enough for them.

*   *   *

Except for one previously unpublished report (which appears here as chapter 9), these essays first appeared in various periodicals and anthologies, and I am grateful for the permissions the original publishers have given for their reuse here. The oldest came forth in 1981, and a half-dozen others during the 1980s, but two thirds of them were published during the past seven or eight years. Almost half were composed for the "Etceteras" feature that I write from time to time in my capacity as editor of *The Independent Review: A Journal of Political Economy*. All are accessible to any intelligent reader with an interest in the topic at hand. Nothing that I have written primarily for professional economists or economic historians appears here. (Another collection to be published soon, *Depression, War, and Cold War: Studies in Political Economy*, contains some of my more demanding and professionally focused papers.)

In preparing the materials of the present volume for republication, I have taken advantage of the opportunity to add documentation, polish the prose, and bring the discussions up to date. Nothing appears here exactly as it did in its first publication. In reworking the seven review essays at the end, however, I have refrained from adding more recent citations to my critical arguments on the grounds that it would be unfair to criticize authors in the light of research that they could not have known about at the time they wrote their own books.

Although I express a definite point of view in these essays, I have also been at pains to present evidence, explanation, and analysis—this book is not just a bunch of op-ed diatribes. Above all, I have sought to express my ideas in clear, forceful, and vivid English. To the extent that I have succeeded in this attempt, the reader may find that at least from time to time the essays provide enjoyment as well as instruction.

Robert Higgs
Covington, Louisiana
February 2004

PART I

Welfare Statism

1

Is More Economic Equality Better?

For most American intellectuals, the answer is obvious. The question itself would strike them as either frivolous or callously reactionary. For the typical intellectual, including the typical economist, it is clear that more economic equality is better. If pressed, the intellectual might offer some kind of argument to support his position, but normally he simply treats it as axiomatic.

I disagree. In doing so, I am not claiming that more economic equality is necessarily worse. I simply insist that the societal distribution of income or wealth itself, whatever it might happen to be, is morally neutral: neither an increase nor a decrease in the degree of inequality has any unambiguous moral meaning. Everything hinges on *why* the distribution changes. Once we know and morally assess the actions that cause the distribution to change, we need go no further. The resulting change in the distribution itself is a statistical artifact, devoid of any moral implications.

The Prevailing Intellectual Position

When I say that the typical intellectual believes more economic equality is better, I am not thinking about wild-eyed radicals or street-corner revolutionaries. I have in mind some of the most respected and influential social scientists in the land. Consider, for example, the statement of Arthur M. Okun, an economist who taught at Yale before serving on the President's Council of Economic Advisers during the 1960s: "Equality in the distribution of incomes ... would be my ethical preference. Abstracting from the costs and the consequences, I would prefer more equality of income to less and would like complete equality best of all."[1]

Henry J. Aaron, an economist and senior fellow at the Brookings Institution who has taught at the University of Maryland and served as assistant secretary for planning and evaluation in the Department of Health, Education and Welfare, has said: "My own perception is that some additional redistribution [from the richer to the poorer via government] will cost almost nothing in freedom, though it will cost something in efficiency, and that it is worth getting."[2]

Christopher Jencks, a Harvard professor of sociology, has gone much further than Okun and Aaron. Jencks concludes his widely discussed (and partially federally funded) book *Inequality* with a remarkable passage urging more government intervention in the distributive process, more envy among the poor, more guilt among the rich, and ultimately a revolutionary restructuring of American society:

> The crucial problem today is that relatively few people view income inequality as a serious problem.... We need to establish the idea that the federal government is responsible for not only the total amount of the national income, but for its distribution ... [;] those with low incomes must cease to accept their condition as inevitable and just.... [T]hey must demand changes in the rules of the game.... [Some] of those with high incomes, must begin to feel ashamed of economic inequality.... [W]e will have to establish political control over the economic institutions that shape our society. This is what other countries usually call socialism.[3]

As a final example, consider the statement of Charles E. Lindblom, a professor of economics and political science at Yale, in his highly acclaimed treatise on the world's political and economic systems *Politics and Markets:*

> It is in communist provision of minimum standards of living and some degree of equality in the distribution of income and wealth that the communist claim to approximate the humanitarian vision ... seems undeniable. On these fronts communist systems have to be credited with great accomplishments, on the whole probably greater than those of the polyarchies.... Inequality in the United States is severe in its [harmful] effects.[4]

Such examples quickly become tedious; their message is clear enough. The prevailing position, not only on the left but also within the mainstream of American social science, is that the existing inequality of income and wealth is unjust. Indeed, most writers routinely employ the words *unequal* and *inequitable* as synonyms, showing no concern for the moral freight borne by this linguistic practice. Hence, not surprisingly, enthusiastic approbation is showered on government policies that promise, either directly or indirectly, to redistribute income from the richer to the poorer.

The Facts about Inequality

Open the *Statistical Abstract* and you will find the "facts" on which most judgments about inequality rest. According to these official data, the lowest fifth of households gets less than 4 percent of the total income (this share having fallen slightly over the past ten years), and the highest fifth gets about 50 percent (this share having risen substantially over the past ten years).[5] The top one percent of households receives about 22 percent of the total income (this share having risen substantially over the past ten years). Economics textbooks reproduce these figures. Economists study and debate them at great length. Intellectuals fashion from them the ammunition for politicians to fire in demagogic salvos.

Yet these figures are virtually worthless. Acceptance of them makes economists either the most gullible or the most dishonest guild on earth. To assess the credibility of the data, one must begin by inquiring into their sources. In fact, they come from the information supplied by people on the census forms collected every ten years or in response to the much smaller Current Population Survey conducted by the Census Bureau as an ongoing project. In both cases, we find out only what people choose to tell us. Of course, people have many reasons to dissemble. A desire to conceal illegally acquired income, a cavalier attitude in responding to the survey, a devotion to privacy in their financial affairs—such are the sources of misreporting. It happens among the rich, the poor, and those in between, but how much is anyone's guess.

Even when people want to be honest and try to be accurate, they forget, miscalculate, or misconstrue the questions. "Household income" is by no means a crystal-clear concept. Just what is a household? And what qualifies as income? Once the data are in hand, should the statistician make his calculations on an annual basis or average them over a longer time span? What adjustments, if any, should be made for differences in age and family size among the income recipients? How much of the money income reported is taken away in individual income and payroll taxes? The answers to these questions are uncertain. To make matters even foggier, the official data neglect whole realms of real income, such as the income in kind received directly from other persons or indirectly in the form of government transfers. As Edgar K. Browning has said, "we really do not know how much redistribution is going on in the present system. . . . How can we talk sensibly about redistributing more if we do not know how much is already being redistributed?"[6]

Still, the statistical issues are secondary. Even if the figures on the societal distribution of income were conceptually unambiguous and numerically precise, the question would remain: Is more equality better? And the answer would still be: not necessarily. To appreciate the basis for this answer, consider some ways in which a more equal societal distribution of income might come about.

Greater Equality: Seven Scenarios

The scenarios I offer here are hypothetical, but they are not impossible. Their lessons, like those of parables, are independent of their degree of descriptive historical veracity.

1. The death rate increases abruptly for persons older than thirty-five. Because older persons have, among other things, accumulated more property and job experience, their average wealth and incomes exceed those of younger persons. To the extent that (average) younger persons inherit the wealth of (average) decedents, the increased mortality among older persons would tend to reduce economic inequality.

2. Young women suddenly find themselves unable to bear children. Because babies do not produce income or accumulate wealth, their presence in society creates economic inequality. Diminished fecundity therefore would tend to reduce economic inequality.

3. A new law requires housewives to enter into paid employment. Because housewives are not rewarded for their efforts in the home by explicit monetary payments, their presence in society increases economic inequality—at least as it is now measured. If all housewives were compelled to earn wages in the paid-labor market, measured economic inequality would decline markedly.

4. A new law requires every worker to switch occupations at least once a year. (Something resembling this requirement has been the policy in communist China at various times during the past fifty years.) Because job experience improves the productivity of workers and leads to higher earnings, the distribution of earnings in an economy where no one could ever escape from the entry level would tend to be more equal, other things being the same.

5. Poor robbers increase their plunder of rich victims. Of course, this reign of Robin Hoods would diminish economic inequality, though the reduction would probably never be detected by the Census Bureau.

6. People develop an aversion to education and training. As in the scenario of annual switching of occupations, the universal refusal to accumulate human capital would tend to place all workers on a more equal footing, and economic inequality would tend to decline.

7. The workweek is legally fixed at twenty hours, and overtime work is outlawed. This trade-union dream come true would tend to equalize the distribution of earnings by making the amounts of labor supplied by various workers more uniform.

To sum up, all of the foregoing scenarios have two characteristics in common. Each entails increased economic equality, and each in its own way is a disaster. Increased mortality, decreased fecundity, forced labor, forced occupational mobility, increased robbery, mass abandonment of education and training, forced unemployment—surely few decent people would argue in their favor. Any increase of measured societal economic equality that arose from such catastrophic events would certainly be considered a spurious indication of increased social well being *if* one knew its origins.

Yet economists and other intellectuals routinely compare the income or wealth distribution between times or places and judge the differences good or bad, depending on whether the measured degree in inequality is less or more, *without giving any consideration to why the differences exist.* This practice bespeaks utter moral blindness. If inequality increases because—in counter-scenarios of those sketched here—older people live longer, women succeed in having the babies they want, more wives choose to work at home, workers switch occupations less frequently, robbery declines, more people acquire advanced education and training, or more workers choose to work full time, can anyone reasonably conclude that society is worse off?

Conclusion

If we know that individual actions are just, that knowledge is all we need in order to make a moral assessment. A supposedly deleterious change in the statistical measure of the societal distribution of income or wealth, should it occur, is simply irrelevant. Changes in such aggregative measures have no moral implications whatever. The error of supposing that more societal equality is necessarily better springs in large part from an even more fundamental error: the implicit assumption that societies are moral agents. Obviously, they are not, nor can they ever be. Society is nothing more than an abstraction, a concept, an intellectual invention. Just as only individuals are economic actors, capable of purposive goal-seeking behavior, so only individuals are moral agents, whose actions we may properly describe as ethical or unethical. Moral individual actions, like immoral individual actions, may produce either more or less societal inequality, depending on their precise character. Some rich individuals steal from some poor persons, and vice versa. Some rich persons voluntarily transfer their wealth to some poor individuals, and vice versa. Any changes in the aggregative statistical profile brought about by such complex and variable individual behavior are wholly uninformative for purposes of a moral assessment. In their simple-minded moral judgments about differences in societal distributions, many intellectuals have committed astonishingly blatant errors. They could have saved themselves from these blunders had they kept their eyes focused on the only true economic and moral agent, the individual human being.

Notes

1. Arthur M. Okun, *Equality and Efficiency: The Big Tradeoff* (Washington, D.C.: Brookings Institution, 1975), p. 47.

2. Comments on a paper by Okun in *Income Redistribution,* edited by Colin Campbell (Washington, D.C.: American Enterprise Institute for Public Policy Research, 1977), p. 46.

3. Christopher Jencks, *Inequality: A Reassessment of the Effect of Family and Schooling in America* (New York: Harper Colophon Books, 1973), pp. 263–65.

4. Charles E. Lindblom, *Politics and Markets: The World's Political-Economic Systems* (New York: Basic Books, 1977), pp. 266 and 268.

5. For data for the period 1967–2000, see U.S. Bureau of the Census, "Historical Income Tables—Households," at http://www.census.gov/hhes/income/histinc.h02.html.

6. Comments on papers by Cohen and Nisbet in *Income Redistribution,* ed. Campbell, p. 208. Attempts to transform the official data into more meaningful distributions include Edgar K. Browning, "The Trend Toward Equality in the Distribution of Net Income," *Southern Economic Journal* 43 (July 1976): 912–23; and Morton Paglin, "Poverty in the United States: A Reevaluation," *Policy Review* 8 (spring 1979): 7–24.

2

The Welfare State
Promising Protection in an Age of Anxiety

More and more we ... debate what government should do—what it should do in a providential manner for people more than people can do for themselves, how it shall confer upon them welfare, security, happiness—forgetting that though an omnipotent government were able to confer these blessings, it would be obliged at the same time to confer upon people also the status of servility.

—Garet Garrett, 1935, *Salvos Against the New Deal: Selections from the* Saturday Evening Post, *1933–1940*

Anxiety, according to *The Random House Dictionary,* denotes "distress or uneasiness of mind caused by apprehension of danger or misfortune." By this definition, the twentieth century qualifies as an age of anxiety for Americans.

There is irony in this condition because in many respects we twentieth-century (now become twentieth-first-century) Americans enjoy much more security than our forebears ever did. Our life expectancy is longer, our work easier and more remunerative, our style of life more comfortable, stimulating, and unconstrained. Yet, notwithstanding all objective indications that our lives are better than those of our ancestors, we have become incessant worriers.

Our predecessors dealt with their worries by relying on religious faith. For tangible assistance, they turned to kinfolk, neighbors, friends, and coreligionists, as well as to comrades in lodges, mutual benefit societies, ethnic associations, labor unions, and a vast assortment of other voluntary groups. Those who fell between the cracks of the families, churches, and voluntary societies received assistance from cities and counties, but governmentally supplied assistance was kept meager and its recipients stigmatized.

In the twentieth century, especially after the onset of the Great Depression, Americans came to place their faith in government, increasingly in the federal government. When Franklin Delano Roosevelt assumed the presidency in 1933, voluntary relief quickly took a back seat to government assistance. Eventually, hardly any source of distress remained unattended by a government program. Old age, unemployment, illness, poverty, physical disability, loss of spousal support, child-rearing needs, workplace injury, consumer misfortune, foolish investment, borrowing blunder, traffic accident, environmental hazard, loss from flood, fire, or hurricane—all became subject to government succor.

Our ancestors relied on themselves; we rely on the welfare state. The "safety net" that governments have stretched beneath us, however, seems more and more to be a spider's web in which we are entangled and from which we must extricate ourselves if we are to preserve or perhaps regain a prosperous *and* free society.

Bismarck, Soldiers, and Mothers

The modern welfare state is often seen as originating in Imperial Germany in the 1880s, when the Iron Chancellor, Prince Otto von Bismarck, established compulsory accident, sickness, and old-age insurance for workers. Bismarck was no altruist. He intended his social programs to divert workers from revolutionary socialism and to purchase their loyalty to the kaiser's regime; to a large extent he seems to have achieved his objectives.

In the late nineteenth century, no aspiring American social scientist regarded his education as complete without a sojourn in a German university, and the impressionable young men brought back to the United States a favorable view of Bismarckian social policies absorbed from the teachings of Deutschland's state-worshipping professoriate.[1] Men such as Richard T. Ely, Edward A. Ross, Henry Carter Adams, and Simon Patten transported ideas and outlooks that persisted through several generations.[2] Consider, as but one example, that Edwin Witte, the chief architect of the Social Security Act of 1935, was a student of John R. Commons, who was a student of Ely, whom Joseph Schumpeter described as "that excellent German professor in an American skin."[3].

While Ely and the others were preaching their Germanic doctrines in the late nineteenth and early twentieth centuries, an incipient welfare state was emerging quite independently in the United States through a far-reaching expansion of the pensions provided to Union veterans of the Civil War. Originally the pensions went only to men with proven service-related disabilities and to their dependent survivors, but politicians, especially the Republicans, soon recognized that they could buy votes by dispensing the pensions more liberally. Eligibility rules were stretched further and further. Eventually no service-related disability needed to be proved, no combat experience was required, and old age alone was sufficient for a veteran to qualify. Some congressmen even went so far as to change the official military records of deserters in order to award them pensions through special acts of Congress.[4]

Between 1880 and 1910, the federal government devoted about a quarter of its spending to veterans' pensions. By the latter date, more than half a million men, approximately 28 percent of all those age sixty-five or older, were receiving pensions, as were more than three hundred thousand dependent survivors of veterans. Moreover, thousands of old soldiers lived in homes maintained by the federal government or by the states.[5]

That politicians turned the legitimate pension system for injured veterans and their survivors into a political patronage machine should hardly come as a surprise. Buying votes and dispensing patronage are what elected politicians normally do unless rigidly constrained. The doleful profligacy of the Civil War pension system might well have served as a warning, and for a while it did, but eventually the lesson was forgotten.

During the first three decades of the twentieth century, when middle-class political groups generally refused to support proposals for comprehensive so-cial-spending programs on the grounds that elected politicians would abuse them, women's organizations including the General Federation of Women's Clubs and the National Congress of Mothers lobbied successfully for the es-tablishment of state mothers' pensions.[6] These small, locally administered stipends went to "respectable impoverished widows" to allow them to care for children at home. Between 1911 and 1928, forty-four states authorized such payments.[7] In 1935, with passage of the Social Security Act, the federal gov-ernment joined forces with the states in financing an extension of the mothers' pensions, Aid to Dependent Children (ADC)—later called Aid to Families with Dependent Children (AFDC), which ultimately became nearly synony-mous with "welfare."

In addition, during the second decade of the twentieth century, all but six states enacted workmen's compensation laws, which removed workplace injury claims from the courts and required that employers carry insurance to pay com-pensation for various types of injury under a system of strict liability.[8]

The First Cluster, 1933–1938

Between 1929 and 1933, the economic contraction left millions of Americans destitute. State and local governments, straining to provide unprecedented amounts of relief while their own revenues were shrinking, called on the fed-eral government for help. President Herbert Hoover opposed federal involve-ment in relief efforts, but he reluctantly signed the Emergency Relief and Con-struction Act of 1932, which transferred federal funds to the states for relief of the unemployed (under the fiction that the transfers were loans).

After Franklin Delano Roosevelt took office, the federal government im-mediately launched vast relief activities. The Federal Emergency Relief Admin-istration (FERA), directed by welfare czar Harry Hopkins, channeled funds to the states—half in matching grants (one dollar for three dollars) and half in dis-cretionary grants. The money went to work-relief projects for the construction of roads, sewers, and public buildings; to white-collar beneficiaries such as teachers, writers, and musicians; and to unemployable persons including the blind, the physically disabled, the elderly, and mothers with young children.[9]

Hopkins's discretionary allocations and his oversight of the federal money embroiled the FERA in political controversy. Politicians fought fiercely for control of the patronage inherent in determining who would get the relief money and the jobs and who would fill the 150,000 administrative positions. According to Jeremy Atack and Peter Passell, "Governor Martin Davey of Ohio had an arrest warrant sworn out for Hopkins should he set foot in the state, and a number of politicians, the most notable being Governor William Langer of North Dakota, were convicted of misusing funds and served time in jail."[10]

Also in 1933, Congress created the Civilian Conservation Corps to put young men to work in outdoor projects under quasi-military discipline; the Public Works Administration to employ people in building public works such as dams, hospitals, and bridges; and the Civil Works Administration to operate hastily contrived federal make-work projects for more than 4 million of the unemployed during the winter of 1933–34.

In 1935, with 7.5 million workers (more than 14 percent of the labor force) still unemployed and another 3 million hired only for emergency relief jobs,[11] Congress passed the Emergency Relief Appropriation Act, under the authority of which FDR created the Works Progress Administration (WPA) to hire the unemployed. The president appointed Hopkins to act as the WPA's administrator. By the time the WPA was terminated eight years later, it had paid out more than $10 billion for 13.7 million person-years of employment, for the most part in construction projects but also in a wide range of white-collar jobs, including controversial support for actors, artists, musicians, and writers.[12]

Like the FERA, the WPA engaged the ambitions of state and local politicians in a "cooperatively administered" arrangement that set a pattern for many subsequent welfare programs. Under federally issued guidelines and with mainly federal funding, state and local officials secured substantial control of the patronage. Local governments usually designed the projects, selecting workers from their relief rolls and bearing a small portion of the costs. The Republicans correctly viewed the WPA as a massive Democratic vote-buying scheme. WPA projects were frequently ridiculed, as in the following stanzas of a contemporary song:

We're not plain every day boys,
Oh, no, not we.
We are the leisurely playboys
Of industry,
Those famous little WPA boys
Of Franklin D.

Here we stand asleep all day
While F. D. shooes the flies away
We just wake up to get our pay
What for? For leaning on a shovel.[13]

The spirit of this song persisted ever afterward, as many tax-paying private employees have resented those employed in government make-work projects (often described in later times as "training" programs).

During the first two years of his presidency, FDR came under growing pressure from more radical politicians. Louisiana senator Huey Long touted his Share Our Wealth Plan for a sweeping redistribution of income and gained a national following in 1934 and 1935. Simultaneously, California physician Francis Townsend recruited millions of supporters for his Townsend Plan, under which people older than sixty years of age could retire and receive from the government a monthly stipend of $200 on the condition that all the money be spent within thirty days. To head off the mass appeal of such outlandish proposals, FDR formed in 1934 the Committee on Economic Security, whose executive director was Edwin Witte, to formulate a plan for a national social-security system.

This planning bore fruit in 1935, when Congress passed the Social Security Act, the foundation of America's welfare state. The act gave federal matching funds to the states for assistance to the aged poor, the blind, and dependent children. It levied a payroll tax, 90 percent of which would be refunded to states that established acceptable unemployment insurance systems. (All of them did.) And it created a national old-age pension program disguised as insurance but actually, especially after amendments in 1939 added surviving dependents as recipients, a scheme for transferring current income from workers to nonworkers.

From that time forward, defenders of the pension system denied that it was a "welfare" program for redistributing income. "It was portrayed instead as a huge set of public piggy banks into which individual prospective 'beneficiaries' put away 'contributions' for their own eventual retirements."[14] In the 1950s, 1960s, and 1970s, congressional incumbents turned the pension system into a fabulous vote-buying machine, as they repeatedly extended its coverage, added disability insurance in 1956, raised the benefits, and even, in 1972, indexed the pensions to protect them from inflation. Only in the 1990s did a substantial portion of the public begin to recognize that the piggy bank depiction was a myth and that the system faced bankruptcy as the ratio of taxpayers to recipients slipped ever lower because of demographic changes.[15]

As the New Deal was breathing its last in 1938, it brought forth the Fair Labor Standards Act. This act established a national minimum wage (originally twenty-five cents per hour for covered employees but scheduled to rise to forty cents over seven years); fixed a maximum work week (originally forty-four hours but scheduled to fall to forty by 1940); set a 50 percent premium for overtime work; prohibited the employment of children under sixteen years of age in most jobs; and authorized the Department of Labor to enforce the law.[16] Afterward, Congress raised the minimum wage repeatedly. It is now (early in 2002) $5.15 per hour. This pseudowelfare measure has proven to be an effective means of actually increasing the unemployment rate of low-productivity workers—those who are young, ill-educated, or inexperienced—but continuing support by leftist politicians and labor unions has prevented its repeal.

The GI Bill

In the spring of 1944, with elections looming and 11.5 million men—most of them draftees—in the armed forces, FDR and Congress saw the wisdom of accepting the American Legion's proposals to create unprecedented benefits for veterans: hence the Servicemen's Readjustment Act, popularly known as the GI Bill of Rights. Besides guaranteeing medical care in special veterans' hospitals, the law provided for pensions and vocational rehabilitation for disabled veterans; occupational guidance; unemployment benefits for up to fifty-two weeks; guaranteed loans for the purchase of homes, farms, or businesses; and stipends and living allowances for up to four years for veterans continuing their education.[17] Most of the 16 million veterans of World War II took advantage of the unemployment and educational benefits. In addition, by 1962 the Veterans' Administration had insured more than $50 billion in loans.[18]

Even though the veterans' program applied to only a minority of the total population, it helped to retain the momentum of the burgeoning welfare state. "When the steam appeared to have escaped from the engine of the New Deal by 1945, the World War II nondisabled veterans' benefits—by design and chance—provided new sources of energy."[19] The GI Bill set an irresistible precedent, and later legislation provided similar benefits for veterans of the Korean War and, in 1966, even for those who served in the armed forces in peacetime.[20]

The Second Cluster, 1964–1972

With the succession of the ambitious New Dealer Lyndon B. Johnson to the presidency, the drive to build the welfare state became ascendant again. The election of 1964 brought into office a large, extraordinarily statist Democratic majority in Congress. Keynesian economists assured the public that they could fine-tune the economy, taking for granted a high rate of economic growth from which the government could reap a perpetual "fiscal dividend" to fund new programs. John Kenneth Galbraith, Michael Harrington, and other popular social critics condemned the market system's failures and ridiculed its defenders. The public seemed prepared to support new measures to fight a "war on poverty," establish "social justice," and end racial discrimination. Hence the Great Society.[21]

Congress loosed a legislative flood by passing the Civil Rights Act of 1964. Among other things, in an attempt to quash racial discrimination this landmark statute set aside private-property rights and private rights of free association. The ideal of a color-blind society, however, died an early death, succeeded within a few years by "affirmative action"—an array of racial and other preferences enforced by an energetic Equal Employment Opportunity Commission and enthusiastic federal judges.[22]

Congress proceeded to pass a variety of laws that injected the federal government ever more deeply into education, job training, housing, and urban redevelopment. The Food Stamp Act of 1964 gave rise to one of the government's most rapidly growing benefit programs: in 1969 fewer than 3 million persons received such stamps, and federal outlays totaled $250 million; in 1981, 22 million persons received the stamps, and federal outlays totaled $11 billion.[23] The Community Action Program aimed to mobilize the poor and raise their incomes. When Congress appropriated $300 million to create community-action agencies, a wild scramble to get the money ensued, led by local politicians and, in some cities, by criminal gangs—as vividly portrayed in Tom Wolfe's tragicomic tale *Mau-Mauing the Flak Catchers* (1970).

In 1965, Medicare was added to the Social Security system, ensuring medical care for everyone older than sixty-five years of age. Medicaid, a cooperatively administered and financed program (state and federal), assured medical care for welfare recipients and the medically indigent. As usual, these programs were not exactly what they were represented to be. "Most of the government's medical payments on behalf of the poor compensated doctors and hospitals for services once rendered free of charge or at reduced prices," historian Allen J. Matusow has observed. "Medicare-Medicaid, then, primarily transferred income from middle-class taxpayers to middle-class health-care professionals."[24]

The federal government's health programs also turned out to be fiscal time bombs. Between 1970 and 2000, in constant (1996) dollars, Medicare outlays increased from $20.8 billion to $181.2 billion; the federal portion of Medicaid from $9.9 billion to $109.8 billion.[25] Like the old-age pensions, these programs achieved rates of growth that could not be sustained indefinitely.

Other Great Society measures to protect people from their own incompetence or folly included the Traffic Safety Act (1966), the Flammable Fabrics Act (1967), and the Consumer Credit Protection Act (1968).

After Richard Nixon became president, highly significant measures continued to pour forth from Congress—the National Environmental Policy Act (1969), the Clean Air Act Amendments (1970), the Occupational Safety and Health

Act (1970), the Consumer Product Safety Act (1972), the Water Pollution Control Act (1972), and the Equal Employment Opportunity Act (1972), to name but a few. Nixon also wielded his congressionally authorized power to impose comprehensive wage-and-price controls between 1971 and 1974, thereby (spuriously) protecting the public from the inflation created by the Federal Reserve System's intemperate monetary policies.

The Welfare State Marches On

Although the growth of the welfare state has slowed during the past twenty years, it has scarcely stopped. The reform of the family-assistance program enacted in 1996 signaled a partial retreat on one front, but the staying power of that reform remains much in doubt,[26] and as I write (early in 2002), unemployment-insurance claims and the welfare rolls are growing rapidly as a result of the national economic recession.[27] Such recent measures as the Clean Air Act Amendments (1990), the Nutrition Labeling and Education Act (1990), the Safe Medical Devices Act (1990), the Civil Rights Act (1991), the Health Insurance Portability and Accountability Act (1996), and the relentless power grabs of the Food and Drug Administration show that our rulers remain as determined as ever to protect us from ourselves—to treat us as a shepherd treats his flock, and with no more regard for our intelligence and our rights.

If we cared nothing for our own freedom, we might be inclined to accept the welfare state's ministrations with gratitude, but even then our contentment would be disturbed by the large extent to which the government fails to deliver what it promises. To be blunt, the government's protection is largely fraudulent. Officials pretend to protect citizens and to promote social harmony while actually accomplishing the opposite. Thus, the government's affirmative action programs have actually fostered racial acrimony and conflict rather than racial harmony.[28] The environmental laws have caused many billions of dollars to be squandered in mandated actions for which costs vastly exceed benefits.[29] And the Food and Drug Administration, far from improving public health, has caused (at least) hundreds of thousands of excess deaths and untold human suffering.[30] It is bad enough that citizens are viewed as sheep; it is worse that they are sheared and slaughtered.[31]

Fifty years ago, Bertrand de Jouvenel wrote, "The essential psychological characteristic of our age is the predominance of fear over self-confidence.... Everyone of every class tries to rest his individual existence on the bosom of the state and tends to regard the state as the universal provider." But this protection costs the public far more than the high taxes that fund its provision because "if the state is to guarantee to a man what the consequences of his actions shall be, it must take control of his activities ... to keep him out of the way of risks."[32]

In the interval since Jouvenel wrote those lines, the demand for government protection has risen to new heights, and the corresponding loss of individual liberties has proceeded apace.

If we are to regain our liberties, we must reassert our responsibilities for ourselves, accepting the consequences of our own actions without appealing to the government for salvation. To continue on the road we Americans have traveled for the past century is ultimately to deliver ourselves completely into the hands of an unlimited government. It will not matter if democratic processes lead us to that destination. As noted previously, the making of the welfare state has been from the very beginning a matter of politicians' corrupt vote buying and patronage dispensing—democracy in action: "And one sad servitude alike denotes / The slave that labours and the slave that votes."[33] We can have a free society or a welfare state. We cannot have both.

Notes

1. Dorothy Ross, *The Origins of American Social Science* (Cambridge, Eng.: Cambridge University Press, 1991), pp. 104–6.

2. Murray N. Rothbard, "Richard T. Ely: Paladin of the Welfare-Warfare State," *The Independent Review* 6 (spring 2002): 585–89.

3. Joseph A. Schumpeter, *History of Economic Analysis* (New York: Oxford University Press, 1954), p. 874.

4. Theda Skocpol, "America's First Social Security System: The Expansion of Benefits for Civil War Veterans," in *Social Policy in the United States: Future Possibilities in Historical Perspective* (Princeton, N.J.: Princeton University Press, 1995), p. 63.

5. Ibid., p. 37.

6. Theda Skocpol, "Gender and the Origins of Modern Social Policies in Britain and the United States," in *Social Policy,* pp. 114–29.

7. Ibid., pp. 74, 76.

8. Herman M. Somers, "Workmen's Compensation," *International Encyclopedia of the Social Sciences,* vol. 16 (New York: Macmillan and the Free Press, 1968), pp. 572–76; Price V. Fishback and Shawn Everett Kantor, *A Prelude to the Welfare State: The Origins of Workers' Compensation* (Chicago: University of Chicago Press, 2000), pp. 103–4.

9. Searle F. Charles, "Federal Emergency Relief Administration," in *Franklin D. Roosevelt: His Life and Times,* edited by Otis L. Graham Jr. and Meghan Robinson Wander (Boston: G. K. Hall, 1985), pp. 132–33.

10. Jeremy Atack and Peter Passell, *A New Economic View of American History from Colonial Times to 1940,* 2d ed. (New York: Norton, 1994), p. 670.

11. Michael R. Darby, "Three-and-a-Half Million U.S. Employees Have Been Mislaid: Or, an Explanation of Unemployment, 1934–1941," *Journal of Political Economy* 84 (February 1976), p. 7.

12. Lester V. Chandler, *America's Greatest Depression, 1929–1941* (New York: Harper and Row, 1970), pp. 203–5.

13. John LaTouche, "Leaning on a Shovel," reprinted in Richard D. McKinzie, "Works Progress Administration," in *Franklin D. Roosevelt,* ed. Graham and Wander, p. 462. Econometric historians have tried to determine how much of the New Deal's relief spending reflects playing politics. See John Joseph Wallis, "Employment, Politics, and Economic Recovery During the Great Depression," *Review of Economics and Statistics* 69 (August 1987): 516–20.

14. Theda Skocpol, with G. John Ikenberry, "The Road to Social Security," in *Social Policy,* p. 162.

15. Bipartisan Commission on Entitlement and Tax Reform, *Interim Report to the President* (Washington, D.C.: Government Printing Office, August 1994), pp. 14–15, 18–19.

16. Chandler, *America's Greatest Depression,* p. 237; Gregory King, "Wages and Hours Legislation," in *Franklin D. Roosevelt,* ed. Graham and Wander, p. 438.

17. Jack Stokes Ballard, *The Shock of Peace: Military and Economic Demobilization after World War II* (Washington, D.C.: University Press of America, 1983), pp. 48–49.

18. "G.I. Bill," in *The Reader's Companion to American History,* edited by Eric Foner and John A. Garraty (Boston: Houghton Mifflin, 1991), p. 449.

19. Davis R. B. Ross, *Preparing for Ulysses: Politics and Veterans During World War II* (New York: Columbia University Press, 1969), p. 290.

20. Ibid.

21. Robert Higgs, *Crisis and Leviathan: Critical Episodes in the Growth of American Government* (New York: Oxford University Press, 1987), pp. 246–51.

22. Nathan Glazer, *Affirmative Discrimination* (New York: Basic Books, 1975); Thomas Sowell, *Civil Rights: Rhetoric or Reality?* (New York: William Morrow, 1984), pp. 38–42.

23. Edgar K. Browning and Jacquelene M. Browning, *Public Finance and the Price System,* 2d ed. (New York: Macmillan, 1983), p. 128.

24. Allen J. Matusow, *The Unraveling of America: A History of Liberalism in the 1960s* (New York: Harper and Row, 1984), pp. 231–32.

25. U.S. Office of Management and Budget, *Budget of the United States Government: Historical Tables, Fiscal Year 2002* (Washington, D.C.: Superintendent of Documents, 2001), pp. 134, 138.

26. Robert Higgs, "Why the Welfare Reform Will Fail," *San Diego Union-Tribune,* October 25, 1996.

27. For a graph of unemployment claims, 1967–2001, see http://www.brook.edu/wrb/resources/facts/claims.htm; on the recent increase in welfare rolls, see Tony Pugh, "Recession Is Testing Welfare Changes. In 33 States, Layoffs and Hiring Freezes Have Triggered a Rise in the Rolls," *Philadelphia Inquirer,* at http://inq.philly.com/content/inquirer/2002/01/28/national/WELFARE28.htm.

28. Thomas Sowell, *Preferential Policies: An International Perspective* (New York: William Morrow, 1990).

29. William C. Mitchell and Randy T. Simmons, *Beyond Politics: Markets, Welfare, and the Failure of Bureaucracy* (Boulder, Colo.: Westview Press, for The Independent Institute, 1994), pp. 146–62.

30. Dale H. Gieringer, "The Safety and Efficacy of New Drug Approval," *Cato Journal* 5 (spring–summer 1985): 177–201; Robert M. Goldberg, "Breaking Up the FDA's Med-

ical Information Monopoly," *Regulation,* no. 2 (1995): 40–52; Robert Higgs, ed., *Hazardous to Our Health? FDA Regulation of Health Care Products* (Oakland, Calif.: The Independent Institute, 1995).

31. The latest flimflam protection is the federal takeover of airport security. See John Tierney, "Is a U.S. Force the Safest Bet for Airports?" *New York Times,* October 16, 2001; and Robert Higgs, "Don't Federalize Airport Security," *San Francisco Business Times,* October 22, 2001. Equipping the pilots with pistols would do more to prevent terrorists from taking over the airplanes than all the costly and degrading procedures put in place by the federal security bosses.

32. Bertrand de Jouvenel, *On Power: The Natural History of Its Growth,* translated by J. F. Huntington (Indianapolis, Ind.: Liberty Fund, 1993; original French edition 1945), pp. 388–89.

33. Peter Pindar's lines as quoted in ibid., p. 353.

3

Nineteen Neglected Consequences of Income Redistribution

Virtually every government action changes the personal distribution of income, but some government programs, which give money, goods, or services to individuals who give nothing in exchange, represent income redistribution in its starkest form.

Until the twentieth century, governments in the United States steered pretty clear of such "transfer payments." The national government gave pensions and land grants to veterans, and local governments provided food and shelter to the destitute, but the transfers to veterans might best be regarded as deferred payments for military services, and the local relief never amounted to much.

Since the creation of the Social Security system in 1935, especially during the past thirty-five years, the amount of income overtly transferred by governments has risen dramatically. In 1965, government transfer payments to persons amounted to less than $36 billion, or 6.4 percent of personal income. In 1999, the total came to $1,016 billion, or 13 percent of personal income. In other words, more than one dollar out of every eight received as personal income now takes the form of old-age, survivors, disability, and health insurance benefits ($588 billion); unemployment-insurance benefits ($20 billion); veterans' benefits ($24 billion); family assistance payments ($18 billion); and miscellaneous other government transfer payments ($366 billion), including government employees' retirement benefits, federal payments to farmers, and state and local public assistance to poor people.[1]

Myth Versus Reality

It is tempting to think about government transfers in a simple way: one person, taxpayer T, loses a certain amount of money; another person, recipient R, gains the same amount; and everything else remains the same. When people view income redistribution in this way, they tend to make a judgment about the desirability of the transfer simply by considering whether T or R is the more deserving. Commonly, in particular when the issue is discussed in the news media or by left-liberal politicians, R is portrayed as a representative of the poor and downtrodden and T as a wealthy person or a big corporation. From this point of view, opponents of the transfers appear callous and lacking in compassion for the less fortunate.

In fact, the overwhelming portion—more than 85 percent—of all government transfer payments is not "means-tested"—that is, not reserved for low-income recipients.[2] The biggest share goes to the elderly in the form of old-age pensions and Medicare benefits, and anyone at least sixty-five years old, rich and poor alike, can receive these benefits. Today, people older than sixty-five have the highest income per person and the highest wealth per person of any age group in the United States. Federal transfer payments to farmers present an even more extreme case of giving to those who are already relatively well off. In 1989, for example, the federal government paid about $15 billion to farmers in direct crop subsidies, and 67 percent of the money went to the owners of the largest 17 percent of the farms. Thus, in many cases, payments to farmers are literally welfare for millionaires.[3] It is simply a hoax that, as a rule, government is taking from the rich for the benefit of the poor. Even people who believe in the rectitude of redistribution à la Robin Hood ought to be troubled by the true character of the redistribution being effected by governments in America today.

Apart from the troubling moral questions raised by redistribution, the issue is far more complicated than ordinarily considered. Beyond the naked fact that T pays taxes to the government and the government gives goods, services, or money to R, at least nineteen other consequences occur when the government redistributes income.

Neglected Consequences

1. Taxes for the purpose of income redistribution discourage the taxpayers from earning taxable income or from raising the value of taxable property through investment. People who stand to lose part of their earnings respond to the altered personal payoff. As a result, they produce fewer goods and services and accumulate less wealth than they otherwise would. Hence, the society is made poorer, both now and later.

2. Transfer payments discourage the recipients from earning income in the present and from investing in their potential to earn income in the future. People respond to a reduced cost of idleness by choosing to be idle more often. When they can get current income without earning it, they exert less effort to earn income. When they expect to get future income without earning it, they invest less in education, training, job experience, personal health, migration, and other forms of human capital that enhance their potential to earn income

in the future. Hence, the society is made even poorer, both now and later, than it would have been—merely because taxes discourage current production and investment by the taxpayers who fund the transfers.

3. Recipients of transfers tend to become less self-reliant and more dependent on government payments. When people can get support without exercising their own abilities to discover and respond to opportunities for earning income, those abilities atrophy. People forget—or never learn in the first place—how to help themselves, and eventually some of them simply accept their helplessness. It is no accident that both material privation and lassitude have distinguished the individuals accustomed to living on payments from Aid to Families with Dependent Children (AFDC) or from its post-1996 successor Temporary Assistance for Needy Families (TANF).

4. Recipients of transfers set a bad example for others, including their children, other relatives, and friends, who see that one can receive goods, services, or money from the government without earning them. The onlookers easily adopt an attitude that they, too, are entitled to such transfers. They have fewer examples of hardworking, self-reliant people in their families or neighborhoods. Hence, a culture of dependency on government transfers can become pervasive when many people in a neighborhood rely on such transfers for life's essentials or—where the recipients are better off—for its comforts.

5. Because some transfers are more generous than others, some classes of recipients come to resent the "injustice" of the distribution of the largess. Hence arise political conflicts. Representatives of discontented groups politicize the determination of the amounts to be transferred and engage in continual jockeying to increase certain kinds of transfers, at the expense of others if necessary. Note, for example, the ceaseless activities of the American Association of Retired Persons, perhaps the most powerful lobby in Washington, as it strives to increase old-age pensions and Medicare benefits, or of the National Association for the Advancement of Colored People as it seeks to increase transfers that benefit blacks in particular. Such political maneuvering creates or exacerbates conflicts among groups defined by their eligibility to receive particular kinds of transfers: old against young, black against white, rural against urban, female against male, northern against southern, homeowner against renter, and so forth without visible limit. In this way, society becomes more contentious.

6. Just as recipients engage in internecine warfare, so do taxpayers, who resent disproportionate burdens in funding the transfers. For instance, young people now learn that their Social Security taxes are going straight into the pockets of retired people who as a group are better off than they are. Young taxpayers also learn that they probably will never recoup their own contributions, unlike the present-day elderly, who have realized an extraordinarily high effective rate of

return on their "contributions." (Recently, the average married couple was getting back everything ever paid in, with interest, in just over four years.)[4] Black Social Security taxpayers learn that because of their lower life expectancy, they cannot expect to receive as much retirement income as the average white person can expect. Taxpayers who consider themselves disproportionately burdened grow to resent their exploitation by the tax-and-transfer system. Therefore, they give more support to politicians who promise to defend their pocketbooks against legislative marauders, and they strive harder to avoid or evade taxes.

7. As a result of the preceding two consequences, the entire society grows more divided and pugnacious. Less and less does the society constitute a genuine community. Rather, it becomes balkanized into bellicose subgroups regarding one another as oppressors and oppressed. People lose their sense of belonging to a common political community with collective interests and joint responsibilities. Instead, fellow citizens regard each other as either patsies or moochers and feel personal hostility toward those who appear to be net gainers from the system. Some actually come to hate the perceived moochers. Witness the palpable hostility when shoppers paying cash wait in the check-out line at the grocery store while someone uses food stamps to make purchases.

8. Among the recipients of transfers, self-help institutions languish. In former days, the burden of caring for the less fortunate outside the family was borne mainly by friends and neighbors acting jointly through churches, lodges, unions, clubs, and other voluntary associations. When individuals can receive assistance directly from the government, however, competing private associations tend to wither and eventually die—at least, their functions as helping institutions disappear. When they are gone, people who need help have nowhere to turn except to the government, which is unfortunate in many ways because what the government does is not really the same. Nor is it as effective, especially in the long run, when private associations have much greater success in making sure that people who recover their capacities then resume taking care of themselves.

In the aftermath of the big Los Angeles earthquake a few years ago, it was noted that "Thousands of forlorn, atomized individuals did nothing but wait for a centralized savior, the federal government. America has been diminished by a system of compulsory compassion that simply wants true communities out of the way so that altruism can be left to the experts."[5]

9. Just as self-help institutions wither among the needy, so do charitable institutions among those who are better off. When government agencies stand ready to attend to every conceivable problem in society, people whose sensibilities incline them toward helping the less fortunate have less incentive to organize themselves for doing so. It is easy to say, "I pay my taxes, and plenty of

them. Let the government take care of the problem." If one contributes to charities, it is as if one were paying twice to accomplish the same objective. Hence, government transfers crowd out private transfers. Coercion, in the form of the tax system, displaces the voluntary provision of assistance, and private charitable institutions wane.

10. As citizens drop out of their involvement in charitable and helping institutions, letting the government take over, they become less self-directing and more accepting of all kinds of government activity. So when someone proposes that the government undertake a function previously carried out exclusively within the private sphere, people are not shocked; they are not even very suspicious of the government's ability to carry out the task. After all, governments now do all sorts of things, from socializing preschoolers to feeding the poor to insuring the medical expenses of the elderly. So what if the government takes on still another responsibility? What was once a prevailing suspicion of the enlargement of government has become a resignation to or even a ready acceptance of its continuing expansion into new areas.

In the nineteenth century, opponents of proposed new government programs would commonly protest: "The government has no business doing that." Now we rarely hear anyone oppose a government initiative on these grounds. That there exists a private sphere into which government ought never to intrude has become a nearly extinct species of thought as governments have spread their programs, activities, and regulations into almost every cranny of society, including (formerly) private life.

11. Hence, people do not mobilize political opposition so readily when new government programs are proposed. Facing less opposition, those who support the new programs are more likely to triumph politically. New government programs proliferate more quickly, restrained somewhat by budgetary limitations but not much by fundamental ideological objections. According to a recent Wall Street Journal/NBC poll, "when Americans were asked whether 'entitlements' should be cut to reduce the deficit, 61% said yes. But when they were asked whether 'programs such as Social Security, Medicare, Medicaid and farm subsidies' should be cut, 66% said no."[6] Most people evidently resent paying for the programs, but they have no objection to the programs themselves.

12. Redistribution involves more than T who pays and R who receives. In between stands B, the bureaucracy that determines eligibility, writes the checks, keeps the records, and often does much more, sometimes intruding into clients' personal lives. The mediating bureaucracies consume vast resources of labor and capital, accounting for much of the gross expense of the transfer system. For the government to transfer a dollar to R, it is never sufficient to take just a dollar from T. A hefty "commission" must also be paid to support B. From a

societal perspective, one must recognize that labor and capital employed by the bureaucracies cannot be used to produce goods and services valued by consumers. Again, the society is made poorer.

13. Once a bureau is created, its staff becomes a tenacious political interest group, well placed to defend its budget and to make a case for expanding its activities. After all, who knows more about the urgent necessity of increasing a bureau's budget and staff than those who carry out its activities? The bureaucrats have a close hold on the relevant data and the ostensible expertise with respect to whatever problem they treat. Therefore, they have potent advantages in the political process when they seek to augment the resources placed at their command. Agency experts will testify that outsiders "just don't know how serious the problem is."

A bureau often constitutes one side of a political "iron triangle," joined with the organized client groups that form the second side and the congressional committees with legislative jurisdiction or oversight responsibility that form the third side. When the bureau becomes politically embedded in this way, as most do, its impoverishment of society can continue indefinitely without serious political challenge.

14. Taxpayers do not simply cough up money to fund the transfers without resistance. Many of them devote time, effort, and money to minimizing their legal tax liability or to evading taxes. They buy books and computer software. They employ financial advisers, lawyers, and accountants. From time to time, they organize political movements to campaign for tax relief à la California's Proposition 13. All the labor and capital employed in connection with tax resistance are unavailable to produce goods and services valued by consumers. Society is made poorer and will remain poorer as long as people continue to devote resources to tax resistance. (However, to the extent that tax resistance succeeds in making tax rates lower than they otherwise would have been, it promotes greater wealth creation in the longer run.)

15. In the end, many citizens will pay taxes to finance the transfers. Even if no one tries to resist the taxes or alters his behavior in supplying labor and capital, the cost to taxpayers will be more than one dollar for each dollar taken by the government because it is costly just to comply with the tax laws. Taxpayers must keep records, research the tax rules, fill out forms, and so forth. These activities require time and effort withdrawn from valuable alternative uses. Many people, even though they intend nothing more than full compliance with the law, hire the expert assistance of accountants and tax preparers—the tax rules are so complicated that mere mortals cannot cope. Use of resources to comply with tax laws makes the society poorer.

According to a study by James L. Payne, just the private compliance expense of taxpayers plus the budgetary and enforcement expense of the Internal Revenue Service add $270 million to the tab for each billion dollars of spending by the federal government.[7]

16. Just as taxpayers do not passively submit to being taxed, so recipients and potential recipients of transfers do not just sit quietly waiting for their ship to come in. They also act politically. They form organizations, attend meetings, employ publicists and lobbyists, and campaign for political candidates who support their objectives. All the labor and capital employed in transfer-seeking activities are therefore unavailable to produce goods and services valued by consumers. Society is made poorer and will remain poorer as long as people continue to devote resources to seeking transfers.

17. Just as taxpayers must employ resources to comply with the tax laws, so transfer recipients must employ resources to establish and maintain their eligibility to receive the transfers. For example, recipients of unemployment insurance benefits must visit the state department of employment security and wait in long lines to certify that they are indeed unemployed; sometimes they must go from place to place applying for jobs, which they may have no intention of accepting, in order to demonstrate that they are "seeking employment." Recipients of disability insurance benefits must visit doctors and other health professionals to acquire certification that they are indeed disabled. In each case, more resources are squandered, and society is made that much poorer.

18. By adopting programs to redistribute substantial amounts of income, a nation guarantees that its government will become more powerful and invasive in other ways. Because government itself is the most menacing interest group in society, nothing good can come of this development, and much evil may come of it. As James Madison remarked more than two centuries ago, "one legislative interference is but the first link of a long chain of repetitions, every subsequent interference being naturally produced by the effects of the preceding."[8] When the government created Medicare and Medicaid in 1965, for example, it set in motion a train of events that led inexorably to the subsequent "crisis" of escalating health-care costs and thence to the bigger government now being wrought by congressional efforts to deal with this artificial crisis, including the ominous, if pleasingly named, Health Insurance Portability and Accountability Act of 1996.[9]

19. Creating a more powerful and invasive government means that citizens' liberties will be diminished. Rights previously enjoyed will be set aside. For a long time, American citizens enjoyed extensive rights in the negative sense—rights to be left alone by governments and by other people as they went about their

lives. All individuals could enjoy such rights simultaneously. With the growth of the transfer society, American citizens have gravitated away from negative rights and toward positive rights, also known as welfare rights, which are in effect claims on other people's resources. One person's welfare right entails other people's corresponding duty to provide the resources necessary to satisfy the claim. As such entitlements have grown, therefore, liberties as negative rights have necessarily diminished.

Culmination

Ironically, in the full-fledged transfer society, where governments busy themselves redistributing income by means of hundreds of distinct programs, hardly anyone is better off as a result. Those who get something of value from the system frequently give up even more in taxes. Further, because many of the consequences of government income redistribution share the common aspect of impoverishing the society, even those who get a bigger slice than they surrender are cutting into a smaller pie. Only the ruling class—those who constitute the government—can confidently expect to gain, as each new program enlarges the number of official jobs and the bureaucracy's budget.

In the transfer society, the general public is not only poorer but also less contented, less autonomous, more rancorous, and more politicized. Individuals take part less often in voluntary community activities and more often in belligerent political contests. Genuine communities cannot breathe in the poisonous atmosphere of redistributional politics. Most important, the society that allows its government to redistribute income on a large scale necessarily sacrifices much of its liberty.

Finally, one must recognize that, notwithstanding what some regard as the institutionalization of compassion, the transfer society quashes genuine virtue. Redistribution of income by means of government coercion is a form of theft. Its supporters attempt to disguise its essential character by claiming that democratic procedures give it legitimacy, but this justification is specious. Theft is theft, whether it be carried out by one thief or by a hundred million thieves acting in concert. And it is impossible to found a good society on the institutionalization of theft.

Notes

1. U.S. Council of Economic Advisers, *Report 2001* (Washington, D.C.: U.S. Government Printing Office, 2001), pp. 308–9.

2. James D. Gwartney and Richard L. Stroup, *Microeconomics: Private and Public Choice*, 6th ed. (Fort Worth, Tex.: Dryden Press, 1992), pp. 409–10.

3. Ibid., pp. 488–89. This form of grand larceny only gets worse. See Michael W. Lynch,

"Money for Nothing: The Joys of U.S. Farm Policy," *Reason* (November 2001), p. 25; "Prairie Plutocrats" [editorial], *Wall Street Journal*, February 1, 2002; and David E. Sanger, "Bush Quietly Signs Farm Bill with Big Subsidies Increase," *New Orleans Times-Picayune*, May 14, 2002, reprinted from *New York Times*.

4. Paulette Thomas, "Bipartisan Panel Outlines Evils of Entitlements, But Hint of Benefit Cuts Spurs Stiff Opposition," *Wall Street Journal*, August 8, 1994.

5. Arianna Huffington, as quoted in John H. Fund, "A Spiritual Manifesto for a New Political Age," *Wall Street Journal*, July 13, 1994.

6. Thomas, "Bipartisan Panel."

7. James L. Payne, "Inside the Federal Hurting Machine," *The Freeman* (March 1994), p. 127.

8. Alexander Hamilton, John Jay, and James Madison, *The Federalist* (New York: Modern Library, n.d.), p. 291.

9. Charlotte Twight, "Medicare's Progeny: The 1996 Health Care Legislation," *The Independent Review* 2 (winter 1998): 373–99; Charlotte Twight, "Health and Human Services 'Privacy' Standards: The Coming Destruction of American Medical Privacy," *The Independent Review* 6 (spring 2002): 485–511.

Our Glorious Leaders

4

The Mythology of Roosevelt
and the New Deal

The Great Depression was a watershed in U.S. history. Soon after Herbert Hoover assumed the presidency in 1929, the economy began to decline, and between 1930 and 1933 the contraction assumed catastrophic proportions never experienced before or since in the United States. Disgusted by Hoover's inability to stem the collapse, the voters elected Franklin Delano Roosevelt as president, along with a heavily Democratic Congress, in 1932 and thereby set in motion the radical restructuring of government's role in the economy known as the New Deal.

With few exceptions, historians have taken a positive view of the New Deal. They have generally praised such measures as the massive relief programs for the unemployed; the expanded federal regulation of agriculture, industry, finance, and labor relations; the establishment of a legal minimum wage; and the creation of the Social Security program with its old-age pensions, unemployment insurance, and income supplements for the aged poor, the physically disabled, the blind, and dependent children in single-parent families. In the construction of the U.S. regulatory-and-welfare state, no one looms larger than Roosevelt.

For this accomplishment, along with his wartime leadership, historians and the general public alike rank Franklin D. Roosevelt among the greatest of U.S. presidents. Roosevelt, it is repeatedly said, restored hope to the American people when they had fallen into despair because of the seemingly endless depression, and his policies "saved capitalism" by mitigating its intrinsic cruelties and inequalities. The very title of the volume in the *Oxford History of the United States* that deals with the Roosevelt era—*Freedom from Fear*—encapsulates the popular as well as the academic understanding of what the New Deal achieved. The author of that volume, David M. Kennedy of Stanford University, concludes that "achieving security was the leitmotif of virtually everything the New Deal attempted.... Its cardinal aim was not to destroy capitalism but to devolatilize it, and at the same time to distribute its benefits more evenly."[1]

This view of Roosevelt and the New Deal amounts to a myth compounded of ideological predisposition and historical misunderstanding. In a 1936 book called *The Menace of Roosevelt and His Policies,* Howard E. Kershner came closer to the truth when he wrote that Roosevelt "took charge of our government when it was comparatively simple, and for the most part confined to the essential functions of government, and transformed it into a highly complex, bungling agency for throttling business and bedeviling the private lives of free people. It is no exaggeration to say that he took the government when it was a small racket and made a large racket out of it."[2]

As this statement illustrates, not everyone admired Roosevelt during the 1930s. Although historians have tended to view his opponents as self-interested reactionaries, the legions of these "Roosevelt haters" actually had a clearer view of the economic consequences of the New Deal. The nearly 17 million men and women who, even in Roosevelt's moment of supreme triumph in 1936, voted for Alfred Landon could not all have been plutocrats.

Prolonging the Depression

The irony is that even if Roosevelt had helped to lift the spirits of the American people in the depths of the depression—an uplift for which no compelling documentation exists—that achievement only led the public to labor under an illusion. After all, the root cause of the prevailing malaise was the continuation of the depression. Had the masses understood that the New Deal was only prolonging the depression, they would have had good reason to reject it and its vaunted leader.

In fact, as many observers claimed at the time, the New Deal did prolong the depression. Had Roosevelt only kept his inoffensive campaign promises of 1932—promises to cut federal spending, balance the budget, maintain a sound currency, and rein in the bureaucratic centralization in Washington—the depression might have passed into history before his next campaign in 1936. Instead, Roosevelt and Congress, especially during the congressional sessions of 1933 and 1935, embraced interventionist policies on a wide front. With its bewildering, incoherent mass of new expenditures, taxes, subsidies, regulations, and direct government participation in productive activities, the New Deal created so much confusion, fear, uncertainty, and hostility among businessmen and investors that private investment and hence overall private economic activity never recovered enough to restore the high levels of production and employment enjoyed during the 1920s.[3]

In the face of the interventionist onslaught, the U.S. economy between 1930 and 1940 failed to add anything to its capital stock: net private investment for that eleven-year period totaled *minus* $3.1 billion.[4] Without ongoing capital accumulation, no economy can grow. Between 1929 and 1939, the economy sacrificed an entire decade of normal economic growth, which would have increased the national income by 30–40 percent.

The government's own greatly enlarged economic activity did not compensate for the private shortfall. Apart from the mere insufficiency of the dollars spent, the government's spending tended, as contemporary critics aptly noted, to purchase a high proportion of sheer boondoggle. In the words of the common man's poet Berton Braley,

> A dollar for the services
> A true producer renders—
> (And a dollar for experiments
> Of Governmental spenders!)
> A dollar for the earners
> And the savers and the thrifty—
> (And a dollar for the wasters,
> It's a case of fifty-fifty!).[5]

Under heavy criticism, Roosevelt himself eventually declared that he was "not willing that the vitality of our people be further sapped by the giving of doles, of market baskets, by a few hours of weekly work cutting grass, raking leaves, or picking up papers in the public parks."[6] Nevertheless, the dole did continue.

Buying Votes

In this madness, the New Dealers had a method. Notwithstanding its economic illogic and incoherence, the New Deal served as a highly successful vote-buying scheme. Coming into power at a time of widespread destitution, high unemployment, and business failures, the Roosevelt administration recognized that the president and his Democratic allies in Congress could appropriate unprecedented sums of money and channel them into the hands of recipients who would respond by giving political support to their benefactors. As John T. Flynn said of Roosevelt, "it was always easy to interest him in a plan which would confer some special benefit upon some special class in the population in exchange for their votes," and eventually "no political boss could compete with him in any county in America in the distribution of money and jobs."[7]

In buying votes, the relief programs for the unemployed—especially the Federal Emergency Relief Administration, the Civilian Conservation Corp, and the Works Progress Administration—loomed largest, though many other programs fostered achievement of the same end. Farm subsidies, price supports, credit programs, and related measures won over much of the rural middle class. The labor provisions of, first, the National Industrial Recovery Act, then later the National Labor Relations Act, and finally the Fair Labor Standards Act purchased support from the burgeoning ranks of the labor unions. Homeowners supported the New Deal out of gratitude for the government's refinancing of their mortgages and its provision of home loan guarantees. Even blacks, loyal to the Republican Party ever since the Civil War, abandoned it in exchange for the pittances of relief payments and the tag ends of employment in the federal work-relief programs.[8] Put it all together and you have what political scientists call the New Deal Coalition—a potent political force that remained intact until the 1970s.

Inept, Arrogant Advisers

Journalists titillated the public with talk of Roosevelt's "Brains Trust"—his coterie of policy advisers just before and shortly after his election in 1932, of whom the most prominent were Columbia University professors Raymond Moley, Rexford Guy Tugwell, and Adolph A. Berle. In retrospect, it is obvious that these men's ideas about the causes and cure of the depression ranged from merely wrongheaded to completely crackpot.

Many of the early New Dealers viewed the collapse of prices as the cause of the depression, so they regarded various means of raising prices, especially cartelization of industry and other measures to restrict market supplies, as appropriate in the circumstances. Raise farm prices, raise industrial prices, raise wage rates, raise the price of gold. Only one price should fall—namely, the price (that is, the purchasing power) of money. Thus, they favored inflation and, as a means to this end, the abandonment of the gold standard, which had previously kept inflation more or less in check.

Later advisers, the "happy hot dogs" (after their mentor and godfather Harvard law professor Felix Frankfurter), such as Tom Corcoran, Ben Cohen, and James Landis, who rose to prominence during the mid-1930s, had no genuine economic expertise but contributed mightily to Roosevelt's swing away from accommodating business interests and toward assaulting investors as a class, whom he dubbed "economic royalists" and blamed for the depression and other social evils.

Early and late, the president's advisers shared at least one major opinion: that the federal government should intervene deeply and widely in economic life; or, in other words, that government spending, employing, and regulating, all directed by "experts" such as themselves, could repair the various perceived defects of the market system and restore prosperity while achieving greater social justice. As Garet Garrett perceived as early as August 1933, the president's academic advisers sought not merely to deal with the emergency. Theirs was "a complex intention, not restoration, not prosperity again as it had been before, but a complete new order, scientifically planned and managed, the individual profit motive tamed by government wisdom, human happiness ascendant on a plotted curve."[9] Even at the time, the overweening haughtiness of these incompetent policy advisers struck many thoughtful onlookers as their most distinctive trait. As James Burnham wrote of them in his 1941 book *The Managerial*

Revolution, "they are, sometimes openly, scornful of capitalists and capitalist ideas. . . . They believe that they can run things, and they like to run things."[10] More recently, even a sympathetic left-liberal historian, Alan Brinkley, wrote that the hardcore New Dealers embraced government planning "with almost religious veneration."[11]

The Misleading Analogy of War

Many of the New Dealers, including Roosevelt himself (as assistant secretary of the navy), had been active in the wartime administration of Woodrow Wilson. Ruminating on how to deal with the depression, they seized on an analogy: the war was a national emergency, and we dealt with it by creating government agencies to control and mobilize the private economy; the depression is a national emergency, and therefore we can deal with it by creating similar agencies. From that reasoning arose a succession of government organizations modeled on wartime precedents. The Agricultural Adjustment Administration resembled the Food Administration; the National Recovery Administration resembled the War Industries Board; the Reconstruction Finance Corporation (created under Hoover but greatly expanded under Roosevelt) resembled the War Finance Corporation; the National Labor Relations Board resembled the War Labor Board; the Tennessee Valley Authority resembled the Muscle Shoals project; the Civilian Conservation Corp resembled the army itself; and the list went on and on.

In his first inaugural speech, Roosevelt declared, "we must move as a trained and loyal army willing to sacrifice for the good of a common discipline." He warned that should Congress fail to act to his satisfaction, he would seek "broad executive power to wage a war against the emergency as great as the power that would be given me if we were in fact invaded by a foreign foe."[12] However stirring the rhetoric, this approach to dealing with the depression rested on a complete misapprehension. The requisites of successfully prosecuting a war had virtually nothing in common with the requisites of getting the economy out of a depression. (Moreover, the president and his supporters greatly overestimated how successful their wartime measures had been— World War I had ended before the many defects of those measures became widely appreciated.)

A Pure Political Opportunist

Roosevelt did not trouble himself with serious thinking. Flynn referred to an aspect of his character as "the free and easy manner in which he could confront problems about which he knew very little."[13] Nor did he apparently care that he knew very little; his mind sailed strictly on the surface: "Fundamentally he was without any definite political or economic philosophy. He was not a man to deal in fundamentals.... The positions he took on political and economic questions were not taken in accordance with deeply rooted political beliefs but under the influence of political necessity.... He was in every sense purely an opportunist."[14] Raymond Moley flaunted "the superb assurances that the President has given the country in connection with some of this [1933] legislation ... that it is frankly experimental."[15] In other words, Roosevelt had no idea how to deal with the situation he confronted, but he determined to launch a thousand ships anyhow in the hope that one of them might reach the promised land and in the conviction that he would be rewarded politically for such mindless activism.

An indifferent student and then a wealthy, handsome, and popular young man about town, Roosevelt had distinguished himself in his early days mainly by his amiable and charming personality. A born politician—which is to say, he was devious, manipulative, and mendacious—he had a flair for campaigning and for posturing before and propagandizing the public. His "first instinct," according to *New York Times* reporter Turner Catledge, "was always to lie," although "sometimes in midsentence he would switch to accuracy because he realized he could get away with the truth in that particular instance."[16] Though millions hated him with a white-hot passion, there is no gainsaying that far more loved him, and millions regarded him as a savior—"the Heaven-sent man of the hour," as the *New York Times* editorialized on June 18, 1933.[17]

If demagoguery were a powerful means of creating prosperity, then Roosevelt might have lifted the country out of the depression in short order. But in 1939, ten years after the onset of the depression and six years after the commencement of the New Deal, 9.5 million persons, or 17.2 percent of the labor force, still remained officially unemployed (of whom more than 3 million were enrolled in emergency government make-work projects). Roosevelt proved himself to be a masterful politician, but, unfortunately for the American people subjected to his policies, he had no idea how to end the depression other than to "try something" and, when that didn't work, to try something else. His ill-conceived, politically shaped experiments so disrupted the operation of the market economy and so discouraged the accumulation of capital that they thwarted the full recovery that otherwise would have occurred—after all, the capitalist machine was not irreparably broken, despite what an emergent school of "stagnationist" economists was saying in the late 1930s. Roosevelt's followers revered him as a great leader then, and many people revere him still, but except for the members of the planner class and their private-sector pets, wrongheaded leadership turned out to be worse than no leadership at all.

Legacies

Although Roosevelt and the New Dealers failed to end the depression, they succeeded in revolutionizing the institutions of U.S. political and economic life and in changing the country's dominant ideology. Even today, sixty-five years after the New Deal ran out of steam, its legacies remain and continue to hamper the successful operation of the market economy and to diminish individual liberties.

One need look no further than an organization chart of the federal government. There one finds agencies such as the Export-Import Bank, the Farm Credit Administration, the Rural Housing and Community Development Service (formerly part of the Farmers Home Administration), the Federal Deposit Insurance Corporation, the Federal Housing Administration, the National Labor Relations Board, the Rural Utilities Service (formerly the Rural Electrification Administration), the Securities and Exchange Commission, the Social Security Administration, and the Tennessee Valley Authority—all of them the offspring of the New Deal. Each in its own fashion interferes with the effective operation of the free-market system. By subsidizing, financing, insuring, regulating, and thereby diverting resources from the uses most valued by consumers, each renders the economy less productive than it could be—in the service of one special interest or another.

Once the New Deal had burst the dam between 1933 and 1938, ample precedent had been set for virtually any government program that could gain sufficient political support in Congress. Limited constitutional government, especially after the Supreme Court revolution that began in 1937, became little more than an object of nostalgia for classical liberals.

Indeed, in the wake of the New Deal, the ranks of the classical liberals diminished so greatly that they became an endangered species. The legacy of the New Deal was, more than anything else, a matter of ideological change. Henceforth, nearly everyone would look to the federal government for solutions to problems great and small, real and imagined, personal as well as social. After the 1930s, the opponents of any proposed federal program might object to its structure, its personnel, or its cost, but hardly anyone objected on the grounds that the program was by its very nature improper to undertake at the federal level of government.

"People in the mass," wrote H. L. Mencken, "soon grow used to anything, including even being swindled. There comes a time when the patter of the quack becomes as natural and as indubitable to their ears as the texts of Holy Writ, and when that time comes it is a dreadful job debamboozling them."[18] Sixty-five years after the New Deal itself petered out, Americans overwhelmingly take for granted the expansive, something-for-nothing character of the federal government established by the New Dealers. For Democrats and Republicans alike, Franklin Delano Roosevelt looms as the most significant political figure of the twentieth century.

However significant his legacies, though, Roosevelt deserves no reverence. He was no hero. Rather, he was an exceptionally resourceful political opportunist

who harnessed the extraordinary potential for personal and party aggrandizement inherent in a uniquely troubled and turbulent period of U.S. history. By
wheeling and dealing, by taxing and spending, by ranting against "economic
royalists" and posturing as the friend of the common man, he got himself
elected time after time. For all his undeniable political prowess, however, he
prolonged the depression and greatly fostered a bloated, intrusive government
that has been trampling on the people's liberties every since.

Notes

1. David M. Kennedy, *Freedom from Fear: The American People in Depression and War,
   1929–1945* (New York: Oxford University Press, 1999), pp. 365, 372.
2. Quoted by Richard M. Ebeling, "Monetary Central Planning and the State, Part XIV:
   The New Deal and Its Critics," *Freedom Daily* 9 (February 1998), p. 15.
3. Robert Higgs, "Regime Uncertainty: Why the Great Depression Lasted So Long and
   Why Prosperity Resumed after the War," *The Independent Review* 1 (spring 1997): -
   561–90.
4. Ibid., p. 567.
5. Berton Braley, "Even Steven," in *Virtues in Verse: The Best of Berton Braley,* selected and
   arranged by Linda Tania Abrams (Milpitas, Calif.: Atlantean Press, 1993), p. 70.
6. John T. Flynn, *The Roosevelt Myth* (Garden City, N.Y.: Garden City Books, 1948), p. 86.
7. Ibid., pp. 127, 65.
8. Paul Moreno, "An Ambivalent Legacy: Black Americans and the Political Economy of
   the New Deal," *The Independent Review* 6 (spring 2002): 513–39.
9. Garet Garrett, *Salvos Against the New Deal: Selections from the* Saturday Evening Post
   1933–1940, edited by Bruce Ramsey (Caldwell, Id.: Caxton Press, 2002), p. 36.
10. Quoted by F. A. Hayek in "Review of Burnham, *The Managerial Revolution,*" in *The Col-
    lected Works of F. A. Hayek,* vol. 10 (Chicago: University of Chicago Press, 1997), p. 251.
11. Alan Brinkley, *The End of Reform: New Deal Liberalism in Recession and War* (New York:
    Knopf, 1995), p. 47.
12. "F. D. Roosevelt's First Inaugural Address, March 4, 1933," in *Documents of American
    History,* edited by Henry Steele Commager (New York: Appleton-Century-Crofts, 1948),
    pp. 421–22.
13. Flynn, *The Roosevelt Myth,* p. 31.
14. Ibid., pp. 77–78.
15. Quoted in Garrett, *Salvos Against the New Deal,* p. 46.
16. Description of what Turner told friends, as reported by Marvin Olasky, "Sex and the
    Presidency," *Wall Street Journal,* January 26, 1998.
17. Quoted in Flynn, *The Roosevelt Myth,* p. 15.
18. H. L. Mencken, *On Politics: A Carnival of Buncombe* (Baltimore: Johns Hopkins
    University Press, 1996), p. 335.

5

Public Choice
and Political Leadership

Public-choice analysts proceed on the assumption that individuals do not differ as they participate in private and public affairs. The man who shops for groceries, they say, is the same man who votes. The woman who decides where to invest her savings is the same woman who serves in the state legislature. In the jargon of economics, each person has a utility function that remains in place whether the person acts in the market or in the political arena. If people behave differently when they possess governmental authority, they do so only because governmental actors have different incentives and constraints than private-sector actors have. Accordingly, public-choice analysts conclude, for example, that it is futile to "throw the rascals out" in elections because the new officeholders will themselves become rascals in response to the incentives and constraints inherent in their offices.

As behooves an operating assumption, this one serves a certain purpose. It allows the analyst to abstract from any differences that do set public and private actors apart and thereby to determine how institutional differences in incentives and constraints alone elicit differing actions even if the actors have identical motives. So far, so good. Unfortunately, here as elsewhere, the analysts tend to fall in love with their theoretical assumption and before long start to think it is actually true, as opposed to merely useful. Moreover, the most cocksure analysts regard any questioning of the assumption as a sign of mental frailty.

Whatever its merits as an operating assumption in positive political analysis, the proposition that the people who wield political power are just like the rest of us is manifestly false. Lord Acton was not just expelling breath when he said that "power tends to corrupt, and absolute power corrupts absolutely." Nor did he err when he observed that "great men are almost always bad men"—at least if "great men" denotes those with great political power.[1]

Among the most memorable lines in Friedrich A. Hayek's *Road to Serfdom* is the title of chapter 10, "Why the Worst Get on Top."[2] Hayek was considering collectivist dictatorships when he noted that "there will be special opportunities for the ruthless and unscrupulous" and that "the readiness to do bad things becomes a path to promotion and power."[3] But the observation applies to the functionaries of less-egregious governments, too. Nowadays, nearly all governments, even those of countries such as the United States, France, or Germany, jokingly described as "free," provide numerous opportunities for ruthless and unscrupulous people. As Robert A. Sirico has said, tipping his hat to Lord Acton, "the corrupt seek power and use it absolutely."[4] Decent people, virtually by definition, do not seek to exercise political power over their fellows. The mystery is that so many citizens continue to admire and defer to the reptilian wretches who rule them.

Of all the accounts of political leadership I have read, most of which obsequiously endorse the myths propagated by the master class itself, the best is anthropologist F. G. Bailey's *Humbuggery and Manipulation: The Art of Leadership*.[5] Bailey gets right to the point by noting in his preface that "leaders and gangsters have much in common."[6] Of course, political leaders are much more ambitious than gangsters. The latter are content to take your money, whereas the former, besides taking far more of your money, have the effrontery to violate your just rights whenever their convenience dictates and even to anticipate your gratitude for their compassionate devotion to your welfare.

To put citizens into a suitably servile and moronic frame of mind, political leaders dish out claptrap day and night. Followers

> are cajoled into devotion by the leader's pretended concern or admiration for them or for some cause in which they believe, by a pretense of virtue; it is mostly humbuggery.... [T]he role of leader requires performances in defiance of truth, ranging from the mild and on the whole inoffensive metaphorical exaggerations ... to actions that are carefully written out of autobiographies because they are shamefully dishonest or even criminal.[7]

Honorable people, taking a wrong turn and blundering into positions of political leadership, would last no longer than a nun in a brothel. If ruthless rivals did not displace them at the earliest opportunity, the scrupulous people would soon remove themselves in disgust. People who lack pugnacity do not succeed as prizefighters; people who lack a talent for lying, stealing, and, if need be, abetting homicide do not succeed in modern politics. As Bailey puts it, "Leaders are not the virtuous people they claim to be; they put politics before statesmanship; they distort facts and oversimplify issues; they promise what no one could deliver; and they are liars.... [L]eaders, if they are to be effective, have no choice in the matter. They could not be virtuous (in the sense of morally excellent) and be leaders at the same time."[8]

Some critics have condemned public-choice analysis for promoting cynicism about politics, government officials, and public affairs in general. They protest: What about all that obvious public spirit?[9] In contrast, Bailey surveys the real political scene through the open and dispassionate eyes of a well-traveled social scientist. "Much of the time," he affirms, "the humbuggery works and the enthusiastic followers are carried on a wave of passion and euphoria until the wave breaks on the rock of reality and they find themselves dumped. The cynics, meanwhile, stay out beyond the surf and stay afloat."[10]

It is true, I think, that public-choice analysis fosters cynicism about political leaders. But not as much as they deserve.

Notes

1. Acton as quoted by James C. Holland in his introduction to John Emerich Edward Dalberg Acton, *The History of Freedom* (Grand Rapids, Mich.: Acton Institute, 1993), p. 2.

2. Chicago: University of Chicago Press, 1944, p. 134.

3. Ibid., p. 151.

4. Robert A. Sirico as quoted in "Notable and Quotable," *Wall Street Journal*, August 20, 1996.

5. Ithaca, N.Y.: Cornell University Press, 1988.

6. Ibid., p. xiii.

7. Ibid., p. 169.

8. Ibid., p. 174. See also Laurie Calhoun, "The Problem of 'Dirty Hands' and Corrupt Leadership," *The Independent Review* 8 (winter 2004): 363–85.

9. Steven Kelman, *Making Public Policy: A Hopeful View of American Government* (New York: Basic Books, 1987).

10. *Humbuggery and Manipulation*, p. 173.

6

Bolingbroke, Nixon, and the Rest of Them

I'm not certain, but I'm willing to conjecture that Genghis Khan's executive office had no position for an assistant to the khan and press secretary; no assistant to the khan for communications; no assistant to the khan for public liaison; no deputy assistant to the khan and director of speechwriting; no deputy assistant to the khan and deputy press secretary to the khan; no deputy assistant to the khan and director of media relations and planning; no deputy assistant to the khan and deputy director of public affairs; no special assistant to the khan for public liaison; no special assistant to the khan and chief speechwriter—all of which, if one merely substitutes the word *president* for the word *khan,* President Ronald Reagan did have in his executive office.[1] Genghis had no need to put a spin on his policy decisions. He expected his reputation to precede him, and, if it didn't, so much the worse for the uninformed.

In the old days, everyone recognized a political leader as, in the words of Bertrand de Jouvenel, the "chief freebooter, leader of forays, director of the nation's strength."[2] For millennia, political leadership simply coincided with personal prowess in murder and mayhem. Although leaders often strove to ease their exploitation of subjects by clothing themselves in religious or other forms of ostensible legitimacy, a clear-eyed subject appreciated that his only real choice was stark: obey or get hurt. Nobody wasted a moment supposing that the leader acted as an agent of the public or sought above all the public's well-being.

In recent centuries, as elected officials displaced absolute monarchs and dictators, people increasingly fell under the illusion that the government served them rather than itself; indeed, some even accepted the absurd claim that they *were* the government by virtue of their periodically casting a vote for one or another of the names placed on the ballot by the political ringmasters. In a flight of wishful thinking, subjects neglected to notice that the government—the collectivity of persons wielding power under color of official authority—even in a democracy "has its own life, its own interests, its own characteristics, its own ends."[3]

To reassure citizens that government's voracious appetites signified nothing more than an earnest desire to promote the public's well-being, governments, especially in the twentieth century, increasingly cultivated the arts of propaganda. Hence the battalions of special deputy assistant undersecretaries for bamboozlement listed earlier. As political leaders surrounded themselves with layer upon layer of mendacious flunkies, citizens came to possess less and less reliable information to assess the fidelity of their "public servants." How could skeptical citizens, perennially immersed in a fog of disinformation, ground their inchoate suspicion that the government actually conducted its affairs far differently than it claimed?

Of course, evidence sometimes does come to light confirming such suspicion, usually long after the deed is done. Lord Bolingbroke (1678–1751), an English politico of considerable clout in the early eighteenth century, penned one of the most forthright confessions in a letter to Sir William Windham:

> I am afraid that we came to court in the same dispositions that all parties have done; that the principal spring of our actions was to have the government of the State in our own hands; that our principal views were the conservation of this power, great employments to ourselves, and great opportunities of rewarding those who had helped to raise us, and of hurting those who stood in opposition to us.[4]

More than a century earlier, the Marquis of Halifax (1633–1695) made a similar observation: "Parties in a State generally, like freebooters, hang out false colours; the pretence is the public good; the real business is to catch prizes; and wherever they succeed, instead of improving their victory, they presently fall upon the baggage."[5]

The antiquity of the preceding quotations does not warrant anyone's dismissal of their applicability to modern conditions. For evidence of their enduring pertinence, consider that most unvarnished of all political records, the Nixon tapes. There, perhaps uniquely, we find the modern politician fully unmasked. In November 1996, after the Nixon estate gave up its fight to keep 201 hours of previously unreleased tapes secret, the National Archives made them public. Among them is a recording of an Oval Office conversation Nixon had with his two top aides, H. R. (Bob) Haldeman and John Ehrlichman, on May 13, 1971. Echoing Bolingbroke, Nixon discussed the sort of person he wanted as commissioner of internal revenue: "I want to be sure that he is a ruthless son of a bitch, that he will do what he is told, that every income-tax return I want to see, I see. That he will go after our enemies and not go after our friends. It's as simple as that."[6]

Nixon seems to have believed that his predecessors had used the Internal Revenue Service (IRS) in the same way. On May 27, 1973, the president asked Ehrlichman if he had ascertained "who ordered . . . the audit of my income-tax returns in 1961."[7] Tricky Dick was not just hallucinating. As Elizabeth Mac-

Donald has shown recently, "the Kennedys were far worse than Nixon in their manipulation of the IRS."[8]

The recently released tapes also reveal that in 1971 the president instructed Ehrlichman to sic the IRS on wealthy Jewish contributors to his Democratic rivals. On September 8, Nixon said: "John, we have the power. Are we using it now to investigate contributors to Hubert Humphrey, contributors to Muskie—the Jews, you know, that are stealing in every direction? Are we going after their tax returns? . . . I can only hope that we are, frankly, doing a little persecuting."[9] On September 13, Nixon told Haldeman: "Now here's the point, Bob, please get me the names of the Jews. You know, the big Jewish contributors to the Democrats." The president wanted them investigated. The next day, talking to Haldeman and presidential aide Charles Colson, he resumed: "What about the rich Jews? The IRS is full of Jews, Bob." Later he admonished, "Go after 'em like a son of a bitch!"[10]

Although some may regard Richard Milhous Nixon as an egregious example, my own hunch is that he differed from most other successful political leaders mainly by extensively recording his private conversations and then failing to destroy the tapes that attest so plainly his motives, methods, and manners.

Of course, one may argue, citizens in a democracy can always "throw the rascals out" at the next election. Here in the United States we have been flinging rascals hither and yon for more than two centuries. But what do we have to show for it?

Jouvenel, whose magnificent book *On Power* I freely employed earlier, had a clear vision of how the circulation of rascals, far from protecting the citizens, only shackles them more severely:

> Every change of regime and, to a lesser extent, every change of government is, as it were, a reproduction, on a more or less reduced scale, of a barbarian invasion. The newcomers wander about the power house with feelings in which curiosity, pride, greed, all have a place. The credit which they then for the first time enjoy enables them to make full use of this formidable machinery, and even to add to it some further controls of their own. In time yet another faction will, by promising to make a better use of it, force its way in turn into the City of Command, which it will find already embellished by its forerunners. So that the hope, always renewed, of stripping from Power all trace of egoism results only in forging ever vaster means of compulsion for the next egoism.[11]

In the United States today, where two revolving factions of a one-party state farcically masquerade as authentic alternatives, the one specializing in crushing economic freedom and the other concentrating on crushing every other form of freedom, we know all too well what Jouvenel meant.

Notes

1. U.S. Office of the Federal Register, *The United States Government Manual, 1983/84* (Washington, D.C.: U.S. Government Printing Office, 1983).

2. Bertrand de Jouvenel, *On Power: The Natural History of Its Growth,* translated by J. F. Huntington (Indianapolis, Ind.: Liberty Fund, 1993, original French edition 1945), p. 96.

3. Ibid., p. 103.

4. Quoted in ibid., p. 126.

5. Quoted in ibid., from *Maxims of State,* a compilation of Halifax's reflections.

6. Quoted in Donald M. Rothberg, "Nixon Felt Cabinet Had Abandoned Him, Tapes Show," *Seattle Times,* November 19, 1996.

7. Quoted in ibid.

8. Elizabeth MacDonald, "The Kennedys and the IRS," *Wall Street Journal,* January 28, 1997.

9. Quoted in "Nixon Urged IRS Audits of Jews," *Seattle Times,* December 8, 1996.

10. Quoted in ibid.

11. Jouvenel, *On Power,* p. 131.

7

What Professor Stiglitz
Learned in Washington

Joseph E. Stiglitz, a professor at Columbia University and the recipient (along with two others) of the 2001 Nobel Prize in Economic Sciences, is a major figure in the mainstream economics establishment. He has been described as "a giant in his profession" and as "perhaps the most prominent economic theorist of his generation."[1] Having been a faculty member at Yale, Princeton, Oxford, and Stanford, a prolific publisher in the leading academic journals, and the recipient of prestigious honors and appointments, Stiglitz moved into elevated positions as a policy adviser during the 1990s. From 1997 to 2000, he served as senior vice president and chief economist for the World Bank. Previously, from 1993 to 1997, he had served on the President's Council of Economic Advisers (CEA), chairing the council during the latter part of that period. Recently, he discussed his experience at the CEA in the annual Distinguished Lecture on Economics in Government.[2]

Stiglitz's academic reputation rests in large part on his construction and analysis of mathematical models from which he has concluded that "the market fails" in ways previously undreamed of by neoclassical welfare economists. "I found a general way," he said, "to model imperfect information. And when you plugged this in [the model], you found markets to be almost always inefficient."[3] So no one will be surprised to encounter his confession that he went to the CEA not just to learn at firsthand about government policymaking but "also [to be] an activist."[4] His appreciation of neoclassical welfare economics had led him to believe that "there will always be some intervention by which the government can make everyone better off."[5]

Even though Stiglitz professes an awareness of "government failure" as well as "market failure," his prior studies, it seems, had not sufficiently prepared him for what he encountered in the highest policymaking circles of the national government. He recalls:

> When I was in the lawyer- and politician-dominated White House environment, I often felt that I had arrived in another world. It was not just that another language was spoken. I understood and expected that;

every culture (including that of economists) creates its own language to set itself apart. It was that often another system of logic, another set of rules of reasoning, applied. I had expected lower standards of evidence for assertions than would be accepted in a professional article, but I had not expected that evidence offered would be, in so many instances, so irrelevant, and that so many vacuous sentences, sentences whose meaning and import simply baffled me, would be uttered.... Empirical evidence—at least beyond an anecdote or two—and theoretical analysis should have been able to shed light on the merit of alternative policies. While that is where the conversation should have begun, it almost never got that far. What occurred was often worse than Gresham's Law: it was not only that bad arguments seemed to drive out good, but good economists, responding to implicit incentives, adopted bad arguments to win their battles. In a process of cognitive dissonance reduction, possibly combined with some intellectual atrophy, sometimes good economists even seemed to come to believe their specious arguments.[6]

Yet, after nearly four years immersed in such Alice in Wonderland jabbering, not to mention the asinine posturing, personal backstabbing, and special-interest grasping that constitute the real world of government, Stiglitz is still able to declare, "Those who said that I would leave the White House with a more jaundiced view of the role of government were only partly correct." The all-too-obvious failures of government, he maintains, "do not undo the great achievements of the public sector."[7] As examples of those great achievements, he mentions mass education and a cleaner environment.

My own reading of the literature on environmental policy leaves me unconvinced that government policy in that area has succeeded, even in the utilitarian terms by which neoclassical economists assess it. Have aggregate benefits really exceeded aggregate costs? With respect to a less ambiguous matter, however, there is no doubt: environmental policies have definitely diminished American liberties, sometimes in grotesquely Stalinistic fashion, as when people have been imprisoned for installing ordinary drainage or filling in mud holes on their own land.[8]

As for the great achievements of government in mass education, I recommend that when Professor Stiglitz has some spare time, he spend it looking into what goes on at a few randomly selected public schools in his own city. I am confident that he will learn a great deal.

Notes

1. Louis Uchitelle, "The Economics of Intervention: A Prominent but Impolitic Theorist Questions the Worship of Free Markets," *New York Times,* May 31, 1998, sec. 3.

2. Joseph E. Stiglitz, "The Private Uses of Public Interests: Incentives and Institutions," *Journal of Economic Perspectives* 12 (spring 1998): 3–22.

3. Uchitelle, "The Economics of Intervention."

4. Stiglitz, "The Private Uses of Public Interests," p. 3.

5. Ibid., pp. 3–4.

6. Ibid., p. 5.

7. Ibid., p. 21.

8. See, for examples, Sigfredo A. Cabrera, "Environmental Law Endangers Property Rights," *The Freeman* 45 (August 1995): 489–92; Marisa Manley, "A Victim of Wetlands Regulations," *The Freeman* 47 (July 1997): 408–12; and James Bovard, *Lost Rights* (New York: St. Martin's Press, 1994), pp. 33–38, 69–76.

8

Great Presidents?

My idea of a great president is one who acts in accordance with his oath of office to "preserve, protect, and defend the Constitution of the United States." Not since the presidency of Grover Cleveland has any president achieved greatness by this standard. Worse, the most admired have been those who, by this standard, failed most miserably. Evidently, however, my standard differs from that employed by others who judge presidential greatness.

In the December 15, 1996, issue of the *New York Times Magazine,* Arthur M. Schlesinger Jr. presented the results of a poll of historians asked to rank the presidents (excepting only William Henry Harrison and Zachary Taylor, who held office very briefly).[1] Thirty historians and—bizarrely—politicos Mario M. Cuomo and Paul Simon were asked to rank the nation's chief executives as Great, Near Great, Average, Below Average, or Failure. The ranking applies to performance in the White House, not to lifetime accomplishments, and the historians used their own judgment as to what constitutes greatness or failure.

The results of the poll correspond well with the results of a number of earlier polls, especially as regards the set of presidents ranked "Great" or "Near Great." The three "Great" ones are Washington, Lincoln, and Franklin D. Roosevelt. The "Near Great" comprise Jefferson, Jackson, Polk, Theodore Roosevelt, Wilson, and Truman. The "Failures" are Pierce, Buchanan, Andrew Johnson, Grant, Harding, Hoover, and Nixon, this last man ranking at the very bottom.

What are we to make of this ranking? Well, it helps to know that the historians (and two politicians) doing the ranking are nearly all left liberals. In this regard, they faithfully represent the history profession in the United States today. In making their judgments, such historians bring to bear left-liberal beliefs and values. Thus, one respondent, James MacGregor Burns, asks: "How can one evaluate such an idiosyncratic President [as Nixon], so brilliant and so morally lacking?"—as if Nixon were, in this crowd, uniquely immoral.[2]

One need not ponder the rankings very long, however, to discover a remarkable correlation: all but one of the presidents ranked "Great" or "Near Great" had an intimate association with war, either in office or by reputation before taking office. Of the top-ranking "nine immortals," five (Lincoln, FDR,

Polk, Wilson, and Truman) were commander in chief when the nation went to war, and three (Washington, Jackson, and Teddy Roosevelt) were best known prior to becoming president for their martial exploits. The one exception, Jefferson, confined his presidential bellicosity to authorizing the naval engagements against the Barbary pirates (of course, he had been a revolutionary official during the War of Independence).

In contrast, of the eleven presidents ranked "Below Average" or "Failure," all but one (Nixon) managed to keep the nation at peace during their terms in office, and even Nixon ultimately extracted the United States from the quagmire of the war in Vietnam, although not until many more lives had been squandered.

The lesson seems obvious. Any president who craves a high place in the annals of history should hasten to thrust the American people into an orgy of death and destruction. Nor does it matter how ill-conceived that adventure may be. Lincoln achieved his presidential immortality by quite unnecessarily plunging America into its greatest bloodbath—ostensibly to maintain the boundaries of an existing federal union, as if those boundaries possessed some sacred status. Wilson, on his own initiative and against the preference of a clear majority of the American people, propelled the country into a grotesquely senseless, shockingly barbarous clash of European dynasties in which the United States had no substantial national interest. On such savage and foolish foundations is presidential greatness constructed.

I hold no brief for John Quincy Adams, Martin Van Buren, or Chester Arthur; but I think we ought to give them their due: at least they did not spill the blood of their fellow citizens.[3] Grant and Harding, who always rank near the bottom, do not deserve such contempt. Schlesinger observes that "their sin was excessive loyalty to crooked friends"—a sin that, in truth, many presidents have committed. Even Schlesinger admits, "Scandal and corruption are indefensible, but they may injure the general welfare less than misconceived policies."[4]

Indeed, scandal and corruption, which not surprisingly have tainted most administrations to some degree, pale by comparison with the damage presidential policy decisions have wreaked. What weight does Grant's Credit Mobilier scandal have in comparison to Lincoln's 620,000 dead in the Civil War? Harding's Teapot Dome affair is but a drop in the ocean of malfeasance compared to the global horrors set in train by Wilson's decision to take the United States into World War I. Why do the historians, and following them the public, place on pedestals the leaders responsible for such monumental catastrophes?

I have a theory: left-liberal historians worship political power and idolize those who wield it most lavishly in the service of left-liberal causes. How else can one account for the worship of Lincoln, Wilson, and FDR? Truman, whose stock now stands so high in the historians' estimation, left office in unpopularity bordering on disgrace because of his Korean War disaster, but the historians admire his half-hearted attempts to preserve and extend the New Deal. Theodore Roosevelt, a bloodthirsty protofascist, evokes admiration because of his public flogging of big corporate business, which is a perennial whipping boy for the left liberals.

Were I to rank the presidents, I would not quite turn the historians' ranking on its head, but I would move in that direction. Certainly Lincoln, Wilson, FDR, Truman, and Lyndon Johnson belong at the bottom for their statist economic policies as well as their utterly catastrophic war policies.

Finding presidents to put at the top of the list poses more difficulty, especially in choosing among those who have held office during the past century. Grover Cleveland, though far from perfect, may have been the best of them all. He kept the country at peace. He respected the Constitution, acknowledging that the national government has only a limited mission to perform and shaping his policies accordingly. He fought to lower tariffs; preserved the gold standard in its time of crisis; and restored order forcibly when hoodlums disturbed the peace on a wide front during the great railroad strike of 1894.[5]

Washington, I think, actually does deserve a high rating—not even the historians can be wrong all the time. He established the precedent of stepping down after two terms, a precedent that lasted until it clashed with FDR's insatiable ambition, and he prescribed a sensible foreign policy, later smeared as "isolationism," that served the nation well for more than a century. Other early presidents who were not entirely reprehensible in office include Jefferson and Jackson, though each committed grave derelictions.

Of the presidents since Cleveland, I rank Coolidge the highest. He sponsored sharp tax cuts and greatly reduced the national debt. As H. L. Mencken wrote, "There were no thrills while he reigned, but neither were there any headaches. He had no ideas, and he was not a nuisance"[6]—high praise in view of the many execrable men who have served as president during the twentieth century. Taft and Eisenhower were a cut above the rest, but that's not saying much.

Unfortunately, under FDR the Constitution suffered damage that none of his successors has repaired and most have made worse. Certainly since 1932— and, one might well argue, since 1896—no president has been true to his oath of office. Bringing to realization the ambitions harbored by Teddy Roosevelt and Wilson, FDR created the "imperial presidency," and we have been the worse for it ever since.

The people who ratified the original Constitution never intended the presidency to be a powerful office that spawns "great men." Article II, sections 2–4, which enumerate the powers of the president, comprise but four paragraphs, most of which deal with appointments and minor duties. The president is to act as commander in chief of the army and navy, but Congress alone can commit the nation to war—that is, "declare war." The president is to "take care that the laws be faithfully executed," but only Congress can enact laws, and then only within the scope of its limited, enumerated powers. The presidency was intended to be a largely ceremonial position whose occupant would confine himself to enforcing federal laws. Over time, however, abruptly during Lincoln's presidency and progressively during the twentieth century, presidents seized more and more power.[7]

Just before Bill Clinton took office in 1993, the *Seattle Times* crowned an opinion article with the stunningly stupid headline "Can Bill Clinton Save America?" I daresay that even devout Christians might have recoiled had the question been "Can Jesus Save America?" But probably few readers reacted as I did to the Clinton headline, because its pathetic presumption—that the federal government, under the command of a glorious new leader, might have the power to salvage our faltering fatherland—only mirrors the country's dominant ideology.[8]

Liberty in the United States will never be reestablished so long as elites and masses alike look to the president to perform supernatural feats and therefore tolerate a virtually unlimited exercise of presidential power. Until we can restore limited, constitutional government in this country, God save us from great presidents.

Notes

1. Arthur M. Schlesinger Jr., "The Ultimate Approval Rating," *New York Times Magazine,* December 15, 1996, pp. 46–51.

2. Quoted in ibid., p. 48.

3. My friend Jeff Hummel does have a high opinion of Van Buren. See Jeffrey Rogers Hummel, "Martin Van Buren: The Greatest American President," *Independent Review* 4 (fall 1999): 255–81.

4. Schlesinger, "The Ultimate Approval Rating," p. 50.

5. Robert Higgs, *Crisis and Leviathan: Critical Episodes in the Growth of American Government* (New York: Oxford University Press, 1987), pp. 77–105.

6. H. L. Mencken, *The Vintage Mencken,* compiled by Alistair Cooke (New York: Knopf, 1955), p. 233.

7. For one of the few scholarly sources that does not glorify this development, see John V. Denson, ed., *Reassessing the Presidency: The Rise of the Executive State and the Decline of Freedom* (Auburn, Ala.: Ludwig von Mises Institute, 2001). Chapter 1 of this collection is especially apt for present purposes: Richard Vedder and Lowell Gallaway, "Rating Presidential Performance," pp. 1–32.

8. I borrow here from my reflection "The Silly Season," *Liberty* (June 1993), p. 11.

PART III
Despotism, Soft and Hard

9

The U.S. Food and Drug Administration
A Billy Club Is Not a Substitute for Eyeglasses

Medical goods—specifically, drugs and devices—have the potential
to benefit users who seek to prevent or treat injuries and illnesses. Before using
such products, users would like to know that the products will serve their intended purpose effectively and will not cause unacceptable side effects. In
short, users value quality assurance for medical goods. Hence, they are willing
to pay for such assurance.

No method of quality assurance is or can be perfect. For some users, under
some conditions, some products will prove ineffective for their intended purposes. For some users, under some conditions, some products will cause unanticipated and sometimes harmful side effects. Largely because of differences
among patients in their physiological responses and their psychological inclination to accept various trade-offs, the typical medical product produces a
range of expected outcomes among its users.[1] No amount of premarket testing
can eliminate all such uncertainties. Therefore, evidence that a particular system of quality assurance has or might have flaws carries little weight in itself.
The critical question is whether another feasible system would perform better.

The U.S. Food and Drug Administration

In the United States, since the enactment of the Food, Drug, and Cosmetic Act
of 1938, the U.S. Food and Drug Administration (FDA) has been authorized
to regulate medical goods, ostensibly to provide potential users with quality assurance. Since 1938, the FDA has required that drug manufacturers produce
evidence that a new drug is *safe* when used as directed. If the agency finds the
manufacturer's evidence of safety unsatisfactory, it may withhold permission for
the would-be seller to place the product on the market. Since amendments to
the legislation in 1962, the FDA has been authorized to require also that drug
manufacturers produce evidence of a new drug's *efficacy* in its intended use.
If the agency finds the manufacturer's evidence of efficacy unsatisfactory, it
may withhold permission for the would-be seller to place the product on the
market. The 1962 amendments also authorized the FDA to regulate the clinical

trials by which the manufacturers generate human evidence pertaining to safety and efficacy. Clinical trials thus may proceed only in the manner approved by the FDA. In 1976, the FDA gained statutory authority to regulate medical devices in a similar fashion—that is, to require acceptable evidence of safety and efficacy before approving the marketing of new devices. The agency has also been authorized to exercise other regulatory powers, including the stipulation of detailed rules for Good Manufacturing Practice (GMP) and the requirement that manufacturers systematically track and report on the use of certain drugs and devices. The FDA may order manufacturers to cease the production or sale of products, to distribute new warnings, or to remove existing products from the market.[2]

Among the most important powers exercised by the FDA is its detailed regulation of the marketing, advertising, and other means by which the manufacturers seek to communicate with potential users and others about their products. Manufacturers are required to say certain things in certain ways, and they are forbidden to say other things or to say those things in certain ways.[3] Thus, all marketing messages—indeed, any communication that the FDA construes as somehow related to the marketing of products—are subject to stringent censorship, notwithstanding the rights of free speech and a free press that, one might have supposed, enjoy protection under the First Amendment.

Putting aside what the FDA is supposed to achieve, and considering instead what it clearly does in actuality, we can see that *its major activity is banning existing products from the market* until their manufacturers adduce satisfactory evidence of efficacy and safety. Auxiliary activities include

1. the agency's *prevention of clinical trials* until manufacturers provide satisfactory plans for the conduct of those trials;

2. its *censorship of product information* until manufacturers comply with its requirements for how such information will be communicated;

3. its *stipulation of manufacturing methods;* and

4. its *requirements for monitoring and reporting on the use of certain products* after the commercial introduction of those products.

FDA officials claim that, by means of these regulatory actions, the agency fulfills its legislative mandate to assure that all medical products available for sale in the United States are safe and effective when used as directed. Agency officials describe their system of regulation as the "gold standard" of regulatory regimes, superior to all those employed elsewhere and, presumably, superior to any feasible alternative system. However, the agency has never seriously undertaken to demonstrate that its regulatory actions generate benefits greater than their costs. When challenged by critics on these grounds, FDA officials resort either to the raw assertion that the agency's actions have positive net benefits or to the declaration that the FDA is only a police agency, that it is merely enforcing the Food, Drug, and Cosmetic Act, as amended, and cannot legally do anything else even if doing something else would be better for those subject to its regulation.

In reality, it is highly unlikely that the benefits of FDA actions exceed their costs. "Unhappily," as Dr. Henry I. Miller, an FDA official from 1979 to 1994, has written, "the 'gold standard' of FDA regulation is fool's gold."[4] Indeed, according to one defensible way of considering the matter, it is logically impossible that the FDA product bans produce a net benefit for anyone.[5] Rather than supplying the quality assurance that people value, the FDA serves, in a sense, as a central planner in the quality-assurance sector of the medical goods economy. The agency imposes a body of rigid, one-size-fits-all rules, binding on everyone regardless of the actual individual differences of people's medical conditions, personal preferences, and attitudes toward bearing risk. Just as the central planning of an entire economy produced not the superior efficiency fantasized by the socialist economists but instead the "planned chaos" predicted by Ludwig von Mises, so the FDA regulatory regime produces only the illusion of superior quality assurance. In fact, the FDA almost certainly brings about vastly more suffering and premature death than would occur in its absence.[6] Like other forms of central planning, it cannot solve the problems of information and incentives inherent in its way of dealing with the issues within its jurisdiction.

The Structure of Incentives at the FDA

Many analysts have described the fundamental incentive problem. The simplest way to describe it is to suppose that a product subject to FDA approval is either safe and effective (SE) or not (NSE), and that the FDA reviewer has two options, approve the product (A) or do not approve the product (NA). In this scenario, four outcomes are possible. In two of them, SE/A and NSE/NA, no problem arises; the agency is doing what it is supposed to do, and no one raises an objection. In the two other possible outcomes, the reviewer makes an error. A Type I error occurs when the reviewer does not approve a product that is in fact safe and effective (SE/NA). A Type II error occurs when the reviewer approves a product that is in fact not safe and effective (NSE/A).

Of course, FDA reviewers do not want to make any kind of error, but the reviewers' incentives lead them systematically to try much harder to avoid a Type II error (possible only when a product is approved) than to avoid a Type I error (possible only when a product is not approved). In the words of a former FDA reviewer, "Any time you approve a new drug you're wide open for attack. If the drug turns out to be less effective than the original data showed, they can nail you for selling out to a drug company. If it turns out to be less safe than anybody expected, some congressman or a newspaper writer will get you. So, there's only one way to play it safe—turn down the application. Or at least stall for time and demand more research."[7] Because commission of a Type II error has great adverse consequences for the reviewer, whereas commission of a Type I error has little or no adverse consequence for the reviewer, the FDA reviewers tend to proceed in a way that protects them from the possibility of approving a bad product: slowly, carefully, demanding more and more testing, more and more data, before giving the manufacturer permission to proceed.

As a result of the operation of this regulatory regime—the world's slowest and most expensive—drug development costs, in both time and money, have risen steadily during the post-1962 era. By the mid-1990s, the average new drug was taking fifteen years to pass from laboratory synthesis to FDA marketing approval, through a process that cost approximately $500 million.[8] More recently, in 2001, Tufts University researchers reported that "the average cost of discovering and developing a new medicine has risen to $802 million," and "the average development time for new medicines is 12 years."[9] Medical device companies have also experienced greater regulatory compliance costs and "increasingly lengthy product development times," often five to ten years for innovative products.[10]

Although the FDA always claims that it is solving its problems, the problem of asymmetric incentives is inherent in the situation. Hence, not surprisingly, the agency continues to operate in the same way. Recently, Dr. Miller referred to "the agency's thirty-year-plus tradition of risk-aversion and foot-dragging." In his view, "What many FDA officials lack in productivity and efficiency, they more than make up for in skills related to obstructionism and self-preservation."[11]

While FDA officials drag their feet, products remain banned from the market, and all consumers who might have benefited from their use must forgo those benefits. Obviously, a course of action that is "safe" for the FDA reviewers themselves is often unsafe—indeed, deadly on a wide scale—for these potential beneficiaries. No one knows just how great the death toll has been, but various estimates of the number of lives that might have been saved, but for the FDA's obstruction, add up to hundreds of thousands during the past four decades. The number of lives saved by FDA regulation is lower by at least an order of magnitude.[12] This difference is almost inevitable, because a dangerous product would be withdrawn from the market quickly, once its dangers were known, whereas the loss of life occasioned by the FDA's withholding of a product from the market typically can continue indefinitely, even as the deaths mount, because hardly anybody holds the agency responsible for the damage caused by its commission of the Type I error (SE/NA).

Individual Heterogeneity Versus Command and Control

The FDA attempts to supply quality assurance by means of command and control, just as (in socialist theory) the central planners of an entire economy attempt to allocate resources efficiently by means of command and control. Long ago, Ludwig von Mises and F. A. Hayek explained that economic central planning would inevitably fail because, among other things, the planners impose a static solution on a problem that is inherently dynamic. Planners cannot keep up with all the ceaselessly changing economic data. Even less can they find out about data that are not only variable but specific to time and place. And in no event can they find out what is known even to the individual economic actors in only a tacit, inarticulable way.[13]

Likewise, FDA decision makers cannot know how much risk individuals prefer to take and therefore at what point in a prolonged process of testing and monitoring those persons would desire to begin using a product. Various individual and group efforts make it clear that many would like to have access to products long before the FDA permits them to have that access. Notice, however, that the FDA's insistence on extensive testing and monitoring provides *no* benefit for individuals who prefer even more assurance: those persons will continue to delay their own individual use of a product even after the FDA has approved its commercial introduction. Thus, no matter at what point the FDA allows a new product to be sold, the outcome is that, in terms of expected utility, some persons are harmed (because they wanted access sooner), but no one is benefited (because other potential users want more than the legally compelled amount of quality assurance before they will use the product).[14]

Like economic central planners, FDA officials speak of the problem they attempt to solve as if it pertained to some gigantic organism. As one FDA official put it, "We believe that benefits which accrue to society because of our regulatory system are worth the cost and far outweigh any risks."[15] This statement refers to the benefits and the costs of FDA regulation as if they were experienced by society at large rather than by specific individuals who differ enormously in their personal valuation of the costs and benefits and in their willingness to bear risk. This FDA official's claim rests on the unspoken assumption that a single rule should apply in all cases, mocking the actual heterogeneity of people's preferences and medical conditions.[16]

Keeping all the actual variation in mind, one realizes that the simple four-cell schema (SE/A, SE/NA, NSE/A, NSE/NA) employed earlier in my analysis fails to capture the essential complications of the situation. Hardly any product that comes before the FDA is either totally safe or totally effective. Rather, it is safe with a certain probability, with respect to a certain adverse side effect, when used by a certain person, under certain conditions. Rather than designating a product as either safe and effective (SE) or not safe and effective

(NSE), as previously, one would need to identify a product as safe for person p with probability q with respect to adverse side effect of type r under condition s—in symbols, S[p, q, r, s]. Similarly, one would have to identity a product as effective for person u with probability v with respect to benefit of type w under condition x—in symbols E[u, v, w, x]. In reality, a medical product does not fall into one or another of *two* classes, but into one class of an *indefinitely large number* of possible classes, depending on the specific user. Each individual potentially constitutes a distinct class.

Only the individual who seeks to use a medical product, perhaps in consultation with his doctors and other medical experts who advise him and his doctors, can make a rational decision about whether the use of an existing product is desirable or not. To suppose that any central planning agency, regardless of its scientific expertise, can arrive at a better decision than the patient and his personal advisers is to misconstrue completely the relevant decision problem. To impose a single decision on the use of the product—either to permit everyone's access or to forbid everyone's access—is to oversimplify drastically and often fatally the potential users' actual situations.[17]

Wanted: Information, Not Dictation

The FDA is a police agency. On the basis of its enabling legislation, it makes rules and it enforces them coercively by threats of administrative, civil, and criminal punishments.[18] When David A. Kessler was seeking reappointment as commissioner of food and drugs after Bill Clinton's first presidential election, "Instead of talking about new drugs approved and lives saved, [he] boast[ed] that 'the number of injunctions, the number of seizures, the number of criminal cases referred to [the Department of] Justice ha[d] all increased' in his term."[19]

Among the most important FDA rules are those expressed as the command "Do not sell product A until we permit you to do so." That kind of police action is the bluntest possible instrument for solving the relevant problem of quality assurance.[20] What the consumer who comes to the market for medical goods actually values is *information* of various sorts and the *freedom* to combine that information with his own subjective valuations of costs, benefits, and risk-bearing in order to arrive at an optimal decision tailored specifically to his unique circumstances. In seeking quality assurance, consumers want "eyeglasses," a means of gaining a clearer vision of the various factors related to their decision problem. In response to that demand, the government gives them the FDA policeman wielding a billy club. A billy club is not just a poor substitute for eyeglasses; it is the wrong instrument for the job at hand.

One might argue, of course, that the FDA does provide quality assurance because it assures every potential user that any product it allows on the market is "safe and effective" when used as directed. No doubt many Americans, having never given the matter much thought, do perceive the FDA's accomplishments in such simple, naive terms. Dr. Louis Lasagna has noted that "in public opinion surveys [the FDA] seems generally perceived as not only performing an important function but as doing it well."[21] Certainly, the agency itself encourages the public to think of its actions in such terms.[22] But even a little thought along the lines I have laid out is sufficient to demolish the FDA's claims.

Anyone inclined to reject my arguments might be surprised to learn that, according to a study published recently (April 1999) in the *Journal of the American Medical Association,* an estimated 106,000 Americans (plus or minus 30,000) die each year *in hospitals* as a result of adverse reactions to drugs prescribed by doctors (this number does *not* include deaths from drug abuse, suicide, and mistaken prescription).[23] If the study is correct—the experts are still arguing over the precise best estimate—then fatal reactions to *FDA-approved* drugs amount to the fourth-leading cause of death in the United States, after heart disease, cancer, and stroke.[24]

Notice that *these deaths, not to mention the estimated 2.2 million serious injuries to hospitalized patients and the unknown but most likely large number of deaths and injuries to nonhospitalized patients from the same cause, adverse reactions to approved drugs, are precisely the sort of harm from which the FDA's vast apparatus of regulation is supposed to be protecting the American public.* Obviously, not only has the FDA failed to consider how much harm it causes by its commission of Type I errors, but it has also failed abysmally in avoiding Type II errors.[25] As David Weimer has noted, without the FDA's premarket approval system, "doctors would no longer be encouraged to equate market availability with safety. Hence, greater care in prescribing could conceivably result."[26]

In reaction to the *Journal of the American Medical Association* study, "The FDA concedes that it doesn't closely track the problem of adverse drug reactions but says it lacks the resources to thoroughly review the 250,000 cases it hears about each year."[27] This excuse rings hollow when one recalls that the FDA has somehow found the resources to engage in a wide range of public-relations stunts, such as that involving the destruction of twelve thousand gallons of perfectly drinkable but allegedly "mislabeled" orange juice;[28] in ideologically inspired regulation, such as that related to silicone breast implants;[29] and in blatantly illegal efforts, such as the regulation of tobacco products, a major agency undertaking later struck down by the U.S. Supreme Court.[30]

In sum, the FDA has failed to provide the quality assurance it pretends to provide; it has caused immense harm by the way its regulations discourage research and development and block the access of new products to the market; and it has occupied itself in activities that only waste public money in carrying out power-grabbing jihads against politically incorrect products or producers. Regardless of the aspect from which one views the FDA, its actions merit only vigorous condemnation.

Quality Assurance Without the FDA

Many have imagined that the FDA might be reformed. As Henry I. Miller and William M. Wardell have written, "for decades, debates about [FDA] regulatory reform have identified the same problems, and the same solutions have been recommended by panel after distinguished panel.... Because the agency has been too slow and obdurate in implementing most of these repeated recommendations, reform must come from outside the agency, via legislative changes."[31] After the Republicans took control of Congress in 1995, they promised to undertake such a reform.[32] They evidently underestimated the resistance of the executive branch and the political adroitness of the FDA itself.

After three years of hearings, spin-doctoring, and deal making, Congress brought forth the impressively titled FDA Modernization Act of 1997, which Dr. Miller aptly describes as "the moral equivalent of the proverbial elephant laboring to bring forth a mouse." It consists of a number of minor changes, but "even the bill's most ardent advocates have not claimed that it will reduce the overall time or costs of drug development."[33] Nor will the token pilot program for third-party review of low-risk medical devices bring about significant change.[34] Under the new law, the FDA retains final say with respect to everything important. The agency's friends even managed to place a provision in the act that substantially expands the FDA's reach by authorizing it to regulate "activities pertaining to any potentially regulated products that occur completely within a single state."[35] Once again, Congress makes a mockery of the Constitution's interstate commerce clause. Although it is easy to understand why the would-be reformers of FDA regulation forsook genuine reform and settled for a mere semblance, the experience only emphasizes anew that the public will never escape the destructive effects of the agency's regulation until the FDA is simply abolished.[36]

Of course, many questions might be raised about how well alternative measures of quality assurance for medical goods would operate. *By far the most important thing to remember, however, is how horribly the present system operates,* how "the FDA's policies have made life progressively more dangerous for patients and difficult for physicians."[37] To falter in endorsing the abolition of the agency would be like declining a truce in 1918 because one was worried about the risks to which the soldiers might be exposed after leaving the battlefield. The difference is that warfare is undeniably destructive and is represented as such, whereas the FDA's regulatory regime, although also undeniably destructive, is represented by government officials and accepted by most members of the public as a life-saving undertaking. Not only does the public suffer the excessive pain, distress, and premature death that result from FDA regulation, but it is also led to play the fool by endorsing the very cause of its misfortune.

In an important respect, the FDA's control over drugs has always been incomplete. Once a drug has been approved, doctors are not restricted to using it solely for the FDA-approved indication; they may prescribe it for other purposes as well. Such uses, known as "off label," account for some 40–50 percent of all prescriptions, including 85–90 percent of those for treating children and 60–70 percent of those for treating cancer.[38] In many cases, an off-label drug use actually constitutes the established standard of care for physicians.[39] Yet, in effect, such medications are "unapproved" because the drugs used have never passed though the Phase II and Phase III clinical studies required by the FDA to establish their efficacy for those particular indications. Nevertheless, there is no evidence that this widespread off-label drug use has given rise to problematic side effects more frequently than has FDA-approved use of drugs. If ordinary people understood better the place of off-label drug use in the current practice of medicine, they might be more willing to contemplate getting rid of the FDA or at least returning its regulatory scope to that of the pre-1962 era.[40]

One also needs to appreciate that because the FDA does not supply the quality assurance people value, many alternative suppliers of quality assessments have *already* emerged. Scientific, medical, and engineering researchers publish vast amounts of information relevant to assessing the quality of medical goods. With the advent of the Internet and the World Wide Web, practically anyone can have cheap, immediate access to this information. American, European, and international organizations have established a multitude of standards that are already being used widely to gauge the quality of products and of manufacturing and related processes. Manufacturers can—and already do— attest the quality of their products by issuing declarations of conformity with appropriate standards, for example, the CE mark, which signifies conformity with the relevant directives issued by the European Union. Organizations such as Underwriters Laboratory,[41] ECRI (formerly, Emergency Care Research Institute),[42] TÜV PS (Technischer Uberwachungsverein Product Service),[43] the more than fifty Notified Bodies authorized to operate in the European Union,[44] and many other organizations already perform many quality-assurance activities, and they might perform far more.[45] Absent the FDA, many quality-assurance organizations currently "crowded out" would enter the market, both complementing and competing with those already in operation.

In the United States and many other countries, patients must have a doctor's prescription to purchase a new drug.[46] Indeed, increasingly, more than a single doctor stands between the patient and the product:

> Typically, today's manufacturer of a new drug must convince a panel of experts who comprise a managed-care organization's formulary committee—a discerning and informed consumer—of the importance of the product. Their evidentiary criteria can exceed those of FDA and they

may call for evidence (such as pharmacoeconomics and comparative efficacy) that is outside the sphere of the drug-approval process. The utilization of new (and other) drugs is becoming more tightly controlled, and the outcomes are being recorded and analyzed in ways that were previously inconceivable. There is, for example, a growing use of computerized control of patient selection, indication, dose, and duration of therapy.

Thus, manufacturers' products and claims, and the evidence supporting them, must meet very high standards to be accepted in today's marketplace. In this exacting environment, government regulation of the product-development process should not add burdens that are no longer necessary.[47]

FDA officials and other supporters of the current regulatory regime would have us imagine that wily and sinister drug companies push their products onto distraught and bewildered consumers who are helpless to defend themselves against such wicked tricksters. Even if the manufacturers of medical goods had no ethics, however, they would still be greatly constrained by the potential damage to their reputations and by the losses they might suffer from lawsuits.[48] Those important considerations aside, prescribing doctors, health-maintenance organizations, and hospital formularies intervene, the latter two evincing "the evolution of various nongovernmental entities into de facto drug-vetting, standard-setting organizations."[49]

More Than Health Is at Stake

It is certainly unfortunate that the FDA's regulatory regime has brought about a silent epidemic of unnecessary suffering and avoidable deaths. I cannot imagine any feasible public-policy change that would so surely enhance the public's welfare as would the abolition of the FDA. Yet great improvement of the public health would not be the only valuable outcome of such an abolition. Liberty would also expand enormously.

At present, the American people are being treated as if they were children or barnyard animals, as if they had no capacity for making their own decisions about their own most vital interests, as if only government bureaucrats have the capacity to deal with the risks people face as consumers of medical goods. Lest I be thought to exaggerate, consider the words of the recent commissioner of food and drugs David Kessler:

> If members of our society were empowered to make their own decisions about the entire range of products for which the FDA has responsibility ... then the whole rationale for the agency would cease to exist. ...

To argue that people ought to be able to choose their own risks, that government should not intervene ... is to impose an unrealistic burden on people when they are most vulnerable to manufacturers' assertions. ... Those are precisely the situations in which the legal and ethical justifications for the FDA's existence is [*sic*] greatest.[50]

Notwithstanding the anguished cries of countless patients and their families who have sought to escape from FDA restrictions of their choice of treatments,[51] Kessler has the audacity to declare that it would be an "unrealistic burden" on them, that it would be unethical if they, rather than he and his subordinates, decided the most vital questions bearing on their well-being and even their very survival. Rarely does one encounter a more grotesque moral arrogance.

Ultimately, abolition of the FDA would amount to the elimination of an insulting and inhumane restriction of individual liberty.[52] It would return the property rights over people's bodies to the legitimate owners. It would be a declaration of independence from those who fancy themselves better equipped than we are to decide how we should manage our own lives and who mercilessly employ the coercive force of government to impose that management on us.

Notes

1. Stephen A. Eraker and Harold C. Sox, "Assessment of Patients' Preferences for Therapeutic Outcomes," *Medical Decision Making* 1 (1981): 29–39; Sally Usdin Yasuda and Raymond L. Woosley, "The Clinical Value of FDA Class C Drugs Approved from 1981 to 1988," *Clinical Pharmacology and Therapeutics* 52 (December 1992): 577–82, esp. p. 581.

2. Peter Barton Hutt and Richard A. Merrill, *Food and Drug Law: Cases and Materials* (Westbury, N.Y.: Foundation Press, 1991). Extensive information, citations, and links regarding all aspects of FDA regulation can now be found at a Web site created by Daniel Klein and Alexander Tabarrok and maintained by The Independent Institute. See http://www.FDAReview.org.

3. Richard M. Cooper, Richard L. Frank, and Michael J. O'Flaherty, "History of Health Claims Regulation," *Food Drug Cosmetic Law Journal* 45 (1990): 655–91; John E. Calfee, "FDA Regulation: Moving Toward a Black Market in Information," *The American Enterprise* 3 (March–April 1992): 34–41; Richard T. Kaplar, ed., *Bad Prescription for the First Amendment: FDA Censorship of Drug Advertising and Promotion* (Washington, D.C.: Media Institute, 1993); Paul H. Rubin, "FDA Advertising Restrictions: Ignorance Is Death," in *Hazardous to Our Health? FDA Regulation of Health Care Products*, edited by Robert Higgs (Oakland, Calif.: The Independent Institute, 1995), pp. 29–53; Robert M. Goldberg, "Breaking Up the FDA's Medical Information Monopoly," *Regulation*, no. 2 (1995): 40–52; John Berlau, "Dr. Kessler, Remove the Gag," *Wall Street Journal*, December 5, 1995; Daniel E. Troy, "FDA Censorship Could Cost Lives," *Wall Street Journal*, July 23, 1999.

4. Henry I. Miller, M.D., *To America's Health: A Proposal to Reform the Food and Drug*

Administration (Stanford, Calif.: Hoover Institution Press, 2000), p. 35.

5. Robert Higgs, "Banning a Risky Product Cannot Improve Any Consumer's Welfare (Properly Understood), with Applications to FDA Testing Requirements," *Review of Austrian Economics* 7 (1994): 3–20.

6. William Wardell, "More Regulation or Better Therapies?" *Regulation* (September–October 1979): 25–33; Paul J. Quirk, "Food and Drug Administration," in *The Politics of Regulation,* edited by James Q. Wilson (New York: Basic Books, 1980), pp. 226–32; Henry G. Grabowski and John M. Vernon, *The Regulation of Pharmaceuticals: Balancing the Benefits and Risks* (Washington, D.C.: American Enterprise Institute, 1983), esp. pp. 46–47; Dale H. Gieringer, "The Safety and Efficacy of New Drug Approval," *Cato Journal* 5 (spring–summer 1985): 177–201; Sam Kazman, "Deadly Overcaution," *Journal of Regulation and Social Costs* 1 (1990): 35–54; Alison Keith, "Regulating Information about Aspirin and the Prevention of Heart Attack," *American Economic Review* 85 (May 1995): 96–99; Robert Higgs, "FDA Regulation of Medical Devices," in *Hazardous to Our Health?* ed. Higgs, esp. pp. 80–82; Robert Higgs, *How FDA Is Causing a Technological Exodus: A Comparative Analysis of Medical Device Regulations—United States, Europe, Canada, and Japan* (Washington, D.C.: Competitive Enterprise Institute, February 1995); Doug Bandow, "The FDA Can Be Dangerous to Your Health," *Fortune,* November 11, 1996; "FDA Slammed in Comparison with Europe," *Clinica* 694 (February 26, 1996): 7; Michael F. Cannon, *The FDA's Report Card Shows Another Failing Grade,* Citizens for a Sound Economy Issue Analysis no. 52 (Washington, D.C.: Citizens for a Sound Economy, April 30, 1997), esp. pp. 7–13; Michael F. Cannon, *Third FDA Report Card Shows Longer Delays for New Drugs in Fiscal Year 1997,* Citizens for a Sound Economy Issue Analysis no. 73 (Washington, D.C.: Citizens for a Sound Economy, August 6, 1998), esp. pp. 11–15; Robert Goldberg, *David Kessler's Legacy at the FDA,* Institute for Policy Innovation Policy Report no. 143 (Lewisville, Tex.: Institute for Policy Innovation, October 1997); Alexander Tabarrok, "Assessing the FDA via the Anomaly of Off-Label Drug Prescribing," *The Independent Review* 5 (summer 2000): 25–53, esp. 29–36, 44, 48.

7. FDA reviewer as quoted by Milton Silverman and Philip R. Lee, *Pills, Profits, and Politics* (Berkeley: University of California Press, 1974), p. 251. See also Dr. Henry I. Miller's recollection of the advice given to him by his FDA superior, in Miller, *To America's Health,* pp. 41–42, and Commissioner Alexander Schmidt's statement quoted by Quirk, "Food and Drug Administration," p. 216.

8. Bertram A. Spilker, M.D., Ph.D., "The Drug Development and Approval Process," retrieved on April 3, 2000, from http://www.phrma.org/charts/approval.html. Dr. Spilker is senior vice president for scientific and regulatory affairs at the trade association Pharmaceutical Research and Manufacturers of America. The original source of the cost estimate is a January 1996 report by the Boston Consulting Group; the original source of the development-time estimate is the Tufts Center for the Study of Drug Development. See also Joseph A. DiMasi, Mark A. Seibring, and Louis Lasagna, "New Drug Development in the United States from 1963 to 1992," *Clinical Pharmacology and Therapeutics* 55 (June 1994): 609–22, esp. pp. 614–17.

9. Tufts Center for the Study of Drug Development, news release, November 30, 2001; Gardiner Harris, "Cost of Developing Drugs Found to Rise," *Wall Street Journal,* December 3, 2001.

10. "FDA Modernization Act: Full Implementation to Improve Patient Access," retrieved on June 27, 2000, from the Web site of the Advanced Medical Technology Association (for-

merly known as the Health Industry Manufacturers Association), http://www.himanet .com. See also Higgs, "FDA Regulation of Medical Devices"; Ralph A. Epstein, "Medical Devices," in Ralph A. Epstein and others, *Advancing Medical Technology: Health, Safety, and the Role of Government in the 21st Century* (Washington, D.C.: Progress and Freedom Foundation, 1996), esp. pp. 65–67; and Charles A. Homsy, *How FDA Regulation and Injury Litigation Cripple the Medical Device Industry,* Cato Institute Policy Analysis no. 412 (Washington, D.C.: Cato Institute, August 28, 2001).

11. Henry I. Miller, "Failed FDA Reform," *Regulation* 21, no. 3 (1998), p. 29.

12. See sources cited in footnote 6.

13. Ludwig von Mises, *Socialism* (Indianapolis, Ind.: Liberty Fund, 1981; 1st ed., in German, published in 1922); F. A. Hayek, "The Present State of the Debate," in *Collectivist Economic Planning: Critical Studies on the Possibilities of Socialism,* edited by F. A. Hayek (London: George Routledge and Son, 1935), pp. 210–43.

14. For a fuller development of this argument, see Higgs, "Banning a Risky Product." See also David Leo Weimer, "Safe—and Available—Drugs," in *Instead of Regulation: Alternatives to Federal Regulatory Agencies,* edited by Robert W. Poole (Lexington, Mass.: Lexington Books, 1982), pp. 240, 253–55, 269, for anticipations of the argument.

15. FDA official as quoted by David Seidman, "The Politics of Policy Analysis," *Regulation* (July–August 1977), p. 31. See also the statement of FDA official Janet Woodcock as quoted in Tamar Nordenberg, "Why Should FDA Regulate Drugs? An Interview with Janet Woodcock, M.D., Director of FDA's Center for Drug Evaluation and Research," *FDA Consumer* 31 (September–October 1997), p. 22: "We at CDER think we've achieved the proper balance."

16. Seidman, "The Politics of Policy Analysis," p. 25.

17. Dale H. Gieringer, *Compassion vs. Control: FDA Investigational-Drug Regulation,* Cato Institute Policy Analysis no. 72 (Washington, D.C.: Cato Institute, May 20, 1986), pp. 5–6.

18. For data on enforcement actions taken during the fiscal years 1997–99, for example, see Tamar Nordenberg, "FDA Takes Action to Enforce the Law," *FDA Consumer* (May–June 2000), pp. 7–8.

19. "Kessler and Clinton" [editorial], *Wall Street Journal,* January 12, 1993.

20. For an important recent example, see "Laboratories Scramble to Find Replacement Supplies Following FDA Ban on 125 Abbott Products," *Clinica* 887 (December 6, 1999): 8–9.

21. Louis Lasagna, "Congress, the FDA, and New Drug Development: Before and after 1962," *Perspectives in Biology and Medicine* 32 (spring 1989), p. 322. A 1995 poll found that 78 percent of respondents considered the FDA necessary. See "Wall Street Journal/NBC News Poll," *Wall Street Journal,* January 20, 1995. A typical view is the editorial "Dangerous Schemes to Overhaul the FDA," *San Francisco Chronicle,* February 5, 1995.

22. Tom Paulson, "Haste with New Drugs Risky, FDA Chief Warns," *Seattle Post-Intelligencer,* November 8, 1994.

23. J. Lazarou, B. H. Pomeranz, and P. N. Corey, "Incidence of Adverse Drug Reactions in Hospitalized Patients," *Journal of the American Medical Association* 279 (1998): 1200–1205.

24. "Deadly Rx: Why Are Drugs Killing so Many Patients?" *USA Today,* April 24, 1998; Terence Monmaney, "Study: Prescriptions May Kill 100,000 a Year," *Seattle Times,* April 15, 1998; "Study Finds Drug-Reaction Toll Is High," *Wall Street Journal,* April 15, 1998.

25. U.S. General Accounting Office, *FDA Drug Review: Postapproval Risks, 1976–85,* GAO/PEMD-90-15 (Washington, D.C.: U.S. Government Printing Office, April 1990): "identifies drugs for which serious risks arose after approval for marketing."

26. Weimer, "Safe—and Available—Drugs," p. 266. See also Leonard G. Wilson, "FDA Red Tape Dooms Transplant Drug," *Wall Street Journal,* June 24, 1993 ("Once approval has been granted, the FDA becomes remarkably tolerant of any shortcomings in a drug that may emerge from further experience"); and Quirk, "Food and Drug Administration," p. 223 ("it is generally easy to keep a drug on the market, once it has been approved").

27. "Study Finds Drug-Reaction Toll Is High."

28. Herbert Burkholz, *The FDA Follies* (New York: Basic Books, 1994), pp. 179–81; James Bovard, "Double-Crossing to Safety," *American Spectator* (January 1995), p. 25.

29. Marcia Angell, M.D., *Science on Trial: The Clash of Medical Evidence and the Law in the Breast Implant Case* (New York: Norton, 1996); David E. Bernstein, "The Breast Implant Fiasco," *California Law Review* 87 (March 1999): 457–510.

30. Eben Shapiro, "FDA Amassing Data in Effort to Gain Power to Regulate Cigarettes as Drug," *Wall Street Journal,* March 28, 1994; Robert S. Greenberger and Gordon Fairclough, "FDA Oversight of Tobacco Struck Down," *Wall Street Journal,* March 22, 2000.

31. Henry I. Miller and William M. Wardell, "Therapeutic Drugs and Biologics," in *Advancing Medical Technology,* p. 48.

32. Laurie McGinley, "GOP Takes Aim at FDA, Seeking to Ease Way for Approval of New Drugs, Medical Products," *Wall Street Journal,* December 12, 1994.

33. Miller, "Failed FDA Reform," p. 28.

34. "FDA Finds Little Response to Third-Party Review Pilot," *Clinica* 820 (August 10, 1998), p. 4.

35. Ibid., p. 29.

36. "FDA Comes under Fire over Implementation of Modernization Act at US Senate Panel Hearing," *Clinica* 881 (October 25, 1999): 3; "FDA Shows Little Desire to Rescind Control in Scientific Disputes Between Companies and Reviewers," *Clinica* 868 (July 26, 1999): 7.

37. Miller, *To America's Health,* p. 56.

38. Miller, "Failed FDA Reform," p. 25.

39. Goldberg, *David Kessler's Legacy,* pp. 8–10.

40. For extended discussion of the evidence and the argument with respect to off-label prescribing, see Tabarrok, "Assessing the FDA."

41. Noel D. Campbell, "Exploring Free Market Certification of Medical Devices," in *American Health Care: Government, Market Processes, and the Public Interest,* edited by Roger D. Feldman (New Brunswick, N.J.: Transaction, 2000), esp. pp. 337–41; "New Notified Body Aims to Be Number One," *Clinica* 899 (March 13, 2000): 7; "TÜV PS Gets a Rough Ride over Its Additional Quality Mark for Devices," *Clinica* 892 (January 24, 2000): 4–5.

42. Bruce Goldfarb, "Technology's Watchdogs: Institute Monitors Safety and Effectiveness

of Medical Devices," *American Medical News,* May 11, 1992; Joan Stephenson, "Medical Technology Watchdog Plays Unique Role in Quality Assessment," *Journal of the American Medical Association* 274 (1995): 999–1001.

43. TÜV Product Service, "Zertificate für Europa/Certificates for Europe," brochure; "EU-COMED Appeals to Companies to Shun Supplementary Quality Marks and Stick with the CE Mark," *Clinica* 866 (July 12, 1999): 6 (concerning the TÜV Mark).

44. G. R. Higson, "Medical Device Regulations in the New Europe," *Journal of Medical Engineering and Technology* 16 (May–June 1992): 107–11; Gordon Higson, "The European Medical Device Directives," *Clinica Supplement* (October 1993); Amanda Maxwell, "Update on Implementation of the Medical Devices Directives," *Clinica Supplement* (October 1995): 1–8.

45. Miller, *To America's Health,* pp. 29–30, 76–81.

46. Sam Peltzman, "By Prescription Only ... or Occasionally?" *Regulation* 11 (1987): 23–28.

47. Miller and Wardell, "Therapeutic Drugs and Biologics," p. 45.

48. W. Kip Viscusi, "Regulatory Reform and Liability for Pharmaceuticals and Medical Devices," in *Advancing Medical Technology,* esp. pp. 81–84; Miller, *To America's Health,* pp. 30–34.

49. Miller, *To America's Health,* p. 29.

50. Kessler as quoted by Goldberg, *David Kessler's Legacy,* p. 1.

51. Jonathan Kwitny, *Acceptable Risks* (New York: Poseidon Press, 1992); Linda DeSpain, "The FDA Snuffs a Ray of Hope," *Wall Street Journal,* June 18, 1996; "Voices in the Health Care Debate," *Wall Street Journal,* February 16, 1993, esp. the statements of James P. Driscoll and Woodrow Wirsig; Lauran Neergaard, "Patients Press FDA to Approve New Drugs to Modestly Extend Life," *Seattle Times,* November 26, 1995; Tom Hazlett as quoted in Peter Brimelow and Leslie Spencer, "Food and Drugs and Politics," *Forbes* (November 22, 1993), pp. 115, 119.

52. Daniel B. Klein, "Liberty, Dignity, and Responsibility: The Moral Triad of a Good Society," *The Independent Review* 1 (winter 1997): 325–51; Daniel B. Klein, "Quality-and-Safety Assurance: How Voluntary Social Processes Remedy Their Own Shortcomings," *The Independent Review* 2 (spring 1998): 537–55, esp. pp. 549–51.

10

Regulatory Harmonization
A Sweet-Sounding,
Dangerous Development

Contemporary social and economic affairs take place within a be-wildering complex of regulatory restrictions and requirements. Already profuse beyond comprehension, the labyrinth grows ever more extensive. In the United States, at the federal level alone, the 4,000–5,000 new final rules put in place each year require some 20,000 pages of the *Federal Register* for their official promulgation.[1] Simultaneously, the 50 states, 3,043 counties, 19,372 municipalities, and 16,629 townships and towns crank out countless new regulations of their own.[2]

All of this regulatory activity, of course, occurs within a single nation-state. Elsewhere in the world, the regulators are not just sitting on their hands, and in certain countries—France springs immediately to mind—the bureaucrats would be outraged by the mere suggestion that the U.S. regulators were surpassing them in the number of regulations. Business firms that operate globally must deal with a vast variety of regulatory restrictions and requirements.

In general, complying with many different bodies of regulation costs more than complying with just one, or so it has often seemed to businesspeople. Hence their inclination to support "regulatory harmonization."

In the United States Historically

In the United States, business support helped to create the very first federal regulatory agency, the Interstate Commerce Commission (ICC), in 1887. As historian Gabriel Kolko has remarked, in the *locus classicus* of this thesis, "The railroads realized long before 1900 that the federal regulation of railroads offered them protection, actual or potential, from harassment by the states," and "it was this threat of state legislative attacks that kept the railroads solidly behind the ICC and federal regulation."[3]

Similarly, as Gary Libecap has shown, butchers and cattle raisers' shift of lobbying efforts from the state legislatures to the U.S. Congress—not consumers' complaints—played a crucial role in gaining passage of the Sherman Antitrust Act in 1890.[4]

Along the same lines, Richard Sylla has argued that efforts toward regulatory harmonization underlay the widespread business support for big federal government that became so evident during the Progressive Era: "How much more efficient and less costly it must have seemed to the businessmen subjected to several state jurisdictions to create an administrative state at the federal level, and to have that state absorb some state activities and override others. That is what they tried to bring about—successfully."[5] Reacting to an earlier, unpublished version of Sylla's article, I agreed that "the managers of the big firms, harassed by dozens of state governments and their rapacious politicos,... began to see the wisdom of federal regulation. Perhaps, they reasoned, they would stand a better chance of escaping the meddlesome, costly, and fluctuating congeries of state regulations if they could deal with a single national regulatory body."[6]

The story, however, did not end at that point. The businessmen who supported the creation of new federal regulatory agencies hoped, of course, to make their lives simpler and their costs lower. Better still, perhaps they could "capture" the agencies and make them serve as, in effect, cartel police, keeping maverick competitors in check and assuring higher rates of return to the cartel members. By no means did they always succeed in that quest,[7] but to the extent that they did succeed, consumers suffered as a result. No doubt, George J. Stigler had just such outcomes in mind when he observed, "Regulation and competition are rhetorical friends and deadly enemies."[8]

Not infrequently, however, business support for regulatory harmonization at the federal level gave birth to an unmanageable offspring. Like Dr. Frankenstein's monster, the newly created federal regulatory agencies often stopped heeding their business progenitors' voice. Within twenty years, for example, the ICC had fallen under the sway of shipper interests, and by refusing to approve reasonable rate increases, the commission proceeded to compress the railroad companies in a merciless cost-price squeeze.[9] So severely had the railroad firms suffered in the decade after 1906 that during World War I they collapsed, financially exhausted, into the loving arms of the U.S. Railroad Administration; afterward, under the terms of the Transportation Act of 1920, they found themselves reduced to little more than regulated public utilities.[10]

In a similar manner, over the past century many a firm must have rued the day that business interests threw their weight behind the enactment of the Sherman Act and thereby gave rise to the galling government harassment that epitomizes everything suggested by the phrase "arbitrary and capricious." Nor have consumers been well served by the rampaging federal trustbusters, as the seemingly endless cases against Microsoft have made crystal clear once again.[11]

On the International Scene Currently

As international commerce has grown in recent decades, more and more firms have found themselves butting up against the obstacles posed by the great variety of regulatory systems in place around the world. Seeking to mitigate the great cost of complying with diverse regulations, businesspeople have lent their support to an accelerating movement toward international regulatory harmonization. Outstanding manifestations of this trend have appeared in the European Union (EU) and its predecessor organizations. As Manfred E. Streit has recently observed, "Almost throughout the whole process of European integration, harmonisation of national laws and regulations was considered a matter of course." There existed "a widespread prejudice ... of assuming quite uncritically that a uniform legal system which covers a large area has a value on its own and that legal harmonisation will lead to the best possible system."[12] However one might characterize the course of economic activity in the EU, no one can deny that "business" has been brisk in Brussels.

Although I find myself in nearly complete agreement with the analysis of harmonization Streit presents in his article, I take issue with his particular conclusion that "taken together, the normative and positive evaluations suggest that harmonisation appears only advisable in those cases in which compelling reasons, *such as the prevention of hazard,* can be given."[13]

In large part, however, my disagreement springs from a recognition of certain tendencies that Streit himself notes, especially the following one: "considering those regulations which have been introduced by harmonisation, it became obvious that in many cases they were more complex and comprehensive than those regulations which were previously in force in the member states."[14] This statement tends to apply to the harmonization process wherever it occurs, not just in the EU. That is, international harmonization of diverse national regulations tends to raise the severity of the regulations at least to the highest level previously reached by a member of the accord—there is, so to speak, a *leveling up*—and frequently to a higher, formerly untried level, so that even the previously strictest regulator becomes stricter still.

Now, it might seem counterintuitive that harmonization would be undesirable—even dangerous—in relation to regulations aimed at the prevention of hazard or the promotion of public health, but at least in certain pertinent areas I have studied in some detail, I am persuaded that such is the case.

Medical Devices as an Example

In the United States, medical devices—thousands of distinct products that now range from bandages, syringes, and latex gloves to implantable defibrillators, CAT scanners, and laser eye-sculpting machines—first became subject to regulation by the Food and Drug Administration (FDA) under the authority of the Food, Drug, and Cosmetic Act (FDC Act) of 1938. The scope and severity of the regulation became much greater under the authority of the Medical Device Amendments of the FDC Act, enacted in 1976, and of later amendments, especially those of 1990. By the early 1990s, firms in the medical-device industry found themselves subject to excruciatingly detailed, unpredictable, very costly, and sometimes strangling regulatory strictures. Worse, consumers of the products—ultimately the sick and injured themselves—suffered because of the regulation's destructive effect on technological development and because of the withholding of already developed products from the market while firms waited, often for years, to receive marketing approval from the FDA.[15]

In Europe, the situation contrasted markedly. Until recently, European countries imposed relatively little regulation on the producers of medical devices. Although the scope, detail, and cost of the regulation varied widely, no European country practiced the sort of rigid, elaborate, legislatively defined, centrally directed and enforced regulation imposed in the United States since 1976. The Europeans relied more on the formulation of technical standards by professional organizations, leaving manufacturers free in most cases to comply or not comply with the established standards. Purchasers, of course, could insist that products meet certain standards, and in some countries major purchasers such as the national health service were either required or urged to do so. In the 1970s, the Europeans began to develop a more restrictive system of regulation, but the adoption of the new system proceeded slowly. Only in the 1990s did EU member states begin to put in place a more systematic and demanding regulatory system.[16]

By the beginning of the twenty-first century, the European situation had changed drastically, especially in countries that previously had little or no regulation. Notably, no evidence exists that European consumers in general had suffered because of the previous, relatively undemanding regulatory environment, and obviously many European patients had benefited by gaining quicker access to new, more effective devices.[17] The recent European changes have been driven not by safety concerns but by the need to make regulations uniform throughout the EU in order to preclude their serving as trade barriers. As the desired uniformity is achieved, the common regulatory system will impose *more* regulation, even in countries such as France and Germany, which already had relatively extensive regulation. Still, when the new EU system is fully in place, it will fall far short of FDA-type regulation, leaving European device manufacturers, purchasers, and patients much better off relative to their U.S. counterparts.

Because regulatory requirements still differ among the major market areas—the United States, the EU, and Japan, not to speak of the rest of the world—producers continue to confront troublesome and costly regulatory diversity. Hence, they continue to press for even greater, ultimately global harmonization of the regulations.[18] The FDA Modernization Act of 1997 directs the FDA to meet with foreign governments to work out harmonization agreements. Earlier, in 1992, a Global Harmonization Task Force—including representatives of industry and regulators from the EU, the United States, Australia, Canada, Japan, and other countries—had been created to chart a course toward that ultimate objective, and its four study groups have been busily emitting documents for potential official adoption by the appropriate government authorities."[19]

A halfway house on the road to global harmonization is the mutual recognition agreement (MRA), a number of which have been reached by various pairs of countries and by the EU and various countries.[20] On May 18, 1998, the United States and the EU signed an MRA and began to work toward its full implementation: "Under the MRA, an EC CAB [European Community Conformity Assessment Body] could conduct quality system evaluations for all classes of devices and premarket 510(k) evaluations for selected [lower-risk] devices based on FDA requirements. Similarly, a U.S. CAB could conduct quality system evaluations for all classes of devices and product type examinations and verifications for selected devices based on EC requirements."[21] In effect, this MRA provides for harmonized regulatory reviews, rather than harmonized regulations; each country retains its own regulations within its own borders. In announcing the U.S.–EU agreement, however, the FDA declared that the MRA "may ... enhance harmonization of U.S. and EC regulatory systems."[22]

Implementation of the U.S.–EU MRA has not been smooth. Once the agreement went into force in December 1998, the FDA threw up a series of obstacles, and European observers concluded that "the FDA only intended to follow through with the MRA on its own terms."[23] "The FDA believed it would be able to use the mutual recognition agreement (MRA) to reinforce the European device regulatory system, which it considers too weak, by ensuring more stringent and more frequent controls on European manufacturers at little extra cost to itself. The FDA also hoped to retain the ultimate say in market authorisation."[24] For some Europeans involved in the process, the FDA's insistence on dominating the implementation of the U.S–EU MRA rendered the arrangement "little more than a charade."[25]

European industry representatives began to view the MRAs as failures and to characterize them as detours from rather than way stations on the road to global harmonization. According to Ian Cutler, the director of regulatory affairs at Smith & Nephew, "As a result of these initiatives the regulatory scene is becoming too complex and there does not appear to be any effective control. This excessive regulation will stifle and retard medical device development, increase the costs of market entry, discourage investment in industry and ultimately deny patients the potential benefits."[26] Most likely, however, such grumbling reflected little more than the frustrations normally associated with constructing any elaborate regulatory arrangement involving many interested parties in many different countries. The trend toward global regulatory harmonization in the medical device industry seems unalterable, if only because so many government bureaucracies around the world have committed themselves to it.

Conclusion

It has been noted that "regulatory harmony, like motherhood and apple pie, is difficult to argue against."[27] Especially for the bureaucratic mind, enforcing one set of regulations seems to make more sense than enforcing many. Business people always resent the costs associated with regulatory multicompliance. With the affected business interests demanding regulatory harmonization and the world's legislators and regulators willing to supply it, who will oppose it? The answer is no one.

The absence of organized, vocal, political opposition does not indicate, however, that regulatory harmonization harms no one. On the contrary, such harmonization holds the potential to harm multitudes. It is a species of cartelization, and just as successful cartelization in ordinary markets harms the consumers, so successful cartelization across regulatory jurisdictions tends ultimately to harm all those whose freedom of peaceful, voluntary action is thereby restrained.

During the first half of the 1990s, when the FDA became even more outrageous than usual in its regulation, many people fled to Europe to gain access to the medical devices to which the FDA denied them legal access in the United States. Medical device companies began to shift their operations, especially their clinical trials, from the United States to Europe.[28] In those days, Americans had somewhere to seek refuge from intolerably harmful regulation. Their pathetic flight served as important evidence when, after the 1994 elections, certain members of Republican-led Congress took the FDA to task, causing it to moderate its most outrageous actions—a reactive "reinvention" eventually codified in the FDA Modernization Act of 1997.

Once global regulatory harmonization has been achieved, however, the FDA's victims will have nowhere to run. They will have no choice but to suffer in silence, or, should they incline toward expressing their political "voice," to plead pitiably for their governmental overseers' mercy. For the most part, these victims will remain unaware of the relation between their plight and the worldwide cooperation of those who claim—counterfactually—that they are only protecting people's health and safety. The costs of regulatory harmonization will have to be counted not only in dollars but in freedom, physical well-being, and life itself.[29]

Even the critics of regulatory harmonization make an exception for regulations affecting the public health and safety. In so doing, they are turning matters upside down. Whereas the public can endure the costs of, say, securities regulation or cable TV regulation, the costs of government regulation of medical goods are far greater. It has been said that war is too important to be left to the generals. Likewise, people's health and survival are far too important to be left to office-holding politicians and their smiley-faced henchmen.

Notes

1. Clyde Wayne Crews Jr., *Ten Thousand Commandments: An Annual Policymaker's Snapshot of the Federal Regulatory State* (Washington, D.C.: Competitive Enterprise Institute, March 1999), pp. 14–15.

2. U.S. Bureau of the Census, *Statistical Abstract of the United States 2000* (Washington, D.C.: U.S. Government Printing Office, 2000), p. 299, for the number of government units as of 1997.

3. Gabriel Kolko, *Railroads and Regulation, 1877–1916* (Princeton, N.J.: Princeton University Press, 1965), pp. 164, 205; see also the section titled "National vs. State Regulation," pp. 217–26.

4. Gary Libecap, "The Rise of the Chicago Packers and the Origins of Meat Inspection and Antitrust," *Economic Inquiry* 20 (April 1992): 242–62.

5. Richard Sylla, "The Progressive Era and the Political Economy of Big Government," *Critical Review* 5 (fall 1991), p. 540.

6. Robert Higgs, "*Crisis and Leviathan*: Higgs Response to Reviewers," *Continuity: A Journal of History*, no. 13 (spring–fall 1989), p. 95.

7. On the early ICC, for example, see Paul W. MacAvoy, *The Economic Effects of Regulation: The Trunk-Line Railroad Cartels and the Interstate Commerce Commission Before 1900* (Cambridge, Mass.: MIT Press, 1965).

8. George J. Stigler, *The Citizen and the State: Essays on Regulation* (Chicago: University of Chicago Press, 1975), p. 183.

9. Albro Martin, *Enterprise Denied: Origins of the Decline of American Railroads, 1897–1917* (New York: Columbia University Press, 1971).

10. Robert Higgs, *Crisis and Leviathan: Critical Episodes in the Growth of American Government* (New York: Oxford University Press, 1987), pp. 152–53.

11. Richard B. McKenzie and William F. Shughart II, "Is Microsoft a Monopolist?" *The Independent Review* 3 (fall 1998): 165–97; and Stan J. Liebowitz and Stephen E. Margolis, *Winners, Losers, and Microsoft: Competition and Antitrust in High Technology* (Oakland, Calif.: The Independent Institute, 1999).

12. Manfred E. Streit, "Competition among Systems, Harmonisation, and Integration," *Journal des Economistes et des Etudes Humaines* 8 (Juin–Septembre 1998), pp. 239, 251.

13. Ibid., p. 250, emphasis added. The same exception for "health or safety" is adduced by Alan O. Sykes in his otherwise well-reasoned discussion in *The (Limited) Role of Regulatory Harmonization in the International System*, Working Paper no. 96/97-23 (Berkeley, Calif.: University of California School of Law, Program in Law and Economics, pp. 21, 24.

14. Streit, "Competition among Systems," p. 252.

15. For a detailed account, see Robert Higgs, "FDA Regulation of Medical Devices," in *Haz-*

ardous to Our Health? FDA Regulation of Health Care Products, edited by Robert Higgs (Oakland, Calif.: The Independent Institute, 1995), pp. 55–95. More recent accounts include Noel D. Campbell, "Exploring Free Market Certification of Medical Devices," in *American Health Care: Government, Market Processes, and the Public Interest,* edited by Roger D. Feldman (New Brunswick, N.J.: Transaction, 2000), pp. 313–44; and Charles A. Homsy, *How FDA Regulation and Injury Litigation Cripple the Medical Device Industry,* Cato Institute Policy Analysis no. 412 (Washington, D.C.: Cato Institute, August 28, 2001).

16. For an account of the development of medical device regulation in Europe, see Robert Higgs, *How FDA Is Causing a Technological Exodus: A Comparative Analysis of Medical Device Regulations—United States, Europe, Canada, and Japan* (Washington, D.C.: Competitive Enterprise Institute, February 1995), pp. 23–34.

17. "FDA Slammed in Comparison with Europe," *Clinica* 694 (February 26, 1996): 7. For many specific examples, see the evidence cited in Higgs, *How FDA Is Causing a Technological Exodus,* p. 48, fn. 107.

18. "Global Harmonisation Is the Only Solution to Escalating Regulatory Costs, Says Industry Executive," *Clinica* 867 (July 19, 1999): 5.

19. "Focus Moves from Mutual Recognition to Global Harmonisation," *Clinica* 815 (July 6, 1998): 6.

20. Egid Hilz, "Mutual Recognition Agreements Set the Scene for Easier Trade," *Clinica Review 1998* (1999): 10.

21. *Federal Register* 63, July 2, 1998, p. 36247.

22. Ibid.

23. Amanda Maxwell, "European Industry Fears the US Is Playing a Cat and Mouse Game with Mutual Recognition Agreement," *Clinica* 843 (January 25, 1999), p. 3.

24. Ibid.

25. Ibid.

26. Quoted in Zoë McLeod, "Tide of European Industry Opinion Moves Against Device MRAs and Global Harmonisation," *Clinica* 853 (April 12, 1999), p. 4.

27. Helen Gavaghan, "Harmony and Regulation Yield to the Need for Payment," *Clinica Review 1996* (1997), p. 3.

28. Higgs, "FDA Regulation," pp. 73–77.

29. See Robert Higgs, "Should the Government Kill People to Protect Their Health?" *The Freeman* 44 (January 1994): 13–17.

11

Puritanism, Paternalism, and Power

"Live and let live" would appear to be a simple, sensible guide to social life, but obviously many Americans reject this creed with a vengeance. They find toleration so unpleasant that they support the imprisonment of hundreds of thousands of individuals whose personal behavior they regard as offensive. Why do so many Americans favor the use of coercive sanctions to enforce repression? Perhaps the answer lies in our history.

Puritanism

Politicians and other patriotic posturers like to declare that the Europeans came to America seeking freedom. The claim is at best a half-truth. In the colonial era, most Europeans arrived in North America bound in some form of indentured servitude, many of them children or convicts put out to work. Disregarding such servants, one finds that the free colonists sought mainly to improve their economic well-being.

To be sure, some of them, including the early arrivals in Massachusetts, were fleeing religious oppression, but the Pilgrim Fathers had absolutely no intention of establishing a community in which individuals would be free to behave according to the dictates of their own consciences. The Puritans had already seen the light, and, by God, they intended to use all necessary means to ensure that everybody comply with Puritan standards. Far from free, their "City upon a Hill" was a hard-handed theocracy.

For them, pleasure seemed the devil's snare. Their vision of the good life was austere, and they looked askance on the possibility that others might embrace hedonism. In H. L. Mencken's famous characterization, Puritanism was "the haunting fear that someone, somewhere, may be happy."[1] Moreover, if the Puritans suspected that someone might be having fun, they had no compunction about using government coercion to knock some sense into the offender. Mencken might have had this proclivity in mind when he observed, "Show me a Puritan and I'll show you a son-of-a-bitch."[2]

In view of the Puritans' dispositions, it is unfortunate that they exerted an immense and lasting influence on American social and political affairs.

Puritanism's "central themes recur in the related religious communities of Quakers, Baptists, Presbyterians, Methodists, and a whole range of evangelical Protestants," and Puritanism "established what was arguably the central strand of American cultural life until the twentieth century."[3] Even today, ghosts of the Pilgrim Fathers haunt the land.

Paternalism

Paternalists are more ambitious than Puritans. Whereas the latter are content to steer people away from sinful behavior, the former go further, seeking also to promote the worldly health, safety, and welfare of their wards, coercively if need be. Of course, paternalists direct their deepest compassion toward saving children.

In the nineteenth and early twentieth centuries, when American social life was more rigidly hierarchical and dominated by WASPs, the paternalistic impulse came naturally to those who took themselves to be the respectable class in society. In their efforts to uplift the rabble, however, they perceived a need to rid the poor wretches of their vices. Hence the succession of campaigns against, among other things, drinking alcohol, smoking cigarettes, and engaging in all unseemly sexual activity, including autoeroticism. A century ago, groups such as the Women's Christian Temperance Society and the Anti-Saloon League enjoyed legions of supporters. The Anti-Cigarette Movement campaigned vigorously, especially against smoking by women and children; and the Social Purity Movement, followed shortly after 1900 by the Social Hygiene Movement, strove to stamp out pornography, prostitution, marital infidelity, and masturbation.

Government Power

As the Eighteenth Amendment of the U.S. Constitution (1919) reminds us, the better sorts did not hesitate to employ government coercion to promote their rehabilitation of society. They previously had saddled the nation with the Comstock Act (1873), which forbade sending sexual information through the mail, and the Mann Act (1910), which banned taking women across state lines for immoral purposes. In many local jurisdictions, they had obtained legal prohibitions of smoking by women and of commerce in liquor.

In these and many other ways, the respectable campaigners shamelessly combined Puritanism, paternalism, and government power. As David Wagner succinctly expresses the matter in his recent book *The New Temperance: The American Obsession with Sin and Vice,* "the Victorian and Progressive Period movements were characterized by what scholarly observers consider an exaggerated ... notion of their ability to change behavior, by a huge faith in government's ability to regulate every aspect of private life, and by a strong ethnocentric belief in the correctness of white, Protestant, middle-class social norms."[4]

These crusaders labored under no burden of doubt about the rectitude of their own standards of personal behavior or about their right to impose these standards on everybody else at gunpoint. Although they ceaselessly proclaimed their Christianity, they overlooked some of Christ's admonitions, especially "judge not, that ye be not judged" and "he that is without sin among you, let him first cast a stone."

Respite and Calamity

In 1933, after a decade of gang warfare and growing disrespect for law, Americans abandoned their "great experiment" and repealed the Eighteenth Amendment. The homicide rate, which had risen by about 50 percent during the previous fifteen years, immediately began a secular decline that continued until the 1960s.[5] Mark Thornton, a careful student of these events, concludes that "the repeal of Prohibition appears to be the best explanation for the dramatic reversal in 1933 and the return to the long-run decline in crime rates" because "alternative theories have a difficult time explaining the continuous decrease in crime during the remainder of the 1930s."[6]

Despite the continuation in force of the Harrison Narcotic Act (1914) and the passage of the prohibatory Marijuana Tax Act (1937), during the 1940s and 1950s the crusading class largely shifted its attention away from domestic uplift and toward resistance to fascism and communism.

In the 1960s, however, the tidy world of the self-righteous came crashing down as antiwar protesters, hippies, and other elements of the counterculture flaunted their disrespect for the bourgeoisie and its standards of conduct. The long-haired, free-loving, dope-smoking scorn of youths, poor people, and blacks—the very groups traditionally regarded as most in need of strict supervision and control—unbearably goaded the guardians of respectable society.

War on Drugs

In response, government officials pandering to the ire of the well-behaved "silent majority" declared a "war on drugs," which meant of course the punishment of selected individuals for the crime of offensive personal behavior, notwithstanding the absence of harm to nonconsenting parties. As a political tactic, this legal offensive was a no-brainer: "For political leaders, temperance wars, like foreign wars, are mobilizations that can serve as strategies to excite the masses of people and, for this reason, enjoy continued use."[7] Hence the Comprehensive Drug Abuse Prevention and Control Act (1970), the Comprehensive Crime Act (1984), and the Anti–Drug Abuse Act (1988), among many other enactments. The drug war helped to divert citizens from dwelling on such annoyances as futile foreign wars, high taxes, obnoxious regulations, poor government services, and meager protection of life and property.

In this so-called war, the police needed no postgraduate training to discern how to promote their own interests. Drug arrests could be arranged virtually at will to bulk up the score sheet of police accomplishments, and once civil forfeitures became an option in the war on drugs, the police possessed the added opportunity of wantonly seizing private property to enhance their resources.[8]

Meanwhile, the police and others could blame the use of drugs for the growing violence among youths, especially big-city blacks, when in reality the increased violence occurred mainly because the drug trade was illegal. As Thornton observes, "violence is used in black markets and criminal organizations to enforce contracts, maintain market share, and defend sales territory.... Street gangs profit and expand based on their role in organizing retail drug sales. Their violent criminal activity has been a growing and very visible result of the war on drugs during the 1980s and 1990s."[9]

As the prohibition of commerce in "controlled substances" has spawned a vast, global black market, recently estimated by the UN International Drug Control Program at $400 billion in annual sales,[10] opportunities for government officials—everyone from street cops to heads of state—to enrich themselves have grown enormously. In several countries, governments appear to be, from top to bottom, in league with the drug merchants. In the United States, the news media routinely report the arrests and convictions of police and other government officials for services to drug dealers, and these reports most likely represent only the unlucky tip of an iceberg of corruption. David E. Sisk writes, "If the true consequences of such laws [and the extent of] police corruption ... were well publicized, supporters of such laws could no longer hide behind a shield of morality."[11]

Endless Crusades

Sisk may be right, but I am inclined to think that no matter how horrible the consequences, the desire to butt into other people's personal affairs, employing the police and even the military as agents, is deeply ingrained in the American national character. Gerald Klerman aptly indicts "pharmacological Calvinism"; J. Weeks refers to "apple pie authoritarianism"; and Ellen Willis likens the contemporary drug test to the McCarthy-era loyalty oath: "When I say pee, you pee."[12] A 1995 Gallup poll found that 85 percent of the respondents were opposed to legalizing drugs and 87 percent were in favor of greater funding for drug police.[13] Search the Western world and you will find no other nation similarly obsessed. Europeans, themselves no strangers to government intervention, often view the United States as a nation of lunatics. Notwithstanding its changing forms and temporal fluctuations, the penchant for acting as self-righteous busybodies has animated the bourgeoisie of this country ever since the Pilgrims set foot on Plymouth Rock in 1620. Because this proclivity provides an irresistible opportunity for politicians to promote their own interests at public expense, one must expect that we Americans are doomed to an endless procession of costly, futile, and destructive crusades.

It hardly comes as a surprise that the government has not stopped with a war on heroin, cocaine, and marijuana. It is now whooping up a jihad against tobacco. Inasmuch as this war, like virtually all contemporary attacks on individual liberty in America, comes disguised as a program for "saving the children," who can object? Once upon a time the do-gooders condemned "demon run"; now they demonize cigarettes.

Although the First Amendment enjoins that Congress "make no law ... abridging the freedom of speech, or of the press," the Food and Drug Administration (FDA) issued detailed regulations governing the advertising of tobacco products, and the agency formulated ambitious plans for more extensive controls. In this disregard for the Constitution, the government was following a pattern set earlier in fighting the war on narcotics. As Judge James P. Gray has distinguished himself by saying, "Our present [drug] policy is directly responsible for the material and demonstrable reduction of our cherished liberties under the Bill of Rights."[14] Although the Supreme Court ruled in 2000 that the FDA lacks statutory authority to regulate tobacco products,[15] the continuing, multifaceted war on tobacco continues to push us farther along the same oppressive path blazed by the drug warriors. (Ever reliable, the FDA actively seeks the necessary authority to carry on its tobacco jihad, and the secretary of health and human services for the George W. Bush administration, Tommy Thompson, agrees, "I think right now we have to do more regulation, yes.")[16]

Upshot

Alexis de Tocqueville foresaw our present condition when, in the penultimate chapter of *Democracy in America,* he considered "what sort of despotism democratic nations have to fear." There he envisioned "an immense and tutelary power ... absolute, minute, regular, provident, and mild ... like the authority of a parent, if, like that authority, its object was to prepare men for manhood; but it seeks, on the contrary, to keep them in perpetual childhood.... [I]t compresses, enervates, extinguishes, and stupefies a people, till each nation is reduced to be nothing better than a flock of timid and industrious animals, of which the government is the shepherd."[17] As if these conditions were not bad enough, Wagner points out, Americans in true Orwellian fashion "have often come to *identify with* powerful social control as being in their own interest. They often *want* the state to expurgate drugs or cigarettes."[18]

At the end of his provocative booklet *Smoking and Liberty: Government as a Public Health Problem,*[19] Pierre Lemieux contrasts two possible worlds. One is the world of invasive paternalism to which governments in the United States—and likewise in Lemieux's homeland, Canada—progressively consign us. In this world, physical and moral dangers are taken to be ubiquitous, and because individuals are presumed to be too foolish and weak willed to protect themselves, government must micromanage everybody's personal affairs. The alternative world differs starkly. In it, "every individual lives his life as he sees fit, assuming the risks of his joys and the anguish of his death." Lemieux points out that "there is a common denominator between these two worlds: the mortality rate is 100% in both. But the men who live and die are not the same: in the first case, they are slaves; in the second, free individuals."[20]

Notes

1. H. L. Mencken, *A Mencken Chrestomathy* (New York: Vintage Books, 1982), p. 624.

2. Ibid., p. 625.

3. Andrew Delbanco, "Puritanism," in *The Reader's Companion to American History*, edited by Eric Foner and John A. Garraty (Boston: Houghton Mifflin, 1991), p. 893.

4. Boulder, Colo.: Westview Press, 1997, p. 18.

5. U.S. Bureau of the Census, *Historical Statistics of the United States: Colonial Times to 1970* (Washington, D.C.: U.S. Government Printing Office, 1975), p. 414.

6. Mark Thornton, *The Economics of Prohibition* (Salt Lake City: University of Utah Press, 1991), p. 124.

7. Wagner, *The New Temperance*, p. 59.

8. Bruce L. Benson and David W. Rasmussen, "Predatory Public Finance and the Origins of the War on Drugs, 1984–1989," *The Independent Review* 1 (fall 1996): 163–89.

9. *The Economics of Prohibition*, pp. 112, 125.

10. Mark J. Porubcansky, "U.N.: Drug Dealing Is 8% of All Trade," *Seattle Times*, June 26, 1997

11. David E. Sisk, "Police Corruption and Criminal Monopoly: Victimless Crimes," *Journal of Legal Studies* 11 (June 1982), p. 403.

12. All as cited in Wagner, *The New Temperance*, pp. 76, 162, 171.

13. Cited by Nick Gillespie, "Uncompromising Position," *Reason* 28 (July 1996), p. 31.

14. "A Fresh Approach to the War on Drugs," *Seattle Times*, September 20, 1996.

15. Robert S. Greenberger and Gordon Fairclough, "FDA Oversight of Tobacco Struck Down," *Wall Street Journal*, March 22, 2000.

16. Sarah Lueck and Gordon Fairclough, "Health and Human Services Secretary Favors Giving FDA Oversight of Tobacco," *Wall Street Journal*, March 1, 2001.

17. Alexis de Tocqueville, *Democracy in America*, edited by Richard D. Heffner (New York: Mentor, 1956), pp. 303–4.

18. Wagner, *The New Temperance*, p. 173, emphasis in original.

19. Montreal: Varia Press, 1997.

20. Ibid., pp. 92, 93.

12

We're All Sick,
and Government Must Heal Us

In recent decades a portentous cultural change has been gathering momentum in the United States, giving rise to dangerous social and governmental developments. Increasingly, Americans have embraced a *therapeutic ethos*. Actions previously understood as irresponsible, imprudent, immoral, or even evil have come to be understood as symptoms of underlying diseases that ought to be treated or cured rather than condemned or punished.[1] More and more people have been declared or have declared themselves "victims." They take themselves to be suffering, if only from hurt feelings, because others—parents, schoolmates, coworkers, people at large—have somehow infringed their asserted personal right to health and happiness. To a growing extent, governments have become involved in "treating" these newly perceived ills, and in doing so they have in effect asserted a novel raison d'etre, a new justification for their claims to legitimacy. Little resistance has arisen to the proliferating therapeutic programs at all levels of government because these new claims to legitimacy have comported so well with the public's own understandings.

James L. Nolan Jr. has written an impressive and disturbing book about these developments, *The Therapeutic State: Justifying Government at Century's End*.[2] Nolan's study is conceptionally well motivated and empirically well validated; his presentation is soberly balanced and smoothly written. Sociological research does not get much better than this. Notably, Nolan concludes the study by considering the implications of the developing therapeutic ethos for liberty, and he finds those implications unsettling.

The Therapeutic Ethos

Everyone will have noticed some aspect of the emerging therapeutic ethos. Where once we had Alcoholics Anonymous and its twelve-step program, we now have countless XYZ Anonymous groups, each with its own twelve-step remedy. No longer is drinking heavily, using cocaine, or pummeling one's spouse merely indicative of the perpetrators' unwise or cruel choices; instead, such behavior is indicative of an underlying disease. Hence, it would be improper, even pointless, merely to censure or penalize the perpetrators. Rather, those who suffer from the diseases of alcoholism, drug addiction, or violent abusiveness of a spouse should be *treated*, and a government operative—a social worker, a judge, a public-health doctor—is an appropriate agent to administer the treatment. Along the way it will prove essential that the sufferer recognize and admit that he has the disease. To do otherwise would be to remain "in denial," perhaps the most abominable and unacceptable condition in the eyes of those who embrace the therapeutic ethos.

Sit Still, Johnny

In the new world of the therapeutic ethos, curing the children plays a leading part. In olden days, some children chafed under the discipline and regimentation of the schools. Some kids just wouldn't sit still; others were downright naughty. No longer. Now they, along with any others who fail to respond with zombielike responsiveness to the school regulations, are diagnosed as victims of attention deficit hyperactivity disorder (ADHD).[3] For ADHD, which "experts" believe afflicts 5 percent of all children, the prescribed treatment is a drug called Ritalin. In some cases, children have been refused admission to schools, which the law requires them to attend (gotcha!), because their parents objected to the children's taking Ritalin.[4]

Build Self-Esteem

For an astonishingly wide spectrum of behaviors, adherents of the therapeutic ethos view the underlying disease as itself the product of deficient self-esteem. To anyone under the impression that the self-esteem movement is little more than another flaky California fad, Nolan's documentation will prove shocking. It seems that everything from mathematical ineptitude to teen pregnancy to first-degree murder is now viewed as stemming from insufficient self-esteem.

> By the middle of 1994, some thirty states had enacted a total of over 170 statutes that in some fashion sought to promote, protect, or enhance the self-esteem of Americans. The majority of these (around seventy-five) are, not surprisingly, in the area of education. There are additionally at least twenty self-esteem-related statutes in health care, over forty in welfare or social services, and approximately sixteen in the area of corrections or criminal justice. (p. 157)

In addition to uncountably large numbers of touchy-feely Democrats, such prominent Republican figures as Jack Kemp, Barbara Bush, and Colin Powell have come out in support of the self-esteem movement.

Not to be outdone by the states, a number of federal government agencies have issued regulations that make reference to the building of self-esteem (pp. 324–26). Believe it or not, one such regulation was the Commerce Department's 1986 "Northern Anchovy Fishery: Notice of Final Harvest Quotas" (51 FR 32334, cited on p. 325). Is nothing sacred?

The Experts Tell Us . . .

In parallel with the spreading therapeutic ethos, psychologists have established themselves as bona fide experts and have played an expansive role as courtroom advocates of tort remedies for persons claiming to have suffered emotional distress. Beginning in 1946 and ending in the 1970s, all the states adopted licensing statutes for psychologists. "Often, state courts justified the admittance of psychologists as expert witnesses on the basis of the licensing statutes passed by their state legislature. Somehow licensing codes gave credence to the idea that the psychologist was a legitimate expert" (p. 70).

One upshot is that now "therapeutic practitioners, with unprecedented 'expert' authority, provide the courts with psychologically inspired interpretations about human behavior, motives, criminal activity, and truthfulness" (p. 76). In such judicial proceedings, "the state becomes involved not only in the evaluation of behavior but in an assessment of the internal processes of individual psyches" (p. 297).

Therapy Will Win the War (on Drugs)

State and federal prisons brim with persons convicted of drug offenses. Those prisoners have become abundant grist for the mills of the therapeutic state. In 1962, the U.S. Supreme Court ruled that "states could compel offenders to undergo drug treatment." In 1966, the federal Treatment and Rehabilitation Act "gave the courts statutory authority to commit drug offenders involuntarily to residential and outpatient treatment programs as an alternative to incarceration." As Nolan remarks, "with these changes, the stage was set for the conflation of criminal law and therapeutic drug treatment. A number of organizations and agencies sprang up to fill this opening" (p. 81).

One such newcomer was the so-called Drug Court, numbers of which have been established in scores of jurisdictions across the country. Despite the failure of these special courts to reduce recidivism, their popularity has grown merely because of their approach, which is to treat drug offenses as pathological outcomes rather than as ordinary crimes. A drug court transforms a judge into a sort of police-backed hyperintrusive schoolmarm who scolds, praises, or threatens the "clients," depending on how well they play along with the program (pp. 78–112, 295–96).

In 1966, the Narcotic Addict Rehabilitation Act required treatment for federal drug convicts in prison, and by 1990 more than 218,000 prisoners were enrolled in related counseling programs (p. 113). In the state prisons, by 1990 more than 42 percent of the inmates were enrolled in a therapy or counseling program of some sort (p. 115). Although the programs take various shapes, common threads include "emphases on the primacy of self and the centrality of emotions, the view of the inmate as a patient in need of healing, and the assumption that abusive and victimized pasts predispose one toward crime" (p. 120). Not even the get-tough-on-crime reaction of recent years has deflected application of the therapeutic ethos to the operation of prisons.

Kid Stuff

In the schools, as in the prisons, the central objective is now to "cure" the children by promoting their self-esteem. According to Rita Kramer, the author of *Ed School Follies,* "Self-esteem has replaced understanding as the goal of education" (quoted on p. 150). One must admit that schoolteachers and counselors have had a large measure of success in their main endeavor: although in international comparisons American students rank very low in math, science, and other educational attainments, they rank very high in their own evaluation of their abilities (p. 169).

Although saving the children has long served to justify extraordinary government measures, this rationale has become well-nigh universal in recent years. Among the sacred cows of the child savers, the Head Start program, begun in 1964 as part of the war on poverty, commands special veneration. Among other achievements, Head Start gave rise to a program known as "Telephone Friends," allowing lonely old people to talk to young children on the telephone. According to Congressman Ben Erdreich, this "truly gratifying endeavor" improved "self-worth and self-esteem for both seniors and children alike" (quoted on p. 216).

Nolan observes that "the state's role toward children was viewed [in congressional debates] as most appropriate when some form of therapeutic assistance was provided" (p. 217). That legislative perspective no doubt contributed to the authorization of federal funding for Parents Anonymous, established in 1974. "Based on the self-help model of AA, the program provided a forum where parents with the 'sickness' of child abuse could get help. Not surprisingly, the help they sometimes needed was assistance in attaining a higher view of the self" (p. 219). One wonders whether any member of Congress has ever introduced a bill to establish Tenth Amendment Violators Anonymous (TAVA); the desperate need for such a group seems obvious.

Don't Worry, It's Good for You

Every smart ruler understands that the best kind of state coercion is the kind that subjects do not regard as coercive. By resorting increasingly to just that sort of coercion, U.S. governments have succeeded in expanding into whole new domains of private life with scarcely a word of protest being voiced. As Nolan explains it,

> The ideals of a "scientifically" based, therapeutic understanding of the world are so embedded in American culture that overt coercion is rarely necessary. Instead, most citizens naturally comply with programs and policies based on therapeutic rationales, because they are so "obviously" plausible. The basic nature of the coercive and expanding state, then, has not changed. What has changed is the source of legitimation by which the state justifies its continued expansion—an expansion that, through use of therapeutic symbols, can move into realms of societal life once left untouched by the state. (p. 298).

Thus, while many freedom-loving citizens have been fighting the growth of government at the front door—many of them even imagining that they are winning the fight—government at all levels has been streaming through the back door. Having supposed that Orwell's *1984* had been averted, people may yet wake up to find themselves situated in Huxley's *Brave New World.*

Notes

1. The outstanding critic of this development has long been Dr. Thomas S. Szasz. For a recent statement of his views, see "The Therapeutic State: The Tyranny of Pharmacracy," *The Independent Review* 5 (spring 2001): 485–521.

2. New York: New York University Press, 1998. Hereafter cited parenthetically by page number in the text.

3. Look it up. The official guide is the American Psychiatric Association's *Diagnostic and Statistical Manual of Mental Disorders,* 3rd ed., rev., commonly called the DSM III-R. In addition, the World Wide Web now has a nearly infinite number of sites devoted to ADHD.

4. Nolan cites Diane Divoky, "Ritalin: Education's Fix-It Drug," *Phi Delta Kappan* 70 (April 1989): 599–605.

13

Lock 'Em Up!

Let's play the old form-a-line game. Suppose you took all the people incarcerated in U.S. jails and prisons as of June 30, 1998, and formed them into a line, with the individuals standing one yard apart. How far would the line stretch? Starting from Boston, it would reach almost to Atlanta. Try to picture it. You can form a long line with 1,802,496 individuals.

Back on December 31, 1985, the line would have stretched less than half that far, only from Boston to the southern suburbs of Baltimore. (See figure 13.1 for a graphic history.) But during the next twelve and a half years, the incarcerated population grew at an average annual rate of 7.3 percent. (In comparison, the entire U.S. population grew about 1 percent per year.) At the end of 1985, of every 100,000 persons, 313 were confined; by the middle of 1998, the incarceration rate had increased to 668. If the incarcerated population continues to grow at the rate experienced since 1985, then by midyear 2008 our imaginary line will be long enough to extend from Boston to Atlanta, then turn west and continue all the way to San Antonio, Texas.

Here's another way to picture the prisoners. If you gathered all of them together in a formerly vacant location, you would have an agglomeration about as populous as Houston, the fourth-largest U.S. city. Add the more than 3 million persons on probation, and you would have an aggregation larger than any U.S. city except New York. (New York City itself would be a good deal smaller, of course, once its convicts and probationers were relocated to Convict City.)[1]

In 1998, men constituted the great bulk—about 92 percent—of the nation's incarcerated population, but as in so many other areas of American life, women have been catching up. In state and federal prisons, women accounted for 4.1 percent of all inmates in 1980, 5.7 percent in 1990, and 6.4 percent in 1998. In the jails—the locally operated penal institutions, as opposed to the federal and state prisons—the number of women increased from 9.2 percent of the adult inmates in 1990 to 10.9 percent in 1998.[2]

Nationally, the jail population in 1998 was 41 percent white, 41 percent black, 16 percent Hispanic, and 2 percent other ethnicities. Unfortunately, this black-white equality is not exactly the sort for which people of goodwill have

Figure 13.1

Inmates in U.S. Prisons and Jails

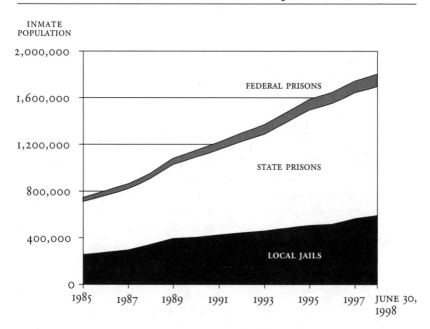

INMATE
POPULATION

been yearning: relative to their numbers in the overall population, blacks are six times more likely than whites to be in jail.[3]

At current rates of imprisonment, federal and state prisons will house 285 of every 1,000 black men, 160 of every 1,000 Hispanic men, and 44 of every 1,000 white men at some point in their lives. For black men, doing time is fast approaching the norm. "The stigma against going into the criminal-justice system is almost gone," according to Harlem youth worker Geoffrey Canada. "It's like going away to war. Everyone gets called. You go, you do your time. It's no big thing."[4]

If the total incarcerated population were to continue to grow by 7.3 percent annually, it would double approximately every ten years, whereas the total population, growing at 1 percent annually, would need some seventy years to double. Hence, in the decade of the 2080s, within the lifetime of many people already born, the prison population would overtake the total population, and the immigration barriers would have to be removed in order to let in enough foreigners to fill the cells. I leave it as an exercise for the reader to determine who will serve as guards.

Why the Upsurge of Imprisonment?

Here is a one-word clue in answer to this question: *drugs*. Of the federal prisoners in 1996, fully 60 percent were serving time for drug offenses; of the far more numerous state prisoners, 23 percent were inside the belly of the beast for drug convictions. Virtually all the growth of the federal inmate population since 1988 has come from adding drug offenders. Between 1985 and 1995, state prisons added 537,000 inmates altogether, an increase of 119 percent. They took in an additional 186,000 inmates convicted of drug offenses, swelling that category by 478 percent.[5] But drug prohibition explains even more of the upsurge than the foregoing data indicate, because many of the persons imprisoned for violent or property offenses would never have committed their crimes but for the illegality of the drug trade, which prompts sellers to settle disputes violently and leads some heavy consumers to steal in order to get the wherewithal to pay for high-priced black-market commodities.

In the 1980s, Americans allowed their political leaders and the news media to stampede them into a full-blown "war on drugs"—more precisely, an attack on the users, buyers, and sellers of a few substances that were officially designated as diabolical. Congress and the states passed mandatory-minimum sentencing laws that required the imprisonment of even first-time drug offenders, often individuals guilty of nothing but possessing the illicit substance. Citizens who have supported this holy war can now take pleasure in pondering the multitude of POWs it has produced.

The simpletons who expected the jihad to create a drug-fee society must be disconcerted that notwithstanding the more than 400,000 persons imprisoned for drug offenses, the drug trade continues to flourish. Although crime rates have dropped sharply in recent years for many categories of crime, including murder, robbery, and assault, close observers report that "drug use has not budged for 10 years."[6] As FBI agent Burdena Pasenelli commented after police in downtown Seattle had made 125 arrests in a "buy/bust" operation in just three days, "the minute a suspected dealer is arrested, another person quickly moves into the area and resumes sales."[7]

Cui Bono?

"We have a failed social policy and it has to be re-evaluated," said drug czar General Barry R. McCaffrey. "Otherwise, we're going to bankrupt ourselves. Because we can't incarcerate our way out of this problem." Echoing the czar's refrain, criminologist Julia Glover Hall has declared: "It's a stupid game we're playing. We're locking up all these nonviolent offenders, pouring money down a rat hole."[8] But one man's failed social policy is another man's road to riches, or reelection. At the bottom of a rat hole, don't be surprised to find a rat.

Just ask the Cleveland police, forty-four of whom were caught in an FBI sting in 1998 and arrested for taking payoffs from drug traffickers in exchange for providing security to those subterranean businessmen.[9] Call me magnanimous, but I'll wager that the cops in other places are just as smart as those in Cleveland when it comes to seizing a convenient opportunity to supplement their salaries.

Indeed, the drug war has been a bonanza even to law-abiding cops, as the altered forfeiture laws have given the police free rein to seize private property more or less at will. If innocent people act quickly and avail themselves of astute lawyers when their property is seized, they may, after much toil and trouble, recover their possessions, but many unfortunates act too slowly or lack adequate legal counsel and therefore never retrieve what the police have snatched. As Bruce L. Benson and David W. Rasmussen explain, "The 1984 federal confiscations legislation followed a period of active advocacy by federal, state, and local law enforcement officials, who emphasized that it would foster cooperation between their agencies and increase the overall effort devoted to and the effectiveness of drug control." Along with other researchers, Benson and Rasmussen have adduced evidence that "law enforcement agencies focus resources on enforcement of drug laws because of the financial gains for the agencies arising from forfeitures."[10] If in the process of padding their budgets the police arrest a throng of street-corner entrepreneurs who subsequently land in prison, well, *c'est la guerre.*

Consider also that every dollar of the estimated $35 billion spent annually on fighting the drug war winds up in somebody's pocket. Hence, we now have what some have dubbed "the prison-industrial complex," in which workers, firms, and entire communities have acquired a vested interest in building and operating prisons.[11] As if this situation were not bad enough, "unions representing prison guards are the fastest-growing public employee associations in many states."[12] With politicians, unions, and construction firms all sleeping in the same bed, the "lock 'em up" policy seems likely to remain ensconced indefinitely.

And make no mistake: the politicians know a good deal when they stumble onto one. Large majorities of voters continue to support the attack on drug users and dealers, notwithstanding the soaring costs of imprisoning more and more people. Says James Alan Fox, dean of the College of Criminal Justice at Northeastern University, "For politicians, the drug debate is driven by the three R's—retribution, revenge, retaliation—and that leads to the fourth R, reelection."[13] Never underestimate the capacity of the American public to cough up money for drum-beating politicos to squander in righteous and futile assaults on sin.

Nor is money the only thing the American public apparently longs to sacrifice. In a 1998 Gallup poll, 62 percent of the respondents agreed that in order to reduce drug use they "would be willing to give up some freedoms."[14] The pollsters ought to have inquired about surrendering some *more* freedoms, because many freedoms already have been obliterated by the fearless drug warriors, who never let a flimsy thing like the Bill of Rights stand in their way.

According to data from a 1997 National Household Survey on Drug Abuse, some 14 million Americans used illegal drugs in the month before the survey was taken.[15] A line formed by these people, with one user per yard, would extend from Boston to Atlanta to Los Angeles to Seattle to Boston and, starting over, nearly to Washington, D.C.—not the sort of image that eases a zealous drug czar into a peaceful night's sleep. Yet the self-reported number of recent users surely falls short of the actual number; and millions of other people enjoyed the forbidden substances in earlier times and may someday wish to indulge again. Despite the desires of many millions of consumers to acquire the products regularly and of millions of others to acquire them occasionally, the local, state, and federal governments of the United States seem hellbent to continue law enforcement that results in the imprisonment of ever larger numbers of these consumers and of the businessmen who cater to their demands.

These facts may incite some spectators to enter into a theological debate about whether a person has a God-given right to choose his own poison. I am inclined to view the whole sad spectacle from a zoological perspective, recalling H. L. Mencken's observation that "men are the only animals that devote themselves, day in and day out, to making one another unhappy."[16]

Postscript 2002

In the three years since I first composed the foregoing screed, the prison population has continued to climb, though at a slower rate, surpassing the 2 million mark early in 2000.[17] In mid-2001, federal prisons alone held more than 125,000 inmates, and more than 56 percent of the sentenced persons in those prisons were confined for drug offenses—a percentage down slightly from a maximum of 61.3 percent in 1994.[18] Besides those behind bars in prisons and jails, nearly 4 million persons were on probation and more than 725,000 on parole in mid-2000, bringing the total number of persons under some form of "correctional" supervision by all levels of government to almost 6.5 million.[19]

It has been reported that some Americans are beginning to worry that the gigantic orgy of imprisonment during recent years reflects not fair retribution but moral righteousness and a desire to toss the rabble into prisons in order to put distance between them and the respectable class.[20] Nothing is new about the respectables' sentiment, of course; only the scale has been unprecedented.

In any event, the party cannot go on forever: rising costs, if not awakening consciences, must eventually bring it to a stop. Perhaps, after the terrorist attacks of September 11, 2001, the respectables will turn their righteous indignation toward other, more menacing targets than their neighborhood drug pushers.

Notes

1. Sources of data for the preceding calculations include U.S. Department of Justice, Office of Justice Programs, Bureau of Justice Statistics, *Bulletin,* NCJ 173414 (Washington, D.C.: U.S. Government Printing Office, March 1999), pp. 2–3; *1996 Rand McNally Road Atlas,* p. A13; and U.S. Bureau of the Census, *Statistical Abstract of the United States 1997* (Washington, D.C.: U.S. Government Printing Office, 1997), pp. 45–47.

2. U.S. Department of Justice, *Bulletin,* NCJ 173414, pp. 4, 6.

3. Statistics retrieved on March 26, 1999, from Bureau of Justice Statistics at http://www .ojp.usdoj.gov/bjs/glance/corr2.txt.

4. Quoted in "Frustration with Crime Wave, and Criminals, Led to a Huge Surge in the Construction of Jail Cells," *Wall Street Journal,* October 27, 1998. On the devastating social consequences of such massive, routine incarceration, especially for the black population, see Ellis Cose, "The Prison Paradox," *Newsweek,* November 13, 2000, pp. 40-49.

5. See the Bureau of Justice Statistics sources cited in fnn. 1 and 3.

6. Timothy Egan, "Less Crime, More Criminals," *New York Times,* March 7, 1999.

7. Quoted in "125 Suspects Arrested in Seattle Drug Sweep," *Seattle Times,* September 20, 1997.

8. McCaffrey and Hall quoted in Timothy Egan, "The War on Crack Retreats, Still Taking Prisoners," *New York Times,* February 28, 1999.

9. Pam Belluck, "Police Caught in Sting," *New York Times,* January 25, 1998.

10. Bruce L. Benson and David W. Rasmussen, "Predatory Public Finance and the Origins of the War on Drugs, 1984–1989," *The Independent Review* 1 (fall 1996): 163–89, quotations on pp. 176, 178.

11. Eric Schlosser, "The Prison-Industrial Complex," *Atlantic Monthly* 282 (December 1998): 51–77.

12. Egan, "Less Crime."

13. Fox quoted in Egan, "The War on Crack."

14. Gallup poll quoted in ibid.

15. Egan, "The War on Crack."

16. H. L. Mencken, *A Mencken Chrestomathy* (New York: Vintage, 1982), p. 617.

17. Drug Policy Alliance, "U.S. Prison Population Passes 2 Million Mark," February 15, 2000, at http://www.lindesmith.org/news/DailyNews/2million_inmates2.html.

18. U.S. Department of Justice, Federal Bureau of Prisons (on-line), at http://www.bop.gov/ fact0598.html, retrieved June 4, 2001.

19. U.S. Department of Justice, Bureau of Justice Statistics, "Key Facts at a Glance: Correctional Populations, 1980–2000," retrieved February 1, 2002, at http://www.ojp.usdoj.gov/ bjs/glance/tables/corr2tab.htm.

20. Drug Policy Alliance, "U.S. Prison Population Passes 2 Million Mark."

14

Government Protects Us?

When I was younger and even more ignorant than I am today, I believed that government (understood conventionally as a monopoly of legitimate coercive force in a given territory) performs an essential function—namely, the protection of individuals from the aggressions of others, whether those others be compatriots or foreigners—and that no other institution can perform this function successfully. Indeed, I once wrote a book whose very first sentence reads, "We must have government."[1] In this belief, I was merely plodding along the path of the great unreflective herd, although, to be sure, many philosophers, social scientists, and other deep thinkers have reached the same conclusion. Growing older, however, has given me an opportunity to reexamine the bases of my belief in the indispensability of the protective services of government (again, as conventionally understood). As I have done so, I have grown increasingly skeptical, and I am now more inclined to disbelieve the idea than to believe it. More and more, the proposition strikes me as almost preposterous.

My skepticism springs in part from my improved understanding of just how horrendously destructive and murderous governments have been, not only by their involvement in wars with other governments, but more tellingly in their assaults on their own citizens. According to the statistics compiled by R. J. Rummel, governments probably caused the deaths of some 170 million of *their own citizens* between 1900 and 1987,[2] and the death toll has continued to rise during the past fifteen years. To this gruesome total must be added some 40 million others who perished in battle in the wars into which the world's governments plunged their populations during the twentieth century.[3]

Yes, yes, you may be saying, *certain* governments surely have acted murderously, but that bad behavior reflects not on government as such, but rather on the bad manners of the Chinese, the Russians, the Germans, and so forth. Or perhaps you are objecting that the fault lies not in government as such, but rather in communism, fascism, or some other ugly ideology that prompted the leaders of certain governments to misbehave so outrageously. These objections, however, cannot bear much weight, because the destructiveness of governments has spanned huge ranges of ethnicity and ideology. In control of egregious governments have been Chinese, Russians, Germans, Japanese, Cambodians, Turks, Spaniards, Vietnamese, Poles, Pakistanis, Yugoslavs, British, Koreans, Croatians, Mexicans, Indonesians, Ugandans, Rwandan Hutus, Nigerians, and a variety of other ethnic or national types. The common denominator would seem to be not ethnicity or nationality, but government in itself. In control of appalling governments have been nationalists, tribalists, fascists, communists, socialists, and adherents of various other ideologies or of none at all. Again, the common denominator would seem to be government itself.

Well, you say, the world has certainly endured more than its fair share of vicious rulers, but our own U.S. government would never commit such crimes. Unfortunately, it has already done so. The attacks by U.S. troops on civilians and their means of subsistence in the Confederate States of America during the War Between the States surely rank as heinous in the highest degree.[4] The devastation wreaked on many native Indian tribes brings no honor and much shame to the history of the U.S. government. In my own lifetime, in the 1940s, the U.S. government was pleased to drop many thousands of tons of high-explosive and incendiary bombs on the residential areas of German and Japanese cities, blasting, suffocating, and incinerating hundreds of thousands of innocent men, women, and children who happened to be living there. Referring to Tokyo, General Curtis LeMay declared, "We knew we were going to kill a lot of women and kids when we burned that town. Had to be done."[5] Ultimately the government capped even this wanton cruelty by exploding atomic bombs above the hapless populations of two large Japanese cities. At Hiroshima, "about 100,000 people (95,000 of them civilians), were killed instantly. Another 100,000, most of these civilians as well, died long, drawn-out deaths from the effects of radiation."[6] The A-bomb dropped on Nagasaki, which was exploded directly above "a suburb of schools, factories, and private houses," killed some 74,000 people and injured a similar number, the great majority of them civilians, "with the affected survivors suffering the same long-term catastrophic results of radiation and mental trauma as at Hiroshima."[7] So where's the essential difference between the actions of those allegedly wicked governments and the actions of our own? Might it be that government itself is the root of the evil?

But without government, the familiar refrain goes, we would be plunged into anarchy—understood conventionally as violent chaos, a Hobbesian war of all against all. Nothing, it is widely assumed, could be worse than the situation that would exist without government (as we know it). Notice, however, that this supposition is just that—a mere supposition. Can we really imagine that the world's people, absent governments to organize and goad them on, would have been so obtuse and antisocial that they would have ended up slaughtering *more than 210 million* of one another in the twentieth century before coming to their senses? Such a vision of haphazard violence boggles the mind. Even though my own opinion of mankind is, I confess, substantially lower than the average opinion, I still have trouble imagining that, without government, people would have done even worse than they did *with* government.

Setting aside the doubts raised by exercises in counterfactual history, we still encounter troubling questions about the government's protective function. One can't help wondering: Why do so many of us continue to fall victim to murder, rape, assault, robbery, burglary, and other crimes too numerous to catalog? Where's the vaunted government protection? According to the Federal Bureau of Investigation's compilation of offenses known to police (the number of offenses that actually occur is far greater), in 1999 the residents of the United States suffered some 16,000 murders, 89,000 forcible rapes, 410,000 robberies, and 916,000 aggravated assaults, not to speak of some 2,100,000 burglaries, 6,957,000 larcenies and thefts, and 1,147,000 motor vehicle thefts.[8]

In truth, most Americans know perfectly well that the government either cannot or will not actually protect them and their property, and therefore they have increasingly resorted to protecting themselves. For the past several decades, the private security industry has been among the fastest growing in the United States (as well as in many other countries, too). According to a 1997 report by *The Economist,* in 1970 government police outnumbered private police by 40 percent, but "now there are three times as many private policemen as public ones. . . . Americans also spend a lot more on private security (about $90 billion a year) than they do, through tax dollars, on the public police ($40 billion). Even the government itself spends more money hiring private guards than it does paying for police forces."[9] Astutely, the reporter notes, "The private sector has rushed into a vacuum of demand for law and order left unfulfilled by the state."[10]

Do you feel safer in a gated residential community protected by private security personnel or on a public street protected by government cops? To ask the question is to answer it. If government had been performing the essential protective function it continually trots out to justify its intrusions and its tax burdens—indeed its very existence—there would have been no "vacuum" for the private security industry to occupy. Government cops may show up, in their own sweet time, to take some notes after a crime has been committed. Private security forces, in contrast, prevent crimes from occurring in the first place. Relying on government police, the public must suffer the insult of paying for the cops in addition to the injuries and losses caused by the criminals, because heaven forbid that government require the guilty parties to make restitution to their victims. Then the wounded public must pay still again, this time to finance the government's prison system, where the inmates while away their time consuming drugs and dreaming of new crimes to commit upon their release.

Worst of all, government police and prosecutors, unlike private protective personnel, busy themselves in committing crimes rather than preventing them. When government agents arrest and prosecute people for actions that those persons have every just right to undertake—from smoking pot to gambling to trafficking in sexual services to selling unlicensed services or "unapproved" medicines—those government functionaries act not as protectors of the public but as agents of naked tyranny—in Gore Vidal's words, "so many Jacobins at war against the lives, freedom, and property of our citizens."[11] No wonder such large swaths of the population view these enforcers with contempt and even hatred. A government that presumes to protect citizens from themselves, jamming its jails and prisons with millions of such inoffensive offenders, has indeed gone to war against its own people. Where is John Locke when we need him?

Almost eighty years ago H. L. Mencken composed what is arguably the most perceptive essay ever written on government. In it he dealt squarely with the alleged protective function of government:

> The citizen of today, even in the most civilized states, is not only se-cured but defectively against other citizens who aspire to exploit and in-jure him ... ; he is also exploited and injured almost without measure by the government itself—in other words, by the very agency which professes to protect him. ... He finds it more difficult and costly to sur-vive in the face of it than it is to survive in the face of any other enemy. ... But he can no more escape the tax-gatherer and the policemen, in all their protean and multitudinous guises, than he can escape the ulti-mate mortician. They beset him constantly, day in and day out, in ever-increasing numbers and in ever more disarming masks and attitudes. They invade his liberty, affront his dignity and greatly incommode his search for happiness, and every year they demand and wrest from him a larger and larger share of his worldly goods.[12]

Since Mencken made these observations in 1924, the situation has only gotten worse—much worse, steadily worse. Powerful elites, especially the in-formation masters of the so-called New Class, beat their tom-toms incessantly to alert us to each new danger de jour—just tune in CNN's *Headline News* on any day of any week—and clamor ceaselessly for new government protections that, in truth, the government cannot or will not actually provide.

The government will never cease, however, to *claim* that it protects the peo-ple and to devote its immense resources to propagandizing and bamboozling the public to prop up that claim. As Vidal has observed, "there is little respite for a people so routinely—so fiercely—disinformed."[13] Will people ever see through this flimflam? Mencken himself held out little hope. "The extortions and oppressions of government will go on," he declared, "so long as such bare fraudulence deceives and disarms the victims,"[14] and for him there was no end in sight. Sad to say, he was probably right.

Notes

1. Robert Higgs, *Crisis and Leviathan: Critical Episodes in the Growth of American Government* (New York: Oxford University Press, 1987), p. 3.

2. R. J. Rummel, *Death by Government* (New Brunswick, N.J.: Transaction, 1994), p. 4.

3. Ibid., p. 3.

4. Thomas J. DiLorenzo, "Waging War on Civilians," in *The Real Lincoln: A New Look at Abraham Lincoln, His Agenda, and an Unnecessary War* (Roseville, Calif.: Forum, 2002), pp. 171–99.

5. Quoted in Sven Lindqvist, *A History of Bombing*, translated by Linda Haverty Rugg (New York: New Press, 2000), p. 109.

6. Ibid., p. 112.

7. "Nagasaki," in *The Oxford Companion to World War II*, edited by I. C. B. Dear and M. R. D. Foot (New York: Oxford University Press, 1995), p. 773.

8. U.S. Bureau of the Census, *Statistical Abstract of the United States 2001* (Washington, D.C.: U.S. Government Printing Office, 2001), p. 182.

9. "Welcome to the New World of Private Security," *The Economist* (April 19, 1997), quoted from on-line text.

10. Ibid.

11. Gore Vidal, *Perpetual War for Perpetual Peace: How We Got to Be So Hated* (New York: Thunder's Mouth Press/Nation Books, 2002), p. 115.

12. H. L. Mencken, "On Government," in H. L. Mencken, *Prejudices: A Selection*, edited by James T. Farrell (New York: Vintage, 1958), pp. 178–79.

13. *Perpetual War for Perpetual Peace*, p. 115.

14. "On Government," p. 188.

15

Coercion Is Not a Societal Constant

Warren Samuels has taken a familiar and defensible idea—that the workings of any market reflect, to some degree, the character of the private-property rights enforced by government—and pushed it to a bizarre and indefensible extreme. "There is something like a constant level of coercive command and control in society," he declares, "some of it in 'private,' some in 'public' hands." Therefore, "even in a libertarian utopia, government intervention, so-called, would be universal, in that the whole system would depend on government determination and enforcement of a certain form of property (and other) rights." The only variables are "who is to control and use government and whose interests is government to promote and whose to inhibit."[1] In short, the only question it makes sense to ask is: Whose ox is to be gored? In this view, a person or group must be either dishing out coercion or taking it, because for societal coercion as a whole, people are playing a constant-sum game.

For Samuels, it makes no sense to divide the socioeconomic world into a private sphere and a public sphere; for him, there's only one sphere, and it's public all the way through—that is, fully determined, either directly or indirectly, by government decisions. It makes no difference whether rights receive their definition and enforcement through common-law courts or through legislatures and administrative agencies. In either case, the ultimate outcome will be decided by the way in which the government stands ready to bring violence to bear on members of society. Regardless of how government sets the rules or in whose interests it does so, the police will stand ready to break *someone's* head to uphold the established rules. "What constitutes 'activist government,' 'freedom,' or 'coercion' is a matter of selective perception" dependent on one's ideology.[2]

Big Government, Small Government—Same Thing?

In Samuels's view, my attempt in *Crisis and Leviathan* to explain the rise of Big Government rested on a "fundamental conceptual error" because the event at issue never happened: the workings of the U.S. economy in 1987 were no more determined by government officials than they had been in 1887. "Higgs's

Big Government merely does, in different ways, what it has been doing all along"; "government influence is now no more fundamental than when it protected certain interests selectively by designating them as property." According to Samuels, my book boils down to "principally an exercise in ideological manipulation."[3]

In my book, I describe Big Government as marked by "the wide scope of its effective authority over economic decision-making, that is, the great extent to which governmental officials rather than private citizens effectively decide how resources will be allocated, employed, and enjoyed."[4] Among my most prominent examples of Bigger Government is military conscription during 1917–18 and 1940–73, which was important both for its immediate effect in raising large armed forces and for its lasting positive effect on the public's attitude toward other extreme measures of government command and control.[5]

I assume, given Samuels's comments, that he would deny that the imposition of the draft constituted an increase in the amount of coercion in American society. To make a case à la Samuels, however, one would have to affirm that in the years without a draft, someone somewhere in America was being coerced by an amount equal to that by which the conscripts were being coerced during the years when the draft was in operation, if indeed "there is something like a constant level of coercive command and control in society." I have tried to imagine who those unfortunates might have been during the years without a draft, but I've come up empty. I know of no one of any ideological stripe who would deny that conscription itself is coercive. Some approve of it, others don't, but all agree that draftees are coerced into service; otherwise, the draft would be pointless because the men would come forth voluntarily to do exactly what they do under the draft, for exactly the same compensation and other terms of "employment." How can anyone deny that conscription added to the overall coerciveness of U.S. society when it was imposed in 1917 and again in 1940?

I am similarly perplexed by Samuels's assertion that "The question is not whether there is to be law and order but law and order on which/whose terms, or which law and order."[6] Samuels seems to be saying that there is a constant amount of order in society, an assertion that is hard to swallow. Take, for example, an episode I discuss in my book, the riots in Chicago and elsewhere associated with the Pullman strike of July 1894.[7] A great deal of looting, arson, and destruction of property (including some two thousand railroad cars) occurred. More than twenty persons were killed and many more injured. Thousands of federal troops and militiamen in twenty states were called into action to suppress the violence. When the authorities had suppressed the disorder, commentators of various political persuasions rejoiced. Would Samuels maintain that 1894 displayed an equal amount of law and order as in any other year?[8] The riots were hardly just a matter of a different interest being served, unless—to use one of Samuels's favorite terms—one "privileges" the interest of the rioters, largely drunken hoodlums and thrill-seeking youths, as against those of the terrified residents of Chicago and the people whose property was being wantonly destroyed. Is it nothing but ideological drivel to say that 1894 ranked relatively low on a law-and-order scale?

Two Misconceptions

In making his arguments, Samuels goes astray in two fundamental respects.

First, he exaggerates the *extent* to which government decisions predetermine the workings of a market society. Government, he asserts, "is the process through which the basic economic institutions are determined." He refers to "the role of government in defining and creating the economy," declaring that "particular markets are a function of particular power structures."⁹ Officially sanctioned property rights are certainly important, but they are not the *only* determinants of how markets will allocate resources. Yoram Barzel has shown, for example, how transaction costs condition the extent to which nominal owners can control and reap benefits from their officially recognized property rights.¹⁰ Customs, mores, religions, cultures, attitudes, tastes, and other attributes of a society also shape the workings of its markets. The rules nominally established and enforced by government are never completely decisive in shaping socioeconomic processes or outcomes. As Douglass C. North has written, "formal rules, in even the most developed economy, make up a small (though very important) part of the sum of constraints that shape choices."¹¹

Second, with regard to the attainment of specific socioeconomic outcomes, government stipulation of private-property rights differs fundamentally from government command and control. In the former case, the government sets rules regarding only *what may not be done*—namely, a person may not take actions that violate the established rights of another. Therefore, the choices people make and hence the outcomes of the socioeconomic process remain open-ended to an enormous degree. The concept of a "spontaneous order"— a pattern of socioeconomic arrangements, transactions, and realizations unforeseen and unforeseeable by anyone, including those who establish the prevailing private-property rights—nicely expresses the workings of a society based on private-property rights.¹² In the command-and-control case, however, the authorities stipulate *what must be done*. If they have sufficient power to enforce their rules, then once we know the rules, we can forecast the socioeconomic outcomes. For example, in the private-property case, wage earners may decide for themselves how much or how little to set aside for their old age; in the command-and-control case of the present-day United States, they must pay a 15.3 percent Social Security tax. In the former case, we cannot predict how much will be set aside by various individuals or in the aggregate; in the latter case, we know that at least 15.3 percent of earnings will be set aside by every wage earner against whom the law is effectively enforced.

The Degree of Societal Coercion Can Change— and Has Changed

For a long time, governments in the United States enforced the institution of slavery. Then, after 1865, they enforced its prohibition. Would Samuels say that post-1865 America was not, in consequence, less coercive than pre-1865 America? Would he insist that the government exerted as much coercion after 1865 in keeping the freed people free as it had exerted before 1865 in keeping them enslaved? Was emancipation simply a matter of switching the oxen subjected to a perpetually maintained amount of goring? I think not. It seems to me a far more sensible representation of reality to say that American society became substantially less coercive as a result of the emancipation, notwithstanding the former slave owners' capital losses and unhappiness. Although the masters lost coercive power over their slaves, the freed people did not acquire an equal amount of coercive power over others. To insist that someone somewhere in the United States exerted as much coercion after 1865 to prevent slavery as the slaveowners and their henchmen had exerted to maintain it before 1865 seems not only to argue for a prima facie implausible proposition but to wander into a sort of Alice in Wonderland world of thinking about social relations in general.

Similarly but in the opposite direction, the many accretions of government economic controls during the twentieth century indeed augmented the degree to which American society is coercively directed toward the performance of specific, officially designated tasks and toward the actual realization of outcomes preordained by official policies. Many people approve of these changes, judging their benefits greater than their costs; a few of us deplore them, judging them too costly in liberty and other values. Only Samuels denies the very existence of their addition to societal coerciveness.

Let Us Reject This Bizarre Conversation Stopper

Not everyone accepts the conventional libertarian concept of coercion, but in scholarly debate even those who prefer an alternative concept generally understand what the libertarians are talking about and do not dispute that the libertarian concept refers to something one can identify empirically, such as slavery or conscription or the enforcement of a tax law. For this widely understood concept, Samuels would substitute a set of assertions—constant governmental coercion, constant law and order—so fundamentally implausible that a scholarly conversation could never be sustained on such terms. Of course, social scientists and historians want to know whose interests a government promotes and whose it thwarts, but investigation of those questions will not be advanced by insisting that a society cannot become what American society manifestly has become in the past century—more coercive overall.

Notes

1. Warren Samuels, "The Growth of Government," *Critical Review* 7 (fall 1993), pp. 459, 453.

2. Ibid., pp. 458–59.

3. Ibid., pp. 452, 454, 455, 459, respectively.

4. Robert Higgs, *Crisis and Leviathan: Critical Episodes in the Growth of American Government* (New York: Oxford University Press, 1987), p. 28.

5. I expand on this theme in my essay "War and Leviathan in Twentieth-Century America: Conscription as the Keystone," in *The Costs of War: America's Pyrrhic Victories,* edited by John V. Denson (New Brunswick, N.J.: Transaction, 1997), pp. 309–22 (included in revised form as chap. 24 in the present collection).

6. "The Growth of Government," p. 453.

7. *Crisis and Leviathan,* pp. 91–97.

8. Allan Nevins called the year that began July 1, 1894, "the *année terrible* of American history between Reconstruction and the World War." See *Grover Cleveland: A Study in Courage* (New York: Dodd, Mead, 1932), p. 649.

9. "The Growth of Government," pp. 452, 455, 458, respectively.

10. Yoram Barzel, *Economic Analysis of Property Rights* (New York: Cambridge University Press, 1989).

11. Douglass C. North, *Institutions, Institutional Change, and Economic Performance* (Cambridge, Eng.: Cambridge University Press, 1990), p. 36. North discusses separately the informal constraints (pp. 36–45) and the formal constraints (pp. 46–53).

12. Steven Horwitz, "From Smith to Menger to Hayek: Liberalism in the Spontaneous-Order Tradition," *The Independent Review* 6 (summer 2001): 81–97, and sources cited there.

PART IV
Economic Disgraces

16

Official Economic Statistics
The Emperor's Clothes Are Dirty

Economists have been grousing a good deal lately about the deteriorating quality of basic economic statistics—official data on prices, incomes, employment, productivity, and poverty, among other things—and about the lack of government funding to remedy the problem. (The first eight articles in the winter 1998 issue of the *Journal of Economic Perspectives* deal with various aspects of this issue.) On its face, the complaint seems reasonable and practical.

But I wonder. Having used official economic statistics from time to time for nearly forty years, I would miss them if they were to disappear. Yet, however put out I might be as an economic analyst, I suspect that the world would be a happier place had these figures never been created. Certainly the statistics are often inaccurate or otherwise flawed and hence misleading. An even more serious consideration, however, is that the official statistics help to provide rationales for pernicious policymaking.

Poorly Defined, Imprecise, and Invidious

Because many official economic statistics are ill defined conceptually, they fail to capture what they purport to measure. Figures on "poverty," for example, are notorious in this regard. Is poverty an absolute or a relative condition? If the latter, what is the proper standard of comparison? Obviously, the living conditions of many Americans described as being "below the poverty line" must seem affluent to billions of submerged denizens of the Third World. Apart from international comparisons, the living conditions of many Americans now classified as poor would have seemed well-to-do in the eyes of, say, their own grandparents.[1] Above a certain absolute income level, "poverty" becomes less a definite condition than a staging area from which armies of redistributionists launch their attacks on higher-income people.

Aside from the conceptual questions, the mere measurement of personal income as currently defined poses nearly insurmountable difficulties. For example, among those in "poverty," illegal (hence unreported) incomes loom large—earnings from drug dealing, prostitution, gambling enterprises, and everyday theft. In any event, you have to wonder: if the poor have only the income they report to the Internal Revenue Service or the Bureau of the Census, how do they come by the automobiles, TVs, jewelry, and other visible adornments of their homes and persons? Of course, the poor are scarcely the only class concealing real income, whether it be honestly or illicitly acquired. The wealthy support an entire stratum of professional attendants—lawyers, accountants, financial gurus—whose sole mission in economic affairs is to remove income from the gaze of the tax collector. Small-business operators notoriously accept payments "under the table," and hosts of carpenters, painters, electricians, plumbers, and gardeners—not to mention the nannies—earn income that goes wholly or partly unreported.

In one of the most important and unjustly neglected economics books of the past fifty years, Oskar Morgenstern warned, "We must carefully distinguish between what we think we know and what we really do and can know."[2] Yet all too often economists avert their eyes, plowing blithely ahead with exquisitely sophisticated econometric analyses of virtually meaningless or inaccurately measured variables. As Michael J. Boskin attests, "Both the economics and statistics professions have become more theoretical and spend less time on the practical issues of sampling, data collection, quality of data, and providing professional rewards in terms of standing in the profession for those who show great skill in finding, developing, or improving data."[3]

One hesitates, then, to blame lay persons for reacting to the drumbeat of media reports of a widening distribution of income during recent decades in the United States. Is this "growing inequality" not a fact? Who really knows? Whether it is or is not, however, it would never have been made the basis for public-policy proposals to "correct" the situation if statisticians had not constructed "the distribution of income" in the first place. It is hard to imagine another statistical artifact better calculated to feed the fires of envy and political rapacity. Such information is completely unnecessary for the conduct of a just government but well-nigh indispensable for the operation of a predatory one.[4]

Nourishing the Mercantilists

In an uncertain world, one thing is for sure: every month, without fail, the press will prominently report the latest official figures for the U.S. international "trade deficit." Even in a relatively intelligent 1998 article, the graph is labeled "That Pesky Trade Deficit."[5] Of course, the very term *deficit* has a negative connotation, suggesting a shortfall of some—no doubt regrettable—kind. Clearly, the journalists, along with the proverbial man in the street, regard the trade deficit as a Bad Thing. Often these reports highlight some ominous bilateral trade imbalance, especially the perennial trade deficit of the United States with Japan. Surely it dampens one's spirits to be told repeatedly that the nation is being "flooded" by imports, that it is "awash" in cheap foreign goods.

Yet anyone who stops to consider how someone might keep track of all the goods and services being exchanged across U.S. borders must develop some fundamental doubts. Upon being informed that the trade deficit is X, well might one ask: How do they know? Of course, the Customs Service generates mountains of data on international trade, but many transactions escape the agency's surveillance—for instance, the sizable commerce in illegal drugs, estimated at $400 billion a year worldwide, in which the United States looms large as a net importer.[6] Nor are illicit drugs the only products covertly imported or exported.

Morgenstern aptly warned against the unreliability of the international trade data when he wrote,

> Any one who has ever sat through meetings (as the author has) in which final balance of payment figures for most invisible items were put together, can only marvel at the naiveté with which these products of fantasy, policy, and imagination, combined with figures diligently arrived at, are gravely used in subsequent publications. . . . Writers on all phases of foreign trade will have to assume the burden of proof that the figures on commodity movements are good enough to warrant the manipulation and the reasoning to which they are customarily subject.[7]

Morgenstern was writing decades ago, but the deficiencies to which he called attention have persisted. According to Boskin's recent assessment, "the trade statistics have serious flaws," and "it is becoming more and more difficult to measure trade accurately."[8]

Actually, the compilers of the international trade statistics openly confess their inability to identify all the relevant transactions or to measure correctly the ones they do identify. Because every exchange has two sides—for every buyer, a seller; for every importer, an exporter—the overall balance of payments must necessarily balance. In practice, however, it never does, and the U.S. Commerce Department reconciles the two sides of the account by inserting a fudge factor called *statistical discrepancy* (formerly called *errors and unrecorded transactions*). In 1996, for example, this discrepancy amounted to minus $46.9 billion, equivalent to 32 percent of that year's deficit on current account.[9] The statistical discrepancy varies widely from year to year. For instance, in 1992 it was negative $43.6 billion, in 1993 positive $5.6 billion. In view of the violent fluctuations of this fudge factor, how much confidence can we place in the "fact" that between 1992 and 1993 the deficit on current account increased by $34.4 billion?[10] Perhaps, despite all the hand wringing occasioned by the increase of the measured current-account deficit in 1993, the true deficit did not increase at all. Moreover, considering the inaccuracy of even the annual data, the monthly reports featured in the press deserve no credence whatsoever.

If balance-of-trade data merely served as one more excuse for econometricians to waste their time, the data would be relatively innocuous. Unfortunately, these figures, by virtue of their routine and widespread dissemination by the news media, play an important role in the politics of rent seeking. As Paul Heyne has written, allegations of a trade deficit

> provide political arguments that can be used by people who want protection from foreign competitors or subsidies for their efforts to sell abroad. For the existence of a trade deficit implies that the ratio of imports to exports *must eventually decline,* since no deficit can continue forever. So we might as well get on with it now: Fund the Export-Import Bank, restrict imports from nations that interfere with our exports, slap penalties on foreign firms that are "dumping" in our markets, and face up in general to the fact that free trade is good trade only if it is fair trade.[11]

Anyone who pays attention to the news will recognize the refrain. As Heyne observes, "the declaration of a trade deficit amounts in practice to a kind of declaration of martial law. What is most dangerous about such a declaration is that it gives government officials a license to subordinate the rule of law and respect for established rights to considerations of political advantage."[12] Far better for both justice and economic prosperity if the international trade statistics had never been collected. They have been and continue to be major means to the thoroughly mischievous ends of pandering politicians and their rent-seeking supporters.

Defining Government Spending as Productive

William Petty (1623–87), an Englishman who practiced "the art of political arithmetic," has been called "the first econometrician" and identified as "the author of the first known national income estimates."[13] It would have been a boon to honest humanity had *political arithmetic* stuck as the name for economic statistics of the sort now assembled in the official national income and product accounts. This designation would have alerted one and all to the political purposes lurking beneath the construction of such figures.

Consider, for example, how the statisticians arrive at the amount of gross domestic product: add the values at market prices of all newly produced, domestic, final goods and services purchased by consumers, investors, and governments, then throw in net exports. So accustomed are we to this setup that no one pauses to ask: Why make government purchases a separate category? Further, if we do include government services, how can we value them at market prices, inasmuch as they are generally provided without charge and financed by taxation? Not even many economists today know that prior to World War II the inclusion of a government category in the national income and product accounts was a hotly debated issue. Now, however, as Ellen O'Brien has written, "it is rare that someone suggests that the current treatment of the government product in national income is flawed and it is nearly inconceivable that it would be suggested that a government product doesn't belong at all."[14]

As O'Brien notes, "the treatment of the government sector put in place in 1947 (which has remained standard practice in the US since that date) was initiated by estimators in order to assess the impact of the tremendous increase in war expenditures on the economy" during World War II. The "theoretical debates from the pre-war period continued through 1947 and were never fully resolved."[15] Simon Kuznets, the principal architect of the early national income accounts in the United States, played David in this David-and-Goliath struggle, but ultimately he could not prevail against the vastly superior resources of the U.S. Department of Commerce, and he retreated from the field of battle.[16]

In reviewing this dispute, O'Brien puts her finger on a critically important but scarcely appreciated consideration: "It seems as if the government bureaucrats were determined to emphasize the importance of government's role in the economy by enlarging the share of government expenditure in the national income. While this official change was motivated by the great increase in government expenditures caused by the war, the underlying explanation must relate to the Commerce estimators' philosophy of the proper role of government in the economy."[17] It is easy to see how postwar Keynesian doctrine and policymaking meshed with a system of national accounts in which *all* government purchases of goods and services—the services of government employees being valued at whatever those employees happen to be paid—count equally with private purchases of only *final* goods and services in the market, where consumers and investors demonstrate their valuations by spending their own money.

Among the many repercussions of adopting the official national income and product accounts was the perpetuation of the myth of "wartime prosperity" during World War II, along with the crackpot theories of "military Keynesianism" that the myth fostered and continues to foster. Eliminate the government component, which during World War II was devoted almost entirely to purchasing munitions and paying the personnel of the bloated, mainly conscripted armed forces, and you are left with national product data indicative of wartime *recession.*[18] Later, especially in the 1950s, the official accounts gave rise to a distorted picture of the business cycle.[19]

For more than half a century, policy warriors have used the official national income and product accounts as a map to plan their assaults on Fine-Tune

Mountain. For this indictment, the annual reports of the U.S. Council of Economic Advisers contain incontestable evidence, as do successive generations of macroeconomics textbooks, written as though intended to serve as cookbooks for policymakers. If the macroeconomic warriors failed to capture the hill, perhaps the blame belongs to their tactics or weaponry as well as to their faulty map. Still, lacking that map, they might have been more reluctant to sally forth, and the U.S. economy might have been spared the ravages of these pretentious idiot savants.

To Conclude

Economists' passive acceptance of economic statistics designed and constructed by government bureaucrats ranks among the more shameful aspects of their professional conduct in the past century. One wonders: Who was using whom? In the post–World War II era, this intermingling of an ever more intrusive government and an economics profession dedicated to instructing the intruders achieved solid institutionalization. It is now the status quo, with every prospect of remaining so. But the economic statistics joining the two sides of this symbiosis are often ill defined, inaccurate, and productive of mischief when used in policymaking.

Morgenstern considered it "necessary that worthless statistics be completely and mercilessly rejected on the ground that it is usually better to say nothing than to give wrong information which—quite apart from its practical, political abuse—in turn misleads hosts of later investigators who are not always able to check the quality of the data processed by earlier investigators."[20] The advice remains sound, however little it has been or will be heeded. Economics would progress more quickly if economists asked more questions before admitting official data into their analyses.

On a wider front, where the interests of the general public come into play, economic statistics might be put to an even more stringent test. Suppose we were to pose seriously the question that journalist Peter Passell asked rhetorically in his discussion of international trade statistics. "The transactions are voluntary and generally take place between consenting adults," Passell observed. "So why is it anyone's business but theirs?"[21] Why indeed?

A just government, one that confines itself to protecting the citizens' rights to life, liberty, and property, has no need for figures on the distribution of personal income; no need for data on international trade and finance; no need for national income and product accounts. None of these statistics can assist in the defense of the citizens' just rights. Such figures belong to "political arithmetic." They are raw materials for rent seekers and government officials who would make the government an engine of predation and a destroyer of just rights.

Notes

1. Nicholas Eberstadt, "A Misleading Measure of Poverty," *Washington Post*, February 17, 2002.

2. Oskar Morgenstern, *On the Accuracy of Economic Observations*, 2d ed. (Princeton, N.J.: Princeton University Press, 1963), p. vii.

3. Michael J. Boskin, "Some Thoughts on Improving Economic Statistics to Make Them More Relevant in the Information Age," prepared for the Joint Economic Committee, Office of the Vice Chairman, United States Congress, October 1997, p. 5.

4. Here I stand by my previous statement, "Is More Economic Equality Better?" *Intercollegiate Review* 16 (spring–summer 1981): 99–102, a revised version of which appears as chap. 1 in the present collection.

5. Peter Passell, "The Fear Is Gone, Not the Danger," *New York Times*, March 1, 1998.

6. Mark J. Porubcansky, "U.N.: Drug Dealing Is 8% of All Trade," *Seattle Times*, June 26, 1997.

7. *On the Accuracy*, p. 180.

8. "Some Thoughts," p. 9.

9. The current account includes investment income and transfers as well as sales of goods and services. For the data, see U.S. Council of Economic Advisers, *Annual Report for 1998* (Washington, D.C.: U.S. Government Printing Office, 1998), p. 399.

10. Ibid., pp. 398–99.

11. Paul Heyne, "Do Trade Deficits Matter?" *Cato Journal* 3 (winter 1983–84), p. 711, emphasis in original.

12. Ibid., p. 715.

13. Phyllis Deane, "William Petty," in *International Encyclopedia of the Social Sciences*, edited by David L. Sills (New York: Macmillan/Free Press, 1968), vol. 12, p. 67.

14. Ellen O'Brien, "How the 'G' Got into the GNP," in *Perspectives on the History of Economic Thought*, vol. 10, *Method, Competition, Conflict, and Measurement in the Twentieth Century*, edited by Karen I. Vaughn (Aldershot, Eng.: Edward Elgar, 1994), p. 247.

15. Ibid., p. 242.

16. See, however, the rearguard action Kuznets mounted in his *Capital in the American Economy* (Princeton, N.J.: Princeton University Press, 1961), pp. 465–84.

17. "How the 'G' Got into the GNP," p. 252.

18. Robert Higgs, "Wartime Prosperity? A Reassessment of the U.S. Economy in the 1940s," *Journal of Economic History* 52 (March 1992): 41–60.

19. Robert Higgs, "The Cold War Economy: Opportunity Costs, Ideology, and the Politics of Crisis," *Explorations in Economic History* 31 (July 1994): 283–312, esp. pp. 297–98.

20. *On the Accuracy*, p. 55; for a similar warning, see Boskin, "Some Thoughts," p. 20.

21. "The Fear Is Gone."

17

A Tale of Two Labor Markets

The post–World War II economic history of western Europe and the United States divides neatly into two halves, which we might call the Golden Age and the Time of Troubles, respectively. In the latter era, Europe achieved only a small increase in employment and suffered a huge increase in the rate of unemployment, whereas the United States achieved a huge increase in employment and kept its rate of unemployment in check.

What Has Happened?

During the Golden Age, from 1945 to 1973, the European economies recovered from the war and enjoyed high rates of economic growth. The United States, having emerged from the war with a relatively smaller loss of human and material capital, experienced somewhat slower economic growth but remained the world's most productive and prosperous nation.

Before 1974, despite concerns about certain lagging industries and regions, unemployment did not constitute a major problem in the North Atlantic economy. In the 1960s, the unemployment rate ranged from 1.3 to 2.6 percent in France, from 0.3 to 1.4 percent in West Germany, from 2.4 to 3.8 percent in Italy, and from 2.0 to 3.4 percent in the United Kingdom.[1] For the group of countries that eventually became the first twelve members of the European Union (EU), unemployment stood at about 2.5 percent from 1960 through 1974.[2] In the United States, the long economic expansion of the 1960s brought the jobless rate down to 3.5 percent by 1969, although it did rise thereafter, reaching 5.9 percent in 1971.[3]

On both sides of the Atlantic, the recession of 1973–75 ushered in the Time of Troubles. The U.S. unemployment rate rose to 8.5 percent in 1975, the EU rate to about 4 percent. After the recession, unemployment fell during the latter half of the 1970s in the United States, but it continued to climb in Europe, and by 1979 the U.S. jobless rate and the EU rate had converged at about 6 percent. With the onset of another recession in 1980, the two rates rose in tandem for three years, reaching nearly 10 percent in 1982.

After 1983, the U.S. recovery pushed unemployment down rapidly, but in Europe unemployment continued to climb until mid-decade. Though European joblessness declined substantially in the late 1980s, it stood about 3 percentage points above the U.S. level when the recession of the early 1990s began to push it up again. In the early 1990s, just as in the early 1980s, Europe's unemployment continued to rise long after the U.S. rate had peaked and begun to fall.[4] By 1997, the U.S. rate had dipped below 5 percent, whereas the EU rate remained well above 10 percent.

France, whose unemployment rate during the past quarter century has closely tracked that of the entire EU, can serve for a comparison with the United States. From the graph in figure 17.1, one gets the clear impression of a widening performance gap between the two job markets, opening in 1984 and yawning ever wider since 1992. By the latter part of 1997, France had an unemployment rate of 12.5 percent (September), the United States 4.7 percent (October).[5] For many French people, unemployment became a way of life. A French politician who preferred to remain anonymous declared that the na-

Figure 17.1

Unemployment Rate (percent), 1970–1997

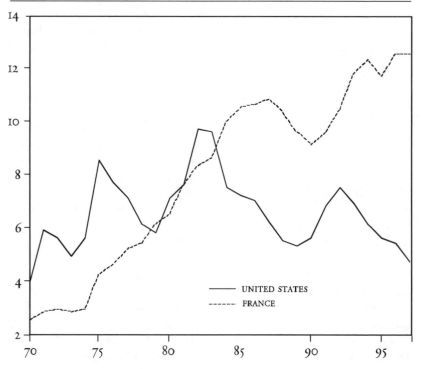

tion's "priority now is not creating jobs but acknowledging that some people will never work."[6]

Among the major European economies in the 1990s, only the United Kingdom (UK) seemed capable of getting a grip on its unemployment problem. By October 1997, the UK jobless rate had dropped to 5.2 percent, just half a percentage point above the U.S. rate. "There's a sense of optimism in this country that is lacking in France," said a French investment banker working in England, where many young French people have moved in search of opportunities unavailable in their homeland. "People [in Britain] take their problems in hand and take care of themselves. In France, people expect smart Government bureaucrats to solve their problems for them."[7]

Among the smaller European economies, some did better, some worse, relative to the big three problem children, Germany, France, and Italy. By the latter part of 1997 (September or October), jobless rates stood at 7.7 percent in Denmark, 7.1 percent in Austria, 6.8 percent in Sweden, 5.3 percent in the Netherlands, and 4.8 percent in Switzerland. At the other extreme, in 1997 Belgium reported 13.4 percent of its labor force unemployed for October, and Spain 20.8 percent for the second quarter, though informal reports indicate that many of the Spaniards reported as without jobs actually work in the underground economy—a phenomenon obviously occurring elsewhere in Europe as well.[8]

Whence the Trouble?

Why the high, persistent, rising levels of unemployment in Europe? The question has a short answer, a long answer, and a fundamental answer. The short answer is that the cost of labor is too high. The long answer, which explains why the cost of labor remains too high to clear the market, pertains for the most part to government policies and their consequences. The fundamental answer has to do with how the political process has given rise to the adoption and maintenance of policies that entail high, persistent, rising levels of unemployment.

As figure 17.1 illustrates, since 1970 the U.S. unemployment rate has varied mainly with the course of macroeconomic fluctuations, although the peaks and troughs of the unemployment rate cycle did tend to rise until the early 1980s and to fall thereafter. For the period from 1970 through 1997, the mean rate was 6.5, the range from 4.0 to 9.7. Of the year-to-year changes, nine were positive, eighteen negative.

European unemployment, in contrast, tended to rise almost relentlessly and displayed only a muted relation to the course of macroeconomic expansion and contraction. In France, for example, from 1970 through 1997, the mean rate of unemployment was 7.9, the range from 2.5 to 12.5. Of the year-to-year changes, twenty-one were positive, five negative, and one approximately zero. Again, figure 17.1 tells the story: a horizontal trend in the United States; a steeply rising trend in France, as in western Europe as a whole.

The figure does not reveal an even more startling fact: during the past three decades, European labor markets have expanded employment by only a tiny amount. Between 1972 and 1992, when U.S. employment rose by 36.4 million persons (44 percent), EU employment rose by only 5.9 million persons (4.8 percent), even though simultaneously the EU population ages fifteen to sixty-four increased by 18.9 million persons (9.7 percent).[9] Why has western Europe virtually lost its capacity to generate new employment?

We can place the causes under two headings: those that deter employers from offering jobs and those that discourage would-be workers from seeking or accepting offers.

Over time European governments have mandated an extensive list of employment benefits that elevate the costs of employing permanent workers—for instance, a month or more of paid vacation annually and a year of maternity leave with 75 percent of pay. "Mandated severance pay and the required period of notice before dismissals can occur are generally greater in Europe than in the United States, and furthermore in some countries these have tended to become more stringent over time."[10] Payroll taxes have reached extraordinary levels—more than 50 percent in France and Italy.[11] Wilfried Prewo reports that "indirect labor costs in Germany [which recently amounted to about 46 percent of total labor compensation] have increased about twice as fast as gross wages since 1966, and this increase is closely correlated with the rise in the unemployment rate."[12] Given the high costs of employing and firing workers, employers are loath to add workers unless they are sure that they will have a long-term need for those workers and confident that the new workers will prove sufficiently productive to warrant the costs and risks of employing them. To some extent, employers can escape the severe legal strictures by hiring temps. By the end of the 1990s, half of all the workers under twenty-five years old in France were officially classified as temporary employees.[13]

Labor unions receive greater privileges in Europe than in the United States, and the European labor force is much more heavily unionized. Unions represent more than 40 percent of European employees, in contrast to fewer than 15 percent in the United States.[14] By pushing wages and benefits above competitive levels, unions discourage hiring and encourage both plant closures and the relocation of production to lower-cost venues. Unemployment in Europe is especially high among heavily unionized manual workers such as miners and shipbuilders.[15]

After the German reunification, Germany's strong unions, seeking as always to foreclose competition in their labor markets, pressed successfully to raise wages in the East, where wages had been (along with labor productivity) much lower. Eastern wages moved toward parity much more quickly than did eastern productivity, so employers soon found many workers in the East too expensive to warrant their hiring. By the late 1990s, the unemployment rate in the New Laender had reached approximately 20 percent—and if we count the "hidden" unemployed in government make-work programs and short-term jobs, the rate came closer to 30 percent.[16]

Minimum-wage laws, which are relatively generous in western Europe, diminish the prospects of unskilled and inexperienced job seekers, especially young people. The French minimum wage, for example, rose from 40 percent of average earnings in the 1960s to 50 percent in the 1980s, whereas the U.S. minimum wage fell relative to the average wage.[17] The socialist government that assumed power in France in 1997 raised the minimum wage further, to 39.4 francs (about $6.20) an hour. That government's plans also included raising corporate taxes, cutting the workweek from thirty-nine to thirty-five hours with no cut in pay, and putting an additional 350,000 persons into make-work programs at taxpayer expense.[18]

In addition to discouraging employers from offering jobs, European public policies also deter potential workers from actively seeking or accepting offers. High proportions of the unemployed—89 percent in Germany, 98 percent in France, as opposed to about 33 percent in the United States—are eligible to collect a dole, and any stigma that might once have attached to taking such government handouts has evaporated.[19] Unemployment benefits replace nearly 60 percent of average earnings and in many countries extend virtually indefinitely. Researchers have found "a very significant relationship between the length of time for which unemployed workers are eligible for benefits (generally much longer in the European Community than elsewhere) and the degree of persistence in the unemployment process across countries."[20] Taking a job means sacrificing the dole *and* becoming subject to heavy income and employment taxes, so the jobless, especially those whose earnings would be relatively low, have little incentive to seek or accept work. In the EU in 1993, 43.3 percent of the unemployed had been out of work for more than a year, as compared to just 11.7 percent in the United States.[21] Although workers who endure prolonged unemployment may get by on the dole, family assistance, and erratic earnings in the underground economy, they tend to lose skills and productive work habits, and they forgo valuable on-the-job training and experience. Employers look askance at job applicants who have not worked for a long time, so long-term joblessness becomes self-perpetuating.[22] To make matters worse, the long-term unemployed tend to occupy a world apart in society and therefore lose touch with the regularly employed, who might provide them with the word-of-mouth information that both job seekers and employers use to fill positions.[23]

As a summary of the long answer to the European unemployment question, Martin Feldstein's 1997 statement serves nicely:

Unemployment rates have been rising for two decades and remain high today because high unemployment benefits and other transfer payments discourage working, high minimum wages and the nonwage costs of employment (like payroll taxes, mandated fringe benefits and work rules) reduce the demand for labor, excessive regulations impede the creation of service jobs, and high income taxes induce the substitution of home production for market services.[24]

Why These Policies?

Identifying the causes of the high, persistent, and rising levels of unemployment in western Europe does not require rocket science, just basic economics. Nevertheless, the fundamental question remains: If Europe's unemployment problem results from its public policies and their consequences, why do its governments maintain and even augment these pernicious policies? Answering this question requires a much deeper and wider analysis. It calls for an explication of the political actions taken in more than a dozen countries over a span of several decades. No short answer can suffice, and I am not so presumptuous as to offer one here.

Some clues, however, should not be ignored. Many observers have noted that Europe's unemployed tend to fall disproportionately into certain classes: younger adults (say, younger than twenty-five); older adults (say, older than fifty), especially those who have been laid off because of plant closures or workforce reductions in declining industries; the unskilled; women; and immigrants. In 1995, for example, the average EU unemployment rate was 9.5 percent for men, 12.5 percent for women.[25] In most European countries, the unemployment rate for young adults recently has stood much higher than the rate for older persons, often more than twice as high. In France, Italy, and Spain, the rate for younger adults has exceeded 25 percent. Persons from fifteen to twenty-four years old accounted for 27.6 percent of all EU unemployment in 1994.[26]

One sees the significance of these data by reflecting on how much political power young people, women, immigrants, and older unskilled men tend to wield in European politics—in general, relatively little. In western Europe's interest-group democracies, as elsewhere, people with the most political muscle control the instruments of government in the service of their own interests. "French politicians," Joel Blocker has reported, "say they won't risk restructuring the national economy by cutting back on their vaunted welfare-state 'social model' and moving toward what they dismiss as the 'Anglo-Saxon model.' They believe they would be committing political suicide if they did."[27] So the politically weak groups seem destined to continue to suffer extraordinarily high rates of unemployment and all the baleful consequences of that condition. Of course, the Europeans would never simply throw the unemployed to the wolves, as they fancy the Americans do. In Europe, governments shower the unemployed with an array of "protections" that—as economic analysis demonstrates and empirical evidence corroborates—contribute to the perpetuation and exacerbation of the unemployment problem.

Postscript 2002

In the four years that have passed since the initial version of the foregoing discussion appeared in print, European unemployment rates have fallen, but not by much. In France, for example, the rate dropped from 11.8 percent in 1998 to 9.0 percent in 2001; in Germany, from 9.3 percent to 7.9 percent; in the EU as a whole, from 9.9 percent to 7.8 percent. Meanwhile, in the United States, the unemployment rate hit a low of 4.0 percent in 2000, then began to climb as the national economic recession began in 2001, and by November 2001 it had reached 5.6 percent—still far lower than the European rate even during the height of the preceding prosperity.[28] Organization for Economic Cooperation and Development projections for 2003 put U.S. unemployment at 6.0 percent and EU unemployment at 8.0 percent.[29] Obviously, the gap between the performance of the two labor markets remains wide, and until Europe (or the United States) alters its basic labor-market and welfare-state policies, that gap probably will remain wide.

Notes

1. U.S. Council of Economic Advisers, *Report 1980* (Washington, D.C.: U.S. Government Printing Office, 1980), p. 326.

2. George Alogoskoufis, Charles R. Bean, Giuseppe Bertola, Daniel Cohen, Juan Jose Dolado, and Gilles Saint-Paul , *Unemployment: Choices for Europe* (London: Center for Economic Policy Research, 1995), p. 6.

3. U.S. Council of Economic Advisers, *Report 1980,* p. 326.

4. Alogoskoufis and others, *Unemployment,* p. 6; Alan R. Townsend, *Making a Living in Europe: Human Geographies of Economic Change* (London and New York: Routledge, 1997), pp. 27, 62; U.S. Council of Economic Advisers, *Report 1997* (Washington, D.C.: U.S. Government Printing Office, 1997), p. 421.

5. Data plotted in figure 17.1 for 1970–96 come from U.S. Council of Economic Advisers, *Report 1997,* p. 420; for September or October 1997, from *The Economist* (November 29, 1997), p. 108.

6. Joel Blocker, "Europe: France—Unemployment as a Way of Life," Radio Free Europe/Radio Liberty, at http://www.rferl.org/nca/features/1998/03/F.RU.980325154028.html.

7. Craig R. Whitney, "Who Said London Is Backward? The French. Now They Flock There," *New York Times International,* March 29, 1998.

8. All 1997 unemployment data in the preceding three paragraphs from the Organization for Economic Cooperation and Development, as reported in *The Economist* (November 29, 1997), p. 108.

9. U.S. Council of Economic Advisers, *Report 1997,* p. 340; Townsend, *Making a Living in Europe,* p. 34.

10. Charles R. Bean, "European Unemployment: A Survey," *Journal of Economic Literature* 32 (June 1994), p. 595; see also the data presented by Alogoskoufis and others, *Unemployment,* p. 63.

11. U.S. Bureau of the Census, *Statistical Abstract of the United States,* 116th ed. (Washington, D.C.: U.S. Government Printing Office, 1996), p. 841.

12. Wilfried Prewo, *From Welfare State to Social State: Empowerment, Individual Responsibility, and Effective Compassion* (Zellik, Belgium: Centre for the New Europe, 1996), pp. 8–9.

13. David Woodruff, "French Firms Embrace Capitalism Despite Government Interference," *Wall Street Journal,* November 24, 1999, p. A15.

14. Bean, "European Unemployment," p. 586.

15. Ibid., p. 590; Townsend, *Making a Living in Europe,* p. 21.

16. Robert Barro, "Why Eastern Germany Still Lags," *Wall Street Journal,* June 11, 1998; Ulrich Witt, "Germany's 'Social' Market Economy': Between Social Ethos and Rent Seeking," *The Independent Review* 6 (winter 2002): 365–75, esp. p. 371.

17. Bean, "European Unemployment," p. 595.

18. Douglas Lavin, "Socialists Sweep to Victory in French Vote," *Wall Street Journal,* June 2, 1997; Douglas Lavin, "Tale of Two Job Markets: Why England Works, France Doesn't," *Wall Street Journal,* August 7, 1997.

19. Sylvia Nasar, "Where Joblessness Is a Way of Making a Living," *New York Times,* May 9, 1999.

20. Bean, "European Unemployment," pp. 586, 610 (quote).

21. Alogoskoufis and others, *Unemployment,* p. 12.

22. Bean, "European Unemployment," pp. 608–10.

23. Nasar, "Where Joblessness Is a Way of Making a Living."

24. Martin Feldstein, "The Political Economy of the European Economic and Monetary Union: Political Sources of an Economic Liability," *Journal of Economic Perspectives* 11 (fall 1997), p. 40.

25. Townsend, *Making a Living in Europe,* p. 28.

26. Ibid., p. 29.

27. "Europe: France—Unemployment as a Way of Life."

28. Organization for Economic Cooperation and Development, "Standardised Unemployment Rates," table, at http://www.oecd.org/oecd/pages/home/displaygeneral/0,3380,EN -document-20-nodirectorat.

29. Organization for Economic Cooperation and Development, *OECD Economic Outlook No. 70,* preliminary ed. (2002), "Summary of Projections."

18

Death and Taxes

An adage affirms that death and taxes are all we can expect with certainty. As maxims go, this one has a superior success record, but the truth it expresses extends far beyond its traditional signification.

Your Money or Your Life

Consider first that despite the insistence of public-choice theorists that political relations have the nature of an exchange in which the subjects pay "tax prices" to acquire the services supplied by the government, the transaction in question bears little resemblance to a free-market exchange. Unlike General Motors or Safeway, whose offers you may take or leave, the government threatens to kill you if you steadfastly resist entering into its deal. Hence, in "political exchange," death and taxes go together just as they do in the Mafia's proverbial "offer you can't refuse."

In the United States, members of Congress and the tax authorities enjoy describing the tax system as one based on voluntary compliance, but everyone of normal intelligence appreciates that this description is pure buncombe. As West Virginia chief justice Richard Neely noted in 1982, "Cheating on federal and state income tax is all pervasive in all classes of society; except among the compulsively honest, cheating usually occurs in direct proportion to opportunity."[1] Without the government's massive surveillance, punctilious penalties, and harsh criminal sanctions, the number of tax-paying citizens would converge toward zero.

Of course, in this country the taxpayers can always protest. At the very beginning of our national life, when Congress enacted an excise tax on whiskey in 1791, the farmers of western Pennsylvania and other frontier areas took offense. For these isolated producers, whiskey served as an important medium of exchange and as a dietary staple. Moreover, they were "reluctant to pay for a central government that delivered no visible services."[2] Denouncing tyranny and waving banners proclaiming such un-American slogans as "Liberty, Equality, and Fraternity," they staged the so-called Whiskey Rebellion during the next three years. To put a point on their protest, the Whiskey Boys, as they called themselves, took to tarring and feathering tax collectors and the sheriffs who accompanied them. At a mass meeting in 1792, they denounced all who might cooperate with the tax collectors: "In the future, we will consider such persons as unworthy of our friendship, have no intercourse or dealings with them, withdraw from them every assistance, and withold [*sic*] all the comforts of life which depend upon those duties that as men and fellow citizens we owe to each other, and upon all occasions treat them with the contempt they deserve."[3] In those days, when men were still men, a tax revolt was an honest-to-God tax revolt, not just a media event.

Treasury Secretary Alexander Hamilton, who had proposed the whiskey tax in the first place, urged President George Washington to suppress the rebellion by armed force in order to teach the people a lesson in submissiveness. As Hamilton explained to Washington in 1792, collecting the whiskey excise was desirable so that "the authority of the National Government should be visible in some branch of internal Revenue; lest a total non-exercise of it should beget an impression that it was never to be exercised & next that it ought not to be exercised."[4] Sufficiently agitated, Washington nationalized almost thirteen thousand state militiamen—a rag-tag, drunken, rowdy, pillaging force comparable in size to the Continental Army he had commanded during the revolution—and General Henry "Light Horse Harry" Lee led them into western Pennsylvania, where nearly all the rebels saw fit to run away or to capitulate and accept an amnesty.[5] Their cause was ultimately vindicated, however, when under President Thomas Jefferson the federal government abandoned nearly all its previous attempts to collect excise and direct taxes.

Your Money and Your Life

Historically, major wars and steep tax increases have coincided. As Bruce D. Porter has written, "War has been the lever by which monarchs and central governments have imposed increasingly larger tax burdens on increasingly broader segments of society, thus enabling ever-higher levels of spending to be sustained, even in peacetime."[6] In the introduction to his three-volume collection of articles on war finance, Larry Neal observes that "many, if not most, of the lasting innovations in the way governments have collected taxes ... have emerged under the duress of war."[7] Neal presents nearly eighteen hundred pages of fascinating documents in support of his claim.

Certainly, in U.S. history, major wars have brought both higher tax rates and new kinds of taxes. During the Civil War, when federal receipts increased tenfold and internal revenues rose from zero to more than $300 million (amounting to more than half of total tax receipts), Congress placed excises on a wide range of goods and services, besides taxing incomes, inheritances, and real estate. According to Republican politico James G. Blaine, the revenue act of 1862 created "one of the most searching, thorough, comprehensive systems of taxation ever devised by any Government."[8]

To collect its new internal taxes, Congress established the Office of the Commissioner of Internal Revenue, a precursor of today's fervently despised Internal Revenue Service. After the war, Congress eliminated most of the new levies but retained the "sin taxes" on tobacco and liquor. These taxes yielded at least a third of all federal tax revenues in the years from the 1870s to World War I. The government financed the Spanish-American War in large part by doubling the taxes on alcohol and tobacco products. In the enforcement of the liquor excise laws, the Treasury's "revenuers," as they became known in the hidden hollows of Appalachia, made themselves a plague upon the numerous operators of illegal stills—spiritual descendants of the Whiskey Boys of the 1790s.

The pecuniary cost of making war increased exponentially. At $3.4 billion, Civil War expenditures exceeded by 90 percent the total spending of the U.S. government in its entire preceding history ($1.8 billion). Roughly speaking, World War I cost ten times more than the Civil War, and World War II ten times more than World War I. Even though the Treasury financed most of its spending for each major war by borrowing, its tax bite still outpaced its war spending: taxes amounted to about 9 percent of federal spending for the Civil War, 24 percent for World War I, and 41 percent for World War II.[9]

In each case, the huge wartime tax burdens gave rise to widespread efforts to escape payment. In turn, the government expanded its tax bureaucracy. The personnel of the Bureau of Internal Revenue increased from about 4,000 in 1913 to 15,800 in 1920. During World War II, the Treasury brought on board another 40,000 employees. Enforcement alone, however, had its recognized limits. Accordingly, during World War I and even more extensively during World War II, the government resorted to insidious propaganda efforts aimed at persuading taxpayers to comply.[10] Moreover, in 1943 Congress enacted a law requiring that taxes due on wages and salaries be withheld at the source, thereby ensuring that workers would have little opportunity to keep their earnings out of the tax collector's clutches.[11]

World War II has often been described as a popular war, but the high wartime taxes were extremely unpopular. In 1944, for the first time ever, Congress overrode a presidential veto of a revenue bill, rebuking President Franklin D. Roosevelt's attempt to raise taxes even higher. Late in the war, tax protesters mounted a major effort to repeal the Sixteenth Amendment, and seventeen states passed resolutions in support of the proposal. In the words of political scientist John F. Witte, these events revealed "the depth of opposition—even during a period of national crisis—to high taxes."[12]

A time-honored means of dealing with opposition to taxation, of course, is to levy the hidden tax by inflating the money stock. U.S. governments did so during each major war. As a result, roughly speaking, the value of the money dropped by about half during the Civil War (excluding the Confederacy, where the paper currency became totally worthless), World War I, and World War II. In the last case, the government concealed the decline of the dollar's value during the war by imposing comprehensive price controls, then allowed the dollar's shrunken value to reveal itself in 1946 and 1947 after the real damage had been done.

Rulers have appreciated how inflation serves as a tax ever since the days when monarchs clipped the coins. Once governments had begun to issue paper currency, the hidden tax became even easier to levy. During the War of Independence, which the Continental Congress and the breakaway states financed overwhelmingly by issuing paper money, Benjamin Franklin wrote that Congress

> hoped, notwithstanding its quantity, to have kept up the value of their paper. In this they were mistaken. It depreciated gradually. But this depreciation, though in some circumstances inconvenient, has had the general good and great effect of operating as a tax, and perhaps the most equal of all taxes, since it depreciated in the hands of the holders of money, and thereby taxed them in proportion to the sums they held and the time they held it, which generally is in proportion to men's wealth.[13]

By supposing that inflation served as a neutral wealth tax, Franklin erred. Obviously, some people held much more of their wealth in the form of money and other assets denominated in nominal units of money than other people did. Moreover, some people surely anticipated the fall in the value of the paper money occasioned by its profuse issue better than other people did. Of course, the Continental Congress had no power to levy explicit taxes, and the states resisted its requisitions, so without inflationary finance it had little capacity to acquire the resources needed to conduct its military operations.

A Warning

In conclusion, for those who may be inclined to tempt fate by asserting a Lockean claim to the fruits of their own labors, a warning: the people who are attempting to tax you are armed and dangerous; proceed at your own risk. Al Capone got away with plenty of murders, but they sent him to prison for tax evasion.

Notes

1. Quoted in Charles Adams, *For Good and Evil: The Impact of Taxes on the Course of Civilization* (New York: Madison Books, 1993), p. 379.

2. Thomas P. Slaughter, *The Whiskey Rebellion: Frontier Epilogue to the American Revolution* (New York: Oxford University Press, 1986), p. 94.

3. Quoted in ibid., p. 116.

4. Quoted in W. Elliot Brownlee, *Federal Taxation in America: A Short History* (Washington, D.C., and New York: Woodrow Wilson Center Press and Cambridge University Press, 1996), p. 18.

5. Slaughter, *The Whiskey Rebellion*, pp. 3, 205–21.

6. Bruce D. Porter, *War and the Rise of the State: The Military Foundations of Modern Politics* (New York: Free Press, 1994), p. 14.

7. Larry Neal, *War Finance* (Aldershot, Eng.: Edward Elgar, 1994), vol. 1, p. x.

8. Quoted in Jeffrey Rogers Hummel, *Emancipating Slaves, Enslaving Free Men: A History of the American Civil War* (Chicago and La Salle, Ill.: Open Court, 1996), p. 222.

9. Claudia D. Goldin, "War," in *Encyclopedia of American Economic History: Studies of the Principal Movements and Ideas,* edited by Glenn Porter (New York: Charles Scribner's Sons, 1980), vol. 3, p. 938.

10. On World War I, see Charlotte Twight, *Dependent on D.C.: The Rise of Federal Control over the Lives of Ordinary Americans* (New York: Palgrave, 2002), pp. 97–98; on World War II, see Carolyn C. Jones, "Class Tax to Mass Tax: The Role of Propaganda in the Expansion of the Income Tax During World War II," *Buffalo Law Review* 37 (fall 1988–89): 685–737.

11. Charlotte Twight, "The Evolution of Federal Income Tax Withholding: The Machinery of Institutional Change," *Cato Journal* 14 (winter 1995): 359–95.

12. John F. Witte, *The Politics and Development of the Federal Income Tax* (Madison, Wisc.: University of Wisconsin Press, 1985), p. 123.

13. Franklin to Thomas Ruston, October 9, 1780, quoted in Margaret G. Myers, *A Financial History of the United States* (New York: Columbia University Press, 1970), p. 51

19

A Carnival of Taxation

Taxes are what we pay for civilized society.

— Oliver Wendell Holmes Jr.

Au contraire.

— Robert Higgs

To determine whether a certain entity is a government, we might first ask: Does it have the power to tax? By this test, for example, the United States of America under the Articles of Confederation (1781–89) was not a government because the confederation lacked the power to tax, whereas the United States of America under the Constitution (1789–) was a government because it did possess that power. Critical minds might conjecture that getting the power to tax was, indeed, the principal point of the Framers' suffering through the hot summer of 1787 with the windows closed.

That certain people have the *power* to tax means, of course, that they will hurt you if you refuse to pay. The rebellious farmers of western Pennsylvania learned that lesson the hard way when they wilted under the weight of the armed forces mobilized by President George Washington in 1794, and a multitude of others have accepted a similar "offer they couldn't refuse" during the ensuing centuries. U.S. governments may be lax in many ways, but tax collection is not one of them. In 1993, the Internal Revenue Service alone had 3,621 employees authorized to carry firearms and make arrests.[1] In 1995, the federal courts alone convicted 866 persons of violating tax laws and sentenced 304 of them to prison terms.[2] State and local governments also work energetically to instruct their subjects in the causal relationship between paying taxes and remaining at liberty. Unfortunately, the *Statistical Abstract of the United States* does not report the number of Americans living in fear of the tax authorities because of offenses real, imagined, or trumped up.

Without doubt, the classic relation of a subject to the government is the payment of tribute in exchange for protection. All too often, however, the protection received by the taxpayer is exclusively against the violence of the tax taker. A question naturally arises, therefore, as to what distinguishes the government from, say, the Mafia, but that question raises issues much too delicate to be resolved here.

In the past century, Americans have endured nearly continuous political rhetoric about tax cuts, and taxes have been cut occasionally, but taking the long view, one sees that the cuts were relatively trifling and transitory (see figure 19.1). In an era marked by the rapid growth of national product, taxes have tended to grow far faster. The tax share of net national product (NNP)—including federal, state, and local taxes—rose from about 8 percent before World War I to 34 percent in 1998. As the figure shows, the twentieth-century rise of the tax share followed a "logistic" curve: the rate of growth was low before the 1930s, accelerated during the 1930s and 1940s, then decelerated during the second half of the century. Despite the deceleration, the tax share con-

Figure 19.1

Taxes as Percent of Net National Product

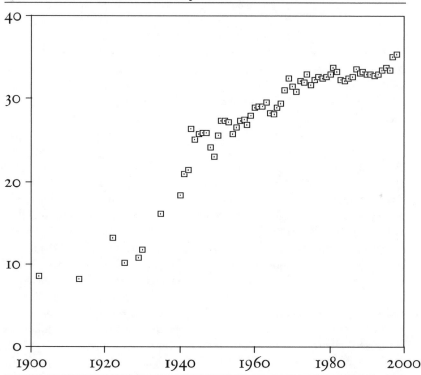

Source: The Tax Foundation (http://taxfoundation.org)

tinued to rise during the postwar era, reaching its all-time high of 35 percent of NNP in 2000.[3]

Before the election of Franklin D. Roosevelt, the tax revenues of state and local governments dwarfed those of the federal government, and the local governments collected by far the largest amount. The New Deal and World War II inverted that longstanding fiscal structure. By 1947, federal revenues were three times greater than state and local revenues combined. The feds have remained the big boys on the block ever since. As table 19.1 shows, the federal government currently absorbs more than two dollars for every dollar taken by state and local governments.

Table 19.1

Taxes by Type and Level of Government, 1998 (in billions of dollars)

	Federal	State & Local	Total
Individual Income Taxes	792.6	169.2	961.8
Social Insurance Taxes	682.2	91.2	773.4
Sales & Excise Taxes	83.0	272.8	355.8
Property Taxes	0	221.3	221.3
Corporate Income Taxes	226.4	40.3	266.7
Other Business Taxes	0	41.5	41.5
All Other Taxes	21.8	24.9	46.7
Total	1,806.0	861.2	2,667.2

Source: The Tax Foundation (http://www.taxfoundation.org)

The table also shows the yield of the major forms of tax. At the federal level, individual income taxes bring in the most, followed closely by payroll taxes. Corporate income taxes rank a distant third, and miscellaneous excises and other taxes round out the total. At the state and local levels, sales and excise taxes yield the most. Property taxes are not far behind; individual income taxes come next; and various other exactions—none of them trivial—add nearly $200 billion to the total.

Table 19.2 displays tax data in snapshots for 1957, 1977, and 1997, revealing several notable facts. First, the median two-income family was already paying a substantial amount of taxes in 1957 (27.8 percent of its total income), but by the time Jimmy Carter took office as president, that family was surrendering a much larger share (36.5 percent) of its much larger income. Looked at another way, the family's nominal income had risen 224 percent, but its nominal tax burden had risen 340 percent. Even though the relative size of the typical tax bite rose much less between 1977 and 1997, the median two-income family continued to lose out to the tax takers, who in the latter year snatched 37.6 percent of the family's income. Figures 19.2 and 19.3 show how taxes compared

Table 19.2

Tax Facts for the Median Two-Income Family

	1957	1977	1997
Median Family Income	$5,776	$18,704	$54,910
Federal Income Tax	$511	$2,102	$4,942
Payroll Tax, Employee Portion	$95	$965	$4,033
Payroll Tax, Employer Portion	$95	$965	$4,033
Total Federal Taxes	$1,167	$4,975	$15,408
State & Local Taxes	$464	$2,205	$6,761
Total Taxes	$1,630	$7,180	$22,169
After-tax Income	$4,240	$12,489	$36,774
Taxes as Percentage of Total Income	27.8%	36.5%	37.6%
Inflation-adjusted Total Taxes (1997$)	$8,281	$17,050	$22,169

Source: The Tax Foundation (http://www.taxfoundation.org)

Note: The burden of federal and state corporate income taxes is included. After-tax income does not deduct employer share of payroll taxes because the burden of the payroll tax is assumed to reduce income before the "gross" seen on paychecks. Total taxes as a percentage of income is calculated by adding the employer's share of the payroll tax to the median family income.

Figure 19.2

Budget of Median Income Family, 1957

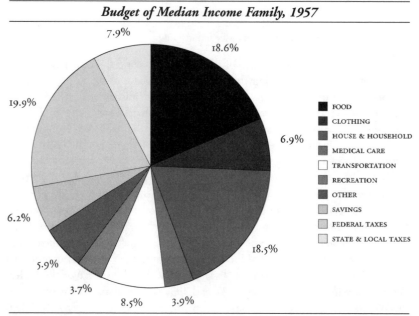

Source: The Tax Foundation (http://taxfoundation.org)

Figure 19.3

Budget of Median Income Family, 1997

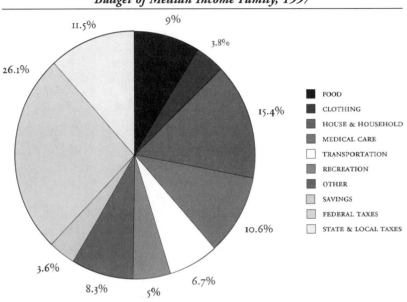

Source: The Tax Foundation (http://taxfoundation.org)

with other major categories of the family budget in 1957 and 1997.

In real dollars, the annual tax burden of the median two-income family increased between 1957 and 1997 by $13,888, or 68 percent, notwithstanding the end of the hugely expensive Cold War. In view of the deterioration of the public schools, the steep increase of crime rates, the crumbling of the public infrastructure, and other adverse developments during those four decades, the typical family might well have asked: What are we getting in exchange for our swollen taxes? However, just as sausage eaters are well advised never to visit a sausage factory, so citizens will surely be more content if they remain largely ignorant of how their governments are disposing of the loot.

Europeans, of course, are not inclined to shed tears for Americans where taxes are concerned. As a rule, European governments take a much larger share of national income than U.S. governments do (see table 19.3). Most Europeans also pay a greater amount of tax per capita than Americans do. (Note, however, that the dollar figures in table 19.3 are sensitive to the exchange rates used to convert local currency units, and exchange rates sometimes change substantially even within the span of a few years.) Contemplating the extraordinary tax burden borne by the Danes, an American taxpayer might wax Shakespearean, concluding that without a doubt, something *is* rotten in Denmark.

Table 19.3

Tax Revenue in 28 Countries, 1994

Country	Total Taxes (billions $)	Taxes per Capita ($)	Tax Revenue as Percent of GDP
Australia	100	5,589	29.9
Austria	85	10,569	42.8
Belgium	106	10,500	46.6
Canada	201	6,858	36.1
Czech Republic	17	1,648	47.3
Denmark	75	14,460	51.6
Finland	46	9,051	47.3
France	586	10,129	44.1
Germany	803	12,197	39.3
Greece	33	3,169	42.5
Hungary	17	1,648	41.0
Iceland	2	7,191	30.9
Ireland	19	5,451	37.5
Italy	424	7,416	41.7
Japan	1,304	10,434	27.8
Luxembourg	6	16,271	45.0
Mexico	71	764	18.8
Netherlands	154	9,983	45.9
New Zealand	19	5,434	37.0
Norway	51	11,706	41.2
Poland	40	1,040	43.2
Portugal	29	2,902	33.0
Spain	173	4,410	35.8
Sweden	101	11,481	51.0
Switzerland	87	12,464	33.9
Turkey	29	480	22.2
United Kingdom	348	5,968	34.1
United States	1,885	7,234	27.6

Source: U.S. Bureau of the Census, *Statistical Abstract of the United States: 1997* (117th ed.). Washington, D.C.: U.S. Government Printing Office, 1997, p. 844.

Still, who can dispute that the governments of the United States constitute the most voracious tax system in the history of mankind? In the year 2000, those governments succeeded in laying hands on more than $3 trillion— almost $11,000 each for the 275 million men, women, and children resident in the country.[4] No other nation-state rakes in an amount even close to the U.S. total. The American revolutionaries, whose tax burden was almost vanishingly small, complained loudly of taxation without representation. If only they could have foreseen the burden of taxation *with* representation.

Notes

1. U.S. Bureau of the Census, *Statistical Abstract of the United States 1997* (Washington, D.C.: U.S. Government Printing Office, 1997), p. 214.

2. Ibid., p. 217.

3. Calculated from data in U.S. Council of Economic Advisers, *Report 2001* (Washington, D.C.: U.S. Government Printing Office, 2001), pp. 304, 371.

4. Ibid., pp. 315, 371.

20

Unmitigated Mercantilism

When my son was growing up, I lived in constant fear that one day he would come to me and ask, "Dad, why do we have an Export-Import Bank?" Fortunately for me, that day never came. If it had, I would have been compelled to make a painful choice: either to lie to him, saying that we need the bank to promote U.S. exports and create jobs, or to hit him with the bitter truth, attesting that the bank is just another contrivance to shift wealth from the politically weak and alienated to the politically strong and connected, while sanctifying the transfer with incantations of economic humbug.

James A. Harmon, the chairman of the Export-Import Bank of the United States (Eximbank) during the late 1990s, demonstrated that he possessed a high threshold for embarrassment. On the home page of the Eximbank's Web site, he declared for all the wide world to see, "Ex-Im Bank Is Vigorously Pursuing Its Mission to Support U.S. Exports and Sustain American Jobs by Offering U.S. Exporters the Loans, Guarantees, and Insurance Products They Need to Compete in the Global Marketplace."[1] Well, okay, not everybody has had the opportunity to take Economics 101.

Someone who, one presumes, has mastered both elementary and advanced economics is the current Harvard University president and former U.S. Treasury secretary Lawrence Summers. After all, Summers was awarded a Ph.D. in economics by Harvard and taught at MIT before returning to Harvard to become the Nathaniel Ropes Professor of Political Economy in 1983.[2] It seemed more than a little odd, therefore, when Summers publicly praised the Eximbank for its stimulation of U.S. exports and its contribution to "our national economic defense." According to Summers, "The virtue of maintaining a strong and credible Export-Import Bank is that it can help to deter abusive subsidies by other countries."[3] It makes you wonder: What have they been teaching in the economics courses at Harvard?

U.S. exports have been running in the neighborhood of $700 billion annually in recent years.[4] According to the Eximbank's 1999 annual report, the bank "supported" in various ways U.S. exports valued at $16.7 billion in fiscal year 1999.[5] Therefore, exports supported by the Eximbank amount to roughly

2 percent of U.S. exports. One strains to imagine how the exporters of the other 98 percent of the stuff managed to arrange financing.

As for the job creation that the bank declares to be its very purpose, one need not pause long over the mathematics. U.S. gross domestic product (GDP) is now approximately $10 trillion. Even if all of the workers required to produce the $16.7 billion of bank-subsidized exports were to become permanently unemployed—a highly unlikely outcome—the resulting increase in the U.S. rate of unemployment would be swallowed up in the rounding error. The repeated claim that the nation needs the Eximbank to create or maintain jobs is not just bad economics—the kind that disregards opportunity cost, among other things—it is also inapt arithmetic.

So what is the real story behind this economic train wreck? We can gain a better appreciation by examining the principal suppliers of the goods whose export the Eximbank effectively subsidizes. Looking through the 1999 annual report (pp. 20–27), one finds the names of such obscure and struggling enterprises as Brown & Root, General Electric, Hughes Space Communications, Westinghouse Electric, Bechtel International, Lockheed Martin Overseas, International Business Machines, Motorola, Federal Express, Case, Caterpillar, and Siemens Westinghouse Power. Would it be heartless of us to insist that these multinational corporate powerhouses line up financing for their overseas sales without dipping into the taxpayers' pockets?

By far the most prominent corporate beneficiary of the Eximbank's largess is the Boeing Company. Its name is attached to thirty-four of the eighty-two deals for loans and long-term guarantees listed by country in the 1999 report. Moreover, for those same eighty-two deals, Boeing's deals accounted for 54 percent of the total amount of loans and 80 percent of the total amount of loan guarantees. Little wonder that the Eximbank has been called "Boeing's Bank."[6] Ten of those thirty-four Boeing loans and guarantees involved sales of aircraft to Chinese airlines, although the company's biggest listed deals, totaling more than $2 billion of loan guarantees, involved sales of aircraft to Saudi Arabian companies. Well might one ask: Can the Saudis not get credit in the ordinary commercial market?

Gather round, children, and I will tell you in words all of you can understand how the Eximbank works. (1) The government takes money from American taxpayers and gives it to the Eximbank. (2) The Eximbank gives the money to the Chinese and Saudi Arabian companies that buy airplanes from the Boeing Company, and those companies promise to hand the money to Boeing and then to repay the Eximbank's loan with (a below-market rate of) interest. (3) The Boeing Company sells (maybe) a few more airplanes than it would have sold in the absence of the export-credit subsidies. (4) A few people work at the Boeing Company who otherwise would have worked elsewhere. (5) Boeing shareholders earn a little more income, which otherwise would have been earned (plus a bit more) by other producers. (6) The total amount of wealth created in the United States—and in the world as a whole—is less than it would have been had these financial shenanigans never taken place. (You kids will understand that last point after you take Economics 101.)

Naturally, any such economically absurd and politically predatory subsidy scheme has a high probability of having been created during the New Deal, and the Eximbank is no exception. Back in 1934, Franklin D. Roosevelt was seeking a way to finance U.S. exports to the Soviet Union. Private financiers, cognizant that the communists had repudiated debts owed by the preceding regime, were unwilling to throw good money after bad. The New Dealers, on the other hand, relished such opportunities, and, as usual, well-connected business interests worked assiduously to get their snouts under the Treasury's tent. In a statement that applies just as well to yesterday as to 1934, historian James S. Olson explains, "American traders began calling for long-term government credit to businesses dealing in foreign markets, particularly since so many foreign governments spared little effort subsidizing their own companies doing business with the United States.... Some form of government insurance or direct lending [the traders argued] was absolutely necessary."[7]

Although political complications sank the USSR loan project that had given rise to the creation of the Eximbank, the bank's all-purpose political serviceability ensured its survival. The first transaction, in 1935, involved a loan that allowed Cuba to purchase silver, a deal that pleased the pressure groups perennially lobbying for subsidies to silver producers in the western states. Continuing to move in accordance with the law of political gravity, most of the bank's early loans "were short-term credit on tobacco and cotton. Commercial banks handled the loans but invariably sold them back. The Export-Import Bank also granted intermediate credit to capital goods exporters, primarily railway and heavy equipment, and advanced long-term credit to exporters and banks against obligations issued by foreign governments in settlement of claims arising out of blocked exchanges."[8]

Later, congressional pressures led the bank to pretend it was helping small businesses and small- and medium-size exporters—in truth, mere dinghies bobbing in the wake of the Boeing battleship.[9] Successive administrations found the Eximbank useful in connection with such political-financial adventures as operating the Marshall Plan, establishing the State of Israel, and, more recently, propping up friends in the successor governments of the old East Bloc and the Asian governments submerged in the financial crisis of the late 1990s.

Although calls for privatizing the Eximbank have been voiced from diverse positions on the political spectrum, the institution continues merrily along its resource-squandering way.[10] Recently, its ambitious chairman, Mr. Harmon, recognizing an opportunity to project his institution into the most politically correct of all causes, announced a campaign to provide Eximbank subsidies in connection with sales of AIDS drugs to African countries.[11] According to a spokesman for Merck & Company, "If Ex-Im Bank really does work to make more resources available to those African countries, then it's very welcome."[12]

Of course, for any political institution, it is important to be seen as doing good while actually doing what all political institutions do. Harmon, ever the aspiring bureaucrat, assured the public that "This country has never needed [Exim] Bank more than it will need it in the years ahead." And right behind him stood that renowned economist Larry Summers, attesting that "The U.S. government has both the responsibility and the tools in hand to protect U.S. exporters from unfair practices that undermine their competitiveness."[13] In short, as long as other governments use subsidies to injure their own economies, never doubt that the U.S. government will match them shot for shot in wounding the U.S. economy.

Postscript 2002

Plus ça change, plus c'est la meme chose, boys and girls. Even though the past few years have brought more than the usual amount of public faultfinding to the Eximbank, this proud ship of state privilege has sailed on unscathed. Because by law the agency requires periodic reauthorization, Congress held hearings on the matter in 2001. This occasion took on additional gravity because the George W. Bush administration had just proposed to cut 24 percent from the Eximbank's subsidy budget in fiscal year 2002 as a token swat at corporate welfare.[14] Big business, as one would expect, cried out in anguish against taking this baby step toward unfettered capitalism, and in due course Congress saw fit to minimize the cut.[15]

The hearings prompted various critics to vent their views. A Green Scissors report endorsed by more than two dozen leftist organizations, for example, included the Eximbank among the government programs it recommended cutting. The report charged that the bank dispenses "polluter pork" by subsidizing exports of goods for environmentally harmful projects such as mines, pipelines, and coal-fired power plants in the Third World, thereby contributing to global warming, among other evils.[16] At the opposite end of the ideological spectrum, Andrew West, a contributing economics editor for *Capitalism Magazine,* also attacked the Eximbank, pointing out that the bank serves as a "key resource for political fund-raising and the spoils system";[17] Ian Vásquez of the Cato Institute testified that "lack of private-sector finance on acceptable terms is not an example of market failure, but rather an important market signal about a project's prospects or a country's investment regime";[18] and libertarian congressman Ron Paul of Texas characterized the arguments in favor of the bank as examples of the broken-window fallacy and the bank itself as immoral "welfare for the rich" and a boon to tyrannical states such as China and Sudan.[19]

Besides the legions of corporate lobbyists, whose interests focused on loot, not logic, other supporters stood up for the Eximbank on public-policy grounds. "It would be a huge mistake for Congress to cut funding for the Export-Import Bank," testified C. Fred Bergsten, director of the Institute for International Economics. Not only should Congress refrain from abolishing the agency or cutting its subsidy budget, but, stated Bergsten, "the Bank's authorization (and appropriation) should instead be increased by about 50 percent." Barring such congressional support, "US exporters will be put at a severe disadvantage in world markets [and] the US economy will suffer substantially."[20] What, one wonders, could cause a professional economist to espouse such intellectually and morally bankrupt views in full sight of his fellow man? I can only speculate. Perhaps it is not entirely out of bounds to note that, as Bergsten himself acknowledged, he was drawing on work presented at a conference hosted by his very own Institute for International Economics in May 2000 "to honor the 65th anniversary of the Export-Import Bank."[21]

Moreover, at that same conference, Eximbank chairman Harmon revealed that the agency had asked the Council on Foreign Relations and the Institute for International Economics to conduct "an independent study" of its operations before the new administration took office:

> We must ensure that this Bank's future lives up to its proud history. We need a no-holds-barred audit of Ex-Im Bank, our programs and the competition, a strong business plan—complete with recommendations—that can be presented to the next President of the United States and to the next Congress on how we can better level the playing field and empower more US businesses to continue growing our economy and creating jobs through exports.[22]

Obviously, the "no-holds-barred audit" was meant to reach predetermined conclusions, justifying the continuing operation of the agency and, in all likelihood, its expansion in size and scope. As Harmon wrote in the annual report for fiscal year 2000,

> When the new Administration and Congress arrive, we will hand to them an independent report on the Bank prepared by the Institute for International Economics with an attached report from the Bank's advisory committee and my own recommendations. *We hope that these reports will serve as the basis for strengthening the Bank,* as part of its upcoming reauthorization, to better serve U.S. exporters in today's environment.[23]

Chairman Harmon was not flying blind. In soliciting an "independent report" from Fred Bergsten at the Institute for International Economics, he was dealing with someone whose ironclad commitment to the agency was a matter of clear public record. Indeed, in a speech given in Washington, D.C., on April 4, 2001, Bergsten boasted, "when I became responsible for Ex-Im Bank policy and the U.S. Government at Treasury in 1977, the program had been cut to a mere pittance. I quadrupled it in 4 years with the support, of course, of the Ex-Im Bank leadership at the time, [and] brought it back into play." In addition, more recently, "We did a big study on this in my institute several years ago and concluded that the earlier era of export controls and inadequate export finance from Ex-Im Bank and other disincentives were costing us $30 to 40 billion a year of potential exports that we would otherwise make to the rest of the world."[24] Clearly, Bergsten and the Eximbank had been cozy for a long time. So much for an "independent study."[25]

When time came for the Bush administration to present its budget proposals for fiscal year 2003, the previous year's assault on corporate welfare had given way to other, more politically promising crusades. This time the budget "not only doesn't seek cuts but, by easing Ex-Im lending requirements, actually will allow as much as a 10% boost in corporate trade financing for such major exporters as Boeing Co. and General Electric Co."[26] Edmund B. Rice, president of the Coalition for Employment Through Exports, a group supported by a number of large corporations, told the *Wall Street Journal* that administration officials had "done a complete 180 and are now supporting expanded Ex-Im lending next year."[27] Cynics might suspect that the Bushies never had their hearts in slashing corporate welfare to begin with and that they lost no sleep agonizing over the unseemly reversal of their position on the Eximbank.

Meanwhile, over at the agency, a new man took the helm as chairman and president: John E. Robson, an establishmentarian extraordinaire who had previously occupied high-level positions as deputy secretary of the Treasury in the earlier Bush administration, president and CEO of drug giant G. D. Searle & Co., dean of the business school at Emory University, and senior adviser with the investment banking firm Robertson Stephens of San Francisco.[28]

Notwithstanding his impressive curriculum vitae, Robson spouted the same sort of economic claptrap his predecessor had routinely dished out: "we play the role of the 'first Marines' to hit the beach for U.S. companies in riskier emerging markets," he wrote in the agency's annual financial report for fiscal year 2001. "We go where the commercial lenders won't. We lead the way into new markets. We take risks that the private sector won't. And we step in where the competition is toughest for U.S. exporters facing competition backed by foreign governments."[29] Brave words, but anyone can be brave when somebody else's resources—in this case, the taxpayers'—are being put at risk. It's fascinating how a government bureaucrat can make wasting the public's money sound like a glorious undertaking.

Although his economic understanding was deficient, Robson showed clear signs of political savvy. He made a point of claiming that "We have helped to create and sustain American jobs in every state *and congressional district,*[30] and a few pages further in the report appears a colorful state map with a list of the dollar amounts of exports from each state "supported" by some form of Exim-bank assistance.[31] This information will come in handy when he hobnobs with members of Congress from time to time, as I am confident he will. After all, as Representative Paul stated, "it is not just any company that receives Eximbank support—rather, the majority of Eximbank funding benefits large, politically powerful corporations."[32] You know, the sort of companies that can afford to keep a congressman or two on tap.

Notes

1. See the Export-Import Bank's Web site at http://www.exim.gov.

2. Biographical information on Summers from *American Economic Review* 87, no. 6 (December 1997), p. 498.

3. Summers as quoted by *Bloomberg News,* May 16, 2000, posted on AOL, retrieved May 27, 2000.

4. U.S. Council of Economic Advisers, *Report 2001* (Washington, D.C.: U.S. Government Printing Office, 2001), p. 392.

5. Report posted at http://www.exim.gov, retrieved May 22, 2000.

6. Janice C. Shields, "Export-Import Bank," *Foreign Policy in Focus* 4, no. 18 (July 1999), p. 2, at http://www.foreignpolicy-infocus.org/briefs/vol4/v4n18exim.html, retrieved May 30, 2000.

7. James S. Olson, *Saving Capitalism: The Reconstruction Finance Corporation and the New Deal, 1933–1940* (Princeton, N.J.: Princeton University Press, 1988), p. 149.

8. Ibid., p. 164.

9. Shields, "Export-Import Bank," p. 3.

10. Ibid., p. 4; Michael M. Phillips, "Ex-Im Chairman Says U.S. Firms Need More Aid to Vie with Foreign Rivals," *Wall Street Journal,* May 15, 2000.

11. Michael M. Phillips, "Ex-Im Bank to Help American Businesses Sell AIDS Treatments to African Nations," *Wall Street Journal,* July 19, 2000.

12. Ibid.

13. *Bloomberg News,* May 16, 2000.

14. James K. Jackson, *Export-Import Bank: Background and Legislative Issues,* Congressional Research Service Report for Congress, 98-568 E (Washington, D.C.: U.S. Government Printing Office, June 14, 2001), p. 1.

15. Jacob M. Schlesinger and Michael M. Phillips, "Bush Budget Underscores His Priorities," *Wall Street Journal,* February 4, 2002.

16. Friends of the Earth, "Environmentalists Agree with President Bush: US Export-Import Bank Needs Appropriations Cut," press release, February 22, 2001, at http:/.www.foe.org/act/gs4pr.html.

17. Andrew West, "Shut Down the Export-Import Bank of the United States," *Capitalism Magazine* (February 21, 2001), at http://www.capitalismmagazine.com/2001/february/aw_shut_down_exp_imp.htm.

18. Ian Vásquez, "Re-authorize or Retire the Export Import Bank?" testimony before the Subcommittee on International Monetary Policy and Trade of the Committee on Financial Services, U.S. House of Representatives, May 8, 2001, p. 3.

19. Ron Paul, "Statement on Funding for the Export-Import Bank," October 31, 2001, at http://www.house.gov/paul/congrec/congrec2001/cr103101.htm.

20. C. Fred Bergsten, "The US Export-Import Bank: Meeting the Challenges of the 21st Century," testimony before the Subcommittee on International Trade and Finance, Committee on Banking, Housing, and Urban Affairs, U.S. Senate, May 17, 2001, pp. 1, 8.

21. Ibid., p. 9, n. 1.

22. Export-Import Bank of the United States, press release, May 15, 2000, at http://www.exim.gov/press/may1500.html.

23. Export-Import Bank of the United States, *2000 Annual Report*, p. 3, at http://www.exim.gov, emphasis added.

24. Export-Import Bank of the United States, press release, April 4, 2001, at http://www.exim.gov/press/apr0401a.html, quotations from pp. 6 and 5, respectively.

25. According to Gary Hufbauer of the Institute for International Economics (telephone interview, February 8, 2002), various attempts to gain funding for the "audit" contemplated by Harmon came to naught, although, as indicated earlier, Bergsten himself did testify before Congress in support of expanding the Eximbank's funding and widening its scope of action.

26. Schlesinger and Phillips, "Bush Budget Underscores His Priorities."

27. Ibid.

28. Biographical information on Robson from "Former Tsy Official Tapped to Head US Export-Import Bk," *Wall Street Journal*, March 28, 2001, at http://www.wsj.com.

29. Export-Import Bank of the United States, *Financial Report FY 2001*, p. 3, at http://www.exim.gov.

30. Ibid.

31. Ibid., p. 15.

32. "Statement on Funding for the Export-Import Bank."

21

Results of A Fifty-Year Experiment in Political Economy

	North Korea	South Korea
Population (millions)	21	46
Life expectancy at birth (years)		
Males	49	70
Females	54	78
Births per 1,000 population	15	16
Deaths per 1,000 population	16	6
Infant deaths per 1,000 live births	88	8
GDP (billions of U.S. dollars, 1996 est.)	21	647
GDP per capita (U.S. dollars, approx.)	1,000	14,000
Military spending (percentage of GDP)	27	3
Active military troop strength	1,054,000	660,000
Television sets per 1,000 population	85	233
Radio sets per 1,000 population	200	928

Note: Data without dates are for circa 1995–97; variables should not be viewed as measured with high accuracy.

Source: *The World Almanac and Book of Facts 1999* (Mahwah, N.J.: World Almanac Books, 1998), pp. 805–6.

22

Results of Another Fifty-Year Experiment in Political Economy

	China (PRC)	*Taiwan (ROC)*
Population (millions)	1,237	22
Population per square mile	335	1,568
Life expectancy at birth (years)		
Males	68.3	73.8
Females	71.1	80.1
Infant deaths per 1,000 live births	45	6
Labor force in agriculture (percentage)	54	10
GDP per capita (approx. U.S. dollars, 1996 est.)		
	2,800	14,700
Military spending (percent of GDP)	5.7	4.9
Active military troop strength	2,935,000	376,000
Passenger cars (millions, total)	4.7	4.3
Television sets per 1,000 population	189	327
Radio sets per 1,000 population	177	402

Note: Data without dates are for circa 1995–97; variables should not be viewed as measured with high accuracy; data for the People's Republic of China do not include Hong Kong.

Source: *The World Almanac and Book of Facts 1999* (Mahwah, N.J.: World Almanac, 1998), pp. 776, 848.

23

Pity the Poor Japanese

All but the very young can still remember the days when the Japanese economy struck fear in the hearts of many Americans. After restoring Japan's war-shattered infrastructure, the Japanese embarked on the most rapid economic growth any large country had ever maintained. By the 1980s, they had transformed their impoverished economy into the wonder of the world, bidding fair to overtake and surpass even the mighty U.S. economy in just a few years. Writers cranked out alarmist books with titles such as *The Japanese Challenge, Japan as Number One, The Enigma of Japanese Power*, and *Power Japan*.[1] During the 1980s, the prices of Japanese real estate and corporate stocks ascended to astronomical heights, and Japanese investors reached out to acquire ownership of landmark properties in the United States and Europe. It seemed that nothing could stop this economic behemoth.

Then the bubble burst, and Japan fell into a slump that has now lasted more than ten years, with no end in sight. The sacrifice of even moderate economic growth for a decade has cost the Japanese people dearly, but that loss has been only one aspect of the failure of Japan's once-vaunted political economy. While asset values have plunged and gross domestic product (GDP) per capita has barely increased, one component of GDP has grown apace: government spending for infrastructure. Indeed, the Japanese government's principal response to the economy's protracted stagnation has been an on-again/off-again program of Keynesian pump priming financed by increased public debt and concentrated on public-works construction projects.[2] Somewhere in hell, Rexford Tugwell, Harry Hopkins, Harold Ickes, and the other New Deal make-work kingpins must be smiling.

In truth, the Japanese were no strangers to such boondoggles even before the great bust. National-accounts data compiled by the Organization for Economic Cooperation and Development (OECD) reveal that as far back as 1965, when Japan still had a relatively low ratio of total government spending to GDP (just 19 percent, compared to an OECD average of 27 percent), the government's spending on fixed-capital projects consumed 5.0 percent of the GDP (compared to an OECD average of 3.5 percent). Such spending rose faster than the national product even during Japan's economic golden age between 1965 and 1990, and by the latter year it amounted to 6.0 percent of GDP (compared to an OECD average of 3.8 percent).[3]

During the 1990s, however, the government-financed bulldozing of dirt and pouring of concrete assumed unprecedented dimensions. By 1995, public-works spending was eating up nearly 8 percent of Japan's GDP, and five years later it remained stuck at that elevated level (relative to an OECD average of 3.4 percent in 2000).[4]

Obviously, all this ostensible pump priming has failed to restore prosperity in Nippon, as anyone with a genuine understanding of economics would have foreseen it would fail. Between 1989 and 1999, Japan's real GDP grew at an average annual rate of only 1.7 percent; between 1995 and 1999 it grew at a rate of just 1.2 percent—less than one-third of the 4 percent growth rate during the 1980s. Among the twenty-nine member states of the OECD, only the Czech Republic did worse during the late 1990s.[5] Between 1980 and 1990, Japan's real GDP per capita, relative to that of the United States, had increased from 69 percent to 81 percent, but by 1999 it had fallen back to 72 percent.[6]

Because a growing proportion of Japan's GDP has consisted of government-financed infrastructure spending, the economy has actually been performing even more poorly than indicated by the commonly cited figures, which count government spending on a yen-for-yen basis with private spending by consumers and investors, who use their own funds to make the purchases and therefore must weigh the personal trade-offs entailed by their choices. Between fiscal year 1990 and fiscal year 2000 (for which only preliminary data are available as I write), Japan's real GDP increased by 13 percent.[7] Because the government share of GDP increased from 31.3 percent to 38.3 percent during that decade,[8] the implication is that the private part of GDP increased by a grand total of just 1.5 percent—that's not 1.5 percent *per year,* but 1.5 percent *in ten years.* Because the population increased by approximately 2.7 percent during the same decade, *private* GDP per capita actually fell. Thus, not only has Japan's economy grown slowly since 1990, but the part of the economy that has some solid meaning has actually contracted on a per capita basis, notwithstanding the inspired Keynesian antics of the politicos and their kept geniuses at the Ministry of Finance.

Like most so-called failed government policies, however, Japan's public-works binge has achieved its actual purpose, as opposed to its declared purpose. In Japan, even more so than in the United States, public-works spending serves as an important means by which politicians reward their friends and supporters. For the oligarchs of the long-entrenched Liberal Democratic Party, building ever more roads, bridges, airports, tunnels, ports, and so forth sustains a sprawling complex of government bureaucrats and hundreds of thousands of small construction companies and materials suppliers beholden to their political benefactors.[9]

In Japan, nearly 10 percent of the labor force finds employment in the construction sector,[10] whereas in the United States the corresponding ratio is less than 5 percent.[11] Much of the government-financed construction work in Japan is, in effect, little more than make-work projects whose costs far exceed their true market value. Their political value, however, is obviously considerable.

Notes

1. Herman Kahn and Thomas Pepper, *The Japanese Challenge* (New York: Crowell, 1979); Ezra Vogel, *Japan as Number One* (Cambridge, Mass.: Harvard University Press, 1979); Karel van Wolferen, *The Enigma of Japanese Power* (London: Macmillan, 1990); and William T. Ziemba and Sandra L. Schwartz, *Power Japan* (Chicago: Probus, 1992).

2. T. Bayoumi, C. Towe, J. Morsink, and I. Oishi, *Japan: Selected Issues,* International Monetary Fund (IMF) Staff Country Report no. 98/113 (Washington, D.C.: IMF, October 1998), pp. 10, 41, 51; J. Morsink, R. Ramaswamy, M. Muhleisen, and I. Oishi, *Japan: Economic and Policy Developments,* IMF Staff Country Report no. 99/114 (Washington, D.C.: IMF, October 1999), pp. 4–9, 14, 24–26.

3. For convenient compilations of the pertinent data, see Paul Atkinson and Paul van den Noord, *Managing Public Expenditure: Some Emerging Policy Issues and a Framework for Analysis,* Organization for Economic Cooperation and Development (OECD), Economics Department Working Paper no. 285 (Paris: OECD, February 8, 2001), pp. 7 and 49; on the Web at http://www.oecd.org/pdf/M00002000/M00002529.pdf.

4. Atkinson and van den Noord, "Managing Public Expenditure," p. 49.

5. OECD, *OECD in Figures: Statistics on the Member Countries,* 2000 ed. (Paris: OECD, 2000), pp. 14, 78.

6. Ratios for 1980 and 1990 calculated from data in U.S. Bureau of the Census, *Statistical Abstract of the United States 1997* (Washington, D.C.: U.S. Government Printing Office, 1997), p. 839; data for 1999 from OECD, *OECD in Figures,* p. 79.

7. Cabinet Office, Government of Japan, national-accounts data at http://www.stat.go.jp/english/data/figures/zuhyou/1624.xls.

8. Atkinson and van den Noord, "Managing Public Expenditure," p. 7.

9. Sheryl WuDunn, "Japanese Liberal Democratic Party Backs $124-Billion Economic Plan," *New York Times,* March 27, 1998, at http://www-personal.umd.umich.edu/~mtwomey/newspapers/0326japa.html; Brian Bremner, "Big Spenders and the Great Seaweed Slaughter," *BusinessWeek Online,* February 6, 2001, at http://www.businessweek.com/bwdaily/dnflash/feb2001/nf2001026_998.htm; Michael Millett, "Deconstructing Japan's Obsession with Public Spending," November 17, 2001, at http://www.theage.com/au/cgi-bin/common.

10. Morsink and others, "Japan: Economic and Policy Developments," p. 25.

11. Calculated from data in U.S. Bureau of the Census, *Statistical Abstract 1997,* p. 424.

PART IV

The Political Economy
of Crisis

24

War and Leviathan in Twentieth-Century America

Conscription as the Keystone

Times of danger, when Power takes action for the general safety, are worth much to it in accretions to its armoury; and these, when the crisis has passed, it keeps. . . . It is impossible to exaggerate the part played by war in the distension of Power.

—Bertrand de Jouvenel, *On Power: The Natural History of Its Growth*

The association of war and the growth of government in the modern era is a commonplace. Randolph Bourne's observation that "war is the health of the state" has become a cliché. Having extensively surveyed the fatal linkage, Bruce Porter concludes that "a government at war is a juggernaut of centralization determined to crush any internal opposition that impedes the mobilization of militarily vital resources. This centralizing tendency of war has made the rise of the state throughout much of history a disaster for human liberty and rights."[1] Porter maintains that much of the history of the West during the past six centuries can be reduced to a simple formula: war made the state, and the state made war. In the process, countless individuals suffered the destruction of their liberties, property, and lives.

Still, as a cause of the development of big government in the United States, war seldom receives its due. Scholars and laymen alike usually trace the origins of our own Leviathan to the New Deal. In doing so, they attribute too much influence to the New Dealers as such. Franklin D. Roosevelt and friends never would—or could—have done what they did in the 1930s without the state-building precedents of World War I, which in many important cases they reinstituted with little more than a change of name. If World War I gets insufficient notice from students of the growth of government, however, World War II gets even less. Too often it is viewed as a discrete event, an episode when government took on awesome dimensions but then relinquished the new powers after the victory had been won, more or less returning the relations between government and civil society to the prewar status quo. Nothing of the sort happened or could have happened. A politicoeconomic undertaking of such enormous magnitude does not just come and go, leaving no trace. In fact, the Big One left a multitude of important enduring legacies.

The government's organization of the economy for war, more than anything else, determined how the central government grew in the United States in the twentieth century, and conscription, more than anything else, determined how the government organized the economy for war. Thus, in a multitude of ways the military draft shaped not only the contours of the nation at war but the course of its politicoeconomic development throughout the past eighty years.

World War I

Notwithstanding the important developments during Woodrow Wilson's first term as president, the federal government on the eve of World War I remained quite limited in size and scope. In 1914, federal outlays totaled less than 2 percent of the gross national product (GNP). The top rate of the recently enacted federal individual income tax was 7 percent on income over $500,000 (equivalent to about ten times that amount in present-day dollars), and 99 percent of the population owed no income tax. The 402,000 federal civilian employees, most of whom worked for the Post Office, made up about 1 percent of the civilian labor force. Nor did the armed forces amount to much, numbering fewer than 166,000 active duty personnel. The federal government did not regulate securities markets, labor-management relations, or agricultural production. It set no minimum wage rate, collected no social security tax, provided no make-work jobs or make-believe job training for the unemployed. Although the feds did meddle in a few areas of economic life, prescribing railroad rates and prosecuting a handful of unlucky firms under the antitrust laws, the central government was for the most part only a small nuisance. It was not very expensive and did not exert an important direct effect on most citizens' daily lives. On the positive side, the government maintained the gold standard and suppressed labor disturbances that threatened to obstruct interstate commerce. The U.S. Supreme Court gave fairly strong protection to private-property rights and freedom of contract, and it generally insisted that state governments not deprive citizens of property rights without substantive due process. After World War I, however, the American people would never again enjoy a government so closely approximating the Jeffersonian ideal.

With U.S. entry into the Great War, the federal government expanded enormously in size, scope, and power. It virtually nationalized the ocean shipping industry and actually did nationalize the railroad, telephone, domestic telegraph, and international telegraphic cable industries. It became deeply engaged in manipulating labor-management relations, securities sales, agricultural production and marketing, the distribution of coal and petroleum, international commerce, and the markets for raw materials and manufactured products. Its

Liberty Bond drives dominated the financial capital markets. It turned the newly created Federal Reserve System into a powerful engine of monetary inflation to help satisfy the government's voracious appetite for money and credit. In view of the more than five thousand mobilization agencies of various sorts—boards, committees, corporations, and administrations—contemporaries who described the government's creation as "war socialism" were well justified.[2]

During 1917 and 1918, the government built up the armed forces to a strength of 4 million officers and men, drawn from a prewar labor force of 40 million persons. Of those added to the armed forces after the U.S. declaration of war, more than 2.8 million, or 72 percent, were drafted.[3] By employing the draft, the government got more men into the army and got them there more quickly than it could have by recruiting volunteers. Moreover, it got the men's services at far less expense to the Treasury. As the army leadership had recommended and President Wilson had accepted even before the declaration of war, the U.S. government obtained its servicemen by following the Prussian model.[4]

Men alone, however, did not make an army. They required barracks and training facilities, transportation, food, clothing, and health care. They had to be equipped with modern arms and great stocks of ammunition. In short, to be an effective fighting force, a large soldiery required immense amounts of complementary resources. As the buildup began, the requisite resources remained in the possession of private citizens. Although manpower could be obtained by conscription, public opinion would not tolerate the outright confiscation of all the property required to turn the men into a well-equipped fighting force. Still, ordinary market mechanisms threatened to operate too slowly and at too great an expense to facilitate the government's plans. The Wilson administration therefore resorted to the vast array of interventions mentioned earlier. All were devices to hasten the delivery of the requisite resources and to diminish the fiscal burden of equipping the huge conscript army for effective service in France. Notwithstanding these contrivances to keep the Treasury's expenses down, enormously increased taxes still had to be levied—federal revenues increased by nearly 400 percent between fiscal 1917 and fiscal 1919—and even greater amounts had to be borrowed. The national debt swelled from $1.2 billion in 1916 to $25.5 billion in 1919.

To ensure that the conscription-based mobilization could proceed without obstruction, critics had to be silenced. The Espionage Act of June 15, 1917, penalized those convicted of willfully obstructing the enlistment services with fines as large as $10,000 and imprisonment as long as twenty years. An amendment, the notorious Sedition Act of May 16, 1918, went much further, imposing the same harsh criminal penalties on all forms of expression in any way critical of the government, its symbols, or its mobilization of resources for the war. These suppressions of free speech, subsequently upheld by the Supreme Court, established dangerous precedents that derogated from the rights previously enjoyed by citizens under the protection of the First Amendment. The government further subverted the Bill of Rights by censoring all printed materials; peremptorily deporting hundreds of aliens without due process of law; and conducting—and encouraging state and local governments as well as vigilante groups to conduct—warrantless searches and seizures, blanket arrests of suspected draft evaders, and other outrages too numerous to catalog here. In California, the police arrested Upton Sinclair for reading the Bill of Rights at a rally. In New Jersey, the police arrested Roger Baldwin for publicly reading the Constitution.[5] The government also employed a massive propaganda machine to whip up what can only be described as public hysteria. The result was countless incidents of intimidation, physical abuse, and even lynching of persons suspected of disloyalty or insufficient enthusiasm for the war. People of German ancestry suffered disproportionately.[6]

The connection of the draft with these official subversions of the Constitution was hardly coincidental; it was direct, intentional, and publicly acknowledged. Consider the statement of a contemporary legal authority, Professor John Henry Wigmore: "Where a nation has definitely committed itself to a foreign war, all principles of normal internal order may be suspended. As property may be taken and corporal service may be conscripted, so liberty of speech may be limited or suppressed, so far as deemed needful for the successful conduct of the war.... [A]ll rights of the individual, and all internal civic interests, become subordinated to the national right in the struggle for national life."[7] The formula, applied again and again, was quite simple: if it is acceptable to draft men, then it is acceptable to do X, where X is any government violation of any individual rights whatsoever. Once the draft had been adopted, then, as Justice Louis Brandeis put it, "all bets are off."[8]

When the war ended, the government abandoned most—but not all—of its wartime control measures. The draft itself ended when the armistice took effect on November 11, 1918. By the end of 1920, the bulk of the economic regulatory apparatus had been scrapped, including the Food Administration, the Fuel Administration, the Railroad Administration, the War Industries Board, and the War Labor Board. Some emergency powers migrated into regular government departments such as State, Labor, and Treasury and continued in force. The Espionage Act and the Trading with the Enemy Act remained on the statute books. Congressional enactments in 1920 preserved much of the federal government's wartime involvement in the railroad and the ocean shipping industries. The War Finance Corporation shifted missions, subsidizing exporters and farmers until the mid-1920s. Wartime prohibition of alcoholic beverages, a purported conservation measure, transmogrified into the ill-fated Eighteenth Amendment.

Most important, the dominant contemporary interpretation of the war mobilization, including the belief that federal economic controls had been instrumental in achieving the victory, persisted, especially among the elites who had played leading roles in the wartime economic management. Economic czar Bernard Baruch did much to foster the postwar dissemination of this interpretation by historians, journalists, and other shapers of public opinion.[9] Many interest groups, however, such as the farmers, needed no prompting to arrive at a Baruchian conclusion. "By the time the Food Administration dropped its wartime controls, it had weakened farmer resistance to governmental direction of their affairs. Having observed how the government could shape wartime food prices, farmers would expect it also to act in peacetime to maintain the prosperity of America's farms."[10] Big businessmen in many industries took a similar lesson away from the war.[11]

The New Deal

In the depths of the Great Depression, the federal government employed the wartime measures as models for dealing with what Franklin Roosevelt called "a crisis in our national life comparable to war."[12] Hence, the War Finance Corporation came back to life as the Reconstruction Finance Corporation, the War Industries Board as the National Recovery Administration, the Food Administration as the Agricultural Adjustment Administration, the Capital Issues Committee as the Securities and Exchange Commission, the Fuel Administration as the Connolly Act apparatus for cartelizing the oil industry and the Guffey Act apparatus for cartelizing the bituminous coal industry. The military mobilization of young men came back as the quasi-military Civilian Conservation Corps. The Muscle Shoals hydroelectric munitions facility became the germ of the Tennessee Valley Authority. The wartime U.S. Housing Corporation reappeared first as part of the Public Works Administration in 1933 and then as the U.S. Housing Authority in 1937. The federal social security program of the New Deal harked back to the wartime servicemen's life insurance and the payments made to the soldiers' dependents. The temporary wartime abandonment of the gold standard became a permanent abandonment in 1933–34, when the government nationalized the monetary gold stock and abrogated all contractual obligations, both public and private, to pay gold. Along with the revived agencies came many of the wartime planners, including Baruch, Felix Frankfurter, George Peek, Hugh Johnson, John Hancock, Leon Henderson, and John Dickinson, not to mention FDR himself, as advisers or administrators. The wartime precedents were obviously crucial in guiding the New Dealers and helping them to justify and gain acceptance of their policies.[13]

World War II

When World War II began in Europe in 1939, the size, scope, and power of the central government of the United States were much greater than they had been

twenty-five years earlier, owing mainly to World War I and its peacetime progeny the New Deal. Federal outlays now equaled 10 percent of GNP. Of a labor
force of 56 million, the federal government employed about 1.3 million persons (2.2 percent) in regular civilian and military jobs, plus another 3.3 million
(5.9 percent) in emergency work-relief programs. The national debt held outside the government had grown to nearly $40 billion. Most important, the
scope of federal regulation had increased immensely to embrace agricultural
production and marketing; labor-management relations, wages, hours, and
working conditions; securities markets and investment institutions; petroleum
and coal marketing; trucking; radio broadcasting; airline operation; provision
for income during retirement or unemployment; and a great deal more.[14]
Notwithstanding these prodigious developments, during the next six years the
federal government would achieve vastly greater dimensions, in many respects
its greatest size, scope, and power ever.[15]

Once again, conscription served as a springboard for the growth of the state.
This time the political pressure to adopt the draft mounted long before the
United States entered the war. In mid-1940, the armed forces had only 458,000
officers and men on active duty. After the great German advances and the defeat
of France in the spring of 1940, proponents of a new draft—including Grenville
Clark, Henry Stimson, and others who had led the charge for conscription before and during World War I—gained greater public support. Opponents fought
hard, however, and a furious national debate raged throughout the summer. Finally, on September 16, Congress enacted the Selective Training and Service Act,
which authorized the conscription of 900,000 men. The law was extended and
amended in the fall of 1941 and again several times after the U.S. declaration
of war. The draftees eventually numbered more than 10 million men, or about
63 percent of all those who served in the armed forces at some time during the
war.[16] Obviously, many of those who volunteered for military service did so to
escape the draft and the consequent likelihood of assignment to the infantry.

As before, a huge conscript-based armed force required enormous amounts
of complementary resources to make possible its housing, subsistence, clothing,
medical care, training, and transportation, not to mention the special equipment, arms, ammunition, and expensive weapons platforms that now included
tanks, fighter and bomber aircraft, and naval aircraft carriers. For the Treasury,
World War II was ten times more expensive than World War I. Many new taxes
were thus levied. Income taxes were raised repeatedly, until the tax rates for individual income extended from a low of 23 percent to a high of 94 percent. The
income tax, previously a "class tax," became a "mass tax," as the number of returns grew from 15 million in 1940 to 50 million in 1945.[17] Even though annual federal revenues soared from $7 billion in 1940 to $50 billion in 1945,
most war expenses still had to be financed by borrowing. The national debt
held by the public went up by $200 billion, or more than fivefold. The Federal

Reserve System itself bought some $20 billion of government debt, thereby acting as a de facto printing press for the Treasury. Between 1940 and 1948, the money stock (M1 measure) increased by 183 percent, and the dollar lost nearly half its purchasing power.

Had the government relied exclusively on fiscal and market mechanisms to marshal the desired resources, the expense of the war would have been far greater, probably much greater than the government could have financed. Accordingly, the authorities resorted to a vast system of controls and market interventions to gain possession of resources without having to bid them away from competing demanders in free markets. Although relatively few resources were simply confiscated or requisitioned, the effect was similar. By fixing prices; directly allocating physical and human resources; establishing official priorities, prohibitions, and set-asides; then rationing the civilian consumer goods in short supply, the war planners steered raw materials, intermediate goods, and finished products into the uses to which they attached greatest importance. Markets no longer functioned freely; in many areas they did not function at all. The economic system was transformed from one in which the market allocated resources, with some peripheral government distortions, to one in which the central government allocated resources, with market (including black-market) influences operating only at the fringes of the command economy.[18]

As before, the draft played a key role in justifying the government's imposition of a command economy. The same formula applied: if the draft is acceptable, then X is acceptable, X being any form of government coercion whatsoever. As the eminent economist Wesley Mitchell put it in 1943, "After common consent has been given to that act [conscription], civilians are morally bound to accept the lesser sacrifices war imposes on them."[19] Even the Supreme Court adopted the argument, as Justice Hugo Black evinced in a 1942 decision: "Congress can draft men for battle service. Its power to draft business organizations to support the fighting men who risk their lives can be no less."[20]

World War II witnessed massive violations of human rights in the United States, apart from the involuntary servitude of the military draft. Most egregiously, about 112,000 blameless persons of Japanese ancestry, most of them U.S. citizens, were uprooted from their homes and confined in concentration camps without due process of law. Those who were subsequently released as civilians during the war remained under parolelike surveillance. The government also imprisoned nearly 6,000 conscientious objectors—three-fourths of them Jehovah's Witnesses—who would not comply with the service requirements of the draft laws.[21] Scores of newspapers were denied the privilege of the mails under the authority of the Espionage Act, still in effect from World War I. Some newspapers were banned altogether.[22] The Office of Censorship restricted the content of press reports and radio broadcasts and censored personal mail entering or leaving the country. The Office of War Information put the government's spin on whatever it deigned to tell the public, and the military authorities censored news from the battlefields, sometimes for merely political reasons. The government seized more than sixty industrial facilities and even entire industries (e.g., railroads, bituminous coal mines, meat packing), most of them in order to impose employment conditions favorable to labor unions engaged in disputes with the management.[23] One indication of the enlarged federal capacity for repression was the increase in the number of Federal Bureau of Investigation special agents from 785 in 1939 to 4,370 in 1945.[24]

At the end of the war, most of the economic control agencies shut down—most, but not all. Some powers persisted—either lodged at the local level, such as New York City's rent controls, or shifted from emergency agencies to regular departments, as when international-trade controls moved from the Foreign Economic Administration to the State Department. The military-industrial complex, which had grown to gargantuan size during the war, shrank, but it survived as top military officers and big contractors, especially the aircraft companies, lobbied hard for new procurements to shore up their bureaucratic clout or financial condition.[25] Federal tax revenues remained very high by prewar standards. In the late 1940s, the Internal Revenue Service's annual take averaged four times greater in constant dollars than in the late 1930s. In 1949, federal outlays amounted to 15 percent of GNP, up from 10 percent in 1939. The national debt stood at what would have been an unthinkable figure before the war, $214 billion—in constant dollars, this was roughly one hundred times the national debt in 1916.

The prevailing interpretation of the wartime experience gave unprecedented ideological support to those who desired a big federal government actively engaged in a wide range of domestic and international tasks. After all, the wartime central planners had just carried out successfully a complex undertaking of enormous dimensions. They had waged a global war, marshaling, organizing, and allocating the requisite resources to defeat two mighty adversaries while leaving American civilian consumers relatively well off, at least by comparison with the suffering populations of the Soviet Union, Japan, Germany, and Great Britain. Surely this great accomplishment testified to the planners' knowledge, abilities, and devotion to the public interest. Surely a central government capable of winning the greatest war in human history could carry out such relatively mundane tasks as stabilizing the business cycle, guaranteeing all citizens a good job and a high standard of living, and regulating the industrial life of the nation to achieve greater fairness than that produced by the unfettered market. Surely. In this spirit, Congress enacted the Employment Act in 1946, pledging the federal government to play a permanent role as macroeconomic savior of the U.S. economy.[26] Thanks to the GI Bill, the Veterans Administration became the overseer of what amounted to a substantial welfare state within a welfare state.

The Cold War

Soon after the Big One ended, the Cold One began. In 1948, the government reimposed the military draft. Then, over the next twenty-five years, conscription was repeatedly extended until the Nixon administration, in the face of massive protests, finally allowed it to expire in 1973. Draftees supplied the principal cannon fodder for the U.S. adventures in Korea and Vietnam, as well as a large part of the standing forces positioned throughout the world to challenge the Soviets and their surrogates. After 1950, the military-industrial-congressional complex achieved renewed vigor, sapping 7.7 percent of GNP on average during the next four decades—cumulatively more than $10 trillion dollars of 1994 purchasing power.[27] During the Cold War, the government's operatives committed crimes against the American people too numerous to catalog here, ranging from surveillance of millions of innocuous citizens and mass arrests of political protesters to harassment and even murder of persons considered especially threatening.[28] These actions warrant close examination by students of the relation between war (or the threat of war) and the growth of the state, but for present purposes we need not dwell on them. So far as the relation between war and the development of America's Leviathan is concerned, the deed had largely been done even before the outbreak of the Korean War.

Legacies of the Age of National Emergencies

Within three decades, from the outbreak of World War I in Europe to the end of World War II, the American people endured three great national emergencies, during each of which the federal government imposed unprecedented taxation and economic controls on the population and accumulated enormous debts. By the late 1940s, these government actions no longer startled the citizenry; indeed, many Americans, including highly regarded intellectuals and top policymakers, had come to regard them as desirable. Even businessmen, many of whom had continued to resist the encroachments of the New Deal bureaucrats throughout the 1930s, now looked on the American Leviathan with an approving eye. The wartime experience, said Calvin Hoover, had "conditioned them to accept a degree of governmental intervention and control after the war which they had deeply resented prior to it."[29] As Herbert Stein has recognized, American businessmen tended to "regard the regulations they are used to as being freedom."[30] Rather than resisting the government's impositions or working to overthrow them, they looked for ways to adapt to them, positioning themselves so that the government policies would provide a tax advantage, channel a subsidy their way, or hobble their competitors.[31] If the business class, with its immense financial resources and its considerable political clout, would not strive seriously to overthrow the Leviathan that had come into being by the late 1940s, there was scant chance that anyone else would mount a substantial attack.

In any event, reactionaries could hardly expect to succeed, because the post–World War II ideological climate showered an active federal government with public trust and approbation. As Ben Page and Robert Shapiro document in their massive survey of public opinion, World War II stands as "the most pervasive single influence on public opinion" since the mid-1930s. Among other things, it "transformed American public opinion concerning virtually all aspects of foreign affairs," opening the way for the imperial presidency and the use of U.S. forces as world police.[32] Opponents of global interventionism were smeared as "isolationists" and "appeasers" and thereby completely discredited. In 1953, Senator Robert Taft died, and his followers, already a dwindling remnant, soon abandoned their former beliefs and political commitments.[33] On the domestic front, the people's devotion to the welfare state solidified. No amount of contradictory evidence seemed to dent the prevailing faith in the government's ability to create personal and social security and to remedy the full range of human problems and pathologies.[34]

Nor did the Constitution serve any longer as a bulwark of protection for individual rights. After World War II, as Edward Corwin observed almost immediately, for the first time in U.S. history after a war the country did not revert to a "peacetime Constitution." Instead, the Supreme Court's wartime surrender to the president combined with the carte blanche it had granted to federal economic regulation in the late 1930s to enhance all of the following:

(1) the attribution to Congress of a legislative power of indefinite scope; (2) the attribution to the President of the power and duty to stimulate constantly the positive exercise of this indefinite power for enlarged social objectives; (3) the right of Congress to delegate its powers *ad labium* to the President for the achievement of such enlarged social objectives ... ; (4) the attribution to the President of a broad prerogative in the meeting of "emergencies" defined by himself and in the creation of executive agencies to assist him; (5) a progressively expanding replacement of the judicial process by the administrative process in the enforcement of the law—sometimes even of constitutional law.[35]

Under these conditions, the only impediment to the relentless growth of the central government consisted of partisan and interest-group opposition to particular proposals. Time would reveal that such obstructionism, ever shifting with the winds of partisan politics and immediate interest-group objectives, could do no more than slow the onrushing Leviathan.

"It is not possible," said William Graham Sumner, "to experiment with a society and just drop the experiment whenever we choose. The experiment enters into the life of the society and never can be got out again."[36] World War I, the New Deal, and World War II gave rise to the greatest experiments in collectivization America had ever experienced. These experiments radically transformed the political economy both institutionally and ideologically. The political economy of 1948 bore scarcely any resemblance to that of 1912, and the changes gave every indication of being irreversible.

In the process by which this radical transformation occurred, the military draft played a central part. Conscription made possible the creation of a huge armed force in 1917–18, which in turn required massive amounts of complementary resources. To get these resources, the government had to raise taxes enormously, to go deeply into debt, and to impose a great variety of controls on the market economy; that is, it had to override traditional limitations on government action and to disallow long-standing economic liberties. In light of the apparent success of the policies employed during World War I, the temptation to impose similar policies during the Great Depression proved irresistible. In large part, the New Deal consisted of quasi-war policies to deal with a pseudowar emergency. Participation in World War II, with its global reach and even more voracious demand for resources, increased every aspect of the process by an order of magnitude: the draft permitted the creation of a huge army, which gave rise to vast military resource requirements that could be met expeditiously only by imposition of a command-and-control system throughout the economy.

By the late 1940s, the three great experiments had entered institutionally and ideologically into the life of the society. With all the fundamental barriers to the growth of government having been battered down during war and pseudowar emergencies, nothing substantial remained to impede the relentless growth of government.[37]

Notes

1. Bruce D. Porter, *War and the Rise of the State: The Military Foundations of Modern Politics* (New York: Free Press, 1994), p. xv.

2. For details, see Robert Higgs, *Crisis and Leviathan: Critical Episodes in the Growth of American Government* (New York: Oxford University Press, 1987), pp. 123–58 and sources cited there; James L. Abrahamson, *The American Home Front* (Washington, D.C.: National Defense University Press, 1983), pp. 101–12.

3. John Whiteclay Chambers III, *To Raise an Army: The Draft Comes to Modern America* (New York: Free Press, 1987), p. 338, n. 68.

4. Ibid., pp. 125–51. One is reminded of Bertrand de Jouvenel's observation that "war is like a sheep-dog harrying the laggard Powers to catch up their smarter fellows in the totalitarian race" (*On Power: The Natural History of Its Growth,* translated by J. F. Huntington [Indianapolis, Ind.: Liberty Fund, 1993; original French edition 1945], p. 157).

5. Michael Linfield, *Freedom under Fire: U.S. Civil Liberties in Times of War* (Boston: South End Press, 1990), p. 65.

6. Ronald Schaffer, *America in the Great War: The Rise of the War Welfare State* (New York: Oxford University Press, 1991), pp. 3–30.

7. Quoted in ibid., pp. 49–50.

8. Quoted in ibid., p. 52.

9. On the various legacies, see Higgs, *Crisis and Leviathan*, pp. 150–56 and sources cited there. On Baruch's public-relations activities, see Jordan A. Schwarz, *The Speculator: Bernard M. Baruch in Washington, 1917–1965* (Chapel Hill, N.C.: University of North Carolina Press, 1981), pp. 193–206, 212.

10. Abrahamson, *The American Home Front*, p. 103.

11. Murray N. Rothbard, "War Collectivism in World War I," in *A New History of Leviathan: Essays on the Rise of the American Corporate State*, edited by Ronald Radosh and Murray N. Rothbard (New York: Dutton, 1972), pp. 66–110.

12. Quoted by Porter, *War and the Rise of the State*, p. 277.

13. William E. Leuchtenburg, "The New Deal and the Analogue of War," in *Change and Continuity in Twentieth-Century America*, edited by John Braeman, Robert H. Bremner, and Everett Walters (Columbus: Ohio State University Press, 1964), pp. 81–143.

14. Higgs, *Crisis and Leviathan*, pp. 159–95 and sources cited there.

15. Abrahamson, *The American Home Front*, pp. 131, 142.

16. Chambers, *To Raise an Army*, pp. 254–55; Higgs, *Crisis and Leviathan*, pp. 200–202.

17. Carolyn C. Jones, "Class Tax to Mass Tax: The Role of Propaganda in the Expansion of the Income Tax During World War II," *Buffalo Law Review* 37 (fall 1988–89): 685–737.

18. Higgs, *Crisis and Leviathan*, pp. 196–236 and sources cited there.

19. Quoted in ibid., p. 202.

20. *United States of America v. Bethlehem Steel Corporation*, 315 U.S. 289 (1942) at 305, quoted in Higgs, *Crisis and Leviathan*, p. 221. For similar argument by the Court in other cases, see ibid., pp. 222–25.

21. Abrahamson, *The American Home Front*, p. 159.

22. Linfield, *Freedom under Fire*, p. 73.

23. Ibid., pp. 102–3.

24. Porter, *War and the Rise of the State*, p. 284.

25. Gregory Hooks, *Forging the Military-Industrial Complex: World War II's Battle of the Potomac* (Urbana: University of Illinois Press, 1991), pp. 225–66.

26. In Abrahamson's words, "World War II . . . validated the Keynesian economic theories that liberal governments would subsequently use to maintain full employment and justify welfare programs" (*The American Home Front*, p. 155). For an argument that this "validation" was invalid, see Robert Higgs, "Wartime Prosperity? A Reassessment of the U.S. Economy in the 1940s," *Journal of Economic History* 52 (March 1992): 41–60.

27. Robert Higgs, ed., *Arms, Politics, and the Economy: Historical and Contemporary Perspectives* (New York: Holmes and Meier, for The Independent Institute, 1990), and Robert Higgs, "The Cold War Economy: Opportunity Costs, Ideology, and the Politics of Crisis," *Explorations in Economic History* 31 (July 1994): 283–312 (see pp. 291–92 for the cumulative cost figures).

28. Linfield, *Freedom under Fire,* pp. 113–67.

29. Calvin B. Hoover, *The Economy, Liberty, and the State* (New York: Twentieth Century Fund, 1959), p. 212.

30. Herbert Stein, *Presidential Economics: The Making of Economic Policy from Roosevelt to Reagan and Beyond* (New York: Simon and Schuster, 1984), p. 84.

31. Higgs, *Crisis and Leviathan,* pp. 243–44, and the *Wall Street Journal,* any day of any week of any year since World War II.

32. Benjamin I. Page and Robert Y. Shapiro, *The Rational Public: Fifty Years of Trends in Americans' Policy Preferences* (Chicago: University of Chicago Press, 1992), p. 332.

33. Justin Raimondo, *Reclaiming the American Right: The Lost Legacy of the Conservative Movement* (Burlingame, Calif.: Center for Libertarian Studies, 1993), pp. 149–56.

34. For extensively documented surveys of modern public opinion on a wide range of policy issues, see Herbert McClosky and John Zaller, *The American Ethos: Public Attitudes Toward Capitalism and Democracy* (Cambridge, Mass.: Harvard University Press, 1984), and Linda L. M. Bennett and Stephen Earl Bennett, *Living with Leviathan: Americans Coming to Terms with Big Government* (Lawrence: University of Kansas Press, 1990).

35. Edward Corwin, *Total War and the Constitution* (New York: Knopf, 1947), p. 179.

36. William Graham Sumner, *Essays of William Graham Sumner,* edited by Albert G. Keller and Maurice R. Davie (New Haven, Conn.: Yale University Press, 1934), vol. 2, p. 473.

37. Higgs, *Crisis and Leviathan,* pp. 20–34, 237–57 and sources cited there.

25

Crisis and Quasi-corporatist Policymaking
The U.S. Case in Historical Perspective

The People versus the Interests, the general welfare versus factional privileges—out of that conflict comes much of the sound and fury of American politics, or of any politics organized in the institutions of representative democracy. The problem arises because what is in the interest of some people may not be in, or may even be adverse to, the interest of others; yet, in many cases, government can establish only a single condition, which all parties must live with, for better or worse.

Because the United States began as a confederation of sovereign states, its Constitution of 1787 gave special status to the representation of sectional interests, distinguishing citizens according to the state government that had jurisdiction over them. The Constitution took no explicit account of the interests associated with various functional economic groups—farmers, sailors, merchants, and so forth. Our system of federalist checks and balances was supposed to solve the problem of rivalrous functional interests by recognizing the police powers of the separate state governments and, within the national government, by establishing three separate but interdependent branches. This plan was intended to frustrate any schemes promoted by economic factions, at least at the national level. For a century and a half, the system worked more or less as intended, but it was never completely successful.

National Economic Interests?

Although the Constitution made no provision for formal economic representation, the politicians and the organized private groups proceeded to establish de facto what the Framers of the Constitution had hoped to prevent. In the late nineteenth century, as the national economy became more tightly integrated, national economic interest groups—manufacturers, railroad companies, investment bankers, farm organizations, trade associations, and labor unions—reallocated their lobbying efforts from the states to the national government. By the early twentieth century, the influence of these broad economic factions on policymaking had become evident. Certain Progressive intellectuals, most notably Herbert Croly, argued that effective government required a reorganized structure that would allow government officials to recognize and deal directly with powerful private actors in the modern, highly organized economy. Proposals proliferated for some kind of formal cooperation or "partnership" of business, labor, and government.

Since then, such proposals have never ceased. In 1988, the *New York Times* surveyed the leaders of several major economic organizations to ascertain what economic policies they thought the next president should adopt.[1] Lynn Williams, president of the steelworkers union, expressed a longstanding proposal when he responded that the next president "should take the lead in setting up tripartite institutions for each economic sector—like steel—to bring together government, industry and labor."

In western Europe, where similar economic development has occurred, the political response has often taken the form of various "corporatist" arrangements. These arrangements provide—sometimes by constitutional authority, sometimes by law, sometimes by informal deals—for the extraparliamentary representation of functional economic interests in policymaking. Corporatism faces the problem of factions directly. In effect, it resolves the problem of the People versus the Interests by forthrightly declaring that the Interests, when properly organized and channeled, *are* the People.

Americans have never been willing to make such a declaration—to do so would too blatantly belie the nation's political mythology; but without ever facing up to what has actually been done, they have come closer to the European practice than they care to admit. If Europeans have developed first corporatism, and then neocorporatism, Americans have developed what might be called quasi-corporatism. By examining just how corporatist our political economy has been, we may gain new insights into the development and present condition of our politicoeconomic institutions.

What Is Corporatism?

Full-fledged corporatism, as a system for organizing the formulation and implementation of economic policies, requires the replacement of political representation according to area of residence with political representation according to position in the socioeconomic division of labor. The citizen of a corporate state has a political identity not as a resident of a particular geographical district but as a member of a certain occupation, profession, or other economic community. He will probably be distinguished according to whether he is an employer or an employee or is self-employed.

One who looks for information about corporatism is frequently referred to fascism.[2] Indeed, the corporatist ideal achieved its fullest historical expression in Italy under Mussolini's regime. There, workers and employers were organized into syndicates based on local trades and occupations. Local syndicates joined in national federations, which were grouped into worker and employer confederations for broad economic sectors such as industry, agriculture, commerce, banking, and insurance. In 1934, the government made peak associations part of the apparatus of state, with one corporation for each of twenty-two economic sectors. The corporations received authority to regulate economic activities, to fix the prices of goods and services, and to mediate labor disputes. In practice, the Italian corporate state operated not as a grand compromise among economic interest groups but as a collection of sectoral economic authorities organized and dominated by the government in the service of the dictatorship's aims. Neither capitalists nor laborers enjoyed autonomy or private rights defensible against the fascist regime.[3] Other fascist regimes in Europe and Latin America operated similarly. In light of this experience, one might judge fascist corporatism to be something of a fraud. The appearance of rationalized popular participation in government failed to mask the dictatorial character of the system.

Not surprisingly, after World War II, *fascism* became a dirty word and full-fledged corporatism a discredited program. Nevertheless, arrangements bearing some similarity to fascism's corporate state developed in the democratic countries of Europe, most notably in Scandinavia, Austria, and the Netherlands, but also to some extent in other countries. No one describes these arrangements as fascist; most commonly they are called *neocorporatist.*

Neocorporatism (also known as liberal, social, or societal corporatism, sometimes as tripartism) shares with fascist corporatism the preference for representation according to membership in functional economic groups rather than according to geographic location. It disavows, at least rhetorically, fascism's totalitarian aspects and fascism's suppression of individual civil and political rights. Neocorporatists support the organization of economic interest groups and the participation of such groups as prime movers in the formulation, negotiation, adoption, and administration of economic policies backed by the full power of the government. Philippe Schmitter, a leading student of liberal corporatism, has defined neocorporatism as

> a system of interest intermediation in which the constituent units are organized into a limited number of singular, compulsory, noncompetitive, hierarchically ordered and functionally differentiated categories, recognized or licensed (if not created) by the state and granted a deliberate representational monopoly within their respective categories in exchange for observing certain controls on their selection of leaders and articulation of demands and supports.[4]

Thus, one might say that, in practical terms, neocorporatists want to be part of the government wherever the powers of government touch the economic interests of their functionally organized groups. They want private-interest groups, such as employers and employees, to deal regularly and directly with one another and with responsible government officials. Together, these tripartite bodies—in certain cases, more than three parties might be involved—would possess sufficient authority to ensure not simply their consultation in policymaking but also their participation in policy adoption and implementation. The ordinary executive and legislative branches of government would stand aside from this process, merely ratifying it or devolving their own authority onto the functional groups directly engaged.[5]

Obstacles to Corporatism in the United States

The United States would seem to offer a relatively inhospitable environment for corporatism because the country's constitutional structure was deliberately constructed to impede political collusion among economic interest groups. James Madison, the leading Framer of the Constitution, worried about the pernicious effects of factions, which he defined in his "Federalist No. 10" as groups of citizens "whether amounting to a majority or minority of the whole, who are united and actuated by some common impulse of passion, or of interest, adverse to the rights of other citizens, or to the permanent and aggregate interests of the community." Madison's *faction* corresponds to what we now call a *special-interest group*. Factions could not be kept from forming; they would inevitably arise among creditors, debtors, landlords, manufacturers, merchants, rentiers, and many other functional groups. Nevertheless, Madison emphatically denied a central premise of corporatist doctrine when he insisted: "It is vain to say that enlightened statesmen will be able to adjust these clashing interests, and render them all subservient to the public good."[6] Instead, wise men would structure the government so that any faction would encounter sturdy barriers to the achievement of its rent-seeking aims.

Two crucial features of the U.S. government help to achieve Madison's objective. First, the governing structure is federal, with powers divided between the national government and the state governments. The powers of the national government, though substantial, are (or at least were in the beginning) limited and enumerated. Originally, thirteen states constituted the Union; now there are fifty. Madison observed that "the influence of factious leaders may kindle a flame within their particular States, but will be unable to spread a general conflagration through the other States."[7] Second, within the national government, powers are separated among the executive, legislative, and judicial branches. Ordinarily, no single branch can do much without the cooperation of the others. To ensure political success, an ambitious interest group must gain the support of all three branches, often a difficult undertaking.

In the nineteenth century, the U.S. economy grew vast and complex, and it spread across an entire continent. Hence, the success of factionalism on the national level became even less likely. Moreover, the dominance of liberal ideology reinforced the resistance to special-interest projects already inherent in the structure of the constitutional arrangements. Of course, the system was not perfect. Some special interests gained political favor in spite of the obstacles.

Moreover, some countervailing developments occurred. The Civil War and the resulting constitutional amendments, especially the Fourteenth Amendment, tended to nationalize policymaking, shifting authority from the states to the national government. Toward the end of the nineteenth century, the ideology of classical liberalism began to lose its hold on opinion leaders and governing elites; during the 1930s, it lost much of its appeal to the middle and working classes as well. After 1937, the Supreme Court interpreted the national government's economic regulatory powers as virtually unlimited, thereby undercutting much of the effect of federalism in relation to economic policy.

Nonetheless, the United States, even in recent times, presents greater obstacles to corporatist modes of interest intermediation than do the relatively small, unitary, parliamentary states of western Europe. There is no attempt at comprehensive central planning; nor is there a persistently maintained wage-price policy. U.S. interest groups, though often powerful, "lack the unity, membership and authority essential for the system to be classified as corporatist."[8] Almost all political scientists seem to agree with Graham Wilson that "there is no corporatism in the United States."[9]

Although I do not disagree completely with this conclusion, I believe that those who have reached it may have overlooked both episodic historical experiences and current practices in certain sectors of the U.S. economy that bear enough similarity to corporatism to be recognized and considered. In the following sections of this chapter, I refer to these features of U.S. policymaking as *quasi-corporatist* and explain what it is about them that warrants such characterization. First, however, I consider briefly the logic of interest-group relations with the government.

General Conditions for the Success of Corporatism

Like Madison, I assume the pervasiveness of latent tendencies for economic interest groups to form and then to use government power in the service of their own ends at the expense of the general public interest. Latent tendencies alone, however, are not enough to prompt the organization of such groups and the effective cooperation of their members. As Mancur Olson argues in detail, latent interest groups must overcome inherent obstacles before they can function successfully enough to gain cartel privileges.[10]

The basic problem confronting a latent interest group is that the privilege it seeks for its members is a collective good (also known in mainstream economic theory as a "public" good)—that is, a condition that applies to all members of the group if it applies to any member of the group. In general, at least some individual members of an interest group—especially if the group has many members—have an incentive to cheat on the agreement whereby the group secures a collective benefit. With sufficient cheating, the arrangement that makes possible the maintenance of the collective benefit collapses. Witness the repeated breakdowns of the agreed-upon supply restrictions in the history of the Organization of Petroleum Exporting Countries (OPEC), which provide a classic example.

This dilemma, which economists call the "free-rider problem," might be overcome in various ways. Olson emphasizes two so-called selective incentives. One is the tying of cooperation to the receipt of privately appropriable goods for the group members. For example, farmers organized to restrict output might form an association offering cheap insurance to members alone. The availability of the cheap insurance might be a sufficient incentive for a farmer to join the association, and the association would then use a portion of the dues received from members to lobby the government for the establishment or the maintenance of a price-support program.

A second selective incentive is coercion, possibly private but usually by the government through legal means. Thus, the collective good of national defense is financed neither by voluntary contributions nor by subscriptions, but by tax revenues paid by citizens on pain of fine or imprisonment. Also, in some circumstances, collective goods may be pursued effectively by groups kept together by informal social sanctions, but this arrangement is less likely to work as the group size increases and the personal interactions of its members become more sporadic and fleeting.

Schmitter has emphasized that for groups to operate successfully within a neocorporatist scheme, they "must get organized, and that requires overcoming the 'free-riding' limitations imposed by voluntary membership and the 'free-booting' temptations inherent in individualistic or particularistic access to political power."[11] Toward this end, they may seek to make member contributions and compliance mandatory. Schmitter surmises that the groups "may eventually come to learn that it is in their interest to have their preferences and behaviors governed by intermediary organizations and subjected to state interests."[12] In any event, the success of a group's project turns critically on compliance with the necessary restrictions on individual members' behavior. If a group fails to enlist the aid of the government in enforcing these restrictions and if incentives for self-enforcement are lacking, then the scheme will fall victim to group members' free-riding actions.

Although I agree with the analyses of Olson, Schmitter, and others regarding the importance of selective incentives—whether they be privately appropriable benefits, government coercion, or informal social incentives—in making possible successful collective action, I have found in my own research in U.S. history another important variable: ideology, especially in its patriotic or nationalistic aspect. On occasion, or in certain sectors for prolonged periods, cooperation with schemes designed to produce collective goods has been elicited by a combination of external conditions and government measures. We are dealing here with what might be called the political economy of national emergency.

Since the early twentieth century, in national emergencies—wars, severe business contractions or rapid inflations, and threatening labor disturbances—the American public has both expected and demanded that the national government do something to allay the perceived threat to national security or economic viability. Governments have responded with policies that entailed widespread costs and heavy burdens, including new demands for citizen compliance with requirements or restrictions. Although such measures have always met some resistance, they have succeeded to the extent that they have received (1) voluntary compliance by the citizens and (2) toleration by the citizens of enlarged government powers employed to gain compliance with the government's emergency measures, even in the face of overt or covert resistance.

When the ideological and political barriers to extended government action are lowered because of prevailing national emergency conditions, interest groups find they can achieve their own ends more readily. First, they can clothe their projects in the rhetoric of public interest, claiming that their own schemes are somehow important in dealing with the emergency. Second, they can more readily secure the delegated or captured powers of the government, which is now more active across the board, to solidify their own projects by suppressing free-riding behavior among their members. The government is usually willing to share its authority with private-interest groups because it needs their expertise and cooperation, or at least their acquiescence, to ensure the success of its own far-reaching emergency program.

At the macrolevel, where societal measures such as comprehensive wage-price controls or central allocations of raw materials are concerned, the success of quasi-corporatist schemes should wane with the passing of the emergency. Of course, to the extent that solid institutions and perhaps even a legal apparatus have been constructed during the emergency, the scheme may persist after the crisis has passed. Insofar as legal sanction is concerned, such arrangements are easier to build during emergencies than they are to tear down afterward.

At the microlevel, in particular sectors, neocorporatist arrangements may survive longer, perhaps indefinitely. Brinton Milward and Ronald Francisco argue that "American policy is forged in a series of policy subsystems, and

... most of these subsystems conform to the major features of corporatism."[13] The conclusion is controversial and subject to a great deal of quarreling based on what exactly is meant by corporatism. Should it be possible, however, to identify a sector where the national emergency never ends, one would expect to find quasi-corporatist arrangements solidly entrenched. I maintain that such conditions have existed in the defense sector of the U.S. political economy. Before that case is considered, however, it might be instructive to survey the episodic experience of quasi-corporatist policymaking in U.S. history.

Precedents for Quasi-corporatist Policymaking

Quasi-corporatist policymaking first appeared in the U.S. labor market in 1916, when the operating brotherhoods of the interstate railroad industry—the four unions whose members manned the nation's trains—threatened to strike. The U.S. economy was extremely dependent on the railroads at that time, and a nationwide strike would have caused devastating harm to the public. The unionists and the national bargaining association of the railroad companies could not agree. However, the very fact that a single bargaining meeting could be convened to deal with wages and working conditions for the entire railroad industry indicated something new in the United States, something suggestive of corporatism.

When the representatives of the employees and the employers reached an impasse, President Woodrow Wilson intervened. He called the bargaining parties to Washington and attempted to persuade them to compromise. When the employers continued to resist, Wilson turned to Congress, securing passage of the Adamson Act, which mandated a 25 percent wage increase. The employers challenged the constitutionality of the act, and the unions continued to threaten a strike. Cabinet officers sought a settlement in compliance with the new law. Finally, on March 19, 1917, the day before the Supreme Court upheld the constitutionality of the Adamson Act, the employers agreed to abide by its terms.

Justice Pitney, who wrote a strong dissenting opinion, complained that the Adamson Act "usurps the right of the owners of the railroads to manage their own properties.... [I]t deprives the carriers of their right to agree with their employees as to the terms of employment." In these respects, it typified American quasi-corporatism in the labor market: whether labor or management comes out ahead, the government ultimately enforces the terms of tripartite "agreements."[14]

The railroad labor troubles did not end. After the United States declared war in 1917, and the nation needed the services of its railroad system more than ever, the unions renewed their threat to strike. Because of government restrictions on company actions and rates charged for services, the employers had little leeway to accommodate the union demands. Finally, at the end of 1917, the government solved the problem by nationalizing the railroads as a war measure. Wages were then raised substantially. The railroad executives continued to manage the properties, subject to the overriding authority of the U.S. Railroad Administration. In 1920, the government returned the companies to their owners, but only after the passage of legislation that placed unprecedented restrictions on the owners' property rights.

During the war, the Wilson administration strongly backed the organization of unions and collective bargaining. More than sympathy for organized labor prompted this support: the government could not risk widespread work stoppages when every effort was needed to convert the economy from civilian production to war production in order to supply both U.S. forces and the Allies. To gain the cooperation of organized labor, the administration placed unionists on many of its wartime control boards, including the Advisory Commission of the Council of National Defense (which included Samuel Gompers, the venerable head of the American Federation of Labor); the Selective Service System, which managed military conscription; the Food Administration; the Railroad Administration; and the War Industries Board. The government's involvement in the wartime labor market eventually led to the creation of the War Labor Administration, headed by the secretary of labor. The secretary appointed a National War Labor Board to provide mediation and conciliation in labor disputes and a War Labor Policies Board to serve as a clearinghouse for all government policies bearing on labor.

While the government was making unprecedented efforts to appease organized labor and to give unionists a voice in policymaking, it was doing even more to accommodate organized business. The key agency was the War Industries Board (WIB), headed during its time of maximum strength, in 1918, by Bernard M. Baruch, a former Wall Street speculator who was destined to become a gray eminence during a long period extending into the 1950s. The WIB divided responsibility for the economy among scores of "commodity sections," each responsible for a specific sector. Each section was managed by experts, almost always businessmen drawn from the sector in question, who decided how industry should manage its assets and produce its outputs to best serve the government's war aims. Historians have generally concluded that these businessmen-turned-bureaucrats used their positions to try to establish and enforce what amounted to cartel arrangements for the various industries.[15]

In addition, the WIB had a price-fixing committee, directly responsible to the president, that set prices for scores of commodities of special interest to the government. Again, businesses often apparently prospered when friendly managers, temporarily invested with the government's wartime powers, could fix their prices and police their markets. Pricing formulas designed to elicit marginal, high-cost supplies sometimes resulted in substantial profits for the established, low-cost producers, although in at least some cases, such as the copper industry, the high wartime taxes and the high wartime rate of inflation took big bites out of what appeared to be extraordinary profits.[16]

Although most of the wartime agencies were closed after the armistice, lessons about the cooperation of government, business, and labor did not go unlearned. Herbert Hoover, who had headed the Food Administration during the war, served from 1921 to 1928 as secretary of commerce. In this capacity, he undertook to organize the U.S. economy on a cooperative basis as no one had ever done before. He sponsored programs to accumulate and disseminate economic information. He worked tirelessly to assist the organization and activities of trade associations. He promoted the standardization of materials, sizes, and designs—a project popular during the war with planners who viewed it as a conservation measure. Hoover believed that laissez-faire was obsolete, or at least that it ought to be made so. He believed that the government should be actively involved in business affairs, not in a dictatorial way but as a mediator, prompter, and helper. Although historians have often characterized the 1920s as a reactionary period in U.S. history, it was in important respects a bridge between the wartime collectivist measures of 1916–18 and the New Deal programs of 1933–38.[17]

Hoover's beliefs in the beneficence of collective bargaining and high wages—a crude form of purchasing-power theory of the business cycle—were put to the test when the economy began to decline in 1929, most noticeably after the October stock-market crash. Now president, Hoover responded by calling a series of meetings in November and December with the leaders of selected businesses, labor unions, and farm organizations. He urged, in particular, that employers maintain real-wage rates and not lay off workers and that unions not strike. Participants in these conferences pledged to abide by Hoover's exhortations; they organized new programs to cooperate in maintaining employment without real-wage reductions. On December 5, Hoover addressed a conference for continued industrial progress attended by some four hundred delegates representing more than three hundred trade organizations. He told them: "The very fact that you gentlemen come together for these broad purposes represents an advance in the whole conception of the relationship of business to public welfare. . . . [T]his is not dictation or interference by the government with business. It is a request from the government that you cooperate in prudent measures to solve a national problem."[18]

However, people often regarded government officials' requests, especially those made at meetings called by the president, as verging on directives. At least, many considered it unpatriotic not to follow the president's suggestions. Whatever the reason, few large businesses cut real-wage rates until well into 1931. By that time, the economy was spiraling rapidly downward, and the financial system had sustained irreparable damage. Ironically, allegiance to

Hoover's program of real-wage maintenance now appears to have been a prime cause of the severity of the employment contraction early in the Great Depression, coming as it did at a critical time when appropriate wage reductions could have restored equilibrium in the labor markets before mass unemployment and all its negative consequences had developed.[19]

By the time Franklin D. Roosevelt assumed the presidency in March 1933, the depression had reached almost unbearable depths. As Justice Brandeis put it, the situation amounted to "an emergency more serious than war." Real gross national product (GNP) per capita was down more than 30 percent; net investment and corporate profits were negative; the financial system was a shambles; unemployment had reached 25 percent; and a substantial number of those people still employed were working part time or living in fear of imminent layoff. In response to these dire conditions, government and private leaders joined to create the most far-reaching quasi-corporatist experiment in the country's peacetime history.

Although agriculture, transportation, finance, and other sectors were placed under quasi-corporatist controls, the centerpiece of the experiment was the 1933 National Industrial Recovery Act (NIRA), which created the National Recovery Administration (NRA) and gave the president authority to create the Public Works Administration. This legislation emerged from a grand compromise of the sort celebrated by corporatists. The most prominent parties to its creation included businessmen seeking higher prices and barriers to competition; labor unionists seeking government sponsorship and protection of their organizing activities and collective bargaining; do-gooders concerned about working conditions and child labor; and proponents of massive government spending for public works. Their model was the WIB of 1918.

Roosevelt placed General Hugh Johnson in charge of the NRA. Businessmen descended on it as they had on the WIB in 1918. It offered them the prospect of government power to control free riding and thereby to solidify cartel arrangements in their industries. The NIRA set aside the antitrust laws. It authorized the president to approve a code of fair competition for each industry or, lacking an acceptable privately tendered code, to impose one of his own making. Every code had to provide for minimum wages, maximum hours, and working conditions satisfactory to the government; each had to guarantee rights of collective bargaining to employees.

NRA bureaucrats worked hard to organize the economy. They eventually approved 557 basic and 189 supplementary codes, covering about 95 percent of all industrial employees. General Johnson made Herculean efforts, verging on the sort of propaganda and intimidation common in the European dictatorships at the time, to stir up enthusiasm for the program and to stimulate compliance with its terms.

Within two years, however, the program had failed: on May 27, 1935, the Supreme Court ruled the NIRA unconstitutional. Few cried at its funeral. It had promised something for everyone—more precisely, for everyone well organized to exert political influence—but its operation had revealed that it actually had little to offer small businessmen, unionists, or consumers. Even big businessmen, who had dominated it, became disaffected—and increasingly irritated by government bureaucrats' chronic interference in their business affairs.[20]

The experiment did leave some quasi-corporatist residues, including a price-fixing scheme in the coal industry and a complicated multigovernmental arrangement for maintaining a national petroleum cartel. Even more important were the labor laws passed to salvage and extend the provisions first enacted as part of the NIRA. In 1935, Congress passed the Wagner Act, creating the National Labor Relations Board and establishing a basic structure for compulsory collective bargaining that has persisted, with only minor amendment, to the present. In 1938, the Fair Labor Standards Act restored the provisions of the NIRA relating to minimum wages, maximum hours, and working conditions. In addition, the basic corporatist arrangements for controlling agricultural production, prices, and marketing, first adopted in 1933, have also survived to the present, though periodic changes in their details have been made.

Surveying the quasi-corporatist legacies of the New Deal, John Commons observed in the early 1940s that economic pressure groups had "become an occupational parliament of the American people more truly representative than the Congress elected by territorial divisions. They are the informal American counterpart of Mussolini's 'corporate state,' the Italian occupational state."[21] The observation was largely wishful thinking but contained a grain of truth.

With the coming of World War II, the Roosevelt administration recovered its zeal for quasi-corporatism, which had waned in the late 1930s. During the so-called defense period, 1940–41, before the United States entered the war as a declared belligerent, public opinion did not support participation in the war unless the country was attacked. The government had to move cautiously in its rearmament program. Conditions were ripe for tripartism: the government lacked the political support simply to order compliance with its program, yet it needed the cooperation of industry and organized labor. Businessmen's expertise and property were essential for rearmament, and work stoppages might jeopardize the whole program. The administration, always friendly to organized labor, continued its strong support of union organization and collective bargaining, support that would persist through the war period. Beginning in 1940, Roosevelt began to woo big business as well.

As the rearmament program developed, businessmen quickly established themselves as its leading managers—subject always to Roosevelt's overriding authority. In 1940, the president revived the National Defense Advisory Commission and gave key positions to U.S. Steel's Edward Stettinius, General

Motors's William Knudsen, and Sears's Donald Nelson. In January 1941, he created the Office of Production Management (OPM) as the chief overseer of the rearmament program and, strangely, put two men in charge of it—the businessman Knudsen and the unionist Sidney Hillman. (The president made clear, however, that because he himself was the real boss at the OPM, the apparently divided authority made no real difference.)

The rearmament agencies enticed many of the nation's leading businessmen to leave their firms in order to take up unpaid service for the government. As early as August 1940, one observer described their gathering as "the greatest concentration of big-business influence ever seen in Washington," with the possible exception of the NRA. A journalist declared the OPM to be "dominated by representatives of du Pont and Rockefeller companies and those dependent upon them." Their numbers grew steadily. By January 1942, almost nine hundred uncompensated businessmen were working for the OPM. When the War Production Board superseded the OPM early in 1942, even more came on board.[22]

This reconciliation between the Roosevelt administration and big business in no way cooled the government's ardor for organized labor. Only ten days after the Japanese attack on Pearl Harbor provoked Congress to declare war, Roosevelt convened a meeting of a dozen employers and a dozen unionists in Washington. They promised, as if they were speaking for all employers and all employees, that they would not resort to lockouts or strikes during the war and would submit to government intervention in unresolved disputes. In January 1942, the president created the National War Labor Board to resolve disputes by mediation or arbitration.

In dealing with union efforts to organize nonunion workforces, the government adopted a formula that made it easy for unions to become and remain the authorized collective-bargaining agents even at workplaces where relatively few employees supported the representation. Under this regime, the unions flourished: during four years of war, union membership increased by more than 4 million persons, or by about 40 percent. Work stoppages did not entirely cease, and the railroad and coal industries continued to thwart the government's efforts to maintain harmony in the labor markets. In general, however, the government's attempt to accommodate organized labor proved compatible with its overall wartime production program—not to speak of with the administration's designs for reelection.

If the unions prospered during the war, big business prospered even more, which explains in large part why businessmen grew more and more comfortable in dealing with the army, the navy, and the Maritime Commission, their major customers. Military spending topped 40 percent of GNP in 1943 and 1944, and most industrial output was going to military uses. As one army historian described it, the relation between the government and the military contractors "was gradually transformed from an 'arm's length' relationship between two more or less equal parties in a business transaction into an undefined but intimate relationship."[23]

Contracts ceased to bind; fixed prices became adjustable; contractual modifications averted looming losses. The important thing was to keep the production lines running. Only the taxpayers stood to lose, and they, as always, had no organized representation in the government. Besides, their patriotism had been aroused, and they were being vigorously propagandized to regard high taxes and forced savings as the necessary price of victory. Rates of return on investment proved extraordinarily high for typical war contractors, particularly in view of the limited risk they bore.[24] Out of this experience emerged the basic structure of the military-industrial complex within which the vast armaments production of the postwar period has been organized.

During the Korean War, the government revived many of the economic controls employed during World War II. Among the agencies created was the Economic Stabilization Agency, which in January 1951 issued regulations to control wages and prices. Of course, the government sought the cooperation of organized business and labor in the implementation of its wage-price controls. Being more favorably inclined toward labor than business, the Truman administration got itself into trouble in applying its incomes policy to the steel industry. It tried to circumvent the lack of business cooperation by nationalizing the steel industry, but in June 1952 the Supreme Court declared that the methods by which the government proposed to take over the industry were unconstitutional, and the administration sustained a major political defeat. Fortunately, the war ended in mid-1953, and the wage-price controls lapsed.

Wage-Price Controls

Quasi-corporatism at the macrolevel next reared its head when the Nixon administration imposed mandatory wage-price controls during the years 1971–74. The program passed through a series of phases, the first being a ninety-day price freeze beginning August 15, 1971. The administration appreciated that a freeze could not be sustained for long without wrecking the price system, so the following phase allowed more discretion and variability in the application of the controls. To make this phase work, the government needed to develop "a broad acceptance of the rules and a willingness to live by them."[25] Wage decisions were made by the tripartite Pay Board, on which "[o]fficial references were made to labor and business representation as though these were organized and duly constituted functional communities."[26] Other prices came under the jurisdiction of a price commission composed entirely of public members, mainly people with business experience.

The third phase, which began in January 1973, involved a shift from administrative review by the government to self-administration (ostensibly of the same rules) by companies and unions. During this phase, prices and wages surged. Dismayed, President Nixon imposed another across-the-board freeze in June 1973, followed by a final phase of bureaucratically administered controls until the program expired on April 30, 1974. The whole program had worked so poorly and had created so many artificial shortages, black markets, and social conflicts that no one minded much when it ended. "[L]abor and management were thoroughly fed up with the whole thing, and the president's Labor Management Advisory Committee had some time earlier publicly recorded its view that controls should end."[27]

Notwithstanding the Nixon program's evident failure, the Carter administration resorted to an even weaker version—unlike the earlier income policies, Carter's policy had no legislative sanction—when inflation began to accelerate in the late 1970s. In October 1978, Carter announced wage-price guidelines, which firms and unions were invited to follow. An executive agency, the Council on Wage and Price Stability (COWPS, pronounced "cops"), took responsibility for haranguing the private sector and monitoring its compliance with the guidelines. As usual, many large firms chose to regard the government's recommendations as directives. Their view is understandable, for the government made clear that it would employ various indirect sanctions to punish noncompliers, including withholding of federal contracts, more enthusiastic exertion of regulatory powers, and publication of an enemies list.

As always, some executives considered compliance merely good citizenship. In contrast, most union leaders, including George Meany, head of the American Federation of Labor and Congress of Industrial Organizations (AFL-CIO), denounced the guidelines. COWPS proceeded to interject itself into several major collective-bargaining negotiations, with counterproductive results. Although, of course, the program had no effect in slowing inflation, it did get the Democratic administration into trouble with its natural allies in the labor unions.[28]

To repair these bruised relations, in the summer of 1979 the administration sought greater union participation in the program by the unions. In response, union leaders proposed creation of a tripartite board to set and modify the wage guidelines and to hear appeals regarding them on an ad hoc basis. The administration liked the idea. Not only would it placate the AFL-CIO, but it would shift the blame for unpopular decisions—indeed for inflation itself—onto the board. Because the board would represent business, labor, and the public, its decisions might appear more equitable and hence receive more compliance.

The culmination of the administration's negotiations with organized labor came on September 28, 1979, when the president announced that the government and the AFL-CIO had entered into a "national accord." This supposedly historic document turned out to be a hodgepodge of highfalutin declarations and vague, mutually incompatible policy proposals. It said nothing specific about the guidelines program except to endorse its continuation with "greater public participation." Its only real accomplishment was expressed in its final paragraph, which declared that "the essence of this National Accord is involvement and cooperation.... It is our purpose to establish procedures for continuing consultations between American labor leadership and the Administration." The Teamsters and the United Auto Workers, large unions that did not belong to the AFL-CIO, also endorsed the accord.

As part of the deal, the president announced the formation of the Price Advisory Committee and the Pay Advisory Committee—the former a pure formality, the latter a key concession to the unions. The tripartite pay board moved slowly. Not until March 1980 was President Carter able to consider and endorse the board's major proposal, which called for a higher range of allowable wage increases under the guidelines. By that time, the program had become almost irrelevant. Absorbed in the reelection campaign, the administration paid little attention to the guidelines—they had never been much more than a device to divert public opinion, anyway. Carter was defeated in November, and one of Ronald Reagan's first acts after becoming president was to abolish the wage-price guidelines program.[29]

With the accession of Reagan, one might have thought that all quasi-corporatist schemes were doomed, but such a supposition would have been mistaken. In one sector, the defense economy, quasi-corporatist arrangements had been entrenched for decades, and during Reagan's unprecedented peacetime military buildup they would flourish.

The Defense Sector

Except during the few years of demobilization in the late 1940s, the United States has maintained a huge military establishment supplied by a correspondingly vast economic sector for the past six decades. During the Cold War years 1948–89, 7.5 percent of the GNP, on average, went toward purchases of military goods and services.[30] After fiscal year 1992, the military share of national product fell steadily until leveling off at 3.2 percent in 1998, but the absolute amount of military expenditure remained at a basic Cold War level, never dropping much below $300 billion per year and then climbing well above that figure in the early 2000s.[31] Although personnel costs account for much of the spending, a substantial portion of the defense budget goes toward research, development, testing, production, deployment, maintenance, and modification of weapons systems. The management and performance of these tasks take place within the unofficial military-industrial-congressional complex (MICC). Universities, research laboratories, think tanks, consultants, labor unions, local government officials, trade associations, and advisory groups also play supporting roles in the MICC.

Despite the multitude of laws supposedly controlling every step taken within the MICC, in practice this conglomeration of overlapping private and government interest groups and military bureaus obscures or obliterates the dividing line between the public and the private: "[T]he procurement of sophisticated weapons systems takes place in a rarified atmosphere in which the distinction between buyer and seller becomes blurred due to the interdependence of the organizations, the growing commonality of goals, and the daily intermingling of personnel from both groups over extended periods of time.... [This is] an environment far removed from the presumed 'arm's length' dealings of the market."[32]

Senator William Roth complained that "one cannot do business in some Army procurements unless one is part of the 'old boy network,'"[33] and Senator William Proxmire pointed to "an active, ever-working, fast moving, revolving door between the Pentagon and its big suppliers."[34] Many of the thousands of high-ranking military officers who retire annually find immediate executive employment in the defense industry, and industry officials routinely take leave from their corporations to occupy high-ranking positions in the Pentagon bureaucracy.[35] Nor is the interchange of personnel confined to the Pentagon and the contractors: academics, consultants, and congressional staffers also play this game. In these circumstances, one easily forgets who is working for whom and where private interest ends and public responsibility begins.

General James P. Mullins, former commander of the Air Force Logistics Command, has written that the defense business "is not business as usual among *independent* parties. This is a family affair among terribly *interdependent* parties." He also affirms that the contractors, far from awaiting government demands, actively generate and shape those demands: "The contractor validates the design [of a weapons system] through the process of marketing it to one of the services. If successful, the contractor gets the contract. Thus, to a substantial degree, the weapon capabilities devised by contractors create military requirements. In the defense business, then, the prime contractors are where the babies really come from."[36]

A senior Pentagon official has spoken with pride of "the complete inter-relationship of the Service/contractor organizations," which are "virtually co-located." The military service "is aware of and, in fact, participates in practically every major contractor decision." In view of this reality, Murray Weidenbaum notes that all defense firms take on a "quasi-public character."[37]

Although the contractors perform much of the research and development to bring forth the weapon systems, numerous midwives attend their labor. Defense trade associations, such as the Aerospace Industries Association, the American Defense Preparedness Association, and the National Security Industrial Association, help to link the industry and the government. Because these associations speak for no particular company, their views appear more neutral, but "sometimes an association in coordination with [government] agency officials can become a de facto policy-maker."[38] The associations sponsor conventions widely attended by both military and private parties, featuring panels, classified briefings, and distribution of information on future weapons programs and policy developments. Association officials regularly testify before congressional committees and meet with executive-branch officials, urging increases in defense spending and greater support for particular research and development (R&D) programs.

Even more significant are the many defense advisory boards, composed of private parties, scattered throughout the defense bureaucracy. An important example is the Defense Science Board, another group described as an "old boy network." James Coates and Michael Kilian report that this board's members "frequently moved in and out of the Pentagon and to and from big jobs with contractors—many of whose weapons they evaluated as board members."[39] The advisory boards ensure a biased appraisal of defense matters and exert a powerful influence in setting the defense-policy agenda. "[T]hey tend to reinforce a closed, interacting network of policy-makers, all of whom have expertise in the area, but who share a similar interest in the preservation of the industry-Government relationship."[40] Their operation exemplifies a clear quasi-corporatist arrangement.

Defense advisory boards have influence in part because their members have security clearances that allow them to gain access to secret information. Indeed, throughout the MICC, secrecy is a significant condition for the intermediation of certain interests and the exclusion of others. As Gordon Adams explains,

> Secrecy permits the contractors and the Department [of Defense] to decide the nation's military future without having to deal with dissent or alternative views.... [N]eeds and fulfillment, missions and weapons systems are so intertwined that it is almost impossible to tell where one stops and the other starts.... Once a major weapons system exists, momentum is created within the company, the DOD and Congress to buy it, particularly since the Government has already heavily invested in the company R&D.[41]

During the late 1980s and early 1990s, for example, defense programs probably included more than $30 billion per year for secret weapons programs unlisted in the official budget documents.[42] As *Washington Post* reporter John Wagner revealed, "The government routinely goes to great lengths to keep the public in the dark about black projects, even authorizing contractors to actively deceive those who inquire about their work, according to an interagency security document produced by the CIA, Energy, Defense and other departments."[43] Secrecy, in combination with the overarching sense of national emergency inherent in the Cold War, helped to sustain the grip of the interfused interests that constitute the MICC and to determine the nation's defense policies and weapons programs practically without challenge or even effective questioning from others.

American-Style Corporatism

Political scientists have concluded correctly that the United States is not a corporate state—certainly not a corporate state comparable to modern Sweden or Austria, nor one that meets the demanding criteria of Philippe Schmitter's definition of *neocorporatism*. U.S. interest groups have been too partial in their membership. Normally, the government power they hope to seize has itself been fragmented, divided at each level among executive, legislative, and judicial branches and dispersed among the national, state, and local levels in a federal constitutional system. Residual allegiance to liberal ideology and to its political norms and practices, including limited government and territorial representation in the legislature, has also impeded the development of corporatism. The U.S. economy is vast and complex. To bring it within the effective control of a few hierarchical, noncompetitive peak associations, as the fascists tried (or pretended) to do in interwar Italy, is almost unthinkable. The closest peacetime experiment, the NIRA of 1933–35, did not work and was collapsing from its own weight when the Supreme Court put an end to it.

Recent U.S. history has brought forth, however, a multitude of little corporatisms, arrangements within subsectors, industries, or other partial jurisdictions. They have drawn on both national and state government powers. They operate effectively in many (but not all) areas of agriculture; in many professional services such as medicine, dentistry, and hospital care; and in a variety of other areas such as fishery management and urban redevelopment. These abundant "iron triangles" normally involve well-organized private-interest groups; government regulatory, spending, or lending agencies; and congressional subcommittees charged with policy oversight. A political economy in which such arrangements predominate, as they do in the United States, is commonly called interest-group liberalism or neopluralism (elsewhere, following Charlotte Twight, I describe it as "participatory fascism"), but it might just as well be called disaggregated neocorporatism.[44]

Under crisis conditions, all the forces normally obstructing the development of U.S. corporatism, whether at the microlevel or the macrolevel, diminish. Since the early twentieth century, in the national emergencies associated with war, economic depression or accelerating inflation, and large-scale labor disturbances, the national government has responded by adopting policies that consolidate power at the top level and extend the scope of its authority. With power more concentrated and more actively employed, the incentive is greater for latent private-interest groups to organize, increase their membership, suppress their internal disputes, and demand a voice in policymaking.

Far from resenting such a private coalescence of interests, the government usually approves, encourages, and sometimes even sponsors it. In a crisis, swift action is imperative, and the government needs private interests with whom it can deal quickly while preserving the legitimacy that comes from giving affected parties a nominal role in policymaking. When the government is imposing unusual restrictions or requirements on the citizens, as it always does during major emergencies, it needs to create the perception, if not the reality, that these burdens have been accepted—better yet, have been proposed and chosen—by those who bear them.

National emergencies create conditions in which governmental officials and private-interest groups have more to gain by striking political bargains with one another. Government gains the private parties' resources, expertise, and cooperation, which are usually essential for the success of government's crisis policies. Private-interest groups gain the application of government authority to enforce compliance with their cartel rules, which is essential to preclude the free riding that normally jeopardizes the success of every arrangement for the provision of collective goods. Crisis promotes extended politicization of economic life, and extended politicization encourages additional political organization and bargaining.

In U.S. history, quasi-corporatism has risen and fallen with the coming and the passing of national emergencies, but each episode has left legacies, accretions of corporatism embedded in the part-elitist, part-pluralist structure of U.S. government. By now these accretions, taking the form of disaggregated neocorporatist arrangements scattered throughout the economy, add up to a significant portion of the political economy.

Overshadowing these developments, and far more significant, is the quasi-corporatism of the military economy. Consuming resources at an enormous rate, the national-security sector manifests most clearly the association between national emergency—for example, the four-decade emergency of the Cold War—and quasi-corporatist arrangements. When the Cold War ended, the system continued to operate almost as if nothing had changed.[45] In defense spending, the lines separating the public sector and the private sector have been almost completely obliterated; and even where they seem to remain, as in the private ownership of the contracting firms, the appearance has little substance. Government involvement infuses every aspect of the operation of these firms. Working from the other direction, the firms have employed a variety of devices, from advisory committees to extensive rotation of their personnel through the Pentagon, to penetrate the military decision-making agencies. No one has a stronger voice in setting the defense production agenda—sometimes the strategic commitments as well—and in directing the R&D that presages future weapons and battlefield scenarios. Other members of the MICC crowd in for their shares of the money and the power, but persons and groups outside this tight circle have little ability to exert influence on the defense sector. Secrecy and old-boy networks deprive outsiders of information, and the outsiders' lack of expertise, credentials, and security clearances ensures that those who would rock the boat will never be allowed on board.

In sum, in the U.S. experience, most quasi-corporatist policymaking has arisen from national emergencies. Should the future bring new crises, as it almost certainly will, we may confidently expect to witness the flowering of still more quasi-corporatism.

Postscript 2002

Early in 2002, the government's conduct of its so-called war on terrorism seems consistent with the foregoing analysis, the initial draft of which was written some fifteen years ago. Government officials, such as Vice President Dick Cheney and Defense Secretary Donald Rumsfeld, have explicitly likened the antiterrorist campaign to the Cold War, representing it as a "new normalcy" likely to continue indefinitely.[46] The government's airline bailout bids fair to become a quasi-corporatist arrangement under the direction of the newly created Air Transportation Stabilization Board, in league with the airline companies and the powerful airline industry labor unions, and subject to chronic meddling by interested members of Congress.[47] Likewise, the government's takeover of airport security activities, under the newly created Transportation Security Administration, would seem to have altered this part of the economy irreversibly—and for the worse.[48] The newly created Office of Homeland Security, with its open-ended mission to "secure the United States from terrorist threats or attacks,"[49] holds the potential to become a focus for a variety of loosely related microcorporatist arrangements.[50] As the *Wall Street Journal* reported early in 2002, "With the government spigot opened wide, the private sector is jostling for position in what many expect to be a transformation of the private security industry." Security-firm executive Chuck Vance told the *Journal*, "There will be plenty to go around. Everybody is working on figuring out how they can fit into the program."[51] Political and regulatory entanglements will follow this economic bonanza as night follows day, and new iron triangles will ultimately be forged. After a century of engagement in the sport of quasi-corporatism, Americans know how the game is played, and they are eager to participate in the next round.

Notes

1. *New York Times,* February 28, 1988.

2. In the *International Encyclopedia of the Social Sciences* (New York: Crowell Collier and

Macmillan, 1968), for example, the entry for *corporatism* reads simply "See Fascism."

3. Mario Einaudi, "Fascism," in *International Encyclopedia of the Social Sciences,* vol. 5, pp. 334–41.

4. Schmitter as quoted in H. Brinton Milward and Ronald A. Francisco, "Subsystem Politics and Corporatism in the United States," *Policy and Politics* 11 (1983): 273-93.

5. Recent surveys of neocorporatism include Wyn Grant, ed., *The Political Economy of Capitalism* (New York: St. Martin's Press, 1985), and Gerhard Lehmbruch and Philippe C. Schmitter, eds., *Patterns of Corporatist Policy-Making* (London: Sage, 1982). See also Eric A. Nordlinger, *On the Autonomy of the Democratic State* (Cambridge, Mass.: Harvard University Press, 1981), pp. 45–46, 166–74.

6. Madison in Alexander Hamilton, John Jay, and James Madison, *The Federalist* (New York: Modern Library, n.d.), pp. 53–62, quotations from pp. 54 and 57, respectively.

7. Ibid., p. 61.

8. Graham K. Wilson, "Why Is There No Corporatism in the United States?" in *Patterns of Corporatist Policy-Making,* ed. Lehmbruch and Schmitter, p. 224.

9. Graham K. Wilson, *Interest Groups in the United States* (Oxford, Eng.: Clarendon Press, 1981), pp. 132–35. See also Wilson, "Why Is There No Corporatism in the United States?" p. 224.

10. Mancur Olson, *The Rise and Decline of Nations: Economic Growth , Stagflation, and Social Rigidities* (New Haven, Conn.: Yale University Press, 1982), pp. 17–74. See also Mancur Olson, *The Logic of Collective Action: Public Goods and the Theory of Groups* (Cambridge, Mass: Harvard University Press, 1965).

11. Philippe C. Schmitter, "Neo-corporatism and the State," in *The Political Economy of Capitalism,* ed. Grant, p. 40.

12. Ibid.

13. "Subsystem Politics," p. 273.

14. Here and later, unless otherwise indicated, quotations and documentation come from Robert Higgs, *Crisis and Leviathan: Critical Episodes in the Growth of American Government* (New York: Oxford University Press, 1987).

15. Robert D. Cuff, *The War Industries Board: Business-Government Relations During World War I* (Baltimore, Md.: Johns Hopkins University Press, 1973).

16. United States District Court, District of Montana, Butte Division, *United States of America v. Atlantic Richfield Company, et al.,* no. CV-89-039-BU-PGH, Expert Report of Robert Higgs, Ph.D., May 14, 1999, pp. 24–30.

17. Murray N. Rothbard, "Herbert Hoover and the Myth of Laissez-Faire," in *A New History of Leviathan: Essays on the Rise of the American Corporate State,* edited by Ronald Radosh and Murray N. Rothbard (New York: E. P. Dutton, 1972), pp. 111–45.

18. Hoover as quoted in Morgan O. Reynolds, "Explaining Wage Rigidity, 1929–31," unpublished ms., Texas A&M University, n.d.

19. Richard K. Vedder and Lowell E. Gallaway, *Out of Work: Unemployment and Government in Twentieth-Century America* (New York: Holmes and Meier, for The Independent Institute, 1993), pp. 74–111.

20. Ellis W. Hawley, *The New Deal and the Problem of Monopoly* (Princeton, N.J.: Princeton University Press, 1966). For a slightly different view of how businessmen viewed the

NRA's demise, see Butler Shaffer, *In Restraint of Trade: The Business Campaign Against Competition, 1918–1938* (Lewisburg, Pa.: Bucknell University Press, 1997), pp. 117–18.

21. John R. Commons, *The Economics of Collective Action,* edited by Kenneth H. Parsons (Madison, Wisc.: University of Wisconsin Press, 1970), p. 33.

22. On the defense period, see Robert Higgs, "Private Profit, Public Risk: Institutional Antecedents of the Modern Military Procurement System in the Rearmament Program of 1940–1941," in *The Sinews of War: Essays on the Economic History of World War II,* edited by Geofrey T. Mills and Hugh Rockoff (Ames: Iowa State University Press, 1993), pp. 166–98 (quotations from p. 189); on the war years, see Higgs, *Crisis and Leviathan,* pp. 196–236 and sources cited there.

23. R. Elberton Smith, *The Army and Economic Mobilization* (Washington, D.C.: U.S. Army, 1959), p. 312.

24. Higgs, "Private Profit," p. 191.

25. George P. Shultz and Kenneth W. Dam, *Economic Policy Beyond the Headlines* (New York: Norton, 1977), p. 69.

26. Theodore J. Lowi, *The End of Liberalism: The Second Republic of the United States* (New York: Norton, 1979), p. 122.

27. Shultz and Dam, *Economic Policy Beyond the Headlines,* p. 75.

28. Robert Higgs, "Carter's Wage-Price Guidelines: A Review of the First Year," *Policy Review* (winter 1980): 97–113.

29. Robert Higgs, "Wage-Price Guidelines: Retreat and Defeat," *The Freeman* 31 (November 1981): 643–52.

30. Robert Higgs, "The Cold War Economy: Opportunity Costs, Ideology, and the Politics of Crisis," *Explorations in Economic History* 31 (July 1994), p. 292.

31. U.S. Office of Management and Budget, *Budget of the United States Government: Fiscal Year 2003, Historical Tables* (Washington, D.C.: U.S. Government Printing Office, 2002), pp. 294–95.

32. Bernard Udis and Murray L. Weidenbaum, "The Many Dimensions of the Military Effort," in *The Economic Consequences of Reduced Military Spending,* edited by Bernard Udis (Lexington, Mass: Lexington Books, 1973), p. 33; see also Jacques S. Gansler, *The Defense Industry* (Cambridge, Mass: MIT Press, 1980).

33. Roth as quoted in Dina Rasor, *The Pentagon Underground* (New York: Times Books, 1985), p. 204.

34. William Proxmire, *Report from Wasteland: America's Military-Industrial Complex* (New York: Praeger, 1970), p. 170.

35. U.S. General Accounting Office, *DOD Revolving Door: Relations Between Work at DOD and Post-DOD Employment,* GAO/NSIAD-86-180BR (Washington, D.C.: U.S. Government Printing Office, July 1986).

36. James P. Mullins, *The Defense Matrix: National Preparedness and the Military-Industrial Complex* (San Diego: Avant Books, 1986), pp. 91, 113, emphasis in original.

37. Murray L. Weidenbaum, *Business, Government, and the Public,* 3d ed. (Englewood Cliffs, N.J.: Prentice-Hall, 1986), pp. 356–58, including quote from the senior Pentagon official.

38. Gordon Adams, *The Politics of Defense Contracting: The Iron Triangle* (New Brunswick,

N.J.: Transaction Books, 1982), p. 156.

39. James Coates and Michael Kilian, *Heavy Losses: The Dangerous Decline of American Defense* (New York: Viking, 1985), p. 207.

40. Adams, *The Politics of Defense Contracting*, p. 166.

41. Ibid., p. 96.

42. Tim Weiner, *Blank Check: The Pentagon's Black Budget* (New York: Warner Books, 1990), p. 16.

43. John Wagner, "Untruth in Government: Feds Write a Guide to the Art of Secrecy," *Seattle Times*, August 6, 1992.

44. For surveys and analyses of the U.S. political economy, see Thomas R. Dye, *Who's Running America? The Conservative Years* (Englewood Cliffs, N.J.: Prentice-Hall, 1986); Peter Navarro, *The Policy Game: How Special Interests Are Stealing America* (New York: Wiley, 1984); Higgs, *Crisis and Leviathan;* Lowi, *The End of Liberalism;* Olson, *The Logic of Collective Action;* Shultz and Dam, *Economic Policy Beyond the Headlines;* Weidenbaum, *Business, Government, and the Public;* and Wilson, *Interest Groups.*

45. Robert Higgs, "The Cold War Is Over, but U.S. Preparation for It Continues," *The Independent Review* 6 (fall 2001): 287–305 (which appears, in revised form, as chap. 30 in this collection).

46. Robert Burns, "Rumsfeld: Terror Fight Like Cold War," Associated Press report posted on AOL, October 4, 2001.

47. Laurence Zuckerman, "U.S. Takes Big Role in Airlines' Crisis," *New York Times* on-line, October 4, 2001.

48. Richard W. Rahn, "Airline Safety: Sense and Nonsense," *Washington Times*, September 24, 2001; Robert Higgs, "Federal Oversight Won't Improve Airport Security," *San Francisco Business Times*, October 26–November 1, 2001; Greg Hitt and Martha Brannigan, "Air-Security Bill Poses Tough Challenges," *Wall Street Journal*, 2001.

49. Executive Order Establishing Office of Homeland Security, October 8, 2001, at http://www.whitehouse.gov/news/releases/2001/10/print/20011008-2.html.

50. George Melloan, "America's Federal Agencies Stake 'Homeland Defense' Claims," *Wall Street Journal*, November 27, 2001; Jim VandeHei and Greg Hitt, "Antibioterror Funding Is Proving to Be a Lure for Many Entities," *Wall Street Journal*, November 20, 2001; Anne Marie Squeo, "Defense Firms Comb Through Arsenals to Pitch Products for Homeland Security," *Wall Street Journal*, November 28, 2001; Steve Hanke and Robert Higgs, "Wake Up to the Law of the Ratchet: National Emergencies Attract Opportunists Who Seek to Profit from the Growth of Government," *Financial Times*, November 26, 2001.

51. Jeanne Cummings, "Bush Allots $37.7 Billion for Homeland Security Budget," *Wall Street Journal*, February 5, 2002.

26

The Normal Constitution
Versus the Crisis Constitution

Few indeed have been the invasions upon essential liberties
which have not been accompanied by pleas of urgent necessity
advanced in good faith by responsible men.

— Justice Frank Murphy

Time and chance have been unkind to the hopes of the Founding Fathers. They
established the Constitution in order to "secure the Blessings of Liberty" to
themselves and their posterity, intending that framework of freedom and government to endure through storm as well as sunshine.[1] The dead, however,
could not bind the living, and during the twentieth century the unfolding of
our history brought into being a second constitution. Besides the Normal Constitution, protective of individual rights, we now have a Crisis Constitution,
hostile to individual rights and friendly to the unchecked power of government
officials. In national emergencies, the Crisis Constitution overrides the Normal
Constitution. The great danger is that in an age of permanent emergency—the
age we live in, the age we are likely to go on living in—the Crisis Constitution
will simply swallow up the Normal Constitution, depriving us at all times of
the very rights the original Constitution was created to protect at all times. This
prospect can only dishearten those who believe that the fundamental purpose
of the Constitution is to protect individuals' rights to life, liberty, and property.

The Historical Record

Although events before the twentieth century, especially during the Civil War,
foreshadowed the Crisis Constitution,[2] World War I gave rise to its unmistak-
able emergence and persistence.

Even before the United States formally entered the war, the railroad labor
troubles of 1916–17 had provoked unprecedented government actions. Facing
the prospect of a nationwide railroad strike when the operating brotherhoods
and the railroad managers could not agree on wages and hours, President
Woodrow Wilson turned to Congress, gaining passage of the Adamson Act in

September 1916. In effect, the act simply imposed on the interstate railroad industry a 25 percent increase in wage rates. The railroads challenged the constitutionality of the law, but the Supreme Court upheld it in *Wilson v. New* (243 U.S. 332 [1917]). The Court's decision emphasized the gravity of the situation—"the impediment and destruction of interstate commerce which was threatened" (p. 352) and "the infinite injury to the public interest which was imminent" (p. 348)—but justified the government's actions by arguing that although the government has no emergency power as such, it has a reservoir of reserved power on which it may legitimately draw during emergencies. The outcome: railroad owners were deprived of a great deal of property, without compensation, for a use not public—namely, to raise the pay of unionized railroad workers holding the economy hostage.

After the United States formally entered the war, the government enacted legislation providing for the conscription of soldiers. Though men had been drafted during the Civil War, the Supreme Court had never ruled on the constitutionality of the draft. Besides, the issues now differed: men were being drafted not to defend the government against violent domestic rebellion or invasion, but to do battle in the trenches of faraway France, ostensibly to foster such abstract ideological aims as "making the world safe for democracy" and securing the "autonomous development" of various European ethnic groups.[3] The Supreme Court, however, readily affirmed the constitutionality of sending men against their will to fight and die in a remote power struggle. Said Chief Justice Edward White: "It may not be doubted that the very conception of a just government and its duty to the citizen includes the reciprocal obligation of the citizen to render military service in case of need and the right to compel it" (*Arver v. United States*, 245 U.S. 366 [1918] at 378). The Court refused to consider seriously the claim that conscription constitutes a form of involuntary servitude forbidden by the Thirteenth Amendment. The outcome: draftees were deprived of liberty, and tens of thousands of them were consequently deprived of life itself by the actions of political authorities intent on the prosecution of the war but unwilling to risk their political positions by imposing enough explicit taxes to hire the desired military personnel.

The Great Depression, which Justice Louis Brandeis called "an emergency more serious than war," prompted a welter of actions by government at all levels. In 1932–34, twenty-five states enacted legislation providing for moratoria on mortgage foreclosures.[4] Such laws appeared to be unambiguous impairments of the obligation of contract and therefore in clear violation of the U.S. Constitution, but when Minnesota's mortgage moratorium law came before the Supreme Court, the majority pronounced this self-declared emergency legislation a valid exercise of the state's police powers (*Home Building and Loan Association v. Blaisdell*, 290 U.S. 398 [1934]). Harking back to the railroad labor case of 1917, Chief Justice Charles Evans Hughes reasoned that "[w]hile emergency does not create power, emergency may furnish the occasion for the exercise of power" (p. 426). The Constitution's clause protecting contracts, said Chief Justice Hughes, "is not to be read with literal exactness" (p. 428). Those mysterious "reserved powers" are to be "read into contracts" (p. 435). In sum, "[a]n emergency existed in Minnesota which furnished a proper occasion for the exercise of the reserved power of the State" (p. 444). The outcome: many thousands of mortgagees were deprived of the rights of foreclosure stipulated in their contracts and compelled to make do with the alternatives provided by the emergency statutes.

In addition, in the depths of the Great Depression, the federal government abandoned the gold standard, nationalized the monetary gold stock, and abrogated the gold clauses of all contracts, public and private, past and future. This "act of absolute bad faith" astonished even some members of Congress. Senator Thomas P. Gore declared it "just plain stealing."[5] Stealing or not, it certainly smacked of what Justice James McReynolds called "arbitrary action, whose immediate purpose and necessary effect is destruction of individual rights" (*Norman v. Baltimore and Ohio Railroad Co.*, 294 U.S. 240 [1935] at 372). McReynolds, however, was speaking in dissent. The majority, for whom Chief Justice Hughes spoke, held that "if the gold clauses . . . interfere with the policy of the Congress in the exercise of that [monetary] authority they cannot stand." The Court recognized that "express stipulations for gold payments constitute property," but it maintained that "[c]ontracts, however express, cannot fetter the constitutional authority of the Congress" (307, 311). The outcome: certainly thousands and perhaps millions of parties to contracts containing gold clauses, including the many holders of U.S. government bonds stipulating payment in gold, were deprived of property rights, victimized by their own government.[6]

In the war emergency that followed the Japanese attack on Pearl Harbor, the government built an awesome command economy, suspending many individual rights. As Clinton Rossiter noted, "Of all the time-honored Anglo-Saxon liberties, the freedom of contract took the worst beating in the war."[7] Ten million men were conscripted. The Supreme Court refused even to review challenges of the constitutionality of the draft. Some 112,000 Japanese Americans, two-thirds of them U.S. citizens and not one of them proved guilty of a crime, were herded into concentration camps, losing their liberty and sustaining property losses estimated at some $400 million.[8] All quite constitutional, said the justices (*Hirabayashi v. United States,* 320 U.S. 81 [1943]; *Korematsu v. United States,* 323 U.S. 214 [1944]). Government orders allocated raw materials and plants; the government seized and operated production facilities and sometimes entire industries; and government officially rationed many consumer goods. None of these actions elicited so much as a ruling from the Supreme Court.[9] The sweeping price and rent controls exercised by the Office of Price

Administration did come before the Court, but the cases focused on procedural, not substantive, questions, and even then the Court found no reason to deny the government any of the powers it was exercising at the expense of private rights.[10] Said Justice Wiley Rutledge, one of the *least* single-mindedly bellicose justices, "Citizens must surrender or forego [*sic*] exercising rights which in other times could not be impaired" (321 U.S. at 461).[11] Justice Owen J. Roberts, in notable dissents, pronounced the Court's review of the government's price and rent controls a sham, "a solemn farce" (321 U.S. at 451, 458–60).

During the Korean War, the government reinstituted controls over raw materials, production, shipping, credit, wages, and prices. When the wage-price controls created a collective-bargaining impasse in the steel industry, threatening a nationwide strike, President Harry Truman ordered the secretary of commerce to seize the industry. In *Youngstown Sheet & Tube Co. v. Sawyer* (343 U.S. 579 [1952]), the Supreme Court, unconvinced that a genuine national emergency existed, ruled that the president had no constitutional authority for the seizure.[12] The ruling, however, in no way signified a triumph for individual rights or a significant check on the exercise of the government's emergency powers.[13] The case actually arose from a power struggle between Truman, by then a very unpopular president, and the Congress.[14] The Court's decision, really a ruling on separation of powers rather than on emergency power as such, found intolerable the president's failure to cite specific legislative authority for his action. On emergency powers, however, the justices' multiple opinions— seven in all—spoke more in favor than in opposition. The three dissenters argued that "a [presidential] power of seizure has been accepted throughout our history" (343 U.S. at 700). Justice Tom Clark, who supported the result but not the reasoning of the majority's ruling, agreed (p. 662). Justice Robert Jackson, in a concurring opinion, emphasized "the ease, expedition and safety with which Congress can grant and has granted large emergency powers" (p. 653). Only two justices, Hugo Black and William O. Douglas, explicitly rejected the claim of inherent presidential power to seize the industry in the absence of congressional authorization.[15] The outcome: the steel seizure itself was forbidden; however, given the justices' reasoning and the fragmentation of their opinions, the vulnerability of private-property rights to emergency suspension remained virtually as great as before.

In the 1970s, the National Emergencies Act (1976) and the International Emergency Economic Powers Act (1977) imposed new procedural requirements but did little to detract from the substance of presidential emergency powers, which continued to be employed routinely.[16] Under emergency decrees, the government subsequently forbade American citizens to engage in a variety of travel, commercial, and financial transactions with the citizens or governments of designated countries, including Cuba, Iran, Libya, Syria, South Africa, and Nicaragua.

In the 1980s, Supreme Court rulings sustained a wide scope for the exercise of presidential emergency powers. The congressional veto case (*Immigration and Naturalization Service v. Chadha*, 103 S. Ct. 2764 [1983]) effectively demolished the check of a concurrent resolution as provided in the National Emergencies Act. In *Dames & Moore v. Regan* (101 S. Ct. 2972 [1981]), the Court gave broad construction to the president's power under the International Emergency Economic Powers Act, endorsing President Jimmy Carter's use of that act first to block Iranian funds held in the United States and later to compel their return to Iran (thereby nullifying certain attachments issued by U.S. courts) as part of his effort to secure the release of American hostages. Equally significant was the Court's ruling on the scope of executive power to deal with such foreign-policy disputes in the absence of statutory authority. While holding that the International Emergency Economic Powers Act gave President Ronald Reagan no statutory authority to "suspend" U.S. citizens' claims against Iran pursuant to President Carter's agreement with the Iranian government, the Court nevertheless ruled that the president did not lack *constitutional* power to terminate the claims. Further erosion of the restraints on the president stipulated in the National Emergencies Act and the International Emergency Economic Powers Act came in *Regan v. Wald* (104 S. Ct. 3026 [1984]), where the Court allowed the executive branch to impose a major new curtailment of private travel to Cuba without a declaration of national emergency or compliance with the procedural requirements of the National Emergencies Act.[17]

The outcome: American citizens have been forbidden to travel to various countries, to borrow or buy from or to lend or sell to the citizens or governments of various countries, to fulfill the terms of valid contracts, or to pursue in U.S. courts legal remedies for injuries and takings. Far from having their rights to life, liberty, and property upheld by the federal government, Americans have been routinely deprived of such rights under declarations of emergency and even by government emergency action absent such a declaration.

Three Loci of the Constitution

Instructed to find the Constitution, most people would go to the bookshelf and take down a copy of the constitutional document. "This is it," they would declare, "and it says right here that. . . ." For some purposes, the constitutional document is all we need to consult. It stipulates that every state shall have two senators, that the vice president shall be president of the Senate, that only natural-born citizens may become president, and so forth. Sure enough, we may confidently expect that all such unambiguous prescriptions will be observed in practice—at all events, they have been for more than two hundred years (except during the upheavals of the Civil War and Reconstruction).

We will search the constitutional document in vain, however, for provisions relating to emergency powers. No such powers are mentioned. If the Framers intended the powers of federal officials or the rights of private citizens to be any different in national emergencies, it is curious that they neglected to express that intention in the Sacred Text.

A slightly more sophisticated searcher, however, would look for the Constitution not just in the document itself but in the several hundred volumes of U.S. Supreme Court reports. The Constitution, as Charles Evans Hughes once bluntly said, "is what the judges say it is."[18] Indeed, it must be so, because, after all, the meanings to be given to such expressions as "commerce among the several states," "due process of law," "necessary and proper," or "cruel and unusual punishments" are far from transparent; indeed, they are, and always have been, vigorously contested. As Charles A. Beard observed, "dispute has raged among men of strong minds and pure hearts over the meanings of these cloud-covered words and phrases."[19] The verbal ambiguities must be clarified if the terms of the constitutional document are to receive practical application. All but the naive and the disingenuous recognize, however, that the justices do not—indeed cannot—merely "interpret" the Constitution, doing no more than "finding" the law it contains. As Lawrence M. Friedman writes, "The Court goes far beyond interpretation. The Court invents and expands constitutional doctrine; some of this doctrine is connected to the text by gossamer threads, if at all."[20] There is nothing especially modern about such judicial practice; the Supreme Court has been making law throughout its history.

The Court has been reluctant to pronounce a clear national-emergency doctrine. To do so would reveal too starkly that the Court effectively disappears from the governmental scene from time to time, an embarrassing admission that would detract from judicial majesty. Even when validating extraordinary government powers—and hence the government's suppression of personal rights ostensibly protected by the Normal Constitution—as it did in *Wilson v. New* and *Blaisdell,* the Court has taken pains to deny that emergency as such alters the Constitution. In constitutional matters as elsewhere, however, actions speak louder than words.

Which brings us to the third locus of the Constitution. Unlike the document itself or the Supreme Court's written decisions, this Constitution is diffuse; it is all around us; it is what we might call the *constitutional system.* Recognition of a constitution in this sense goes back at least as far as Aristotle, who remarks in his *Politics* that "[t]he words constitution and government have the same meaning." In this most fundamental sense, the Constitution is, as Beard observed, "what living men and women think it is, recognize as such, carry into action, and obey."[21] The constitutional system comprises "the entire network of attitudes, norms, behaviors, and expectations among elites and publics that surround and support the written instrument,"[22] as well as, one might add, the

Court's pronouncements. Herman Pritchett observes that "[t]he constitutional system is not separate from the political system, but a necessary part of it, performing the vital function of giving order and structure to the processes of policy formation."[23] The constitutional system, then, is nothing less than the conglomerate of beliefs, behaviors, and institutions that actually determine the structure of government powers and enforceable private rights and the processes whereby these powers and rights are altered.[24]

Clearly, the Crisis Constitution is and long has been as much a part of the American constitutional system as the Normal Constitution. If you cared to place a bet, you could confidently put your money on the prospect that in the next national emergency—real or contrived—the federal government will extend its powers at the expense of private rights to life, liberty, and property. Indeed, as I write, early in 2002, we are in the midst of just such an episode.[25]

Why the Crisis Constitution?

Perhaps the best way to understand how the Crisis Constitution became embedded in the constitutional system is to examine the major episodes of its development, asking of each: Might it have been different? For each episode, it turns out, one can scarcely imagine that, given the political realities and the prevailing crisis conditions, the outcome could have been avoided. By considering why these events were so likely to happen as they did, one may gain a deeper appreciation of the U.S. constitutional system and the Supreme Court's role in it.

Consider first whether the Court might have found the Adamson Act unconstitutional in 1917. What would have been the consequence of such a ruling? Presumably a national railroad strike would have occurred, causing, as the Court put it, the "destruction of interstate commerce" and the "infinite injury to the public interest" that the Court considered imminent. Bad enough, but even greater disaster loomed. The United States stood on the brink of war. (The Court announced its decision on March 20; the United States declared war on April 6.) Thomas Gregory, the attorney general at the time, later recalled that Chief Justice Edward White "knew, as we all knew, that we were on the very verge of war; for the moment he forgot the facts of the case that was before him and his prophetic eye was resting on the immediate future when every proper energy of our country would be called upon to sustain it in its hour of greatest need."[26] The Court's majority was unwilling to issue a ruling fraught with danger to the military strength of the nation, no matter what the Normal Constitution might require. In retrospect, the most remarkable aspect of the ruling in *Wilson v. New* is that four justices dissented, William R. Day and Mahlon Pitney recording vigorous opposition to the majority's derogation from private-property rights in the crisis.

The division within the Court disappeared completely, however, when the justices ruled on the constitutionality of the military draft in 1918: that decision was unanimous. Under the prevailing political and social conditions, permeated by war hysteria, superheated patriotism, and vigilante attacks on "slackers," the ruling was well-nigh inevitable.[27] Men were, after all, being thrown into jail merely for questioning the constitutionality of the draft. The attorney general went so far as to request the aid of the American Protective League, a private organization of superpatriots, to locate draft resisters. Members of the league conducted numerous "slacker raids," made some forty thousand citizens' arrests, and investigated about 3 million suspected subversives.[28] Leon Friedman argues that the draft-law cases "were based upon superficial arguments, disregard of substantial historical evidence, and undue deference to the exigencies of the First World War—in short, that they were incorrectly decided."[29] Nonetheless, one can understand why the justices chose to transcend the Normal Constitution and to uphold the draft: without it, the government's war effort would have collapsed. The 2,820,000 draftees made up about 70 percent of the U.S. Army,[30] and no doubt many of the volunteers came forward only because of the draft. Patriots themselves, the justices simply were not willing to pay such a high price to sustain the Normal Constitution, especially when political elites throughout the land were howling for conscription. Besides, had the Court declared the draft unconstitutional, the executive branch probably would have ignored the ruling, leaving the Court defeated, embarrassed, and diminished in constitutional status. "[I]t is an axiom of constitutional justice that any decision which the Court thinks will not be enforced will probably not be made";[31] and "judges who find themselves 'powerless in fact' are apt to declare themselves 'powerless in law.'"[32]

Might the Supreme Court have upheld private-property rights in the Minnesota mortgage-moratorium case? Of course, it might have—where human judgment is determinative, anything is possible, and the actual decision rested on only a five-to-four margin. Again, however, the Court's ruling accords well with a view of the Court as belonging to, rather than hovering above, the constitutional system. Farmers had suffered disproportionately in the Great Contraction of 1929–33. Caught between drastically reduced farm prices and less-deflated nonfarm prices, and faced with fixed (nominal) dollar obligations for taxes and for interest and principal on mortgage loans, hundreds of thousands had lost their homes and sources of livelihood at a time when alternative opportunities were diminishing daily. Angry and frustrated, some had resorted to violence, and many others had brought ominous political pressures to bear on state legislatures.[33] To strike down, in January 1934, the mortgage-moratorium laws already enacted by twenty-two states would have risked setting off an explosion of farmer protest and perhaps widespread violence. The Court's ruling, in Chief Justice Hughes's words, would allow Minnesota—and by implication, all other states—to prevent "the immediate and literal enforcement of contractual obligations by temporary and conditional restraints where vital public interests would otherwise suffer" (*Home Building v. Blaisdell*, 290 U.S. at 440). Forced to choose between upholding the Normal Constitution and averting a potential social and political calamity, the majority decided to avert the calamity.[34]

When the Court ruled on the gold-clause cases early in 1935, it faced—as it often does in cases involving public policies with pervasive impacts—an executive fait accompli. The government had taken possession of the nation's monetary gold stock; it had voided all contractual gold clauses and thereby prompted a multitude of changes in specific contractual performance. Was the Court now to say that the government must return gold coins and certificates to millions of citizens who had surrendered them and that all those who had paid legal tender instead of gold must turn around and pay the gold as initially stipulated in their contracts? The far-reaching economic consequences of such a ruling—the business chaos of which Attorney General Homer Cummings had warned the Court—must have given the justices pause.[35] The administration was terrified of an adverse decision. "Roosevelt and some of his advisors considered trying to destabilize the gold market ... in order to suggest to the Supreme Court and the public the extent of the chaos that might occur if the government lost."[36] So disastrous did the president consider an adverse ruling on the gold clause of government bonds that, in anticipation, he prepared a radio address announcing that he would not enforce such a ruling.[37] Beyond the utter confusion of the marketplace lay the disruption of the administration's monetary policy, now almost two years old. The attorney general's argument before the Court emphasized the doctrine of emergency powers and the gravity of the prevailing depression crisis; the "power of self-preservation," he declared, required transcending the "supposed sanctity and inviolability of contractual obligations." Again, given the prevailing economic and political conditions, the remarkable aspect of the decision is that four justices dissented—Justice James McReynolds read their objections with muttered asides that "the Constitution is gone" and "this is Nero at his worst."[38]

The Supreme Court's virtual abdication during World War II reflected, even more clearly than the gold-clause cases, a fait accompli by the legislative and executive branches of government. The political branches had created a full-blown command economy, complete with conscription of soldiers; physical allocations of raw materials; confiscation of private facilities; controls of wages, prices, and rents; rationing of consumer goods; and a great deal more.[39] Was the Court, deciding cases in 1944 after such policies had been in force for years, to say that they were unconstitutional? It is inconceivable. It would, in any event, have been futile, as the Court well understood. "[M]ost judicial leaders hoped at all cost to avoid finding themselves in situations of judicial defiance of measures and actions clearly geared to the war effort and national security."[40] The Court occupied "the position of a private on sentry duty accosting a commanding general without his pass."[41] The best that it could do was to continue to go through the motions of judicial review, biding its time in anticipation of the return of normal conditions, when the Normal Constitution would reassert itself over the Crisis Constitution and genuine judicial review would again become feasible.[42]

Besides, as Clinton Rossiter noted in 1948, "the Court, too, likes to win wars."[43] Edward Corwin, expressing himself somewhat more circumspectly, observed in 1947 that "in total war, the Court necessarily loses some part of its normal freedom of decision and becomes assimilated, like the rest of society, to the mechanism of the national defense." Thus, "the restrictive clauses of the Constitution are not ... automatically suspended, but the scope of the rights to which they extend is capable of being reduced in the face of the urgencies of war, sometimes even to the vanishing point.... [T]he Court will not intrude its veto while war is flagrant."[44] For the most part, the suppression of private rights during the war was not even challenged in the courts; or, if challenges arose, the Supreme Court, dominated by the so-called War Hawks (Frankfurter, Stone, Black, and Douglas), chose not to review them.[45]

Events during World War II demonstrate in its clearest form the logic of the Crisis Constitution.[46] When elites and masses alike believe that national emergency is upon them, they call on the government to "do something." The political branches, acting more or less autonomously, adopt policies. By their very nature, such policies place burdens on the public. The greater the burdens, the more likely is public resistance. In the extreme, public resistance jeopardizes the government itself. Anticipating such resistance, governments take steps to conceal or obscure the sacrifices entailed by its policies, invariably substituting (cost-hiding) command-and-control measures for (cost-revealing) fiscal-and-market means of resource allocation. The necessary implication of this substitution is the attenuation or destruction of private rights that the Normal Constitution previously protected.

After the fall of France and even more so after the Japanese attack on Pearl Harbor and the ensuing declarations of war, Americans demanded effective military action to defend the nation and to subdue its powerful enemies. The political branches responded by imposing a sweeping command-and-control system. The Supreme Court could not have prevented this development even had it wanted to do so. "The country at large was prepared to accede to the law of [perceived] necessity rather than to cogent constitutional analysis."[47] The Court must rely on the executive branch for the enforcement of its rulings.[48] As Aristotle said, "[T]hose who carry arms can always determine the fate of the constitution." Even more fundamental than arms themselves, however—because arms must be wielded by people conscious of what they are doing—is the dominant ideology. Therefore, "[m]etaconstitutional limits determine what constitutional provisions [can] be tolerated if enacted."[49] Those limits change during national emergencies. People anxiously seeking security against looming threats to the economic viability, independence, or survival of the nation submit far more readily to a deprivation of normal private rights. Many people who ordinarily would have refused to comply with intrusive government directives accepted them during World War II as appropriate to the prevailing national condition.[50] Only because of such public support did the government's emergency measures prove reasonably effective.

In sum, the Crisis Constitution, like the Normal Constitution, rests on a broad ideological base. Public attitudes, values, norms, and expectations condition the structure and processes of government powers and private rights in both cases.[51] In the twentieth century, the American people came to expect, tolerate, and in many instances demand that the Normal Constitution be displaced during national emergencies.[52] Government officials understand this public disposition and accordingly seek their own objectives within the altered constraints. The dualism of our fundamental institutions might conceivably be unproblematic: we would act according to the Crisis Constitution during national emergencies and according to the Normal Constitution at all other times.[53] History, however, has not conformed to such a simple pattern.

A Merger of the Two Constitutions?

In fact, the Normal Constitution to which we revert after a national emergency is never the same as it was before the crisis. To some degree, aspects of the Crisis Constitution, as expressed in judicial interpretation and even more so in the body of belief that supports the constitutional system, are incorporated into the Normal Constitution.[54] Such legacies marked the aftermaths of both world wars and the Great Depression.

After World War I, the Normal Constitution included massive government participation in credit markets, communications, and transportation industries as well as enduring judicial precedents for rent controls, military conscription, and the suppression of free speech.[55]

The Great Depression, of course, brought a profusion of government restraints and regulatory agencies as well as a corresponding constriction of private-property rights. Rossiter noted that "the emergency practices of the Year of Crisis [1933] wrought several lasting alterations in the Constitutional structure," including "important permanent delegations of crisis power . . . ; a greatly expanded administration; a marked breakdown of the federal principle; and a general increase of presidential power based on executive leadership in the lawmaking process and the delegation of power."[56] Between 1937 and 1942, as nearly all constitutional scholars acknowledge, a veritable Constitutional

Revolution took place—"the product of emergency conditions, the threat to the Court and the reconstruction of its personnel by President Franklin D. Roosevelt"[57]—submerging the doctrine of substantive due process in economic matters and giving unrestricted scope to federal regulatory power.

Then the events of World War II carried the Crisis Constitution to new heights, and the legacies were legion. Even after enactment of a joint resolution repealing many of the wartime statutes in July 1947, more than one hundred wartime statutory provisions remained in force; official states of emergency continued; and various new emergency measures, including a rent-control act and a peacetime military conscription law, were enacted.[58] Corwin observed that after the war, for the first time in U.S. history, the country did not return to a "peacetime Constitution." Instead, the Normal Constitution now included, in his words:

1. the attribution to Congress of a legislative power of indefinite scope;

2. the attribution to the President of the power and duty to stimulate constantly the positive exercise of this indefinite power for enlarged social objectives;

3. the right of Congress to delegate its powers ad libitum to the President for the achievement of such enlarged social objectives ... ;

4. the attribution to the President of a broad prerogative in the meeting of "emergencies" defined by himself and in the creation of executive agencies to assist him;

5. a progressively expanding replacement of the judicial process by the administrative process in the enforcement of the law—sometimes even of constitutional law.[59]

In the fifty-seven years that have passed since Corwin drew up this summary, nothing has changed.[60] Thus, the Normal Constitution of the post–World War II era has fully validated big government in the sense of an active, powerful, highly arbitrary government far less restrained by the constitutional checks and balances of the old Normal Constitution, a system that once restrained government officials' interventions if not their ambitions.

Emergency powers as such continue to undergird the government's denial of numerous private rights, especially in relation to international commercial and financial transactions and travel. In upholding government actions under the International Emergency Economic Powers Act, the Court quoted with approval a lower-court decision noting that the act's language "is sweeping and unqualified. It provides broadly that the President may void or nullify the 'exercising [by any person of] any right, power or privilege with respect to ... any property in which any foreign country has any interest'" (*Dames & Moore v. Regan*, 101 S. Ct. 2972 [1981] at 2982). Thus, even in the early 1980s, as normal a time as one can expect in our era, the Crisis Constitution continued to override and displace the Normal Constitution.

Can Anything Be Done?

Effective protection of private rights against future government invasion under color of emergency is unlikely. The experience of the recent past has shown that the procedural safeguards stipulated in the National Emergencies Act have no substantive effect. In any event, the problem is not procedure; it is substance— and the abuse of substantive powers.

Not much hope can be placed in a reconstituted Supreme Court, one more devoted to individual rights and the restoration of the old Normal Constitution. Even if such judges might be found and appointed—a tremendous long shot—their resistance to the Crisis Constitution would not have more than a temporary effect in an emergency. This lesson we have learned from the constitutional crisis of the mid-1930s.[61] Even a Court that included the Four Horsemen, a Court willing to plunge a constitutional dagger into the collectivist heart of the New Deal, could not hold out indefinitely in the face of preponderant public support for the government's policies. Even if stubborn justices do not buckle under to public opinion in an emergency, they must eventually retire or die—to be replaced by more pliant judges, such as Black, Reed, Frankfurter, and Douglas. Although the Court does not simply follow the election returns, neither does it completely ignore them (indeed, it may on occasion even decide them, as it did in 2000). Even George Sutherland, as staunch a friend as the Normal Constitution ever had, expressed doubt that judges "are indifferent to what others think about their decisions" and avowed that he himself was not indifferent.[62] Justice Owen Roberts, the "swing man" who more than anyone else bore responsibility for the Court's turnaround in 1937, later observed: "Looking back, it is difficult to see how the Court could have resisted the popular urge." He referred obliquely to the "tremendous strain and the threat to the existing Court, of which I was fully conscious."[63] On the Court, as in other branches of government, good men are not enough. Before the fierce winds of adverse political actions and hostile public opinion, even the best judge will eventually bend and break.

The Normal Constitution can be preserved against the inroads of the Crisis Constitution only if the politically influential elites who make policies and mold the opinions of the masses are willing to resist the passions of national emergency. (Such resistance is, or at least once was, possible. Recall how Grover Cleveland's administration and the Supreme Court dealt with the crisis of the 1890s.)[64] People must understand that reversion to the status quo ante will not occur, that private rights once surrendered are unlikely ever to be recovered fully. If such understanding and a concomitant commitment to individual rights were widespread, we would have little to fear. If the dominant ideology gives strong support to the Normal Constitution, it will survive, no matter what else happens.

If the dominant ideology does not give strong support to the Normal Constitution, however, that constitution will eventually be overwhelmed by the Crisis Constitution. Step by step, a ratcheting loss of private rights will attend each episode of national emergency—and we may as well admit that such emergencies are inevitable. (The current one, of course, was precipitated by the September 11, 2001, attacks on the World Trade Center and the Pentagon.) Unfortunately, at present, elites and masses in the United States, with only a few notable exceptions, have neither an appreciation of the ratchet process nor a strong commitment to the protection of individual rights to life, liberty, and property.[65] Therefore, the most likely prospect is for further expansion of the Crisis Constitution and a corresponding loss of private rights. Today, in connection with the U.S. government's so-called war on terrorism, this prospect is becoming a reality before our eyes.

Notes

1. Alexander Hamilton, John Jay, and James Madison, *The Federalist* (New York: Modern Library, n.d.); *Ex parte Milligan*, 4 Wallace 2 (1866); *Home Building and Loan v. Blaisdell*, 290 U.S. 398 (1934) at 448-83 (Sutherland dissenting).

2. Clinton Rossiter, *Constitutional Dictatorship: Crisis Government in the Modern Democracies* (Princeton, N.J.: Princeton University Press, 1948), pp. 223-39, 241-42; Alfred H. Kelly, Winfred A. Harbison, and Herman Belz, *The American Constitution: Its Origins and Development* (New York: Norton, 1983), pp. 229-327; Jeffrey Rogers Hummel, *Emancipating Slaves, Enslaving Free Men: A History of the American Civil War* (Chicago and La Salle, Ill.: Open Court, 1996), pp. 254-59, 265-68.

3. Edward S. Corwin, *Total War and the Constitution* (New York: Knopf, 1947), pp. 87-88; Paul L. Murphy, *The Constitution in Crisis Times, 1918-1969* (New York: Harper Torchbooks, 1972), p. 13, n. 34.

4. Lee J. Alston, "Farm Foreclosure Moratorium Legislation: A Lesson from the Past," *American Economic Review* 74 (June 1984), p. 446.

5. Gore as quoted in Benjamin M. Anderson, *Economics and the Public Welfare: A Financial and Economic History of the United States, 1914-46* (Indianapolis, Ind.: Liberty Press, 1979), pp. 316-17.

6. According to Randall Kroszner, "Roughly $100 billion (nominal) of debt with gold clauses was outstanding during this period." See "Is It Better to Forgive Than to Receive? Repudiation of the Gold Indexation Clause in Long-Term Debt During the Great Depression," unpublished ms., November 1999, p. 2.

7. *Constitutional Dictatorship*, p. 279.

8. J. Woodford Howard Jr., *Mr. Justice Murphy: A Political Biography* (Princeton, N.J.: Princeton University Press, 1968), p. 301.

9. Alpheus Thomas Mason, *Harlan Fiske Stone: Pillar of the Law* (New York: Viking Press, 1956), pp. 696–97.

10. Clinton Rossiter, *The Supreme Court and the Commander in Chief,* exp. ed. with additions by Richard P. Longaker (Ithaca, N.Y.: Cornell University Press, 1976), pp. 97–100.

11. Leading cases were *Yakus v. United States*, 321 U.S. 414 (1944), *Bowles v. Willingham*, 321 U.S. 503 (1944), and *Steuart v. Bowles*, 322 U.S. 398 (1944).

12. Maeva Marcus, *Truman and the Steel Seizure Case: The Limits of Presidential Power* (New York: Columbia University Press, 1977), pp. 225–27.

13. Edward S. Corwin, *The Constitution and What It Means Today,* revised by Harold W. Chase and Craig R. Ducat (Princeton, N.J.: Princeton University Press, 1974), pp. 112, 157.

14. Marcus, *Truman and the Steel Seizure Case,* pp. 17–37, 83–101, 258–59.

15. Ibid., pp. 216; Alan I. Bigel, *The Supreme Court on Emergency Powers, Foreign Affairs, and Protection of Civil Liberties, 1935–1975* (Lanham, Md.: University Press of America, 1986), pp. 135–50.

16. Robert Higgs and Charlotte Twight, "National Emergency and the Erosion of Private Property Rights," *Cato Journal* 6 (winter 1987), pp. 757–62; Michal R. Belknap, "The New Deal and the Emergency Powers Doctrine," *Texas Law Review* 62 (1983), pp. 100–101.

17. Higgs and Twight, "National Emergency," pp. 769–71.

18. Hughes as quoted in Corwin, *The Constitution and What It Means Today,* p. xv.

19. Charles A. Beard, "The Living Constitution," *Annals of the American Academy of Political and Social Sciences* 185 (1936), p. 30.

20. Lawrence M. Friedman, *American Law* (New York: Norton, 1984), p. 181.

21. "The Living Constitution," p. 34.

22. Walter Dean Burnham, "The Constitution, Capitalism, and the Need for Rationalized Regulation," in *How Capitalistic Is the Constitution?* edited by Robert A. Goldwin and William A. Schambra (Washington, D.C.: American Enterprise Institute, 1982), p. 78.

23. Herman Pritchett, "Constitutional Law: I. Introduction," in *International Encyclopedia of the Social Sciences,* edited by David L. Sills (New York: Crowell Collier and Macmillan, 1968), vol. 3, p. 298.

24. Herman Belz, "Changing Conceptions of Constitutionalism in the Era of World War II and the Cold War," *Journal of American History* 59 (December 1972), p. 664; James Dale Davidson, "The Limits of Constitutional Determinism," in *Constitutional Economics: Containing the Economic Powers of Government,* edited by Richard B. McKenzie (Lexington, Mass.: Lexington Books, 1984), pp. 61–87.

25. Dana Milbank, "In War, It's Power to the President. In Aftermath of Attacks, Bush White House Claims Authority Rivaling FDR," *Washington Post,* November 20, 2001; Robert Higgs, "Crisis-Induced Losses of Liberties," *Wall Street Journal,* January 31, 2002.

26. Gregory as quoted in Belknap, "The New Deal and the Emergency Powers Doctrine," p. 80, n. 93.

27. Rossiter, *The Supreme Court and the Commander in Chief,* p. 95; Murphy, *The Constitution in Crisis Times,* pp. 12–13; Kelly, Harbison, and Belz, *The American Constitution,* pp. 447, 526–30; Robert Higgs, *Crisis and Leviathan: Critical Episodes in the Growth of American Government* (New York: Oxford University Press, 1987), pp. 123–58.

28. Herbert McClosky and John Zaller, *The American Ethos: Public Attitudes Toward Capitalism and Democracy* (Cambridge, Mass.: Harvard University Press, 1984), p. 40.

29. Leon Friedman, "Conscription and the Constitution: The Original Understanding," *Michigan Law Review* 67 (May 1969), reprinted in *The Military Draft: Selected Readings on Conscription,* edited by Martin Anderson (Stanford, Calif.: Hoover Institution Press, 1982), p. 233.

30. U.S. Bureau of the Census, *Historical Statistics of the United States, Colonial Times to 1970* (Washington, D.C.: U.S. Government Printing Office, 1975), p. 1140.

31. Philippa Strum, *The Supreme Court and "Political Questions": A Study in Judicial Evasion* (Tuscaloosa: University of Alabama Press, 1974), p. 4.

32. Howard, *Mr. Justice Murphy,* p. 337.

33. Joel Francis Paschal, *Mr. Justice Sutherland: A Man Against the State* (Princeton, N.J.: Princeton University Press, 1951), p. 167; Charles A. Leonard, *A Search for a Judicial Philosophy: Mr. Justice Roberts and the Constitutional Revolution of 1937* (Port Washington, N.Y.: Kennikat Press, 1971), p. 82; Murphy, *The Constitution in Crisis Times,* p. 110, n. 28; Lee J. Alston, "Farm Foreclosures in the United States During the Interwar Period," *Journal of Economic History* 43 (December 1983), p. 886; and Alston, "Farm Foreclosure Moratorium Legislation," p. 447.

34. Samuel Hendel, *Charles Evans Hughes and the Supreme Court* (New York: King's Crown Press, 1951), pp. 180–81.

35. Paschal, *Mr. Justice Sutherland,* p. 181; Leonard, *A Search for a Judicial Philosophy,* p. 57; Kelly, Harbison, and Belz, *The American Constitution,* p. 489.

36. Kroszner, "Is It Better to Forgive than to Receive?" p. 11 (relying on the diary of Treasury Secretary Henry Morgenthau).

37. Merlo J. Pusey, *Charles Evans Hughes* (New York: Columbia University Press, 1963), pp. 735–36.

38. Cummings and McReynolds as quoted in Murphy, *The Constitution in Crisis Times,* pp. 137–38.

39. Higgs, *Crisis and Leviathan,* pp. 196–236 and sources cited there.

40. Murphy, *The Constitution in Crisis Times,* p. 224.

41. Mason, *Harlan Fiske Stone,* p. 665.

42. Corwin, *Total War and the Constitution,* p. 177.

43. *The Supreme Court and the Commander in Chief,* p. 91.

44. *Total War and the Constitution,* pp. 177, 131, respectively.

45. Mason, *Harlan Fiske Stone,* pp. 675, 679–81.

46. Higgs, *Crisis and Leviathan,* pp. 62–67.

47. Kelly, Harbison, and Belz, *The American Constitution,* p. 553.

48. Strum, *The Supreme Court and "Political Questions,"* p. 3; Friedman, *American Law,* p. 196; Bigel, *The Supreme Court on Emergency Powers,* pp. 190–93.

49. Davidson, "The Limits of Constitutional Determinism," p. 68.

50. Rossiter, *Constitutional Dictatorship*, pp. 4, 11, 276, 305; Bernard Schwartz, *The Supreme Court: Constitutional Revolution in Retrospect* (New York: Ronald Press, 1957), p. 293.

51. Mancur Olson, "Comment," in *Constitutional Economics*, ed. McKenzie, pp. 93–94.

52. Kelly, Harbison, and Belz, *The American Constitution*, pp. 554, 556.

53. Strangely, in view of the voluminous evidence to the contrary in their own book, Kelly, Harbison, and Belz assert that the U.S. constitutional system has in fact demonstrated such "remarkable flexibility." They claim that "it could adjust rapidly to the requirement of war and then return as rapidly to the institutions of peace." See *The American Constitution*, p. 571.

54. Corwin, *Total War and the Constitution*, p. 172; Rossiter, *Constitutional Dictatorship*, pp. 13, 295, 313; Kelly, Harbison, and Belz, *The American Constitution*, pp. 517, 519, 565, 574–75; Higgs, *Crisis and Leviathan*, passim.

55. Higgs, *Crisis and Leviathan*, pp. 148–56.

56. *Constitutional Dictatorship*, p. 264.

57. Hendel, *Charles Evans Hughes*, p. 275.

58. Kelly, Harbison, and Belz, *The American Constitution*, pp. 574–75.

59. *Total War and the Constitution*, pp. 172, 179.

60. Higgs, *Crisis and Leviathan*, pp. 237–57.

61. On the pressures that promoted the Constitutional Revolution, see Hendel, *Charles Evans Hughes*, pp. 250–53; Paschal, *Mr. Justice Sutherland*, p. 206; Mason, *Harlan Fiske Stone*, pp. 437–39, 456, 463; Pusey, *Charles Evans Hughes*, p. 747; Leonard, *A Search for a Judicial Philosophy*, pp. 2, 56, 92–93, 124–25, 136–57; Murphy, *The Constitution in Crisis Times*, pp. 154–69; and Frankfurter as quoted in Marcus, *Truman and the Steel Seizure Case*, p. 334 n. 25.

62. Paschal, *Mr. Justice Sutherland*, p. 200.

63. Roberts as quoted in Leonard, *A Search for a Judicial Philosophy*, pp. 144, 155.

64. Higgs, *Crisis and Leviathan*, pp. 77–105.

65. McClosky and Zaller, *The American Ethos;* Antonin Scalia, "Economic Affairs as Human Affairs," *Cato Journal* 4 (winter 1985): 708–9; Higgs, *Crisis and Leviathan*, pp. 192–95, 233–34, 256–57; Robert Higgs, "The Era of Big Government Is Not Over," *The Good Society* 9 (1999): 97–100 (chap. 33 in the present collection), and sources cited there.

27

The Myth of War Prosperity

On October 22, 1990, while the Bush administration was hurrying to build up military forces in Saudi Arabia and its environs, the *Wall Street Journal* sounded a sour note. A three-column headline proclaimed, "Gulf War Might Not Aid U.S. Economy." The subhead explained, as if it were solving a puzzle, "Mideast Scenario Differs from Past Conflicts." Clearly, the presumption was that war and economic prosperity go together, that any other relationship would be an anomaly. The experts quoted in the article agreed that previously war had been an "unmitigated plus." Historically, they averred, military buildups had been "stimulative," putting the economy "on an upward track."

The *Journal* story began by stating matter-of-factly that "it took World War II to pull the U.S. out of the Great Depression." Undoubtedly, this episode serves as the classic case. Although people may argue about the economic effects of World War I or the Vietnam War, almost everyone—expert and lay person alike—believes that the experience of World War II is unambiguous: the war unquestionably got the economy out of the depression. History texts tell the tale in dreary monotony. The experience is commonly regarded as the strongest evidence in support of the Keynesian prescription for curing lackluster macroeconomic performance.

Despite its nearly universal acceptance, however, the standard interpretation is wrong. It rests on evidence that will not bear scrutiny. It exemplifies bad economics and bad history. In large part, the prevailing misconceptions arise from the uncritical use of aggregative concepts and measures of economic performance. Rarely does anyone bother to ask what these familiar indexes really measure or what they really mean. Yet the standard concepts and measures of national income accounting and the explanations derived from orthodox macroeconomic theories, whatever merits they may have in application to a peacetime market economy, lose their meaning in application to a command economy. The prevailing misinterpretations of the performance of the U.S. economy during the 1940s have arisen because economists and historians have failed to appreciate that the U.S. economy during the war was a command economy.

The Consensus

What makes people believe that "the war got the economy out of the depression"? The evidence adduced usually features (1) a great decline in the standard measure of unemployment, (2) a great increase in the standard measure of real gross national product (GNP), and (3) a slight increase in the standard measure of real private consumption.[1]

Most writers understand the entire episode of apparent business-cycle boom during the war years as an obvious validation of the simple Keynesian model: enormous government spending, financed mainly by selling bonds and creating new money, spurred the military economy itself and had multiplier effects on the civilian economy, the upshot being increased real output and employment and decreased unemployment.

The authors of economic history textbooks rely on data taken from standard statistical compilations, either the Commerce Department's *Historical Statistics* or the annual reports of the President's Council of Economic Advisers (CEA), to document their accounts of economic performance during the 1940s. No one expresses any awareness that those data—for example, the GNP measures based on the Commerce Department's concept of national product—might be problematic. The standard numbers receive almost universal acceptance at face value.

Employment and Unemployment

The standard measure of the unemployment rate (the number of persons officially unemployed as a percent of civilian labor force) shows that the rate fell greatly between 1940 and 1944, from 14.6 percent to 1.2 percent. Michael Darby's measure of the unemployment rate, which does not count those in New Deal "emergency government employment" as unemployed, shows that the rate fell from 9.5 percent to 1.2 percent. Either measure signals a virtual disappearance of unemployment during the war, but in the circumstances neither measure means what it is commonly taken to mean.

The buildup of an armed force of more than 12 million persons by mid-1945 made inevitable an enormous decline of the standard unemployment rate. The welfare significance of this decline, however, is far from the usual one. Of the 16 million persons who served in the uniformed armed forces at some time during the war, 10 million were conscripted, and many of those who volunteered did so only to avoid the draft and the consequent likelihood of assignment to the infantry. The civilian labor force during 1940–45 ranged from 54 million to 56 million. Therefore, the 12 million serving in the armed forces in 1944–45, most of them under duress, constituted about 18 percent of the total (civilian plus military) labor force, itself much enlarged during the war.

In short, the country started in 1940 with an unemployment rate (Darby Concept) of 9.5 percent; the government then pulled the equivalent of 22 percent of the prewar labor force into the armed forces; and voilà, the unemployment rate dropped to a very low level. No one needs a macroeconomic model to understand this sequence of events. Given the magnitude of the draft, no plausible view of the economy is incompatible with the observed decline of the standard unemployment rate. Whether the government ran deficits or not, whether money stock increased or not, massive military conscription was bound to decrease dramatically the standard rate of unemployment.

Although the tight civilian labor market during the war reflected the creation of huge military employment, military "jobs" differed categorically. They ranged (sometimes within the same job) from the abjectly disgusting to the intolerably boring to the unspeakably horrifying. Whatever their qualities, they lasted for "the duration." Often they entailed substantial risks of death, dismemberment, and other physical and psychological injury; sustained involvement in combat drove many men insane. Physical casualties included 405,399 dead and 670,846 wounded. Thousands had to endure psychic and physical abuse, even torture, as prisoners of war. To make the military "jobs" commensurable with the civilian jobs—a common statistical procedure in studies of the war labor market—betrays a monumental obtuseness to the underlying realities. Too often have economists and historians appraised the economic benefits of the war to the civilian population as if those benefits had no causal connection with the horrors of the battlefield. In reality, all these events—economic as well as political and military, at home as well as overseas—were threads in the same blood-soaked tapestry.

To see more clearly what happened to the labor force, one can examine the part of the total (civilian plus military) labor force composing the labor "residuum"—that is, all those who are in the labor force but not in nondefense employment. This residuum includes the civilian unemployed plus uniformed members of the armed forces plus civilian employees of the armed forces plus everyone employed in the military supply industries. This measure rises from 17.6 percent in the fiscal year 1940 to more than 40 percent during the fiscal years 1943–45, then drops abruptly to about 10 percent during the fiscal years 1946–49.[2] The extraordinarily high level of the labor residuum during 1942–45 signals that the "prosperous" condition of the labor force during the war was spurious: official unemployment was virtually nonexistent, but four-tenths of the labor force was not being used to produce either consumer goods or capital goods capable of yielding consumer goods in the future. The sharp drop in the labor residuum between the fiscal year 1945 and the fiscal year 1946 marks the return of genuine prosperity.

Real Output

To find out what happened to real output during the war, historians usually consult *Historical Statistics*. Economists typically reach for the latest issue of the CEA annual report. Which source one consults makes a difference. Although the two series show roughly the same profile of real GNP during the 1940s, the Commerce Department version shown in the 1990 CEA report indicates (when indexed as 1939 = 100) a peak value of 192.7 in 1944 versus a peak value of 172.5 in 1944 in the series taken from *Historical Statistics*. The 12 percent difference is hardly negligible, even though it reflects only statistical, as opposed to conceptual, revisions made between 1970 and 1990. Both series show a sharp drop of real GNP between 1945 and 1946: 12 percent in the older series, 19 percent in the newer.

Economists and historians who employ the standard real GNP series seem generally unaware that the numbers may be conceptually problematic. By contrast, Simon Kuznets, a leading figure in the development of the national income accounts, expressed many concerns. In his monograph *National Product in Wartime* (1945), Kuznets discussed a number of issues that analysts must consider when deciding how to construct national-product measures for a nation at war. Noting that the "complexity of observable reality compels the investigator to select one set of assumptions from among many concerning the purpose, value, and scope of the economic activity," he observed that "a major war magnifies these conceptual difficulties, raising questions concerning the ends economic activity is made to pursue ... [and] the distinction between intermediate and final products." He noted that "war and peace type products ... cannot be added into a national product total until the differences in the valuation due to differences in the institutional mechanisms that determine their respective market prices are corrected for."[3]

In refined estimates of national product that Kuznets later produced, he made an adjustment for the steep decline in the relative prices of munitions during the war, and he deleted nondurable war output (pay and subsistence of the armed forces) from his estimate. The result was to eliminate most of the bulge of real GNP during the war years shown by the official Commerce Department data. He might have gone even further, however, to delete *all* government outlays for war purposes. The crucial question is: Does government war expenditure purchase a final good, and hence belong in GNP, or an intermediate good, and hence not belong?

William Nordhaus and James Tobin, in a monograph published in 1972, made numerous adjustments to the standard GNP concept to transform it into what they called a measure of economic welfare (MEW). They aimed to eliminate from GNP certain "activities that are evidently not directly sources of utility themselves but are regrettably necessary inputs to activities that may yield utility"; that is, they sought to eliminate spending that is "only instrumental."[4] Accordingly, they deleted—along with various other items—all national defense spending.

Following the lead of Nordhaus and Tobin, one arrives at a measure of real GNP that shows no wartime prosperity whatsoever. Now one sees that real GNP in 1944, which the Commerce Department variant shows at a peak, was 12 percent *lower* than it had been in 1941. Only with the end of the war did the economy at last break out of its fifteen-year substandard performance, jumping nearly 27 percent between 1945 and 1946.

Finally, one can make an even stronger argument for rejecting the orthodox account of changes in real GNP during the war. One can simply argue that outside a more or less competitive market framework, prices become meaningless; all presumption that price equals marginal cost vanishes, and therefore *no* theoretically justified estimate of real national product is possible. Although mainstream economists cannot be expected to accept this argument, I believe it is sound.

Real Consumption

Some writers who recognize that the expansion of real GNP during the war consisted overwhelmingly of military outputs nevertheless insist that real private consumption also increased. In Seymour Melman's colorful but otherwise representative portrayal, "the economy [was] producing more guns and more butter. Americans had never had it so good."[5]

This view is wrong. It fails to take sufficiently into account (1) the understatement of actual inflation by the official price indexes, (2) the deterioration of quality or disappearance from the market of many consumer goods, (3) the full effects of the rationing of many widely consumed items, and (4) the additional transaction costs borne and other sacrifices made by consumers in getting available goods. When one corrects the data to provide a more defensible estimate of real consumer well-being during the war, one finds that it declined.

During the war years, consumers suffered extraordinary welfare-diminishing changes. To get the available goods, millions of people had to move, many of them long distances, to centers of war production. After bearing extraordinary costs of relocation, they often found themselves crowded into poorer housing. Because of the disincentives created by rent controls, the housing got worse each year, as landlords reduced or eliminated maintenance and repairs. Transportation, even commuting to work, became difficult for many workers. No new cars were being produced. Used cars were hard to come by because of rationing, and they commanded steep prices on the black market. Gasoline and tires were rationed. Public transportation was crowded and inconvenient for many, as well as frequently preempted by the military. Of course, in addition to these privations, in literally thousands of particular ways, consumers lost their freedom of choice.

One must also recognize that while consumers were actually getting less, they were working harder, longer, and at greater physical risk in the workplace to get the available goods. The ratio of civilian employment to population (age fourteen and over) increased from 47.6 percent in 1940 to 57.9 percent in 1944, as many teenagers left school, women left their homes, and older people left retirement to work. The average workweek in manufacturing, where most of the new jobs were located, increased from 38.1 hours in 1940 to 45.2 hours in 1944; and the average workweek increased in most other industries as well, in bituminous coal mining by more than 50 percent. The rate of disabling injuries per hour worked in manufacturing rose by more than 30 percent between 1940 and a wartime peak in 1943. It is difficult to understand how working harder, longer, and more dangerously in return for a diminished flow of consumer goods comports with the description that "economically speaking, Americans had never had it so good."

Inappropriate Theories

None of the standard macroeconomic theories employed to account for the wartime experience provides an acceptable explanation. The standard models cannot do the job because none is a model of a command economy, and the United States during the years 1942–45 was a command economy. Regardless of the peculiarities of their assumptions, all the standard macroeconomic models presume the existence of genuine markets for commodities, factor services, and bonds.

None of these assumptions even approximates the conditions that prevailed during the war. Commodity markets were pervasively subject to controls: price controls, rationing, and in some cases outright prohibition in the consumer-goods markets; as well as price controls, prohibitions, priorities, conservation and limitation orders, quotas, set-asides, scheduling, allocations, and other restrictions in the markets for raw materials, components, and capital equipment. While taxes were raised enormously, many foods and raw materials received subsidies so that the price controls at the retail level would not drive suppliers from the market. Factor-service markets were no freer, and in some respects were less free, than the commodity markets—recall the 10 million men conscripted. Credit markets experienced total control, as the Federal Reserve undertook to reduce and allocate consumer credit and pegged the nominal interest rate on government bonds at a barely positive level. Two-thirds of the investment in manufacturing plants and equipment from July 1940 through June 1945 was financed by the government, and most of the remainder came forth in response to tax concessions and other de facto subsidies authorized in 1940 to stimulate the rearmament.

In sum, the U.S. economy during the years 1942–45 was the exact opposite of a free-market system. Every part of the economy was either directly controlled by the authorities or subject to drastic distortion because of its relations with suppliers and customers who were tightly controlled. To suppose that the economy allocated resources in response to prices set by the free play of demands and supplies in underlying markets for commodities, factor services, and bonds is to suppose a complete fiction. Hence, the assumptions that underlie standard macroeconomic models are unsatisfied by the empirical reality of the wartime economy.

The upsurge of military commodity production during the war—undeniably an awesome accomplishment when measured piece by piece in physical units of munitions—should not be viewed as an expansion phase of the ordinary business cycle, a phase that fits into the longer-term ebb and flow of the economy before and after the war. The war production surge was sui generis and must be understood on its own unique terms. Examining it carefully, we find that it bore no resemblance to what is normally understood by the term *prosperity.* The U.S. economy during the war was exactly what the slogan said, an arsenal. As such, it produced what the authorities ordered, using the materials and methods they required and charging the prices they dictated.

Caveat and Conclusion

I would not want my argument to be understood as pacifistic, and anyone who viewed it as such would be missing the point. In certain circumstances, people may prefer to turn away from their usual economic pursuits and to take up the production and use of weapons. I am not saying that people who make such a choice are necessarily making a mistake.

The point is simply that choices have costs. World War II has been portrayed as what amounts to a case of something for nothing: more guns *and* more butter—"the good war"—but it was no such thing. Nor can we expect any future war to be so costless. People cannot spill their enemy's blood and eat it too.

Notes

1. This chapter is a "popular" version of a fuller, more rigorous, and fully documented professional paper: "Wartime Prosperity? A Reassessment of the U.S. Economy in the 1940s," *Journal of Economic History* 52 (March 1992): 41–60. For the fullest understanding of my views on "wartime prosperity," readers should also consult two other articles I have written: "Regime Uncertainty: Why the Great Depression Lasted So Long and Why Prosperity Resumed after the War," *The Independent Review* 1 (spring 1997): 561–90; and "From Central Planning to the Market: The American Transition, 1945–1947," *Journal of Economic History* 59 (September 1999): 600–623.

2. In those days, the government's fiscal year ended in the middle of the calendar year. Thus, for example, the fiscal year 1940 runs from July 1, 1939, to June 30, 1940.

3. New York: National Bureau of Economic Research, 1945, pp. viii–ix.

4. William Nordhaus and James Tobin, *Is Growth Obsolete?* (New York: National Bureau of Economic Research, 1972), pp. 7–8, 26, 28.

5. Seymour Melman, *The Permanent War Economy* (New York: Simon and Schuster, 1985), p. 15.

28

To Deal with a Crisis: Government Program or Free Market?

National emergencies are inevitable. Our history is replete with them, and the future will certainly bring new ones. During the past century, Americans have suffered the unanticipated shocks of great strikes, wars, economic contractions, terrorist attacks, and various lesser crises.

It is instructive to consider how we have dealt with past crises. Since the early twentieth century, the usual method by which Americans (and many others) have responded—namely, by creating emergency government programs— has resulted in permanent losses of economic freedoms and permanent impairments of economic institutions. If we can learn from our past mistakes, perhaps we can avoid such unfortunate developments when we must cope with a crisis again.

Above all, we need to understand that the choice is not one between a government program and an unrelieved calamity. Rather, the choice is one between remedial actions taken by government officials, who can wield coercive powers, and remedial actions taken by private citizens, who must confine themselves to voluntarily accepted arrangements. In either case, something will be done. The critical questions have to do with the effectiveness and the long-run consequences of the actions taken.

Suppose a crisis strikes, for example, in which foreign supplies of oil are drastically reduced. Industries using oil as a raw material must reduce their rates of production. Workers will be laid off, and hence their earnings will decline or disappear. Oil-related industries and businesses dependent on the patronage of the laid-off workers will feel the impact. They too must cut back. Economic decline spreads like ripples from a stone tossed into calm water. Something must be done, but what should it be?

Some people are likely to propose, indeed to insist, that the government "do something." An emergency program might assign the available supplies of oil to the users that government officials consider most important, including perhaps hospitals, police, fire departments, and farmers. The authorities might undertake to restore the domestic equilibrium upset by the foreign shortfall. They might, for example, compel refiners using domestic oil to give up some of their supplies to refiners dependent on foreign sources. Of course, some method of compensation would have to be devised; someone would have to administer the rules to ensure compliance; and someone would have to make adjustments to unforeseen changes in domestic patterns of demand and supply. In short, a government program to "do something" about the import cutback would probably lead to creation of pervasive rules, a large administrative corps, and a suppression of free-market arrangements over a substantial part of the economy. (Those old enough to recall the events of the 1970s will understand that my account here does not spring entirely from my own fevered imagination.)

Do we have any alternative course of action? Given the dire consequences of the import shortfall, how can we refuse to acknowledge the need for a government program? Will not catastrophe result in the absence of an emergency government response? The short answers to these questions are: an alternative way to deal with the crisis does exist; a government program may not be needed; a market-oriented response probably will work; and people left to work out their own salvation will not simply surrender to despair and disaster.

The essence of many crises is *shortage:* the quantity supplied of something—oil, opportunities for employment, soldiers—falls short of the quantity demanded at the prices prevailing in the market. However, if prices are free to adjust, markets naturally tend to eliminate shortages. In fact, the very existence of a shortage tells us that the prevailing price is too low. When the price rises, two things happen. First, demanders reduce the amounts they want to buy. Second, suppliers increase the amounts they want to sell. Given a sufficiently large price increase, a new equilibrium results in which the quantities demanded and supplied are the same, and thus the shortage disappears. This adjustment process is exactly what is meant by the phrase "the workings of the laws of demand and supply."

Sometimes, however, the process does not appear to be working. Prices quickly rise, but little else seems to happen. Complaints arise that sellers are enriching themselves by "ripping off" the buyers. Political pressures may be exerted to keep the prices from rising further or to force them back to previous levels on the grounds that price increases, even if they eliminate the shortage, only transfer income from buyers to sellers while doing nothing to restore the amounts of the good previously available in the market. But wait.

Laws of Demand and Supply

The laws of demand and supply have two parts. The first law of demand states that, other things being equal, people want to buy less when the price is higher. The second law of demand states that the longer the time for adjustment, the greater is the reduction in quantity demanded for a given increase in price. Similarly with supply. The first law of supply states that, other things being equal, people want to sell more when the price is higher. The second law of supply states that the longer the time for adjustment, the greater is the increase in quantity supplied for a given increase in price.

The message is clear: be patient. The market will move toward the restoration of equilibrium, and conditions will steadily improve. With sufficient time, suppliers will bring forth more of the good in short supply or good substitutes for it. Demanders will find increasingly satisfactory ways to do without the good in reduced supply, often by substituting other goods for it.

In an emergency, however, many people do not want to wait for the second laws of demand and supply to come into play. Markets, we are often told, work too slowly. An emergency government program is said to have the important attribute of speeding the process of adjustment. Undeniably, coercive programs often work more quickly, but is this aspect of their operation really an advantage?

Coercive programs "save time" only because they compel wastefully hasty adjustments. They do not save valuable resources. Rather, they redistribute the costs of adjustment in comparison with the distribution of costs when responses are determined by voluntary arrangements in free markets.

Suppose, for example, that in an oil crisis created by an import shortfall the government orders domestic oil producers to bring forth immediately larger deliveries of oil than they would supply voluntarily in response to the higher price of oil (assuming the government allows the price to rise freely in the market). Does not the government's order hasten the process of adjustment, and is not such a speed-up desirable?

To see what really happens, consider why the oil producers do not supply the government-ordered amount voluntarily. When the price rises, they of course want to increase the amounts they supply. An increase of the amounts supplied can be brought about by various means—for example, by drawing down on inventories stored in tanks, by increasing the rate of pumping from established wells, by drilling more wells into known underground reservoirs of oil, by searching for new oil fields, by extracting oil from shale, and so forth. Each source can be tapped, but in the short run it is wasteful to draw on those that require more costly development—that is, more research, planning, reorganization of facilities, and reallocation of resources. It may make good economic sense to proceed with additional exploration and the development of new oil fields, but to make these options yield oil quickly is possible only at extraordinarily high costs—for hiring and training inexperienced workers, bidding the use of materials and equipment away from other industries, paying employees higher wages to get them to work overtime. In the very short run, it is economically justifiable to bring forth only the extra oil available in existing inventories in storage tanks. Later the other sources of additional supply can be tapped at a measured and therefore cheaper pace.

Coerced haste only makes waste. *Faster adjustments are more costly, and someone must bear the additional costs.* The government can compel a faster adjustment, to be sure, but no valuable resources are saved because of that compulsion. Rather, someone is compelled to bear costs of adjustment that are not worthwhile. To satisfy the government's requirement, resources are shifted from socially more valuable uses to socially less valuable uses. The government gets a faster reallocation of resources not because its emergency programs "save" anything, but only because its coercive power allows it to impose wasteful reallocations on the private owners of labor and capital. Society makes a faster adjustment at the cost of becoming, all values being taken into account, worse off.

Emergency government programs, then, offer exceptional opportunities for those who would substitute their own values for those ordinarily guiding the allocation of resources in the market. When the cry of "Emergency!" goes up, the public's resistance to government takeovers comes down. Hence, aspiring redistributors of income, collectivist planners, and do-gooders at other people's expense rush in to exploit the unusual opportunity for replacing market processes with government controls. Whatever one may think about the *immediate* desirability of an emergency government program, however, one must recognize that the program is almost certainly only a beginning; and what follows in its train may be far less desirable.

Unintended Consequences

At the very start, one often gets something one doesn't want along with something one does. Because government programs are created by politicians who seldom give their assent gratuitously, proponents of a government program of type X may be able to marshal a majority in favor of it only by adding a government program of type Y. For example, when Congress passed the National Industrial Recovery Act (NIRA)—a paradigmatic emergency program—in 1933 to restore business profits by establishing cartels in every industry, provisions were included to promote collective bargaining and establish wage and hour rules in the labor markets. The labor provisions bought the acceptance of the act by congressmen responsive to the interests of labor unionists and thereby ensured its passage. When the Supreme Court invalidated the NIRA in 1935, Congress immediately reestablished and even strengthened its labor provisions by passage of the Wagner Act. In this instance, as often happens, the original emergency program had attached to it, as the outcome of a political "horse trade," a government program that persisted long after the original program had disappeared.

Emergency programs frequently do not work as intended. Government officials attempting to control the market discover that it is a moving target. As George Shultz and Kenneth Dam explain, "To every government action the private sector reacts or accommodates, and the government further reacts as the private economy 'talks back' to the government."[1] The government tries harder and harder to outwit the people subject to its controls. The people try harder and harder to anticipate what the controllers will do next. Although the process may result in a stand-off, it consumes ever more resources on both sides. For example, when the Reagan administration announced new import restrictions on steel in 1984, "steel-making nations around the world began shipping more steel to the United States to establish higher benchmarks from which their steel export limits would be set," thereby bringing about the opposite of what the program was designed to achieve.[2] In consequence, domestic steel producers and labor organizations naturally called for a stronger program to deal with this unforeseen development. American farmers subject to acreage controls have been playing a similar game since 1933.

Creation of an emergency program usually leads to the entrenchment of the connected special interests, both governmental and private. Everyone knows that "infant industries" granted tariff protection never mature to the point that they are willing to give up the "temporary" protection they sought in the beginning. Truckers who got protection from free-market competition during the Great Depression were, fifty years later, fighting to maintain their privileges against those seeking to deregulate the industry. Farmers provide perhaps the most notorious example. Although the number of farmers has declined greatly and the typical farmer's income has risen dramatically since the 1930s, the bureaucracy at the U.S. Department of Agriculture has become vastly larger, and the farm "crisis" seems to be everlasting, no matter how often the government undertakes to deal with it.

The farm programs also illustrate how emergency government programs, when maintained long after the events that prompted them, can lock the government into an almost inescapable position. All parties come to expect the benefit of government subsidies, so it gets "capitalized" into the value of farm land. Current farmers, who must bear the higher cost of land use, get no extra benefit by operating land subject to the subsidies—all the benefits were captured by those who owned the land at the time the new subsidies were first announced. Should the government discontinue the subsidies, however, current farmers would be hurt; the value of their wealth would fall. Naturally they fight to maintain the existing programs. The only way the government can rectify its initially bad choice of policies is by harming innocent parties, which seems manifestly unfair. Thus, the programs go on and on even after almost everyone has recognized their ineffectiveness, inequity, and waste of resources.

Of course, no matter how the programs work out, the administrative corps tends to grow. If there are far fewer farms to serve, well, the people at the Agriculture Department can find other things to do, such as operating the food-stamp program or distributing pamphlets to urban gardeners or studying the international commodity markets. The U.S. Department of Energy grew out of a so-called energy crisis in the 1970s, yet today, decades after oil prices have returned to normal levels and at a time when no one even claims the existence of an energy crisis, the department thrives with thousands of employees and a budget of billions of dollars—for the fiscal year 2003, the Bush administration requested $21.9 billion, $8 billion of which would go toward supporting the department's current nuclear weapons activities.[3]

Suppressing Flexibility

Ultimately, the most unfortunate aspect of emergency government programs is that they suppress or crowd out flexible, creative, voluntary market responses to the crisis. When the energy programs of the 1970s controlled the prices of petroleum products and allocated the products among different classes of users and different areas of the country, the market could not work. Indeed, every aspect of the controls, especially the so-called entitlements program that was developed to make the controls "fair" to different classes of refiners, was socially perverse. Consumption and imports were encouraged; domestic production was discouraged. William E. Simon, the famous energy "czar" of the early crisis period, later declared that "[t]here is nothing like becoming an economic planner oneself to learn what is desperately, stupidly wrong with such a system."[4] Economic history is replete with successful market adjustments to shortages of all kinds: coal was substituted for wood as a fuel; steam engines for animal and water power; an ingenious assortment of machinery for human labor; the list is virtually limitless. Yet such adjustments hinge on the presence of market incentives and the economic liberties that permit voluntary rearrangements to emerge.

The first and second laws of demand and supply cannot come into play unless shortages are allowed to express themselves in the form of price increases and surpluses are allowed to express themselves in the form of price decreases. Ultimately, the most damaging aspect of emergency government programs is that they prevent the fundamental forces of the price system from doing the job that they, and only they, can do while preserving our economic freedoms.

Having witnessed decades of episodic crises, economist Calvin Hoover wrote in the late 1950s: "At the time of economic crisis ... critical extensions of governmental power are likely to occur.... [T]here is likely to be an insistent demand for emergency action of some sort and relatively little consideration of what the permanent effect will be."[5] The outcome is almost always the same. As Clinton Rossiter observed in the late 1940s, "No constitutional government ever passed through a period in which emergency powers were used without undergoing some degree of permanent alteration, always in the direction of an aggrandizement of the power of the state."[6] In U.S.

history, these observations are undoubtedly valid.[7]

Yet the pleas persist. Even in the early 1980s, hardly a time of genuine national emergency, there were calls for emergency government programs to deal with unemployment, mortgage interest rates, the airlines, oil, and, as always, the farmers.[8] The rhetoric of crisis apparently never ceases to promise a positive political payoff, no matter how visibly grasping are the special interests who mouth it.

The government will be less likely to use its powers in the service of these special interests if the general public keeps calm. When we hear the claim that a crisis is upon us, we would be justified in remaining skeptical, for the serviceability of a genuine crisis to those who would set aside the free market has led them to attach the crisis label to almost all their pleas. Even when a genuine crisis occurs, we might well consider whether the best way to deal with it is simply to let the market work. By considering all costs and benefits and all consequences in the long run as well as the short run, we shall be less inclined to place our trust in emergency government programs.

Notes

1. George P. Shultz and Kenneth W. Dam, *Economic Policy Beyond the Headlines* (New York: Norton, 1977), p. 8.

2. "Foreign Steel Still Flooding U.S., 'Voluntary Restraint' on Imports Makes Little Impact," *Easton Express* (Pennsylvania), May 10, 1985.

3. U.S. Department of Energy, "Secretary of Energy Unveils DOE '03 Budget," press release, February 4, 2002, at http://www.energy.gov/HQPress/releases02/febpr/pr02016.htm.

4. William E. Simon, *A Time for Truth* (New York: Berkley Books, 1979), p. 50.

5. Calvin B. Hoover, *The Economy, Liberty, and the State* (New York: Twentieth Century Fund, 1959), pp. 326–27.

6. Clinton L. Rossiter, *Constitutional Dictatorship: Crisis Government in the Modern Democracies* (Princeton, N.J.: Princeton University Press, 1948), p. 295.

7. Robert Higgs, *Crisis and Leviathan: Critical Episodes in the Growth of American Government* (New York: Oxford University Press, 1987).

8. Dennis Farney and Rich Jaroslovsky, "Reagan, Democrats Seeking Compromise to Produce an Emergency Jobs Program," *Wall Street Journal*, February 10, 1983; "Senate Unit OK's $5 Billion Housing Program," *Seattle Times*, April 22, 1982; "House OK's Bill to Aid Housing Industry, Measure Would Pump $1 Billion into Mortgage-Interest Subsidies," *Seattle Times*, May 12, 1982; Dennis Farney, "House Sustains Veto on Mortgage Subsidy Aiding Reagan Bid to Stem 'Bailout' Bills," *Wall Street Journal*, June 25, 1982; "Airline Unions Ask for 'Re-regulation' of Ailing Industry," *Wall Street Journal*, October 5, 1983; "Analysts See Oil-Shortage Problem If Emergency Powers Lapse," *Seattle Times*, September 9, 1981; "Oil Emergency Rules End as World Supply, Price Outlook Eases," *Wall Street Journal*, October 1, 1981; "Senate Self-Embarrassment" [editorial], *Wall Street Journal*, October 12, 1981; "House Votes President Oil-Embargo Powers," *Wall Street Journal*, December 15, 1981; "Return to Rationing?" [editorial], *Wall Street Journal*,

March 16, 1982; "Reagan Vetoes Bill to Give President Powers in Oil Crisis," *Wall Street Journal,* March 22, 1982; "Senate Upholds Veto of Bill on Oil-Crisis Action," *Seattle Times,* March 25, 1982; Andrew H. Malcolm, "In Farm Crisis, the Land Itself Becomes a Liability," *New York Times,* October 9, 1983; "FmHA to make Emergency Loans to Farmers in '84," *Easton Express,* December 28, 1983; "House Panel Clears Measure to Expand Credit for Farmers," *Wall Street Journal,* March 18, 1983; "House Panel Orders More Farm Emergency Help," *Easton Express,* September 22, 1983.

29

Beware the Pork Hawk
In Pursuit of Reelection,
Congress Sells Out the Nation's Defense

With regard to spending for national defense, we are accustomed to perceiving some people as hawks, others as doves. These birds disagree sharply in their answers to the question, How much defense spending is enough? In the 1980s, a new bird, the *cheap hawk,* began to be sighted with growing frequency. This one wants a strong defense. He may or may not want more spending for the military, but he definitely wants more bang for the buck. He worries about weapons that don't work as they are supposed to and about spending for purposes that deliver less military punch than other programs sacrificed in the budget process.

The advent of the cheap hawk pushed the defense budget debate beyond the old question of how much is enough and raised to the forefront the more important question of how we should spend whatever amount is available. Obviously, the nation's security is not promoted simply by spending money under the heading of defense.

Unfortunately, a great deal of the budget is soaked up by items that masquerade as defense but actually make little or no contribution to national security. Many of these spending programs are, in effect, welfare programs—not for ghetto dwellers, homeless people, or other unfortunates, but welfare nonetheless.

In contriving and delivering this pseudodefense largess, another common defense bird enters the picture. Though informed bird-watchers all know about this one, it has yet to receive an accepted name. I propose to call it the *pork hawk.*

In Congress, the pork hawk may appear to be a hawk, a dove, or a cheap hawk. You can't tell by the plumage or the call. You have to check its nesting and feeding habits. You can identify it in many cases by its tendency to lie down very close to constituents and political action committees and by its constant twittering about reelection. If you observe its behavior in the defense field, you'll find it pecking away at the tiniest details. The pork hawk thrives on micromanaging the defense program, stipulating not only how much will be spent for certain broad defense purposes but how much will be spent for each of the several thousand line items in the annual defense budget and exactly how the Pentagon must manage that spending.

The A-7 Stretchout

The habits of the pork hawk can be observed, for example, in the history of the A-7. This subsonic attack plane, produced by the Vought Corporation and first used in the late 1960s by both the navy and the air force for close air support, was an effective weapon in its day. By the mid-1970s, however, Pentagon planners considered it obsolescent. The navy wanted to start acquiring the F/A-18, the air force the F-16. In the late 1970s and early 1980s, the Air National Guard was the only military service that wanted more A-7s, and even the Guard wanted only the two-seat trainer.

Nevertheless, Congress continued to fund the program for years. Why? Because Dallas-based Vought, the Guard, and the powerful Texas congressional delegation demanded it. Such a three-sided coalition is aptly described as what political scientists call an iron triangle.

The Texas delegation is one of the largest and most cohesive in Congress. At the time, it included the venerable George Mahon (D), who chaired the House Defense Appropriations Subcommittee for three decades before retiring in 1979, and Senator John Tower (R), a senior member of the Armed Services Committee and its chairman in the early 1980s. Whereas some senators are known to favor one weapon or another, one service or another, Tower was said simply to "favor Texas."[1] Of course, the Texans always claimed that the A-7 still had substantial military value.

The purity of the coalition's motives was put to a test in the House of Representatives in July 1981. Representative Toby Moffett (D-Conn.) offered an amendment to the authorization bill that would switch funds from A-7s to more modern F-16s for the Air National Guard. The beauty of the proposal was that the Guard would get its planes, better ones at that; it would get more planes, because thirteen F-16s, coming from a big production run, could be purchased for the same price as twelve A-7s from a small production run; and to top it off, the F-16 was also manufactured in Texas.

It was a deal no one could refuse—unless, of course, the real issue was the fortunes of Vought and its congressional allies. Sure enough, the Texas delegation opposed the amendment, concerned that keeping Vought going had more political value than giving a bit more business to General Dynamics, which produced the F-16 at a Texas plant. Vought's friends in Congress were joined by the Guard, which was intent on fulfilling its plans for acquiring the A-7K two-seat trainer. (Several sources, including Defense Secretary Harold Brown, alleged that the Guard wanted the A-7Ks because its commanders were too old to fly high-performance aircraft by themselves.)[2] Moffett's amendment went down on a vote of 148 to 268.

Without doubt, the A-7s funded in fiscal years 1978–81 resulted from congressional micromanagement. (Arguably, many of the planes bought earlier also sprang from this source.) Altogether, the Pentagon got fifty-six aircraft it did not want—twenty-four A-7Es for the navy and thirty-two A-7Ks for the Air National Guard.[3]

Many defense commentators tend to dismiss such congressional micromanagement as "small potatoes." They admit that many members of Congress, especially the chairmen and the senior members of key defense and appropriations committees, make their little grabs and carry the loot back to the home folks to buy votes. These experts believe, however, that the real action, the truly massive waste and mismanagement in the defense budget, lies elsewhere—in the millions that Litton Industries overcharged the Pentagon for military electronics products, for example, or in the several billion required to fix the poorly performing B-1.

Yet the A-7s procured by the pork hawks cost the taxpayers hundreds of millions of dollars. Although it is difficult to identify the costs specifically attributable to adding the fifty-six unwanted planes to the inventory, it appears from scattered information presented by the services to congressional committees that the total cost was approximately $575 million—equivalent to more than $1 billion in today's dollars. Because those aircraft crowded out more effective weapons, their net contribution to the nation's military might was actually *negative*. One can hardly say that such waste is small potatoes.

The Rise of Congressional Defense Micromanagement

Congressional micromanagement of the defense program, on the increase since the early 1970s, burgeoned in the 1980s. Within Congress, its sources included growing committee rivalries, fragmented power, and proliferating staff. The momentous shifts of the political landscape associated with the Vietnam War and the Watergate scandal added impetus to the growth of micromanagement. By diminishing the prestige of the military establishment and the executive office of the president, those forces gave rise to a more assertive and resourceful legislative branch. In the new environment, the pork hawk soared.

Congressional micromanagement reveals itself in various forms. One is the requirement that the Pentagon take specific actions. Once, for example, Congress ordered the Department of Defense (DOD) to double its purchases from minority suppliers during the next year. On another occasion, Congress dictated how many European-made subsystems to include in the U.S. version of the Roland missile—not less than 350. At various times, Congress prohibited the Pentagon from developing a second source for M-1 tank engines, ordered the air force to maintain air transport it didn't want at McChord Air Force Base, and prohibited the army's proposed relocation of helicopter maintenance from Pennsylvania to Texas. In several different years, it directed DOD to purchase three hundred thousand tons of expensive anthracite coal—

produced in Pennsylvania—for shipment to bases in Europe.[4]

The variety of such actions makes them impossible to summarize, but without doubt they increased tremendously. In 1970, Congress required 82 specific actions; in 1976, the number increased to 304, and in 1987 to 807.[5]

An even more important development than specific mandates was Congress's mounting compulsion to adjust the line items of the defense budget—such as appropriating funds for the fifty-six A-7s that the Pentagon didn't want. Again, 1970 provides a base year for comparisons. In that year, Congress made 830 adds or cuts to line items in authorization and appropriations acts. By 1976, the number had climbed to 1,254, and in 1987 Congress micromanaged 3,422 line items.[6]

This form of congressional involvement in the details of the defense budget doesn't just add to spending. It can also undermine effective management at DOD, the armed forces, and the contractors. Interconnected parts of the budget are thrown out of proper relation to one another. For example, Congress directs the Pentagon to buy additional M-1 tanks, but not more of the support vehicles that are needed to operate them; or additional aircraft carriers, but not more of the naval aircraft that use them. It slashes the ammunition budget in order to buy more guns. It stretches out the planned purchases of F-14s, and therefore Grumman's production lines are no longer used at an optimal rate. Such juggling of the budget makes effective planning nearly impossible.

Although most of the micromanagement has taken place in the Armed Services Committee and the Defense Appropriations Subcommittee of each house of Congress, activity on the floor of the House and the Senate has also escalated. Before 1969, the House usually considered only a handful of amendments to the authorization bill, the Senate none at all. By 1985, each house was considering more than one hundred amendments and spending more than a week debating the bill. Many of the amendments were position-taking actions on broad policy matters, such as nuclear weapons or arms control, but a look at the legislative history of the authorization bill for any recent year reveals that many of the amendments amount to pure micromanagement.

The pork hawk flies over the entire defense field, including research and development (R&D) and the procurement of major weapons systems. However, even if we look only at pork barreling in the "soft underbelly"—the construction, operations, and maintenance accounts—huge amounts of spending are at stake and up for congressional grabs.

Former Senator Barry Goldwater (R-Ariz.), one of the few recent members of Congress to speak frankly, was not afraid to take aim at the pork hawk. He was uncommonly well informed about the military, and shortly after his retirement from the Senate in 1987 he wrote an article for *Armed Forces Journal International* in which he blasted Congress for promoting "instability, inefficiency, delay, and confusion." He pointed to "the increasing number of legislators who want to play 'pork barrel' politics with the defense budget" and warned that "their patronage appetites continue to grow."7

Even Senator Goldwater, however, had an ambiguous record. His role in another pork-hawk case illustrates that ambiguity.

The A-10 Stretchout

The story of the A-10, another subsonic attack plane, resembles the story of the A-7 in important respects. After buying some seven hundred A-10s in the late 1970s and early 1980s, the air force decided that acquiring more of them was less important than purchasing other weapons, especially F-16s, adaptable to the same close air-support mission but capable of effective battlefield air interdiction as well. Of course, people with a stake in continued production of the A-10 fought to keep it going. The large New York delegation and its powerful committee heads—Joseph Addabbo (D), chairman of the House Defense Appropriations Subcommittee from 1979 to 1986, and Samuel Stratton (D), chairman of the House Armed Services Committee's Subcommittee on Procurement—intervened to stretch out the procurement program. It was, observed journalist Hedrick Smith, "a case study in protecting pork for the home folks."8

Addabbo, who represented a Queens district, was certainly no hawk, but he was manifestly a pork hawk. Although he opposed many programs pushed by the Pentagon, he invariably promoted military installations and contractors, especially Grumman Corp. and Fairchild, located in or near his district. A *New York Times* reporter described him as "a champion of Long Island military projects," and fellow New York congressman George J. Hochbrueckner (D) praised Addabbo as "the big savior of Long Island."9 When Hedrick Smith questioned Addabbo about the apparent inconsistency of his dovishness and his support for military pork-barrel projects, he shrugged and responded: "Why not build them in your own area, the same as everyone else does?"10

For a while, Goldwater, a senior member of the Armed Services Committee, gave the A-10 strong support, but in 1982 he abruptly turned against further acquisitions. Addressing air force witnesses at a hearing, he made an extraordinary statement. "I know what you are up against," he told the generals. "You have the parochial problem of Massachusetts, New York, Pennsylvania, and Maryland, all wanting to keep that A-10 going just like they bought A-7s to keep Texas happy." Goldwater, however, now thought the time had come to just say no. "I know most of you [in the air force] think you don't need them, but you come over here to tell us you do need them just to keep some people [in Congress] happy."11

Ultimately, Goldwater did use his influence to shut down the A-10 line, which received no procurement funding after 1982 despite the determined efforts of the New Yorkers and their allies, but the A-10 program staggered to its demise in a way that reflected credit on no one.

Through 1980, the program was defensible. It allocated resources to an important and neglected military mission. It was, in defense analyst Richard Stubbing's words, "a rare managerial success—coming in close to cost and performing as well as promised."[12]

The trouble arose when the plane approached the end of its planned production run. Members of Congress and contractors tried to prolong its life, and the stretch-out began. Unit costs soared. In 1980, the air force procured 144 planes for about $6.3 million each. The next year, when procurement fell to 60 planes, the cost jumped to $8.7 million per plane. By 1982, the Pentagon was down to 20 planes, each one costing $10.5 million. Only a modest fraction of the cost escalation reflected inflation. Had the friends of the A-10 succeeded in spending the $357 million appropriated but, owing in large part to Goldwater's opposition, not authorized in fiscal 1983, the unit cost would have been almost $18 million—for an airplane a committee of military men believed could be replaced with a better attack plane that could be produced for less than $3 million.

Although the administration's budgetary shifts and air force gamesmanship contributed to the debacle, certain members of Congress deserve much of the blame. Addabbo, Senator Alfonse D'Amato (R), and others in the New York coalition hardly bothered to conceal their attempt to turn the A-10 into a pure make-work program, but Goldwater's actions also raise questions. In 1982, he was remarkably frank about the parochialism involved in prolonging acquisitions, but his own behavior had been erratic, swinging from emphatic support in 1981 to ridicule in 1983—a switch that lacked a compelling military rationale and seemed capricious.

The T-46 Debacle

Whatever else one might say about the A-7 and the A-10 programs, the planes did have some military utility. The same could not be said about the T-46 trainer aircraft program, which consumed several hundred million dollars, then sank in an ignominious denouement that featured contractor incompetence and congressional parochialism. After T-46 supporters had taken extraordinary measures to salvage the program, although it was manifestly not worth saving, a congressional compromise finally terminated it. Altogether, the T-46 line had brought forth only two prototypes and a single production-model aircraft.

Did the termination signify that lawmakers had spared the taxpayers some wasteful military spending? Not exactly. The fix was itself a monument to congressional parochialism, and the cure was only a little better than the disease.

The air force awarded the T-46 development contract to Fairchild in 1982, but the program never really got going. In 1985, air force examiners reported that approximately 40 percent of the hardware was defective and that company inspectors were passing 24 percent of the defective items. Fairchild's costs were running 80 percent above budget, and the project had fallen behind schedule. The examiners rated the company unsatisfactory in all eight areas of management and contract compliance they checked.[13]

The air force expressed its displeasure by halving its progress payments to Fairchild and by asking Cessna how much the company would charge to upgrade the existing trainer fleet of T-37s. Under increasing pressure to restrain spending, the air force recommended that the T-46 be dropped from the service's five-year budget plan or, alternatively, that the program be switched to another contractor. Congressional friends of the T-46 swung into action.

Not surprisingly, its chief proponents were the New Yorkers, especially Representative Thomas Downey (D), whose district included Fairchild's plant on Long Island, where various military projects were winding down and thereby threatening to wipe out "the vast majority of the 3600 jobs" (and a corresponding number of votes?).[14] Production of the T-46 would provide continued employment.

Downey exemplified the dove as pork hawk. Like his colleague Addabbo, he often opposed the Pentagon's favored projects, but he never failed to support military programs promising jobs and income for his constituents. A paradigmatic "case-work congressman," Downey was willing to ignore the national interest and to forget his ideology when it clashed with the demands of politically active constituents. Although the T-46 eventually went down, it went down with Downey fighting for it all the way.

On October 16, 1986, congressional conflict over the T-46 program came to a remarkable climax in the Senate. The coalition there included the two New York senators, the two Maryland senators (Fairchild had a facility at Hagerstown, Maryland), and Senator Dennis DeConcini (D) of Arizona, where Garrett Corp. was to build T-46 engines. Besides these five, each of whom had a transparent parochial interest in preserving the troubled trainer, only a handful of senators supported keeping the program alive. A few can often prevail, however, especially in the Senate, where the rules allow even a single member to perform miracles of obstruction that induce others to fall into line. Leading the opposition to the T-46 were Goldwater and Robert Dole, acting on this occasion as the senator from (Wichita-based) Cessna.

Goldwater fired the first shot, offering an amendment to prohibit spending money for the T-46 either from funds previously appropriated but withheld by the air force or from funds under debate for 1987. Opponents let loose a procedural barrage. The amendment also faced the impatience of senators who had no particular interest in it but just wanted to pass a spending resolution. The latest of four stopgap funding resolutions that had carried the government into he 1987 fiscal year would expire at midnight, and unless new appropriations were made, the government would have to shut down all nonessential activities and send its employees home.

In a last-ditch effort to save the T-46, Senators D'Amato, Patrick Moynihan (D-N.Y.), and DeConcini waged a filibuster lasting almost twenty-four hours, and the government did shut down. Federal workers were sent home on October 17.[15] It was estimated at the time that such shutdowns cost the government—that is, the taxpayers—some $60 million a day.

Finally, the staffs in the cloakroom arrived at a compromise. It provided that no 1987 money be spent on the T-46 and that the previously appropriated funds could be drawn on to pay for a "fly-off" in which the T-46, the T-37, and any other suitable trainers would compete for the air force contract.[16] This compromise gave the T-46 a faint hope of survival.

The air force subsequently appealed to Congress to release it from the fly-off requirement. Having a competition made no sense when the service no longer planned to procure a new generation of trainers in the next five years. In March 1987, the air force and Fairchild announced that they had reached an agreement whereby the service would cap its payments to the company at $159 million, approximately what had been paid already, and Fairchild would terminate its T-46 line. To cut its losses, Fairchild would close the Long Island plant. "A very black day for Long Island," lamented Downey, "a human tragedy of the first order."[17]

In the spring of 1987, the Senate did release the air force from the obligation to conduct the fly-off, and this action survived in the final defense bill for 1988–89. The pork hawks had extracted a price for their agreement, however: a total of $300 million previously appropriated but not spent for the T-46 was reallocated to navy aircraft programs—the EA-6B, the A-6, and the E-2C—all the business of the Grumman Corp. on Long Island. As a House source told *Armed Forces Journal International*, "The New York delegation is not concerned about the competition. What they were concerned about is what happened to the [T-46] money."[18]

What should we make of the T-46 story? The program was stopped, a great deal of money was saved, the air force was rescued from acquiring an airplane it did not want. Still, several hundred million dollars went down the drain, including the costs of the government shutdown when the T-46 coalition's filibuster held up passage of a funding act for the entire federal government. In the end, $300 million was reallocated from air force to navy aircraft in a fashion that, from a military standpoint, can only be called arbitrary and capricious.

Of course, the reallocation made perfect political sense, which is precisely the point. The whole story illustrates how different and conflicting are the dictates of congressional politics and the dictates of a sensible, economical national defense program.

It's Treachery, but Nobody Minds

Wise men say that complaining about Congress is as futile as complaining about the weather. For as long as anyone can remember, members of Congress have been plundering the public to finance the largess they trade for reelection. By now, they have nearly perfected their system, as almost all incumbents who seek reelection are reelected, especially in the House. We are talking about a ruling class that approximates a self-perpetuating group about as closely as one can imagine in a democracy. So perhaps nothing can be done about the mismanagement and waste that attend congressional micromanagement of the defense program.

Some commentators have gone so far as to argue that we should be happy with the system as it is. After all, the guns do shoot some of the time. We do enjoy some national security. Moreover, given the institutional realities, it is impossible to imagine a reform that would improve on the existing system, because the reformers would face the same incentives and constraints that got us where we are now. Reforms would only make the situation worse.[19]

Maybe the pessimists are right. Their arguments are certainly weighty. My hunch, however, is that a slight chance exists to alleviate the ills associated with congressional micromanagement of defense.

A necessary condition for pork-barrel defense procurement is acceptance—by members of Congress and by the informed public—of what amounts to treachery. Members of Congress, with only a few exceptions, routinely betray the public's trust. In pursuit of their very private interest in reelection, they sell out the national defense of the United States. They know they are doing it; their colleagues know they are doing it; and the public, if it pays any attention at all, knows they are doing it. Yet everyone accepts it.

When opinion leaders, and hence the public, start to view these acts as treachery rather than as politics as usual, the incentives will change for members of Congress. They are sensitive to public opinion; they will not continue to act as they do when people view their actions as intolerably reprehensible and treat the guilty parties accordingly.

What I am contemplating would amount to ideological change on a fairly wide scale, so it is hardly likely, but ideological changes have occurred in the past, and they may occur again. Until they do, however, Congress will go on micromanaging the defense program for parochial purposes, and the resulting waste will continue. Doves and hawks will coo and shriek, while the pork hawks bring home the bacon at taxpayer expense.

Notes

1. Craig Liske and Barry Rundquist, *The Politics of Weapons Procurement* (Denver: University of Denver, 1974), pp. 39–47, 76, 87.

2. U.S. House of Representatives, Defense Appropriations Subcommittee, *Hearings on Department of Defense Appropriations for Fiscal Year 1981*, Pt. 1, 1980, p. 585.

3. Bill Keller, "Reagan, Like Previous Presidents, Fails to Cut Guard's A-7 Jet Fighter," *Congressional Quarterly Weekly Report* 39 (July 18, 1981): 1280–81.

4. Robert Higgs, "Hard Coals Make Bad Law: Congressional Parochialism Versus National Defense," *Cato Journal* 8 (spring–summer 1988): 79–106.

5. Figures for 1970 and 1976 from U.S. General Accounting Office, *Legislative Oversight: Congressional Requests for Information on Defense Activities*, GAO/NSIAD-86-65BR (Washington, D.C.: U.S. Government Printing Office, February 1986), appendix 3; figures for 1987 from James M. Lindsay, "Congress and the Defense Budget," *Washington Quarterly* (winter 1988), p. 61.

6. Figures from U.S. Department of Defense, Office of the Controller, as printed in Lindsay, "Congress and the Defense Budget," p. 61.

7. Barry Goldwater, "Overdose of Oversight and Lawless Legislating," *Armed Forces Journal International* (February 1987), pp. 54, 56.

8. Hedrick Smith, *The Power Game: How Washington Works* (New York: Random House, 1988), p. 178.

9. John Markoff, "Long Island Inquiry Widens in Arms Purchases," *New York Times*, July 17, 1988.

10. Addabbo as quoted in Smith, *The Power Game*, p. 179.

11. U.S. Senate, Armed Services Committee, *Hearings on Authorization for Department of Defense Appropriations for Fiscal Year 1983*, Pt. 4, 1982, pp. 2594–96.

12. Richard A. Stubbing, with Richard A. Mendel, *The Defense Game: An Insider Explores the Astonishing Realities of America's Defense Establishment* (New York: Harper and Row, 1986), p. 142.

13. *Congressional Record* 132 (October 17, 1986), pp. S16589, S16597; "Fairchild Tightens Procedures Following Air Force Review," *Aviation Week and Space Technology* (September 9, 1985), pp. 18–19. According to Bob Malanga, who worked for Fairchild at the time, the Air Force inspection was itself a politically motivated sham: "every one of their findings were ludicrous and a reach to please their top brass." Malanga to Robert Higgs, December 14, 2002.

14. *Congressional Record* 132 (October 17, 1986), p. S16602; Smith, *The Power Game*, p. 178; "New York Legislators Ask for Fairchild Reprieve," *Aviation Week and Space Technology* (September 9, 1985), p. 18; Tracy White, ed., *Power in Congress* (Washington, D.C.: Congressional Quarterly, 1987), p. 71.

15. Elizabeth Wehr, "Congress Clears $576 Billion Spending Measure," *Congressional Quarterly Weekly Report* 44 (October 18, 1986): 2584–85.

16. *Congressional Record* 132 (October 17, 1986), p. S16603.

17. Tim Carrington, "Air Force Renews Campaign to Scrap Fairchild Industries' T-46 Trainer Jet," *Wall Street Journal*, December 10, 1986; Glenn W. Goodman Jr., "Wide Open USAF Trainer Competition Likely If Service Recalcitrance Blunted," *Armed Forces*

Journal International (January 1987): 56; Clifford D. May, "2,500 to Lose Jobs in L.I. Plant as U.S. Ends Jet Contract: Fairchild Republic to Shut by End of Year after Halt in Air Force T-46 Work," *New York Times,* March 14, 1987.

18. Michael Ganley, "Congress Appears Close to Reversing Its Call for a USAF Trainer Competition," *Armed Forces Journal International* (July 1987), p. 8.

19. Dwight R. Lee, "Public Goods, Politics, and Two Cheers for the Military-Industrial Complex," in *Arms, Politics, and the Economy: Historical and Contemporary Perspectives,* edited by Robert Higgs (New York: Holmes and Meier, for The Independent Institute, 1990), pp. 22–36.

30

The Cold War Is Over, but U.S. Preparation for It Continues

As George W. Bush's administration took office in January 2001, you could almost hear the sighs of relief coming from the Pentagon and the corporate headquarters of Lockheed Martin, Boeing, Raytheon, General Dynamics, Northrup Grumman, Litton Industries, and other big defense contractors. After all, the Bush campaign had championed a $45 billion increase in annual military spending over the next decade. Appearing at a Senate confirmation hearing on his nomination as secretary of defense, Donald Rumsfeld advocated an even greater increase, remarking that "it is not a time to preside and tweak and calibrate," though the administration's tactics dictated that the big increase not be requested immediately.[1] Just eleven days later the press disclosed that "the dash for missile-defense profits is on."[2] Nor were the missile defense system contractors the only ones who stood to benefit from the new administration's defense program. Bush's budget, introduced at the end of February, called for an increase of $14.2 billion, or 4.8 percent, in defense spending, but the budget's proposed "contingency reserve" held additional funds that could be tapped by the military,[3] and the Pentagon has been no stranger to supplemental appropriations. As the preliminary maneuvering proceeded, with an eye toward fiscal year (FY) 2003 and beyond, Rumsfeld's staff produced a plan to increase the weapons-procurement budget by 42 percent over seven years, "with big increases for fighter jets, ballistic-missile defense, cargo planes and bombers."[4] Throughout the military-industrial-congressional complex (MICC), the pork hawks preened their feathers and prepared to take flight.[5]

The Latest Cycle

The MICC, it seemed, was setting out on another of the recurrent upsurges that have marked the history of defense spending since the onset of the Cold War. The first such upsurge—the most significant one, in view of its long-term consequences—occurred concurrently with the Korean War, though much of it pertained to the buildup of forces intended for deployment in Europe and elsewhere, not in Korea. The second buildup financed the U.S. misadventure in Vietnam. The most recent upswing was the Reagan buildup of the 1980s, which receded in the first half of the 1990s. Examining what might be viewed as the Cold War norm or baseline of defense spending during FY 1955–65 and 1974–80, when neither substantial mobilization nor demobilization was occurring, we find that real defense spending during those years averaged $281 billion (dollars of 1999 purchasing power) per year.[6] On a graph, the three upsurges and their subsequent abatements appear as discrete hills sitting on that Cold War plateau.[7]

If the Cold War had continued to the present, we might have expected that defense spending during the past several years would have returned to the level of the Cold War norm, and indeed it has done so, despite no Cold War. During the six fiscal years from 1995 through 2000, the average level of annual defense spending was $278 billion (dollars of 1999 purchasing power)—almost exactly equal to the Cold War norm.[8]

Such an equality, however fitting it might seem in the sense of conformity to a statistically descriptive pattern, raises a serious policy question: Given that the Cold War ended a decade earlier, why was the defense establishment plowing ahead as if nothing had changed and even starting to enlarge its bite on the taxpayer's purse? After all, it had been to fight the Cold War that the historically extraordinary magnitude of defense spending had been ordained in the first place, back in the early 1950s. That immense rate of spending was continuously maintained, even when the United States was not engaged in a hot war or other military upsurge, in order, one presumes, to meet the continuing threats posed by the USSR, its satellites, and its proxies, and especially to deter an attack on the North Atlantic Treaty Organization (NATO) domain by the mighty Soviet forces in Europe. Today, however, the Soviet Union is a receding memory; more than a decade has passed since it disintegrated. The Soviet forces that remained in the hands of the Russians have suffered decay, disorganization, and demoralization. In the words of Lieutenant General Alexander I. Lebed, "Russia doesn't have an army anymore. It has only toy soldiers, formations of boys with no capacity."[9] Of the USSR's formidable navy, "little remains but rusting surface vessels and old, undermaintained submarines."[10] Moreover, the Russians, no longer the avowed enemies of the West, have entered into extensive economic, scientific, cultural, and even military cooperation with the United States and other Western nations. In view of all these developments, where is the present threat, the one so large and menacing that it requires military spending equal to that with which the United States waged the Cold War?

Is the United States Militarily Weak?

The United States suffers no shortage of defense Jeremiahs. In their circle, the Munich analogy remains ever fresh, the danger of appeasement and isolationism ever present. Thus, for example, retired Lieutenant General William E. Odom, though conceding that "today the Russian military does not present a serious threat to NATO," has warned that Russia's armed forces are "down but not out."[11] (Don't tell that story to the crew of the *Kursk.*) Former secretary of the navy John F. Lehman and Harvey Sicherman, writing in February 2001 and drawing on their forthcoming book titled *America the Vulnerable,* fretted about the erosion of U.S. military capacities and urged various maneuvers "to steer clear of the 'Pearl Harbor' cycle whereby only a disaster brings effective action."[12] The title of one recently published alarm speaks for itself: *While America Sleeps: Self-Delusion, Military Weakness, and the Threat to Peace Today,* by Donald Kagan and Frederick W. Kagan.[13]

Conservative organizations such as the Heritage Foundation have never met a military budget big enough to satisfy them. In 1996, Heritage analyst Baker Spring perceived "a serious mismatch between [U.S.] security commitments and the military capabilities needed to fulfill those commitments." Soon, he anticipated, the United States "will have to decide between remaining a global power capable of preventing wars or [*sic*] becoming a mere regional military power, condemned to fight and possibly lose them." In his view, projected defense budgets placed the nation "on a forced march along the path to military weakness and withdrawal."[14]

Neoconservatives, worried about what they perceive to be the flabby character of contemporary Americans, have urged greater military spending as support for a Teddy Roosevelt–style interventionist foreign policy, notwithstanding the enormous costs of such forthrightly macho globalism and its negligible likelihood of success in carrying out the neoconservative quest to spread "democracy."[15]

Although their fighting spirit no doubt merits a standing ovation, such observers of the contemporary military scene deserve low marks for their appreciation of the relevant facts. The United States today is anything but militarily weak. It bestrides the globe better equipped to defend its vital national interests than any preceding imperial power ever was. One has only to consider some pertinent comparisons.

According to data compiled by the Stockholm International Peace Research Institute (SIPRI), in 1999 the United States accounted for 36 percent of world military expenditure. U.S. allies Japan, France, Germany, the United Kingdom, and Italy ranked second through sixth, respectively, and, as a group, accounted for 26 percent. Russia ranked seventh, with military spending that amounted to 3 percent of the world total, and China ranked eighth, spending substantially less than Russia.[16] Russia "experienced sharp cuts in its military expenditure and arms procurement during the 1990s."[17] At the end of the 1990s, the United States was spending twenty-two times more than a group of seven so-called rogue states—Iran, Syria, Iraq, Libya, North Korea, Cuba, and Sudan.[18]

Because world military spending fell faster than U.S. military spending between 1985 and 1999, the U.S. share of the world total increased, from 30 percent to 36 percent.[19]

It is possible, of course, that the amounts spent might fail to reflect differences in actual military capabilities, but other data show that U.S. capabilities are genuine. Whether one considers active troop strength, reserve troop strength, heavy tanks, armored infantry vehicles, airplanes, helicopters, or major warships, the United States and its allies possess a preponderance of the warriors and the tools of war, greatly exceeding the troop strengths and the number of weapons platforms in the hands of all potential adversaries combined.[20] Beyond this numerical dominance, the United States and its allies possess important additional advantages of superiority in weapons technology as well as in communications, intelligence, logistics, training, maintenance, and mobility.

Listening to recent defense critics and presidential challengers, we might suspect that U.S. forces lack readiness to fight, but for the most part such suspicions have no sound basis. Readiness, as former assistant secretary of defense Lawrence J. Korb has commented, "is a slippery and poorly understood concept" as well as "a hot-button political issue, subject to unlimited manipulation." In 1995, Korb concluded that "the current readiness gap, like others since the 1970's, was designed and manufactured by the Pentagon to serve its political agenda—to maintain the cold war status quo."[21] Other analysts, writing from a variety of ideological positions, have reached similar conclusions with regard to more recently alleged readiness gaps.[22]

The argument that without a substantial military buildup the United States will soon find itself unable to defend its vital national interests simply cannot withstand scrutiny. Now that the USSR has fallen apart politically, economically, and militarily, no great threat looms.[23] Yes, of course, serious new threats may arise—lately the scare mongers have served up China as the bugbear du jour—and wise management of the defense establishment dictates that efforts be made to anticipate such threats and to prepare to meet them. Yes, the world remains a dangerous place, as the conservatives never tire of reiterating, but which of the existing dangers constitutes a *serious* threat to the vital national interests of the United States? Unless one defines those interests in an absurdly expansive, globally imperious manner, it seems clear that the United States is now well prepared to deal with all genuine present and prospective military threats. Of course, the United States lacks the power to resolve every dispute among the world's warring ethnic groups, to rescue every unfortunate victim of human or natural disaster, and to set every primitive nation on a smooth road to modern democratic capitalism. But no such power could be achieved in any event, and we would be foolish to gauge the adequacy of the U.S. defense establishment by such grotesquely bloated standards. The present forces are more than sufficient to protect U.S. citizens and their property within their national territory from attack by hostile states—as distinct from episodic terrorist attacks. One suspects that, down deep, nearly all those who advocate increased military spending understand that reality. Perhaps, nonetheless, they have other reasons to favor a big military buildup.

If the Nation Were Truly Imperiled, Would They Manage Defense This Way?

The U.S. defense establishment must be enormous and correspondingly expensive, one presumes, because the nation faces grave threats from its enemies abroad. Ostensibly, we are dealing with, in the words of Heritage analyst Baker Spring, a "potentially life-or-death issue."[24] But you have to wonder: If a genuine threat exists, why are defense decision makers managing the military establishment in such a slipshod and irresponsible manner? If the nation's security is really at stake, why do the national-security elites treat defense resources as if those resources serve only one purpose—namely, to feather the various parties' own political, bureaucratic, and economic nests? Danger is supposed to focus the mind. Why hasn't it?

Mismanagement of defense procurement is legendary. Over the years, several so-called blue-ribbon commissions, each composed of zealous, well-informed experts, have investigated the acquisition of military goods and services. Their reports have identified the same shortcomings again and again; their recommendations make for redundant reading. The Pentagon's standard response has been to make profuse promises followed by cosmetic changes, then to hunker down until the disturbers of the status quo lose interest, as they invariably do. The 1955 Hoover Commission, the 1970 Fitzhugh Commission, and the 1986 Packard Commission—all rang the same tocsin.[25] The fifteen-year periodicity of the appointment of such commissions held true to form on October 31, 2000, when President Bill Clinton signed legislation "to set up a 12-member commission with the aim of recommending improvements to the sometimes troubled relationship between the federal government and the nation's aerospace and defense companies."[26] Disinterested observers who know something about the history of such futile endeavors face a vexing choice: laugh or cry? In 1986, General James P. Mullins, former head of the Air Force Logistics Command, made a statement that remains as valid today as it was at the time: "we're still living in the past in the area of weapons procurement and support. We don't do things differently today. We do them just like we did them decades ago—in another day and age."[27] Korb opines that "getting the Pentagon to be more businesslike could save about $100 billion over the next five years,"[28] but what incentive exists to elicit businesslike behavior from a vast bureaucracy fueled by taxpayer money and accountable to neither customers nor shareholders?

In any event, the Department of Defense (DOD) lacks the basic information about its own affairs necessary to conduct them in a businesslike way. More than twenty years ago, air force whistle-blower Ernest Fitzgerald discovered that "feeble audit control by the government was one of the great flaws that allowed the whole scandalous system to flourish."[29] That weakness has persisted. On April 16, 1998, Eleanor Hill, the Pentagon's inspector general, testified to Congress: "I cannot yet report to you that the Department has successfully corrected the many shortcomings in its accounting and financial systems. The financial statement data for most DOD funds remain unreliable and essentially not in condition to audit."[30] Recently, Defense Secretary Donald Rumsfeld admitted, "According to some estimates we cannot track $2.3 trillion in transactions."[31]

The official overseer of the DOD, of course, is Congress. Yet Congress, everyone agrees, is more a problem than a solution. A moderate-size library could be filled with books, articles, and reports detailing congressional mismanagement of the defense program.[32] As always when one uses the term *mismanagement* in this context, one must recognize that the actions qualify as mismanagement only in relation to the ostensible objective of producing the most national security from the resources made available for that purpose.

As a rule, however, the actual objective of congressional actions is the reelection of incumbents, and viewed in that perspective the actions make good sense. In countless ways, big and small, members of Congress treat the defense budget as a big slush fund to be used for winning the favor of constituents and others whose support would improve the members' reelection prospects. As Richard Stubbings, a long-time defense analyst at the Office of Management and Budget, has observed, "this concern for the public-works aspect of the budget—this intramural scramble for resources—often leaves the Congress unable or unwilling to make hard choices on defense issues, particularly on issues with large dollar implications."[33]

Each year Congress adds billions of dollars to the request submitted by the DOD. Some of the add-ons amount to nothing more than a thinly veiled hoax with which the Pentagon plays along—much of the funding for National Guard and Reserve equipment and for military construction projects, for example, belongs in this category.[34] Other add-ons by Congress, however, amount to overrides of the military authorities' judgment, often for obvious pork-barrel projects. As a DOD budget document notes, "unrequested spending is especially damaging when it fails to take account of the future spending that it will generate."[35] Seawolf attack submarines, B-2 stealth bombers, and V-22 Osprey tilt-rotor aircraft come readily to mind as recent examples of this sort of add-on.

A sure sign of congressional hanky-panky is the addition of funds by the conference committee on the defense appropriations bills. Conferees throw in personal favorites not requested by the Pentagon and not included in either the House bill or the Senate bill being reconciled. In the FY 2001 budget, for example, the conference committee added almost $350 million for a long list of pet projects, supplementing the $3,313 million of add-ons already approved by the House and the Senate in their separate bills.[36]

Perhaps the clearest case of all pertains to congressional obstruction of military base closures. To fight World War II, the United States created an armed force of more than 12 million men and women and a multitude of bases to accommodate them and their equipment. After the war, the armed forces shrank drastically, and the number of bases greatly exceeded the number needed; hence, the closure of bases became a routine activity, though never a popular one with the members of Congress in whose districts the bases were being closed. Finally, between 1977 and 1987, an obstinate Congress brought major base closures to a complete halt.[37] In 1988, Congressman Dick Armey, with important support from Senator Barry Goldwater, managed to create and gain congressional approval of a clever arrangement for bringing about additional base closures, managed by the nonpartisan Commission on Base Realignment and Closure. Four rounds of the commission's procedure have now been undertaken, resulting in 222 major and 291 minor base closures or realignments and yielding annual recurring savings of approximately $6 billion, according to the DOD's estimate.[38] Despite the success of the commission—or perhaps because of it—Congress lately has lost its taste for additional closures, although the armed forces, whose ranks have diminished even further during the past decade, continue to urge more closures in order to divert funds from the maintenance of unnecessary bases to other uses.[39]

In examining congressional oversight of the defense program, we might easily fall into thinking that Congress is the mischief maker and the Pentagon is the long-suffering soldier just trying to do his job, but such a view has little to recommend it. In fact, the military departments are no less culpable than Congress. DOD decision makers are as self-interested as others involved in the defense program. Just consider that in 1998, after the active personnel strength of the military establishment had fallen by a third during the preceding decade, the DOD requested approval of fifty-four new slots for generals and admirals.[40]

Conduct a thought experiment: imagine that you are the czar of the U.S. defense program, with plenary power to decide how the limited resources available for defense purposes will be used to protect the nation from powerful external enemies. Would you choose to purchase and maintain more than one hundred "luxury jets used to fly generals and admirals," including seventy-one Learjets, thirteen Gulfstream IIIs, and seventeen Cessna Citations?[41] How about "234 golf courses maintained by the U.S. armed forces worldwide"?[42] Are such uses of resources consistent with the notion that the armed forces are spending the taxpayers' money wisely while dealing with life-and-death threats to U.S. national security?

No matter how objectionable Gulfstreams and golf courses may be as objects of military funding, however, they lie far from the heart of the Pentagon's most momentous misallocation of resources. To appreciate the most consequential mismanagement, one must focus on the big items, starting with the division of funds among the military services.

Interservice rivalry is as old as the republic. It can be and has been defended as an important element in generating innovation and in maintaining morale among the troops.[43] However, as Stubbing has commented, it "can go too far, especially when the services are unable to settle major disputes—over roles and missions, resources, and operations—in an efficient manner. Unfortunately, this has been the case throughout the post–World War II era."[44] Creation of an independent air force in 1947 only complicated and exacerbated the traditional rivalries of the military departments.

On the back side of the Reagan buildup, interservice rivalries became even fiercer in the 1990s as each service adopted the posture, "Hold onto everything you've got and fight the other services to the death."[45] One consequence has been a great deal of needless duplication of the research and development (R&D), production, and maintenance of weapons systems. Currently, for example, three competing tactical fighter aircraft and a variety of theater missile defense systems are being developed. Why, one might ask, must each branch of the military have its own tactical air force? Why maintain all the different medical corps and base structures? Surely costs could be lowered by the standardization of certain equipment, the combination of some R&D programs, and at least a selective sharing of repair facilities, depots, and the like.[46]

Interservice rivalries find their resolution in peace pacts, or cartel agreements—the so-called Key West Accords of 1948 being the most noteworthy—that stipulate how the rivals will divide tasks or resources. That such an agreement has long been in effect with respect to the overall DOD budget seems plain. As Richard J. Sherlock observed in 1997, "The relative portions of the Pentagon budget assigned to the Army, Navy and Air Force have not varied more than 2% over the past 25 years. Today, the Army continues to receive approximately 24%, the Air Force 29%, and the Navy (including the Marine Corps) 30% of the overall Defense budget."[47]

How well has the armed services cartel operated since Sherlock's 1997 observation? As table 30.1 shows, nothing has changed recently. During FY 1998–2001, the spending percentages of the three major services never deviated by as much as two percentage points from the cartel norm. Notice, too, that during recent years the deviations from the norm that did occur left undisturbed the established *relative* positions of the major services—lately, the percentage slice of *each* service has exceeded its cartel norm, and defensewide organizations have absorbed the loss.

Table 30.1

Percentage Distribution of DOD Outlays, by Service,
FY 1998–2001

Service	FY 1998	FY 1999	FY 2000	FY 2001	Cartel Norm
army	25.2	24.4	25.5	25.2	24.0
navy and marines	30.5	31.5	31.0	31.0	30.0
air force	30.4	29.4	29.3	29.9	29.0

Source: Calculated from outlay data in U.S. Department of Defense, Office of the Under Secretary of Defense (Comptroller), *National Defense Budget Estimates for FY 2000* (March 1999), p. 98. Cartel norm from Richard J. Sherlock, "New Realities, Old Pentagon Thinking," *Wall Street Journal*, April 24, 1997.

Return now to the previously described thought experiment: you are the Pentagon czar, intent on managing the DOD exclusively with an eye to the optimal employment of its budget in the service of maximizing national security. How likely is it that despite countless changes in specific threats, technologies, resource costs, and military experience, you would never have occasion to change the interservice distribution of total resources by more than a trivial amount? How likely is it that you would find it sensible even to preserve the traditional army–navy–air force arrangement itself?

The answers are obvious. Clearly, the management of the military establishment reflects not the outcome of a search for the optimal provision of national security, subject to an overall budget constraint. Rather, it reflects the outcome of a bureaucratic rivalry in which each competing organization strives to maintain—and succeeds in maintaining—its organizational integrity and its share of the loot regardless of whether an organizational redesign or a substantial redistribution of resources would enhance national security. Fifteen years ago General Mullins reached the same conclusion, though he expressed it in vaguer and more forgiving language: "Like all large bureaucracies, the military-industrial complex does have its share of problems. It is particularly prone to focusing on internal, organizational interests often to the detriment of the output the organization is designed to produce. In other words, its structure and operation have often evolved without enough regard to its function."[48] Safely in retirement, Admiral Bill Owens, former vice chairman of the Joint Chiefs of Staff, recently felt free to recommend that the services be stripped of their control over the choice of new weapons. "If we don't get some major reform . . . in the way we buy weapons systems," he warned, "we will pass some critical point where we no longer can do what the nation needs us to do."[49]

The Nature of the Beast

The evidence presented in the preceding section, which composes only a small selection from the enormous amount that could have been adduced, suffices to answer the question I posed at the outset: no, if the nation were truly imperiled, defense decision makers would not manage the military establishment as they do. Notwithstanding repeated exposés, critiques, and blown whistles, far too many grievous organizational defects have remained in place for decades, far too many seemingly inexcusable actions have been taken time after time. As an important Senate study concluded in 1985, "Past mistakes—whether in the procurement of a weapon system or in the employment of forces during a crisis—do not receive the critical review that would prevent them from recurring. ... The lessons go unlearned, and the mistakes are repeated."[50] Evidently, the system remains impermeable to genuine reform for a reason: the status quo must be serving somebody's interest.

The concept of the MICC is best understood as nothing more than a suggestion of who the main interested parties are. Members of Congress and the military authorities themselves we have already glimpsed in action, the former seeking for the most part to enhance their reelection prospects and the latter doing for the most part what good soldiers must do to climb the ladder of bu-

Table 30.2

Top Ten DOD Prime Contractors, FY 2000

Company	Awards ($ billions)	Major Products
Lockheed Martin Corp.	15.1	F-16, AH-64 Apache, Trident, and Hellfire missiles
Boeing Company	12.0	F/A-18, F-15, V-22 Osprey, RAH-66 Comanche, C-17
Raytheon Corp.	6.3	Patriot, AMRAAM, and Hawk missiles
General Dynamics Corp.	4.2	nuclear submarines, DDG-51 destroyer
Northrop Grumman Corp.	3.1	B-2 bomber, F-15, F/A-18
Litton Industries, Inc.	2.7	DDG-51 destroyer, LHD amphibious assault ship
United Technologies Corp.	2.1	aircraft and helicopter engines, UH-60, C-17
TRW Incorporated	2.0	electronic systems and support
General Electric Co., Inc.	1.6	aircraft and helicopter engines
Science Applications International Corp.	1.5	programmatic, logistical, and technical support

Source: U.S. Department of Defense, *Companies Receiving the Largest Dollar Volume of Prime Contract Awards—Fiscal Year 2000*. Available at: http://web1.whs.osd.mil/peidhome/ procstat/p01/fy2000/top100.htm, and Center for Defense Information, *Fact Sheet: Top 15 U.S. Defense Contractors*. Available at: http://www.cdi.org/issues/usmi/complex/top15FY99.html.

reaucratic success. We come now to the "industrial" part of the complex. This is where we would have ended up anyhow had we only complied with that ancient maxim of social science research, "follow the money."

Although the MICC shelters a variety of creatures—little rats as well as fat cats, hoot owls among the operation and maintenance accounts as well as lion kings of the major R&D and procurement programs—it is the latter, the big defense companies whose activities are reported in the *Wall Street Journal* on any given day, who occupy the high ground. They are the prime contractors who preside over the design, production, and deployment of the fabulously expensive whiz-bang weapons systems that define the activities of a modern armed force: tanks, ships, aircraft, missiles, satellites, and high-tech equipment for carrying out surveillance, communication, and targeting. Table 30.2 presents some details about the contractors presently leading the pack.

The big defense companies are, in General Mullins's apt phrase, "where the babies come from." As he explains,

> the contractor has already often determined what it wants to produce before the formal acquisition process begins.... The contractor validates the design through the process of marketing it to one of the services. If successful, the contractor gets a contract. Thus, to a substantial degree, the weapon capabilities devised by contractors create military requirements.... For years now, as a customer for the prime contractors, [the military] has placed major emphasis on operational performance. The result was often adoption of immature technologies that are unreliable and difficult to support.[51]

Today's U.S. warriors, regardless of the type of weapon they wield, increasingly resemble space cadets. The V-22 Osprey's cockpit, "with its bank of colored computer displays, ... looks more like the flight deck of a modern jet-liner than a Spartan warbird."[52] Brigadier General Russel L. Honore has complained recently that the army's M1A2 tank "is more like an F-16 jet fighter than it's like an M1A1 tank, and this should sort of scare us."[53] Indeed, it should scare us, in view of the half-educated boys at the controls of those multi-million-dollar behemoths.[54] More than twenty years ago, Secretary of Defense Harold Brown called attention to "the difficulties of training realistically with high-priced weaponry where the potential cost of losing or expending expensive weapons inhibits training realism."[55] As the conduct of the 1999 war against Serbia revealed, U.S. combat commanders have become loathe to risk their hyperexpensive high-tech weapons too close to an actual enemy, even a pathetically inferior one.

Because both the contractor and the military service emphasize pushing the technical-performance envelope, a next-generation weapon typically takes ten, fifteen, or even twenty years to develop and, after finally being deployed, often works poorly and demands frequent, expensive maintenance. Military spokespersons try to cover up the failures of their cutting-edge weapons systems by faking test results and by lying about actual battlefield performance—anything to keep the program rolling. As Fitzgerald has reported, "Government officials, from the majestic office of the president to the lowest, sleaziest procurement office, lie routinely and with impunity in defense of the system."[56] Colonel James G. Burton, an air force officer who spent fourteen years at the Pentagon working with a handful of others trying to reform the system from within, ultimately concluded: "The business of buying weapons that takes place in the Pentagon is a corrupt business—ethically and morally corrupt from top to bottom. The process is dominated by advocacy, with few, if any, checks and balances. Most people in power like this system of doing business and do not want it changed."[57] Because so few powerful people want it changed, it has not been changed in any fundamental respect since it first took shape sixty years ago.[58] Even the rare reform effort that is not a mere public-relations ploy is almost dead on arrival. It twitches for a while and emits a big report, which is promptly filed and forgotten.

Notwithstanding everything that might be said, and time and again has

Table 30.3

Total Projected Program Costs of Selected Weapons Systems

Cost	Weapons Systems	Units
$219.0 billion	Navy–Air Force Joint Strike Fighter (JSF)	3,000 planes
$79.5 billion	Navy F/A-18E/F Hornet tactical fighter	1,000 planes
$70.9 billion	F-22 Air Force advanced tactical fighter	440 planes
$67.0 billion	Navy NSSN new attack submarine	30 submarines
$56.5 billion	Navy DDG-51 AEGIS destroyer	57 ships
$48.0 billion	Army RAH-66 Comanche helicopter	1,292 helicopters
$45.5 billion	Navy (marine) V-22 Osprey	523 planes
$44.4 billion	Air Force B-2 strategic bomber	21 planes
$41.4 billion	Air Force C-17 airlift aircraft	120 planes
$27.5 billion	Navy Trident II (D-5) missile	462 missiles
$5.4 billion	CVN-77 nuclear aircraft carrier	1 ship

Sources: Selected Acquisition Reports, September 30, 1997, and, for JSF and Comanche, cost estimates from Congressional Budget Office, as compiled by Council for a Livable World Education Fund, *Fiscal 1999 Military Budget at a Glance*. Available at: http://www.clw.org/ef/dodbud99.html.

been said, about the deficiencies of the weapons-procurement process, the MICC forges ahead fundamentally inviolate, pouring a vast stream of taxpayer money into the acquisition and deployment of high-tech weaponry. Much of that money the big contractors find some way to absorb:

> The techniques are many—buy-ins during competition, overpriced design changes, charges of unanticipated inflation, creative overhead accounting, sole-source contracts for follow-on modifications and spare parts—but the end result is the same: the large contractors survive and prosper without being held accountable for their performance.... At times the weapons acquisition process appears to be geared far more to protecting and fostering the major defense firms than to arming the military with high-quality weapons at a reasonable price.[59]

Table 30.3 displays information on the costliest programs now under way. High-performance aircraft, ships, and missiles—those are the end products that bring in the big bucks. As a glance back at table 30.2 confirms, the prime contractors of those products are the kingpins of the defense industry.

Mulling over the information displayed in table 30.3, one might wonder: What sort of war, against what enemy, is the DOD preparing to fight? The answer is all too obvious. The Pentagon is preparing to fight the Cold War! Which is not really so surprising. An old aphorism tells us that the generals always prepare to fight the last war. And why not? All significant participants in the MICC continue to serve their own interests best by doing so.[60]

As the prospect brightens for a new infusion of defense spending under the Bush administration, the leading aerospace companies anticipate receiving the biggest slice of those additional funds. The administration's commitment to the development of a national missile defense system (NMD), in particular, promises to serve as a bottomless reservoir of corporate revenue for the top missile and electronics companies and their legions of subcontractors. According to a 1995 Congressional Research Service report, the Pentagon spent $70.7 billion on ballistic-missile defense activities from FY 1984 through FY 1994, with very little to show for it.[61] Current projections place the cost of further NMD development at some $60 billion,[62] but only a dreamer would bet on that figure. If an effective NMD system is ever successfully produced—a big "if"—it will certainly cost far more than the presently projected amount.[63] Unfortunately, that vast expenditure will avail little or nothing in the provision of genuine national security, for an enemy can always choose to play a different game, foiling the best-laid NMD plans by firing a nuclear-armed *cruise* missile from a ship lying off New York, or by delivering a chemical or biological weapon of mass death tucked into a shipment of cocaine bound for Los Angeles, or by taking any number of other actions immune to the NMD system.[64]

Conclusion

After a much-troubled career in the belly of the beast, Ernest Fitzgerald aptly commented that "peacetime military spending has little to do with foreign policy or the world situation.... [I]t is largely driven by domestic politics."[65] Which is to say, it is driven by a combination of ideology (especially among the fleeced taxpayers) and the self-interest of the millions of people who populate the MICC,[66] for whom jobs, career advancement, reelection to political office and, above all, corporate profits turn on feeding more money into the maw of the MICC.[67]

Such facts of life do not imply that no national security gets produced; it does, even if it gets produced as a by-product and in an outrageously wasteful manner.[68] The United States possesses a tremendously wealthy economy. The nation can and does sustain huge losses as resources pass through a MICC replete with foolishness, corruption, and cupidity, yet the nation still emerges on the other side of the process as a great power.[69] The present U.S. military establishment is overwhelmingly the most powerful the world has ever known, and it has ample capacity to defend the nation against the military forces of any present or prospective foe *in the kind of wars it is dedicated to fighting*.

If an enemy should decide to wage a different kind of war, however, such as really serious terrorism, the armed forces are not configured to deal with that kind of threat;[70] "the most powerful weapons available to them, including specifically the heavy ones which account for the bulk of their budgets, are entirely useless" against such a threat,[71] and everyone appreciates that the public-relations noises the Pentagon makes about antiterrorism activities are not intended to be taken seriously by those in the know. The system has no constituency for the nitty-gritty, low-tech activity that an effective antiterrorism program would call for, such as the maintenance of a massive global corps of unsavory informants on the ground; there's no money in it for Lockheed Martin, Boeing, and the rest of the boys. But if you want to talk about a Star Wars system that stretches from here to Mars, they'll say, "Hey, let's talk!"

Postscript 2002

The preceding discussion, almost exactly as it appears here, was completed early in 2001 and published in the fall 2001 issue of *The Independent Review*, which was passing through the mail to subscribers when the terrorist attacks of September 11 took place. My observation that the U.S. military establishment was not being managed so as to provide security against terrorist attacks then seemed prophetic, but I was scarcely a lone voice crying out in the wilderness. Others had been warning for years of precisely the same misallocation of defense resources.

The Hart-Rudman Commission, for example, had highlighted the threat of international terrorism, noting that Americans no longer enjoy a "relative invulnerability of the U.S. homeland to catastrophic attack" and predicting that "[a] direct attack against American citizens *on American soil* is likely over the next quarter century." The DOD, the commission concluded, "appears incapable of generating a strategic posture very different from that of the Cold War, and its weapons acquisition process is slow, inefficient, and burdened by excess regulation." Declaring that the DOD "needs to pay far more attention to this [homeland defense] mission in the future," the commission recommended that "a new office of Assistant Secretary for Homeland Security be created to oversee DOD activities in this domain and to ensure that the necessary resources are made available."[72] Such reports, one comes to expect, are duly noted by the press and then pass into obscurity more or less ignored by the busy people who populate the MICC, and this particular report was no exception.

Shortly after the September 11 attacks, President Bush did move in the direction recommended by the Hart-Rudman Commission when he created the Office of Homeland Security. One wonders how many Americans have stopped to ponder the meaning of that action? For more than fifty years, the United States has maintained an active—some might say hyperactive—DOD. If *it* does not defend our homeland, what *does* it defend?

Whatever the answer might be, the Pentagon has not been shy about spending our money. During the more than forty years of Cold War, annual military spending averaged 7.5 percent of gross national product (GNP),[73] and just in the past five years, military spending has cumulated to more than $1.5 trillion.[74] You'd think that so much money would purchase a great deal of national security. Yet, apart from the catastrophic attack on New York City, the defense establishment, including its numerous "intelligence" agencies, failed even to anticipate or to defend against the devastating attack on its own headquarters.

On October 1, 2001, the Pentagon issued its Quadrennial Defense Review. As *New York Times* reporter Thom Shanker noted, this review "restores the defense of the United States as the department's primary mission."[75] One can't help wondering: What was its primary mission before the attack? Would you believe these imperial objectives: stationing forces worldwide, propping up allied governments, deterring threats to U.S. interests *abroad,* and, should the need arise, fighting a couple of those ever-popular foreign wars?[76]

On October 23, 2001, the DOD issued an announcement seeking contract proposals for "combating terrorism, location and defeat of hard or difficult targets, protracted operations in remote areas, and countermeasures to weapons of mass destruction." It seemed the Pentagon was—*finally*—in a hurry in its counterterrorism efforts, because it sought "near-term solutions" to be developed in twelve to eighteen months.[77] You don't need to be a defense specialist to see that the Pentagon was caught off-guard by the September 11 attacks on the United States, by the manner in which they were carried out, and by nature of the perpetrators. So you have to wonder: What were all those defense bigwigs doing with all that money during the preceding decade?

Well, as we have just seen, they were continuing to fight the Cold War, even though that conflict had ended in the early 1990s with the disintegration of the Soviet Union. Notwithstanding the evaporation of the once-mighty Red Army, the lion's share of recent defense spending has gone—*and continues to go*—toward maintaining a force equipped with Cold War weapons—high-tech combat aircraft, warships, missiles, satellites, and so forth.[78] A politically entrenched defense industry makes sure that such spending continues at a high level, and pork-dispensing congressmen grease the wheels, buying a few votes in the process.

Even though the September 11 attackers launched their mission with decidedly low-tech weapons—box cutters—the MICC, in defiance of all logic, has redoubled its efforts to milk the established high-tech cash cows. For example, Northrup Grumman and its friends in high places now perceive an opportunity to resume production of the quintessential Cold War weapons platform, the B-2 bomber, at a cost of some $28 billion for gearing up the assembly line and turning out another forty aircraft. According to Congressman Duncan Hunter (R-Calif.), chairman of the House Armed Services Committee's Subcommittee on Research and Development, the war on terrorism has shown that "long-range and precision-strike capabilities are going to be even more valuable than before."[79] Yeah, sure.

According to the *Wall Street Journal,* "the F-22 and nearly every other expensive Pentagon weapon suddenly has become immune to major budget cuts" since the terrorists commandeered the four airliners in September. For DOD and its contractors, "that means keeping every current big-ticket item and adding a few new ones." In the immortal words of Boeing vice chairman Harry Stonecipher, "the purse is now open," and members of Congress who oppose the new spending frenzy by arguing that "we don't have the resources to defend America . . . won't be there after November" 2002.[80] Bizarrely, even the granddaddy of all military boondoggles, the ballistic-missile defense system, has regained its momentum in the aftermath of the terrorists' use of nonballistic missiles conveniently made available by United Airlines and American Airlines.[81]

As defense analyst Ivan Eland recently remarked of the Bush administration's proposal to increase defense spending by $45 billion, or 13 percent, during FY 2003, "Most of the defense budget increase has little to do with winning the war on terrorism."[82] Just as the Korean War once served as the pretext for vastly increasing military spending on forces positioned worldwide, the so-called war on terrorism now serves as the pretext for throwing money at every constituent in the MICC. The *Wall Street Journal* confirms, "The antiterror campaign is making for some remarkably flush times for the military, and the need for hard choices on weapons systems has all but evaporated."[83] For all the big weapons systems and all the big contractors, the threat of project cancellations or spending cutbacks is now a thing of the past.

Leading defense contractors have undertaken to broaden the markets for their products in connection with the so-called war on terrorism. However, according to the *Homeland Security Monitor,* "While defense contractors have allocated some resources to selling repackaged products for homeland security purposes, none are staking too much on the effort, as the homeland security funding proposed by President Bush for 2003 is $37.7 billion, only about a tenth of the $379 billion proposed for defense spending."[84] As usual, defending the empire gets the bulk of the budget, whereas defending the American people at home gets a relatively wee amount, and the defense companies, with bloodhound noses for taxpayer loot, follow the scent of the money.

Members of Congress, never satisfied until a maximum amount of the defense budget has been diverted toward buying votes for their reelection, are not objecting to the huge increase in military spending, but they want no reallocations whatsoever away from the established Cold War programs that currently channel taxpayer money to their political backers: "In a bipartisan voice," reports James Dao of the *New York Times,* "lawmakers on Capitol Hill are telling the Pentagon that they want to increase spending on conventional big-ticket weapons programs, particularly warships and planes, raising new questions about Defense Secretary Donald Rumsfeld's ability to revamp the military with newer types of technology."[85] According to an unpublished report by "an anonymous well-placed aide" whose pen name is Spartacus, members of Congress also larded the post–September 11 defense bills with "hundreds of 'irrelevancies' such as museums, chapels and gyms." For Congress, this disgusted insider wrote, "War is not Hell; it's an opportunity."[86]

And so it goes. For those with an appreciation of the past sixty years of U.S. history, its déjà vu again. This time, however, Americans may have to pay a higher price in blood as well as in money for the maintenance of their blessed MICC. The Pentagon's business-as-usual defense policy—*obviously*—failed to defend the American people on September 11. Nor can we expect it to defend us in the future. Just possibly, what's good for Lockheed Martin, the top brass at the Pentagon, and the congressional representatives in cahoots with them is not necessarily good for national security. But then, why worry? We've now got the Department of Homeland Security to protect us.

Notes

1. Rumsfeld as quoted in Greg Jaffe and Jacob M. Schlesinger, "Pressure for More Defense Funds Collides with Other Bush Pledges," *Wall Street Journal,* January 19, 2001. See also Greg Jaffe and John D. McKinnon, "Defense-Budget Request Is Likely to Be Delayed," *Wall Street Journal,* February 6, 2001.

2. Greg Jaffe and Anne Marie Squeo, "Missile-Defense Contract Contest Begins for Lucrative Projects," *Wall Street Journal,* January 30, 2001.

3. "Bush's Budget Balance: Some Numbers Go Up, Others Go Down," *Wall Street Journal,* March 1, 2001.

4. Greg Jaffe, "Pentagon Plan Sees 42% Rise in Arms Budget," *Wall Street Journal,* May 1, 2001.

5. The allusion is to my article "Beware the Pork-Hawk," *Reason* (June 1989): 28–34 (a revised version of which appears as chap. 29 in this collection).

6. U.S. Department of Defense, Office of the Under Secretary of Defense (Comptroller), *National Defense Budget Estimates for FY 2000* (Washington, D.C.: U.S. Government Printing Office, March 1999), pp. 202–3, figures adjusted to 1999 dollars according to the change in the implicit gross domestic product (GDP) deflator reported by U.S. Council of Economic Advisers, *Report 2000* (Washington, D.C.: U.S. Government Printing Office, 2000), p. 310. Throughout this chapter, unless otherwise indicated, *defense spending* refers to actual outlays, not to appropriations, budget authority, obligational authority, or any other accounting measure.

7. Robert Higgs, "The Cold War Economy: Opportunity Costs, Ideology, and the Politics of Crisis," *Explorations in Economic History* 31 (July 1994), p. 288.

8. Defense spending data for FY 1995–99 from U.S. Department of Defense, Office of the Under Secretary of Defense, *National Defense Budget Estimates for FY 2000,* p. 203, adjusted to 1999 dollars according to the change in the implicit GDP deflator reported by U.S. Council of Economic Advisers, *Report 2000,* p. 310; defense spending data for FY 2000 from U.S. Department of Defense, news release, February 7, 2000, adjusted to 1999 dollars by assumption of 2 percent increase in the implicit GDP deflator between FY 1999 and FY 2000.

9. Lebed as quoted in Robert Higgs, "A Strong Defense Against Whom?" *St. Louis Post-Dispatch,* February 6, 1995. See also Adi Ignatius, "Russia Now Fields a Potemkin Military: Armed Forces, Except Nuclear Units, Grow Hollow," *Wall Street Journal,* July 2, 1993.

10. Martin Creveld, *The Rise and Decline of the State* (Cambridge, Eng.: Cambridge University Press, 1999), p. 345.

11. William E. Odom, "Russia's Military: Down but Not Out," *Wall Street Journal,* August 27, 1996.

12. John F. Lehman and Harvey Sicherman, "America's Military Problems and How to Fix Them," *Wire 9,* distributed via the Internet by the Foreign Policy Research Institute, February 17, 2001.

13. New York: St. Martin's, 2001.

14. Baker Spring, *Will Clinton Pay the Price for America to Remain a Global Power?* Heritage Foundation Backgrounder no. 1083 (Washington, D.C.: Heritage Foundation, 1996), pp. 1, 7.

15. Joshua Muravchik, *The Imperative of American Leadership: A Challenge to Neo-isolationism* (Washington, D.C.: American Enterprise Institute, 1996). For a compendium of recent essays along these lines, see Robert Kagan and William Kristol, eds., *Present Dangers: Crisis and Opportunity in American Foreign and Defense Policy* (San Francisco: Encounter, 2000).

16. SIPRI, "Military Expenditure: Recent Trends in Military Expenditure," at http://projects.sipri.se/milex/mex_trends.html. According to data compiled by the Center for Defense

Information (whose sources are the U.S. Department of Defense and the International Institute for Strategic Studies), both Russia and China spent substantially more than the SIPRI data show, but the difference has no substantive bearing on any conclusions reached here. For the alternative data, see the figures at http://www.cdi.org/issues/wme/spendersFY01.html.

17. SIPRI, "Military Expenditure."

18. Center for Defense Information, "Last of the Big Time Spenders," at http://www.cdi.org/issues/wme/spendersFY01.html.

19. Center for Defense Information, "World Military Expenditure: US vs World," at http://www.cdi.org/issues.wme/.

20. Center for Defense Information, "Military Strengths of U.S., Allied, and Selected Other Armed Forces," at http://www.cdi.org/issues/wmke/oob.html.

21. Lawrence J. Korb, "The Readiness Gap: What Gap?" *New York Times Magazine,* February 26, 1995, pp. 40–41. See also David Isenberg, *The Misleading Military "Readiness Crisis,"* Cato Institute Foreign Policy Briefing no. 35 (Washington, D.C.: Cato Institute, 1995).

22. Michael O'Hanlon, *Ready for Action,* Brookings Institution In Brief (Washington, D.C.: Brookings Institution, December 29, 1996); Harvey M. Sapolsky and Eugene Gholz, "The Defense Monopoly," *Regulation* 22 (1999), p. 43; Gregg Easterbrook, "Apocryphal Now: The Myth of the Hollow Military," *New Republic,* September 11, 2000; and Ivan Eland, *A Hollow Debate on Military Readiness,* Cato Institute Foreign Policy Briefing no. 62 (Washington, D.C.: Cato Institute, 2000).

23. The only important exception to this declaration pertains to the continued maintenance of huge battle-ready nuclear forces by both the United States and Russia, but the threat posed by this condition relates to the potential for a catastrophic accident or a failure of the command-and-control systems, not to the likelihood that Russia will launch a deliberate attack on the United States. For informed observations on this danger by the former commander in chief of the U.S. Strategic Command, see George Lee Butler, "Time to End the Age of Nukes," *Bulletin of the Atomic Scientists* (March–April 1997): 33–36. See also Brian Hall, "Overkill Is Not Dead," *New York Times Magazine,* March 15, 1998, pp. 42–49, 64, 76, 78, 84–85; Carla Anne Robbins, "U.S. Nuclear Arsenal Is Poised for War—Is It the Right One?" *Wall Street Journal,* October 15, 1999; and Geoffrey Forden, *Reducing a Common Danger: Improving Russia's Early-Warning System,* Cato Institute Policy Analysis no. 399 (Washington, D.C.: Cato Institute, 2001). Early in 2004 the danger remained as great as ever, and perhaps even greater. See Alexander Zaitchik, "Hair-Trigger Planet: Old Nukes Don't Die. They Just Sit Around and Wait to Be Launched," *New York Press* 17, no. 7 (2004), accessed February 18, 2004, at http://www.nypress.com/print.cgm?content_id=9632.

24. *Will Clinton Pay the Price?* p. 7.

25. William E. Kovacic, "Blue Ribbon Defense Commissions: The Acquisition of Major Weapon Systems," in *Arms, Politics, and the Economy: Historical and Contemporary Perspectives,* edited by Robert Higgs (New York: Holmes and Meier for The Independent Institute, 1990), pp. 61–103.

26. "Commission to Study Relationship Between U.S., Defense Firms," *Wall Street Journal,* November 1, 2000.

27. James P. Mullins, *The Defense Matrix: National Preparedness and the Military-Industrial Complex* (San Diego: Avant, 1986), p. 49.

28. Lawrence Korb, "The Myth of the Two-Front War," *Washington Monthly* (March 1997), p. 25.

29. Ernest A. Fitzgerald, *The Pentagonists: An Insider's View of Waste, Mismanagement, and Fraud in Defense Spending* (Boston: Houghton Mifflin, 1989), p. 165.

30. Hill as quoted in Council for a Livable World Education Fund, "Pentagon: Part of the Problem as Well," at http://www.clw.org/ef/caution/pentagon.html.

31. CBS News, "The War on Waste: Defense Department Cannot Account for 25% of Funds—$2.3 Trillion," *CBS Evening News,* January 30, 2002, at http://www.cbsnews .com/now/story/0,1597,325985-412,00.shtml?

32. In addition to the essays by James M. Lindsay, Kenneth R. Mayer, and Charlotte Twight in *Arms, Politics, and the Economy,* ed. Higgs, see Robert Higgs, "Hard Coals Make Bad Law: Congressional Parochialism Versus National Defense," *Cato Journal* 8 (spring–summer 1988): 79–106; Higgs, "Beware the Pork-Hawk"; James M. Lindsay, "Congressional Oversight of the Department of Defense: Reconsidering the Conventional Wisdom," *Armed Forces and Society* 17 (fall 1990): 7–33; James M. Lindsay, *Congress and Nuclear Weapons* (Baltimore: Johns Hopkins University Press, 1991); Kenneth R. Mayer, *The Political Economy of Defense Contracting* (New Haven, Conn.: Yale University Press, 1991); and Richard A. Stubbing, with Richard A. Mendel, *The Defense Game: An Insider Explores the Astonishing Realities of America's Defense Establishment* (New York: Harper and Row, 1986), chap. 5.

33. Stubbing with Mendel, *The Defense Game,* p. 90.

34. Michelle Cottle, "High on the Hog," *New York Times Magazine,* November 22, 1998, pp. 58–59.

35. U.S. Department of Defense, "The FY 1999 Defense Budget and Future Years Defense Program," at http://www.dtic.mil/execsex/adr98/chap21.html.

36. Center for Defense Information, "Fiscal Year 2001 Add-Ons: Congress' Unrequested Spending for the Pentagon," at http://www.cdi.org/issues/budget/add-ons01.html.

37. Charlotte Twight, "Department of Defense Attempts to Close Military Bases: The Political Economy of Congressional Resistance," in *Arms, Politics, and the Economy,* ed. Higgs, pp. 236–80.

38. Center for Defense Information, "Base Realignment and Closure Statistics," at http://www .cdi.org/issues/brac/bracstat.html.

39. Kenneth R. Mayer, "The Limits of Delegation: The Rise and Fall of BRAC," *Regulation* 22 (1999): 32–38.

40. Council for a Livable World, "Pentagon: Part of the Problem as Well."

41. "Congress Report Says Military Uses Luxury Jets for Top Brass," *Seattle Times,* May 30, 2000.

42. Center for Defense Information, "Tee-ing Off the Taxpayer," at http://www.cdi.org/adm/ Transcripts/948/.

43. Sapolsky and Gholz, "The Defense Monopoly," pp. 41–43.

44. *The Defense Game,* p. 133.

45. Thomas E. Ricks, "Armed Forces Prepare to Battle One Another for Funds," *Wall Street Journal,* February 6, 1997. See also Michael Killan, "Chief Defines New Navy Role," *Seattle Times,* May 6, 1997, and Mayer, "The Limits of Delegation," p. 33.

46. U.S. Senate, Committee on Armed Services, *Defense Organization: The Need for Change.*

Staff Report. 99th Cong., 1st sess., S. Prt. 99-86, October 16, 1985, pp. 539–41.

47. Richard Sherlock, "New Realities, Old Pentagon Thinking," *Wall Street Journal,* April 24, 1997. See also Stubbing with Mendel, *The Defense Game,* pp. 71–72.

48. Mullins, *The Defense Matrix,* p. 3.

49. Owens as quoted in Tim Weiner, "How to Build Weapons When Money Is No Object," *New York Times,* April 16, 2000.

50. U.S. Senate, Committee on Armed Services, *Defense Organization,* p. 8.

51. Mullins, *The Defense Matrix,* pp. 91, 93.

52. J. Lynn Lunsford, "Osprey under Fire," *Seattle Times,* February 20, 2001.

53. Honore as quoted in Council for a Livable World, "Pentagon: Part of the Problem as Well."

54. Stubbing with Mendel, *The Defense Game,* p. 131.

55. Ibid., p. 154.

56. *The Pentagonists,* p. 312. See also Dina Rasor, ed., *More Bucks, Less Bang: How the Pentagon Buys Ineffective Weapons* (Washington, D.C.: Fund for Constitutional Government, 1983); Dina Rasor, *The Pentagon Underground* (New York: Times Books, 1985); James G. Burton, *The Pentagon Wars: Reformers Challenge the Old Guard* (Annapolis, Md.: Naval Institute Press, 1993); Tim Weiner, "Stealth, Lies, and Videotape," *New York Times,* July 14, 1996; and Lunsford, "Osprey under Fire."

57. *The Pentagon Wars,* p. 232. On corruption, see also CBS News, "The War on Waste."

58. On the origins of the modern military acquisition system, see Robert Higgs, "Private Profit, Public Risk: Institutional Antecedents of the Modern Military Procurement System in the Rearmament Program of 1940–1941," in *The Sinews of War: Essays on the Economic History of World War II,* edited by Geofrey T. Mills and Hugh Rockoff (Ames: Iowa State University Press, 1993), pp. 166–98.

59. Stubbing with Mendel, *The Defense Game,* p. 212.

60. Sapolsky and Gholz, "The Defense Monopoly," pp. 40, 43; Steven Lee Myers, "Getting More Bang for the Armed Forces Buck," *New York Times,* February 18, 2001.

61. Physicians for Social Responsibility, "Issue Brief: Ballistic Missile Defense (BMD)," at http://www.psr.org/bmd.htm.

62. International Institute for Strategic Studies, "The Military Balance: The Regions: United States," at http://www.iiss.org/pub/mbregion.asp#arrow.

63. Peter H. Rose, "Bush Should Tone Down National Missile Defense," *Seattle Times,* March 14, 2001.

64. James Dao, "Please Do Not Disturb Us with Bombs," *New York Times,* February 11, 2001; William J. Broad, "Smaller, Cheaper, Stealthier, Deadlier," *New York Times,* February 11, 2001; and Ivan Eland, "Bush's Grandiose Missile Defense Scheme," distributed via Internet by the Cato Institute, May 3, 2001.

65. *The Pentagonists,* p. 132.

66. On the ideological impetus, see Higgs, "The Cold War Economy," and Robert Higgs and Anthony Kilduff, "Public Opinion: A Powerful Predictor of U.S. Defense Spending," *Defence Economics* 4 (1993): 227–38.

67. On the corporate profitability of defense contractors, see Robert Higgs and Ruben Trevino, "Profits of U.S. Defense Contractors," *Defence Economics* 3 (1992): 211–18.

68. On national security as an incidental output, see Dwight R. Lee, "Public Goods, Politics, and Two Cheers for the Military-Industrial Complex," in *Arms, Politics, and the Economy*, ed. Higgs, pp. 22–36.

69. Sapolsky and Gholz, "The Defense Monopoly," p. 43.

70. Matt Kelley, "Pentagon: Anti-terrorist Units Unfit," *Seattle Times*, February 26, 2001.

71. Creveld, *The Rise and Decline of the State*, p. 400.

72. United States Commission on National Security/21st Century, *Road Map for National Security* (February 15, 2001), pp. 8 and viii–ix, respectively, emphasis in original.

73. Higgs, "The Cold War Economy," p. 292.

74. U.S. Office of Management and Budget, *Budget of the United States Government: Fiscal Year 2003, Historical Tables* (Washington, D.C.: U.S. Government Printing Office, 2002), p. 294.

75. Thom Shanker, "Defense Review Reflects Terrorism Threats: Domestic Protection Raised to Top Mission," *New Orleans Times-Picayune*, October 2, 2001, reprinted from the *New York Times*.

76. Ibid.

77. U.S. Department of Defense, Under Secretary of Defense for Acquisition, Technology, and Logistics (USD [AT&L]) and Combating Terrorism Technology Support Office Technical Support Working Group (TSWG), *Broad Agency Announcement 02-Q-4655* (Washington, D.C.: U.S. Government Printing Office, October 23, 2001), p. 17.

78. Council for a Livable World, "Fiscal Year 2003 Military Budget at a Glance," at http://www.clw.org/milspend/dodbud03.html.

79. Andy Pasztor and Anne Marie Squeo, "B-2 Bomber Emerges as Focus of Budget Battles," *Wall Street Journal*, October 24, 2001.

80. Anne Marie Squeo and Andy Pasztor, "Terrorist Attacks Have Made Pentagon Weapons Budget Bulletproof," *Wall Street Journal*, October 15, 2001.

81. Anne Marie Squeo and Greg Jaffe, "Pentagon Enlists Defense Companies' Aid As It Weighs Missile-Defense Restructuring," *Wall Street Journal*, November 8, 2001; Anne Marie Squeo, "Pentagon to Create National Team to Steer Missile-Defense Programs," *Wall Street Journal*, December 24, 2001.

82. "Bush Defense Budget Based on Vested Interests, Not War on Terrorism, says Cato Analyst," Cato Institute press release, February 4, 2002, distributed via Internet.

83. "Rumsfeld Raised the Prospect of Terrorist Attacks Even Deadlier Than Sept. 11," *Wall Street Journal*, February 1, 2002. See also Anne Marie Squeo and Jacob M. Schlesinger, "Budget Plan to Brighten Skies for Defense Contractors," *Wall Street Journal*, February 1, 2002; Greg Jaffe and Anne Marie Squeo, "Bush's Proposed Defense Budget Includes Big Increases for Weapons, Antiterrorism," *Wall Street Journal*, February 5, 2002.

84. "Defense Contractors Shift Resources to Homeland Security," *Homeland Security Monitor*, March 21, 2002, distributed via Internet from intellibridgeteam@intellibridge.com.

85. James Dao, "Some Lawmakers Looking for More Warships, Planes. Too Little Equipment in Budget, They Say," *New Orleans Times-Picayune*, February 17, 2002, reprinted from the *New York Times*.

86. "'Spartacus' Revolts Against the Masters Again, This Time in Congress," *Wall Street Journal*, March 15, 2002.

PART VI

Retreat of the State?

31

Leviathan at Bay?
(As Viewed in 1991)

We Americans have cheered the collapse of socialism in eastern Europe and the Soviet Union. We celebrate as the people of those unfortunate places, long bound and exploited by their governments, strive to create institutions more compatible with individual freedom and economic prosperity. Ironically, however, we Americans ourselves seem hell-bent on making our own governments ever larger and more intrusive. As much of the world makes a U-turn on the road to serfdom, Americans plod doggedly toward that dismal destination. The prospect has driven some libertarians to despair.

But now, like a shaft of light penetrating the darkness, comes *Quicksilver Capital,* a new book by political economists Richard B. McKenzie and Dwight R. Lee.[1] Where there was gloom, McKenzie and Lee see only brighter tomorrows. Despite what many of us thought and feared, Leviathan, the authors assure us, is actually on the road to extinction.

The key to their arguments is the character of recent technological changes. McKenzie and Lee (hereafter M&L) explain that in the past governments have grown by fastening themselves onto an economy characterized by large production units that employ immense amounts of immobile physical capital. For a long time, such production facilities made sense because they allowed firms to benefit from economies of scale. When governments taxed and regulated economic activities more and more, the owners and workers had no easy means of escape because of the high cost of moving the capital essential to their productive activities, but during the past three decades technological changes have been cumulating to alter the old conditions of a capital-intensive, mass-production, industrial economy.

The information revolution associated with computers and miniaturization has changed the character of the economic world. Plants are getting smaller and more specialized. Mass production is losing, custom production is winning. Physical capital is relinquishing its central place in the technology of production. The crucial resources are now information and human capital (people's embodied skills and knowledge).

Resource mobility has become much greater, especially among nations. People can move themselves far more easily than they can move factories, and information can now be flashed around the world at nearly the speed of light. No longer do national boundaries limit transactions. Economic activities all over the planet are being drawn into an ever denser network of interdependence. Nations are becoming increasingly irrelevant to prevailing patterns of economic cooperation and coordination.

Because of the increasingly international character of business competition, the nation-state is losing its hold over the resources it exploits by means of taxation and regulation. M&L argue:

> Governments are not completely autonomous, self-controlling social institutions in which only politically devised, formal constitutional precepts constrain policy choices. On the contrary, governments are constrained by economic forces that, to a significant degree, exist outside of political systems, regardless of their conservative or liberal stripes. These exogenous economic forces have changed, giving rise to changes in direction for government policies. (p. xi)

Sooner or later, Goliath governments will be slain by computer nerd Davids hurling microchips.

M&L devote a substantial portion of their book to describing the technological changes that undergird their argument. Although most of these changes are more or less familiar, the details still boggle the mind. Consider, for example, the increase in the number of international phone calls, from 3.3 million in 1960 to 478 million in 1986 (p. 73). Today, a single computer chip with 10 million transistors can perform electronic operations in four billionths of a second (p. 41). As the microprocessors have become more powerful, the cost of information processing has fallen to a tiny fraction of what it was just twenty years ago, and it shows no sign of stopping its descent. International travel and business transactions have grown apace, much faster than economic activity as a whole. International investment has mushroomed. "Today," M&L remark, "the Japanese would probably have second thoughts about bombing Pearl Harbor simply because so much of Japan is already in Hawaii via the buildup of Japanese investments" (p. 244). The same argument might be made, of course, about many other formerly hostile countries.

Governments now confront a new reality about the resources they tax and regulate; if you abuse them, you lose them. Firms will look abroad for a safer haven, subcontracting portions of their activity or even relocating entire facilities abroad where governments will treat them with greater solicitude. The New York Life Insurance Company now has its claims processing done in Ireland. Instant electronic communications and regular air express service make this alternative cheaper than domestic processing (p. 51). American Airlines employs more than a thousand people in Barbados to enter data into its computers (p. 52). As economic activity moves abroad, it escapes the tax touch and regulatory reach of the government at its origin, weakening that government accordingly. A government had best tread lightly lest all its victims flee. Such considerations are now causing governments around the world to reduce their burdens on domestic economic activities, to privatize state enterprises, and to give greater scope to markets.

Reining in Government, Herding the Evidence

The foregoing is M&L's argument in brief. In its main outlines, it is sound. To some extent one can perceive that international business competition is fostering international government competition in today's world. If this claim were all that M&L contend, one would have little to quarrel with, but they go further. They argue that the process is already well advanced and that even in the United States the prospect that resources will flee if treated too harshly is visibly restraining the growth of government. Because M&L's book is likely to receive—and well deserves to receive—considerable attention, this thesis merits careful scrutiny.

Throughout the book, M&L make exaggerated statements about the extent to which governments, including those in the Western mixed economies, are being reined in. They say that "government's role is being constricted, and much is being done to privatize remaining government activities" (p. 13). Margaret Thatcher and Ronald Reagan, they assert, "cut government power in their respective countries" (p. 22). M&L portray entrepreneurs as "ready to jump jurisdictions in response to the slightest policy provocation" (p. 83). They claim that Gorbachev has "demonstrated that greater prosperity could be had by reducing the onerous burden imposed by government" (p. 158)—this in a chapter entirely too worshipful of Gorbachev, the most hated man in the Soviet Union. "Workers from around the world," say M&L, "can immigrate to this country via modern electronics," and "foreign firms can readily shift production around the world to circumvent trade restrictions" (pp. 232–33). "In the last decade or so, governments appeared to have passed through a 'competitiveness threshold' that has caused something of a quantum leap in their concern for efficiency and their responsiveness to one another" (p. 156). Each of these statements is an exaggeration, if true at all.

To their credit, M&L make many qualifying statements—acknowledging, for example, that "the world will likely be beset for a long time to come by governments holding enormous power to tax and regulate" (p. 16) and that "admittedly, much capital, particularly in the form of factories and workers, is still difficult to move or altogether immobile" (p. 18). They concede that "not all plants and firms are getting smaller. Economies of scale still exist for a number of industries.... Not all equipment has become miniaturized" (p. 46). They admit that the data they present in support of their thesis are "inherently limited" and "do not measure all dimensions of the changes in governments' influence in their respective economies" (p. 116). In the end, however, even though they recognize the existence of countervailing "political moves to extend government regulation" (p. 145), they insist that "markets are being progressively freed" (p. 145) and that "government growth is certainly waning, relative to the size of the national economy" (p. 18).

This last claim carries a major part of the burden of supporting their thesis. Near the end of the book, while making a final qualification of their argument, M&L say that, "to date, the evidence only supports constrained growth relative to national income" (p. 248). In other words, despite some claims they make along the way, M&L refrain from claiming that Western governments have ceased to grow, either absolutely or relatively. They claim only to have documented a slowdown in the rate of growth of government relative to the economy. This is a weak claim, even if it is true.

To see why the claim is weak, just imagine a simple hypothetical case. First, measure the relative size of government as M&L do—by the amount of government spending as a fraction of national income. Then construct a case in which this fraction starts at zero and increases each year by one percentage point. Obviously, this sort of increase will eventually result in the government's spending becoming equal to the entire national income, and, by construction, the result will have been attained in a steady fashion. Notice, however, that the *percentage* rate of growth of the *relative* size of government declines each year. For example, in the second year, the growth rate is 100 percent (that is, the relative size of government increases from 1 percent to 2 percent); in the fifty-first year, the growth rate is 2 percent (relative size increases from 50 percent to 51 percent); and in the one hundredth year, it will be just slightly more than 1 percent (relative size increases from 99 percent to 100 percent).

Substituting actual for hypothetical data, this way of measuring a slowdown is precisely the one that M&L employ. Even if government spending as a percentage of national income were an acceptable index of the true relative size of government—which it is not, because governments have so many alternate ways to control resources besides spending money—a decline of the growth rate of government's relative size becomes virtually inevitable at some point. This sort of evidence just does not carry much weight, yet it is the strongest sort M&L offer.

They understand, of course, that governments can compel private citizens to carry the load by means of regulation or mandated private expenditures (for example, required pollution-abatement costs or mandatory health insurance for employees), and they pay some attention to what has been happening on the regulatory front. The trouble here is that there is no index of regulation even vaguely resembling the orthodox measures of government spending and taxing. Regulations come in nearly limitless variety, from the trivial to the very important. Busy bureaucrats alter them constantly, making some more demanding and others less demanding. Some they enforce vigorously, others laxly, some not at all. Make-believe measurement, such as counting the rate of growth of pages in the Federal Register (p. 183), is just silly.

One has little choice but to rely on experts' judgment as to the weight of the evidence. Remarkably, M&L cite two experts who contradict their thesis. William Niskanen, a member of Reagan's Council of Economic Advisers for several years, opines that "the regulatory momentum was clearly slowed, but it was not reversed" (p. 186); and Murray Weidenbaum, Reagan's first chairman of the Council of Economic Advisers, wrote that "on balance it is clear that the United States has become more protectionist since Ronald Reagan moved into the Oval Office" (quoted on p. 189). In view of these claims by exceptionally well-informed observers, one wonders how M&L can conclude that "the late 1970s and the whole of the 1980s have witnessed a significant containment, at least, of the relative expansion of governmental . . . regulatory powers" (p. 100). Are M&L still playing that little trick with the relative increase of the fraction?

Whatever they may have in mind, no one can talk about the trend of regulation as a whole with much confidence. Unlike height or weight, regulatory constraints cannot be measured on an unambiguous cardinal scale, so speculations about the relative rate of growth of the overall regulatory burden are necessarily pretty airy. My own opinion, for what it is worth, is that on balance the extent of regulatory constraints on the U.S. economy—whether at the federal, state, or local level—has continued to increase during the past decade, just as it did earlier. As to the rate of increase, I would not even hazard a guess.

In making their arguments, M&L blur certain related ideas or actions that differ in important ways. For example, the collapse of socialism in the East Bloc is not directly comparable to the retrenchment of government in the West. The headline of a recent article by James M. Buchanan in the *Wall Street Journal* (July 18, 1990) made the point succinctly: "Socialism Is Dead; Leviathan Lives."

Outside of university campuses in the Western countries, hardly anyone embraces socialist ideology anymore, and the regimes of the centrally planned economies are beating a retreat, although where they will end up remains to be seen. Full-fledged central planning is dead as an idea and dying as a practice. Nevertheless, as Buchanan noted, "there remains a residual unwillingness to leave things alone, to allow the free market, governed by the rule of law, to organize itself." It is quite possible that while governments are surrendering power in the East Bloc, they are still gaining power in the West, at least in the United States.

Finer distinctions need to be made as well between information and human capital. Most forms of information can be moved around the world almost instantly at very low cost, but the knowledge, skill, and other productive attributes embodied in human beings (human capital) can be moved only at considerable cost. It will not do to suppose that any given package of human capital can be shifted from country to country for the price of an airline ticket. Most people prefer to live in their own culture. Barriers of language and culture, among others, impede the flow of people around the world.

Likewise, one must distinguish between financial capital and physical capital. The former can be electronically shifted at will in many instances, but the latter is much more costly to transfer abroad and often is not mobile at all (for example, railroads, highways, dams, water and sewer systems, electrical and gas utilities, networks of telephone lines, large plants and most other structures). Nor is it necessarily the case that a flow of financial capital must entail the potential for a subsequent flow of physical capital (p. 59).

M&L fail more than once to distinguish between the location of capital and the location of the title holder of the capital. The Japanese-owned hotels in Hawaii are not really little pieces of Japan, as M&L seem to suggest in their quip about Pearl Harbor. These properties are completely subject to U.S. tax and regulatory powers, and the Japanese cannot pick up the hotels and carry them back to Tokyo in the event that the local regulations become too onerous. Regardless of the hotel owners' citizenship, the hotels will stay where they are. (Of course—and this may be the stronger point in favor of M&L's thesis—investors will refrain from making new investments in a jurisdiction where the government has treated or threatens to treat them abusively.)

The authors fail to give the devil of nationalism its due. In their view, "The distinction between 'us' and 'them' has simply become muddled" (p. 10); "the 'national interest,' once a unifying banner, no longer elicits automatic accord among citizens of many nations. . . . Citizens now have economic and social ties to countries other than their own" (p. 65); and "[m]any domestic voters will, no doubt, identify with the economic interests of their foreign sources of supply, jobs, sales, and incomes, and will vote accordingly" (p. 76). Even without dwelling on this simplistic vision of how people decide to cast their votes, I find these claims remote from reality. Around the world, as socialism recedes and police states loosen their grips, ethnic groups tear at the throats of their ancestral enemies. Just consider the events in the Soviet Union and Yugoslavia. If nationalism is in decline, I would like to see some evidence. Perhaps the formation of the new arrangements in western Europe is consistent with the view that nationalism has diminished, but we must wait to see how durable the new European Community proves to be. In the United States, the outbreak of rabid nationalism associated with the Gulf War should convince everyone that American nationalism is as robust as ever.

In discussing tax policies, M&L insist, just as they do with regard to the growth rate of relative government spending, that "the pace of growth in taxes has slowed" (p. 195). Again, this claim is a weak one because such a slowing of the growth *rate* of taxes measured as a *fraction* of national income is inevitable at some point; the test is biased toward supporting their hypothesis. Moreover, M&L recognize and document that both the absolute real tax bill and the relative tax burden have continued to grow in the Western countries, including the United States (pp. 127, 194–95). The total U.S. tax burden, relative to gross national product, was higher during the 1980s than during any previous decade.

Furthermore, federal budget deficits began to grow during the 1960s, became much larger during the 1970s, and reached extraordinary levels (more than $200 billion per year) during the mid-1980s. The Bush budget deficits to come will far outdistance those regarded as astronomical during the Reagan years, reaching perhaps as high as $350 billion in a single year. This evidence of accelerating fiscal irresponsibility offers very cold comfort to those expecting an imminent retrenchment of government.

Even when M&L make unobjectionable arguments concerning the direction of causes or effects, they often rely on mere assertion regarding the magnitudes. Thus, when told that technology "has reduced the required scale of operation for many businesses, enabling them to disperse their activity to the corners of the earth" (p. 35), one wants to ask: *How many* firms fit this description? With reference to the "growing hordes of people who have little economic allegiance except to the concept of meeting competition on a world scale" (p. 80), one wonders just *how big* those hordes are. Presented with the claim that "greater capital mobility incorporates a nontrivial, potentially powerful inducement for governments to at least consider lowering their tax prices" (p. 101), one is curious about *how M&L know* the inducement is nontrivial.

Lost Horizons

M&L are well-known members of the public-choice school, but in this book they have taken off their public-choice hat; at any rate, they do not wear it on every page. As a result, they fail to provide a convincing argument regarding the mechanism by which the pressures of international business competition will be transmitted to government policies. Again and again they say that the government will "have to" lighten up, that it "must" lower taxes or regulatory burdens, that it will be "forced" to do so (pp. 57, 85, 105, 111, 235, 237, 239, 240). But why must it? Governments have been abusing their subjects from time immemorial. Why must they act differently now?

Part of the answer, of course, lies in M&L's claim that recent technological changes have pushed people beyond some "threshold" (p. 156), and therefore in the future they will be able to shift their resources at such drastically reduced cost that resource withdrawals will radically diminish the tax base, inducing rulers to back off for fear of impoverishing themselves. Although the broad logic of this argument makes sense, its quantitative sufficiency is debatable, as already noted.

Furthermore, as M&L recognize in a footnote, "in response to growing economic constraints, governments, under some circumstances, may seek to substitute more covert regulations for more overt taxes" (p. 273). This admission is an important public-choice argument that works against their thesis. Other public-choice arguments also contradict or at least diminish the force of the thesis once we get into the details of the transmission process.

To abstract from minor complications, a public-choice analyst supposes that elected politicians, and hence bureaucrats, do what they do because they are rewarded in various ways for doing it. They get campaign contributions (and ultimately the power, pleasure, and perks of office), bribes, adulation, and so forth from those—predominantly organized special interests—who "buy" the policies that government officials create or maintain.

Suppose that people can now take their resources out of the country more readily. What happens in the political "exchange" process? People who reward politicians in exchange for tax breaks, regulatory constraints on competitors, subsidies, income supports, and other largess will continue to do so, although a few may conclude that such political payoffs are no longer the best option and depart the country. In any event, concentrated benefits will continue to trump dispersed costs in determining who organizes effectively for political action.

Even more important, politicians will continue to act based on a very short time horizon. They will worry more or less exclusively about winning the next election, even if they must do so by enacting policies that, in the long run, will destroy the economy and the politicians who feed off it. If incumbents fail to act in this shortsighted manner, they will tend to be displaced by challengers who will make commitments to do so. (The underlying institutional flaw, we may note in passing, is the absence of a "political capital market" in which politicians can gain wealth and other objects of their desire by paying attention to the longer-run future.)

The sorts of pressures M&L's argument requires must necessarily act slowly because not enough resources are sufficiently mobile in the short run. It is easy to imagine the politicos going down with the ship, as they have more than a few times in recorded history. The authors have not convinced me, even granted the technological and economic changes they so convincingly document, that anything in the established political system precludes this dire outcome.

They argue that "technology can give rise to new methods and sources of competition that were not envisioned when special-interest government programs were passed" (p. 106); that "technology has enhanced the relative political weight of the general interest of the larger voting public, *vis à vis* all of the various narrow concerns of special interest lobbies," giving rise to what they call "new-breed lobbying" aimed at the masses rather than at the smoke-filled rooms (p. 107); that "governments are now less able to respond to special-interest political demands" and "interest groups are now less able and willing to bribe or pay off" the politicians (p. 108).

Perhaps these declarations are correct, but where's the evidence? Certainly not in the data on political contributions by special-interest groups. Certainly not in the daily news reports of politicians repeatedly preferring the special interests to the public interest. M&L recognize that, contrary to their thesis, "well-organized interests will often effectively exploit the opportunities offered by the new technology to engage in 'new-breed' lobbying for purposes that expand government programs and increase the scope of government waste." Yet they conclude that "on balance ... new-breed lobbying has forced greater restraint in government" (p. 107). This conclusion is sheer wishful thinking.

Just consider some current events in the United States. The savings-and-loan bailout grows ever larger, reaching into the hundreds of billions of dollars—far greater than all previous bailouts combined in U.S. history. In addition, the Treasury is being called upon to shore up the Federal Deposit Insurance Corporation, as commercial bank failures threaten to bankrupt the fund.

Environmental regulations grow tighter almost daily. Last year's Clean Air Act, for example, requires the public to take extreme measures to combat a trivial acid-rain problem that could be dealt with at far lower cost. Perhaps the most troublesome recent environmental development is the imposition of severe restraints on real-estate developments and farming activities in order that so-called wetlands not be disturbed. In addition, the Endangered Species Act is being used to close millions of acres of federal forest lands to logging, driving the timber industry of the Northwest nearly out of existence ostensibly for the sake of keeping a few "northern" spotted owls at ease.

Antitrust actions are making a comeback under the Bush administration. The Microsoft Corporation, the most gloriously successful competitor in a gloriously competitive industry, is now being investigated and harassed by federal antitrust officials, and it may be restricted in some way or even broken up to give less successful competitors a better chance. Also, the federal government has just injected itself deeply into the child-care business. Regulatory standards are sure to follow, thereby ensuring that the care of children, especially poor children, will suffer. The potential nationalization of health insurance looms just over the horizon. In view of these events and of so many others pointing in the same direction, how can M&L conclude that "on balance, markets are progressively being freed" (p. 145)?

Ideology Has Consequences

M&L have little to say about ideology; there is no entry for it or any of its synonyms in the index. This is a crucial omission. So long as the dominant ideology gives supports to an active, intrusive government, mere political or even constitutional impediments can do little to restrain the government's interventions. Nor, as I've already argued, can economic pressures of the sort M&L emphasize be relied on to push politicians far from their accustomed course. M&L appear to believe that the past decade or so has witnessed an ideological turnaround. I am persuaded that no such turnaround has occurred.

Linda L. M.. Bennett and Stephen Earl Bennett recently published *Living with Leviathan: Americans Coming to Terms with Big Government*,[2] a book that exhaustively examines public-opinion survey data regarding Americans' views on big government. The findings, though not without certain ambiguities, will not encourage friends of liberty.

For one thing, during the past twenty-five years increasing proportions of the randomly sampled respondents have had no opinion at all about the size and power of the national government in the United States. They evidently view it either as a fact of nature or as beyond conceivable change. Maybe they just don't care.

The trend in the 1980s was toward greater approval of the idea that the federal government should use its powers more vigorously (p. 33). In 1989, large majorities favored more government spending for environmental protection, health care, fighting crime, reducing drug addiction, and education. Only on foreign aid did a majority think the government spends too much money (pp. 90–91). Reporting on a 1987 poll, the Bennetts note that "at the same time that majorities said government controls too much of people's daily lives, majorities—sometimes over-whelming majorities—called for more governmental activism" (p. 106). Survey indexes show that younger people were more egalitarian and less individualistic than older people in the 1980s (pp. 124–25).

Where is the hope for the future of liberty? The Bennetts conclude:

> The increasing belief in egalitarianism, particularly among younger Americans, means that there will be no constituency for smaller government in the foreseeable future.... Americans are coming to terms with the leviathan they have helped to create.... Many of those who complained about too much federal control of their lives nonetheless favored increased federal involvement in a wide range of domestic issues. Today, those who call themselves liberals and conservatives no longer dispute whether the government should or should not be involved in almost every aspect of life.... Even as government expanded to do more, Americans saw less reason to be concerned about that expansion.

...There is no longer any sizable constituency in the United States committed to major, across-the-board cuts in governmental spending for a host of domestic programs. In fact, at the end of the 1980s, there [was] a growing public cry for more spending to address domestic problems, particularly drugs.... In all likelihood, future office seekers and their public opinion advisers will quickly take into account America's willingness to accept a permanent service state. (pp. 134–37, 142, 145)

Obviously, these findings flatly contradict M&L's claim that there is an "expanding view in the West that government cannot be the solution to all social ills" (p. 18).

Conclusion

Quicksilver Capital is a major contribution to the ongoing debate about the growth of government in the United States and elsewhere. McKenzie and Lee's central thesis makes sense. I know of no other argument of equal force that forecasts an imminent cessation of the growth of government in the Western world. Their argument is weak, however, in its account of the transmission mechanism from international business competition to international government competition; just saying that governments will "have to" restrain their predations is insufficient. The argument needs to consider more seriously the counterarguments of the public-choice school, especially with respect to politicians' foreshortened time horizon. Moreover, it must somehow resolve the tension between its vision of a contracting government (if not already, then soon) and the brute fact of a dominant ideology in the West that insists on using government as the social and economic "problem solver" of universal first resort. McKenzie and Lee have written an enormously provocative book, filled with fascinating facts and arresting insights, but they have argued more as advocates than as social scientists dispassionately testing a hypothesis. It remains for others to rise to that challenge.

Notes

1. Richard B. McKenzie and Dwight R. Lee, *Quicksilver Capital: How the Rapid Movement of Wealth Has Changed the World* (New York: Free Press, 1991). Hereafter cited parenthetically by page number in the text.

2. Lawrence: University Press of Kansas, 1990. Hereafter cited parenthetically by page number in the text.

32

Escaping Leviathan?

In the terminology made famous by Albert Hirschman, people who are fed up with a government have two options: exit and voice. Political scientists and public-choice analysts have concentrated heavily on the latter, especially on the use of electoral means of transmitting the citizens' "voice" to the government. Scholars have been slow to appreciate that elections are and always have been for the most part a sham—a mere ceremony intended to make people believe they have some control over their fate even as they are mercilessly bullied, bamboozled, and fleeced by their rulers. Whatever the efficacy of political voice as a means of avoiding oppression by government, however, scholars have traditionally paid much less attention to the alternative option, exit.

During the past decade, a growing number of analysts have begun to repair that neglect. Indeed, increasingly, the argument one hears is not that the voters will elect representatives who will "get the government off their backs," but that the people will, as it were, just walk away from oppressive governments, thereby compelling the oppressors to lighten the burdens placed on their remaining subjects before they also flee. As the information revolution has proceeded apace, especially as the scope and activity of the Internet have expanded, the argument has become not so much about people's physically leaving the jurisdiction as about their electronically withdrawing their (taxable) commercial transactions and financial holdings. The logic, many have assumed, holds equally in either case.

Montesquieu and Smith's Version

The gist of the argument goes back at least to the time of the Baron de Montesquieu, who, recognizing merchants' ability to move their financial capital away from jurisdictions with high confiscatory risks, wrote in *De l'esprit des Lois* (1748) that "only good government brings prosperity [to the prince]."[1]

Not long afterward, in *The Wealth of Nations,* Adam Smith presented a characteristically clear statement:

The proprietor of stock is properly a citizen of the world, and is not necessarily attached to any particular country. He would be apt to abandon the country in which he was exposed to a vexatious inquisition, in order to be assessed to a burdensome tax, and would remove his stock to some other country where he could either carry on his business, or enjoy his fortune more at his ease.... A tax which tended to drive away stock from any particular country, would so far tend to dry up every source of revenue, both *to the sovereign* and to the society.[2]

Like Montesquieu, Smith seems to have believed that at least some rulers would have enough sense to realize that impoverishing the realm was not in their own interest and therefore they would respond to the removal of mobile resources by lightening the burdens they laid on the owners of such resources.

McKenzie and Lee's Version

Among the more notable contributors to the recent resurgence of this venerable argument are Richard B. McKenzie and Dwight R. Lee, who laid out their views in 1991 in a book called *Quicksilver Capital:*

The increased mobility of capital, coupled with the growing economic integration of national economies, has dramatically expanded the scope and intensity of competitive markets. This growth in business competitiveness has necessarily forced governments into a competitive struggle for the world's human and physical capital base. As a consequence, governments have lost much of the monopoly power that undergirded their growth in earlier decades. World governments have had to compete against one another by seeking more efficient policies in order to lure and retain the physical and human capital that is now so crucial to modern production processes and to the tax bases on which governments depend.

In general, governments have been forced to lower tax rates, deregulate industries, and privatize services in order that the productive facilities within their borders can remain competitive on a world scale. Governments at all levels—local, state, and national—have lost the vestiges of unchecked economic sovereignty.[3]

Although the argument has its charms, it has serious shortcomings as well.[4] Most important, it exaggerates the magnitude of the effects of the ostensible competitive pressures.

Seldon's Version

Near the end of the 1990s, the argument surfaced again, in Arthur Seldon's monograph *The Dilemma of Democracy*.[5] In Seldon's view, "There are enough escapes from over-government for the people to be able to end its long tolerance of over a century.... If a North Atlantic Union is not formed the political powers of the nation states of Europe will be escaped by the resort to trading by electronic money, barter or the multiplying new devices that ease the rejection of oppressive national laws and invasive taxes."[6] Thus, in Seldon's estimation, the prospect for freedom is sanguine. "The question for the future is increasingly not 'What *should* government do now?' but increasingly 'What *can* government do?'"[7]

Seldon concedes that "national governments, perhaps in league with other governments, will attempt international regulations" to thwart the escape of their victims.[8] A plethora of tax treaties and the ongoing international "harmonization" of regulations are examples that come readily to mind. These sorts of international "cooperation" amount to cartelization by which national governments seek to suppress policy competition among themselves, the better to exploit the resident owners of mobile resources.[9] Nonetheless, Seldon expresses confidence that "science and the human spirit will remain two or three decisive steps ahead of the slower-moving machinery of international politics."[10] Well, one can wish.

Big Government on the Ropes?

In all its recent manifestations, this line of argument has contained a large element of wishful thinking. "Before long," writes Seldon, "there will be increasing public understanding that the expansion in the state over the decades was unnecessary."[11] Don't hold your breath. The evidence of the public-opinion surveys, for example, suggests that the bulk of the American public is incapable of contemplating life without big government. To be sure, most Americans express agreement with the abstract idea that government is now too big and too intrusive, but ask these people about a *specific* government program, and they overwhelmingly support it and even its expansion.[12] Europeans, having recently elected socialist governments throughout the Continent, present an even more hopeless case. In Brussels, the Eurocrats build their Tower of Regulatory Babel ever higher.

Even if the public did not clamor for bigger government, the normal operation of contemporary special-interest politics—the only kind of politics that consistently packs a punch nowadays—would ensure that such government was foisted on them anyhow. Experience in modern representative democracies shows that once a government program has been instituted, it is well-nigh impossible to root it out, no matter how destructive it is in the aggregate or how unpopular it is with the general public.[13]

Skeptics will have no difficulty in raising various objections to the argument that "exit" is taming Leviathan. For an American, the most obvious objection rests on the raw reality of the relentless growth of government. Each year, the more than eighty thousand government entities in the United States spend vastly more money, take in vastly more tax dollars, and promulgate thousands of new regulations. In these circumstances, it is an odd mentality that imagines the government is struggling to survive. The *logic* of the argument for the containment of government growth by exit-related forces is sound, but its quantitative sufficiency must be doubted. So far, at least in the United States, the pressures eventuating in the growth of government have manifestly overwhelmed all countervailing forces. Though the future may be different, currently observable trends give us little reason for optimism.

Black Markets

Seldon considers some fascinating data pertaining to illegal market activity, traditionally called "the black market" but dubbed by Seldon "the parallel economy" to remove the implied moral shadow. Drawing on estimates made by *The Economist* and by Friedrich Schneider, Seldon presents data that indicate parallel economies running from a range of 5–10 percent of gross domestic product in Japan, the United States, Austria, and Switzerland to 10–20 percent in Canada, Britain, France, and Germany and to more than 20 percent in Belgium, Spain, and Italy.[14] Although such estimates, by their very nature, must be viewed as subject to a wide range of error, their orders of magnitude accord, I dare say, with what would seem plausible to an experienced traveler or international businessperson.[15]

By including the parallel economy under the rubric of "escapes from overgovernment," Seldon seems to view the participants in that economy as having successfully "voted with their feet" against the existing regime. The parallel economy, he notes, "produces no taxes on a wide and accelerating range of productive activity."[16] Here, however, he goes too far. It is true that *some* participants in black markets escape taxation, but by no means all do so. The distinction is between escaping the payment of *official* taxes, which black marketers do by definition, and escaping the demands of state officials altogether, which some black-market participants do but others do not. Anyone who reads the newspapers will have seen reports of government officials so unfortunate as to have been exposed taking payoffs from the participants in illegal or tax-evasive economic activities. In many countries, for example, government officials, even at the highest levels, operate in close cooperation with illicit drug traffickers and reap handsome rewards for doing so. The workday nips taken out of merchants and others by local police and politicians are a staple in many societies—in Mexico, for example, *la mordida* (literally, the bite) is a way of life. Just because those exactions go unrecorded in the official government accounts does not mean that government officials have failed to wrest wealth from the populace. Black markets may be a fine thing, as far as they go, but their operation per se does not constitute strong evidence of "escape from over-government."

Nor does their recent growth in the wealthier countries, which Seldon notes and projects to continue in the future, necessarily signify that governments are suffering from a withering exploitative arm. In general, black markets appear when government prevents people from doing what they prefer to do—for example, when it prevents them from buying a commodity without paying an excise tax or from exchanging a commodity banned by the government or restricted to certain transactors, such as licensed dealers. The more the government intrudes into the marketplace, the greater is the incentive for people to resort to the black market. In the Heritage Foundation's annual index of economic-freedom rankings, the black-market scores are, as a rule, much higher for countries with relatively little overall economic freedom.[17] Therefore, growing participation in black markets may signal only that the government in a particular country is becoming more oppressive in its taxing and regulating, and thereby is creating an incentive for more people to resort to illegal transacting. Possibly, however, as the government becomes more oppressive, it does succeed in catching more victims in its enlarged official web. That some people escape, at least to a degree, does not necessarily indicate that, on balance, the government has fallen flat in its additional grasping.

A Never-ending Struggle

As long as governments have existed, some people have been voting with their feet against the established regimes. As economic, ideological, and technological changes have occurred, the balance has shifted many times, sometimes becoming more favorable to the escapees, sometimes more favorable to the regime. Recent increases in the mobility of financial capital and in access to information resulting from technological advances in communications and information processing have raised many observers' expectations that a new age of freedom is about to dawn, that soon governments will be unable to extract rents from their subjects at the old rate, certainly unable to increase the rate of exploitation. But governments are not, as the saying goes, rolling over and playing dead in the face of these developments. Everywhere they are striving to solidify their control over people and resources. Which side will win in the near term remains open to conjecture. Whether the near-term winner turns out to be the oppressor or the oppressed, however, we can be certain that the struggle will continue.

Notes

1. Quoted in Stefan Sinn, "The Taming of Leviathan: Competition among Governments," *Constitutional Political Economy* 3 (spring–summer 1992), p. 190.

2. Adam Smith, *The Wealth of Nations* (New York: Modern Library, [1776] 1937), p. 800, emphasis added.

3. Richard B. McKenzie and Dwight R. Lee, *Quicksilver Capital: How the Rapid Movement of Wealth Has Changed the World* (New York: Free Press, 1991), p. xi.

4. Robert Higgs, "Leviathan at Bay?" *Liberty* 5 (November 1991): 64–70 (a revised version appears as chap. 31 in this collection).

5. Arthur Seldon, *The Dilemma of Democracy: The Political Economics of Over-government* (London: Institute of Economic Affairs, 1998).

6. Ibid., pp. 26, 98.

7. Ibid., p. 26.

8. Ibid., p. 97.

9. Sinn, "The Taming of Leviathan," pp. 188–91; and Manfred E. Streit, "Competition among Systems, Harmonisation, and Integration," *Journal des Economistes et des Etudes Humaines* 8 (Juin–Septembre 1998): 249–51.

10. *The Dilemma of Democracy,* p. 97.

11. Ibid., p. 104.

12. See, for example, Karlyn Bowman, "At War with Washington?" *The American Enterprise* (November–December 1997), p. 93.

13. Milton Friedman and Rose Friedman, *The Tyranny of the Status Quo* (San Diego: Harcourt Brace Jovanovich, 1984), pp. 41–51.

14. *The Dilemma of Democracy,* pp. 79, 82.

15. Somewhat different estimates appear in the graphs of Simon Johnson, Daniel Kaufmann, and Pablo Zoido-Lobatón, "Regulatory Discretion and the Unofficial Economy," *American Economic Review* 88 (May 1998), pp. 390–91.

16. *The Dilemma of Democracy,* p. 76.

17. See also the similar findings reported by Johnson, Kaufmann, and Zoido-Lobatón, "Regulatory Discretion and the Unofficial Economy," pp. 388–91.

· 33

The Era of Big Government
Is Not Over

In his State of the Union address in 1996, President Bill Clinton fa-
mously declared, "The era of big government is over." Putting aside the evident
insincerity of the declaration, we understand that the president was merely acknowledging what many commentators had been saying since the early 1980s.
In light of the adoption of more market-friendly policies in the United States
under Ronald Reagan and in Great Britain under Margaret Thatcher, the pri-
vatization of many state enterprises in Latin America and Europe, the gradual
relinquishment of central planning in China, the overthrow of the communist
regimes in eastern Europe, the demise of the Soviet Union, and seemingly similar developments elsewhere, many commentators concluded that collectivist
economic policymaking had been routed and that, before long, free-market
regimes would hold sway around the world.

As the 1990s drew to a close, however, it became clear that too many observers had been too quick to project a continuation of movement in the direction indicated by limited and short-term policy changes. No country went
all the way; nowhere did laissez-faire take hold as the prevailing guide to government (in)action. Indeed, no country even approached that ideal. Everywhere, big government remains firmly in place. Indeed, in a variety of dimensions, government continues to grow as fast as or faster than it did previously.
Worse, in the wake of the September 11, 2001, attacks on the World Trade Center and the Pentagon, a new surge of government growth has begun in the
United States.

In a short comment, I cannot deal with the whole world. Accordingly, I
focus on the United States. If the Americans cannot block the march of
Leviathan, others are even less likely to do so.

Government Continues to Grow

In the 1990s, U.S. government spending continued to increase rapidly. Despite
the end of the Cold War and a consequent 32 percent reduction of real defense
spending, total federal outlays (in constant 1998 dollars) increased from

$1.49 trillion in fiscal 1989 to $1.67 trillion in fiscal 1998—so much for the "peace dividend." Federal nondefense outlays rose during that nine-year period by 28 percent—far more than the 9 percent increase in population.[1] State and local governments raised their spending even more quickly than did the federal government.[2]

Tax revenues more than kept pace, as the federal government moved from a deficit of $152.5 billion (current dollars) in fiscal 1989 to a surplus of $71 billion in fiscal 1998.[3] According to preliminary estimates by the Tax Foundation, taxes at all levels of government combined, relative to net national product, reached an all-time high of 35.4 percent in 1998.[4] In the United States in the 1990s, taxes rose more quickly than the population, more quickly than the price level, more quickly than the net national product. Not since World War II had government loomed so large—even *during* that great war the government was smaller in some respects.

Despite the increased taxing and spending, fiscal constraints seemed to weigh more heavily on Congress and the states in the 1990s, and legislators turned increasingly to rewarding their supporters by nonfiscal means, mainly by authorizing new regulations. Each year the Federal Register prints some seventy thousand pages just to give notice of the new edicts issued by federal agencies. State and local governments churn out enormous volumes of similar directives. The public's costs of compliance with the proliferating regulations at the federal level alone are now estimated to amount to more than $700 billion per year.[5] Costs entailed by the Americans with Disabilities Act, new "civil rights" regulations, new environmental rules, and new health-care regulations—in considerable part, for record keeping and legal expenses—are but a few of the regulatory burdens that mounted during the 1990s. Even if the explicit tax burden had not risen, Americans would have paid substantially more hidden taxes in the form of the costs associated with regulatory compliance.

Evidence That Government Is Receding?

Apart from sheer wishful thinking, which has been conspicuous in certain pro-market circles, three developments help to explain the widespread impression—illustrated by Bill Clinton's declaration—that the growth of government had been checked. All three, however, pertain more to rhetoric than to substance.

First, the academic climate changed. I am old enough to recall a time when, in nearly all university milieus, one dared not say a kind word about the ideas of, say, the likes of Milton Friedman. To do so was to commit an unforgivable faux pas, jeopardizing one's future invitations to faculty cocktail parties if not one's chances of promotion or tenure. Although such oppressive conditions persist in many academic venues, the climate became somewhat more agreeable for pro-market professors during the past twenty years, especially in departments of economics. Generalizing from the increased tolerance of pro-market ideas in their immediate surroundings, some professors—economists in particular—concluded that pro-market thinking had become intellectually competitive if not triumphant. Such academics now enjoy observing that socialism, as an intellectual doctrine, has been cast into the dustbin of history.

In the wider society as well, public opinion certainly seemed to become less favorable to government social and economic interventions. For example, in a 1964 poll, although 36 percent of the respondents agreed that "government in Washington is getting too powerful for the good of the country and the individual," 30 percent agreed that "government in Washington is not getting too strong." In 1997, however, 64 percent agreed that "government in Washington has too much power," and just 27 percent disagreed. In 1995, 72 percent of those polled thought that "the federal government creates more problems than it solves," and just 21 percent thought it "solves more problems than it creates." During the 1990s, far more respondents favored "smaller government with fewer services" than "larger government with many services," and far more believed "government is trying to do too many things that should be left to individuals and businesses" than believed "government should do more to solve our country's problems."[6]

Undoubtedly, many politicians whistled a new tune during the past twenty years, especially since the Republican electoral victories of 1994. The legislative halls rang with proposals to cut taxes and spending, to deregulate, to privatize, and in general to "get government off the people's backs." Seemingly radical opponents of big government, such as Dick Armey and John Kasich, achieved positions of leadership in Congress. Similar voices became more prominent in many state legislatures.

From the foregoing sorts of evidence, one might have concluded that the volume of pro-market talk rose substantially during recent decades. To espouse reining in the government no longer automatically signified that one was a political Neanderthal or a social pariah. But does the foregoing rhetorical evidence reveal anything about the more decisive actions taking place below the noisy surface? In my judgment, the recent antigovernment talk was largely just hot air; it counted for very little in actually constraining the growth of government.

The Ideological Whole Is Less Than the Sum of Its Parts

The economists need to get out more. Were they to venture beyond their own university departments, especially into departments of comparative literature, sociology, and history, they would discover that even though old-fashioned Marxists are harder to find nowadays, the great majority of their colleagues in the social sciences and the humanities espouse ideologies that, insofar as they bear on one's inclination to support the free market, are no less hostile and, indeed, in various respects are even more antithetical to free societies than they used to be.[7]

Of course, the academics still swim, as they have since the early twentieth century, mainly along the left bank, so one needs to examine more closely the ideological mainstream. In doing so, one quickly finds that the seemingly preponderant commitment to individual responsibility and free markets affirmed by ordinary people and many of their elected representatives resembles the proverbial Missouri River—it's a mile wide and an inch deep.

When the pollsters ask questions about specific government measures, it turns out that the public overwhelmingly supports virtually every aspect of big government, unless the named beneficiaries are blatant ne'er-do-wells (and sometimes even if they are). Thus, in a 1996 poll, government support for "unemployment benefits for workers whose employers went out of business" was endorsed by 86 percent of respondents; "medical care for people who got AIDS through blood transfusions" by 89 percent; "medical care for elderly people who have lung cancer" by 84 percent; "welfare payments to divorced mothers" by 57 percent; and "special education for children of legal immigrants trying to learn English" by 81 percent.[8] The slightest linguistic ingenuity suffices to characterize the recipients of government largess of any kind whatsoever as deserving, and most Americans agree that recipients so characterized ought to receive support at the taxpayers' expense.

President George W. Bush recently has declared himself perfectly at ease with this Santa Claus conception of the role of government: "We have a responsibility," he told an Ohio audience, "that when somebody hurts, government has got to move."[9] Grover Cleveland must be spinning in his grave.

In a notable 1996 poll, respondents were invited to choose either (1) the federal government, (2) the state government, (3) the local government, or (4) individuals in deciding where responsibility for various actions should repose. The most remarkable aspect of the responses is not the way in which the respondents selected one or another level of government, but the fact that in no case did more than 30 percent identify individuals, rather than some level of government, as the party that ought to bear the responsibility.[10] Whether the issue was paying for health care, providing food for the poor, paying for college education, or deciding when to permit smoking in public, an overwhelming majority of the American people (if this sample is representative) believes that some level of government, not individuals, ought to exercise the main responsibility.

People who hold such beliefs cannot sustain a free society. Hence, it should come as no surprise that, increasingly, they have not done so.

What Can Stop the Growth of Government?

Even apart from the so-called war on terrorism that now gives new impetus to the growth of government, the probability that government will soon stop growing in the United States is very slight. Ultimately, of course, government must stop growing: no society can persist if everybody is a predator and nobody is the prey. In my judgment, however, the ultimate limit is so remote that it affords little promise of binding the further growth of government in the next few decades.

So long as the prevailing ideology imposes no general (that is, constitutional-level) constraint on the size, scope, and power of government, then the continued growth of government will flow naturally from the workings of the present political system, as public-choice analysts have made sufficiently clear.[11] Concentrated benefits and dispersed costs for projects championed by special interests; real and trumped up emergencies; scheming, self-serving, strategically situated bureaucracies; and paternalistic projects seemingly without end—all nourish the government's addition of muscle and fat. Why should that deeply institutionalized process cease to operate?

Scenarios can be imagined, of course, in which the growth of government comes to an end in the United States. One such scenario, beloved by generations of gloom-and-doom writers, involves some sort of systemwide breakdown: financial collapse, great depression, terrorist-provoked chaos—take your pick. Only the survivalists seem to put much weight on such contingencies. I myself do not foresee such societal breakdown, but even if one were to occur, it would probably bring about more government rather than less, as genuine national emergencies always have in the past.[12]

In a second scenario, about which a great deal has been written recently, the growth of government stops because the owners of private resources, both human and material, remove those resources from the government's jurisdiction in order to escape additional taxation or regulation, and this flight of people and property teaches the government the wisdom of backing off. Although such "Tiebout-type" movement certainly does occur—people do sometimes vote with their feet, and financial capital can now be reallocated internationally with the click of a mouse—its potential for constraining the growth of government in the United States seems to me to have been greatly exaggerated by those who have discussed it most extensively.[13] In a world of countries nearly all of which have even more oppressive government than the United States, Americans have few good options to which they might escape, and most people have strong emotional ties to their homeland. Nor can physical property be transmitted via the Internet. A vast accumulation of it just sits there, waiting for government to tax or regulate it, sometimes until all its value has been destroyed.

In a third scenario, a sort of libertarian dream, the dominant ideology changes. Both elites and masses rediscover the supreme value of free markets, individual responsibility, and limited government. It might happen, to be sure, but the likelihood that it will happen seems to me to be negligible. For more than a century, the American people have been gravitating, when they were not lurching, further and further away from the ideals of classical liberalism. Not only have they grown accustomed to pervasive government involvement in virtually every aspect of social and economic life, but increasingly they have adopted a perspective on social life that regards more and more kinds of malicious, unwise, or merely unsuccessful human behavior as "sickness" and thus looks to government agents to effect a cure.[14] Arriving at a condition against which Alexis de Tocqueville warned long ago, the American people have now become for the most part "a flock of timid and industrious animals, of which the government is the shepherd."[15] That such people stand on the verge of a libertarian ideological conversion is a prospect too preposterous to take seriously.

Notes

1. U.S. Congress, Joint Economic Committee, "Trends in Congressional Appropriations: Fiscal Restraint in the 1990s," press release no. 105-124, April 6, 1998, p. 9.

2. U.S. Council of Economic Advisers, *Report 1997* (Washington, D.C.: U.S. Government Printing Office, 1997), p. 394.

3. U.S. Office of Management and Budget, *Budget of the United States Government: Fiscal Year 1998, Historical Tables* (Washington, D.C.: U.S. Government Printing Office, 1997), p. 23.

4. Estimates displayed on July 30, 1998, at http://www.taxfoundation.org.

5. According to *government* estimates cited in Brian Doherty, "The Price of Controls," *Reason* (April 1998), p. 19.

6. Poll findings presented by Karlyn Bowman, "At War with Washington?" *The American Enterprise* (November–December 1997), pp. 91–92.

7. See, for well-documented examples, David O. Sacks and Peter A. Thiel, *The Diversity Myth: "Multiculturalism" and the Politics of Intolerance at Stanford* (Oakland, Calif.: The Independent Institute, 1995), and Darío Fernández-Morera, *American Academia and the Survival of Marxist Ideas* (New York: Praeger, 1996).

8. Poll findings presented by Bowman, "At War with Washington?" p. 93.

9. "President Bush Makes Labor Day Remarks to Union Workers in Ohio," September 1, 2003, at http://www.georgewbush.com/News/read.aspx?ID=1997.

10. Ibid., p. 94

11. For an introduction to the principles of public choice, see William C. Mitchell and Randy T. Simmons, *Beyond Politics: Markets, Welfare, and the Failure of Bureaucracy* (Boulder, Colo.: Westview Press, for The Independent Institute, 1994).

12. Robert Higgs, *Crisis and Leviathan: Critical Episodes in the Growth of American Government* (New York: Oxford University Press, 1987).

13. Along these lines, a good book is Richard B. McKenzie and Dwight R. Lee, *Quicksilver Capital: How the Rapid Movement of Wealth Has Changed the World* (New York: Free Press, 1991). For a critique of the book, see Robert Higgs, "Leviathan at Bay?" *Liberty* 5 (November 1991): 64–70 (a revised version of which appears as chap. 31 in this collection).

14. James L. Nolan Jr., *The Therapeutic State: Justifying Government at Century's End* (New York: New York University Press, 1998); Thomas S. Szasz, "The Therapeutic State: The Tyranny of Pharmacracy," *The Independent Review* 5 (spring 2001): 485–521.

15. Alexis de Tocqueville, *Democracy in America,* edited by Richard D. Heffner (New York: Mentor, 1956), p. 304.

PART VI
Review of the Troops

34

The Bloody Hinge
of American History

The Civil War was the Great Event of American history. Much of what happened in the preceding centuries can be seen as part of a process that culminated in the war, and much of what has happened since can be seen as, directly or indirectly, a consequence of the war. Before the war, millions toiled in legally sanctioned lifetime slavery; afterward, the laws permitted slavery only as punishment for crime. Before the war, the country was constitutionally a federation of sovereign constituent states (*these* United States); afterward, it was de facto a unitary state with a dominant central government (*the* United States). Before the war, individual freedom had tended to expand; afterward, it tended to shrink.

No subject in U.S. history has given rise to as much writing—thousands of books and countless articles—as the Civil War. Why do writers continue to grind out still more? Haven't previous authors viewed the great conflict from every conceivable perspective, supported judgments for and against every significant politician and general, and traced the paths of thousands of others involved in the fray? Surely, one might have thought, at this stage no one can do much more than sweep up the crumbs.

Yet, notwithstanding the enormous literature, the publication of Jeffrey Rogers Hummel's *Emancipating Slaves, Enslaving Free Men: A History of the American Civil War* is a major event in Civil War scholarship.[1] I know of no other book like it in perspective, structure, or conclusions. It will have an invigorating and altogether healthy effect on lay and scholarly understanding of America's pivotal cataclysm.

Hummel's book is simultaneously elementary and advanced, thanks to its unique architecture. Each of the thirteen chapters presents a succinct, clearly written narrative of the relevant historical developments that fall under its rubric. The first five chapters cover antebellum developments; the next five, the war itself; and the last two, postbellum developments. Well-chosen contemporary quotations add luster to the narrative. The sources of the quotations appear in twenty-two pages of notes at the back of the book, leaving the text itself uncluttered by scholarly apparatus or intramural quibbling.

Immediately following each chapter, as well as the prologue and the epilogue, is a bibliographical essay. Here Hummel displays not only a mastery of the vast literature but also an extraordinary analytical ability. Experts will relish these essays for their discriminating descriptions of hundreds of books and articles and even more for the light they shed on prevalent misconceptions, errors, and oversights. The bibliographical essays occupy 110 pages, and the narrative chapters 255 pages, but the essays, owing to their smaller print and more closely spaced lines, actually account for more of the book than the page counts suggest. Readers with limited interest can skip these scholarly essays. Those who want to look up a particular point will find the 33-page index is excellent.

Conventional Wisdom

History tends to be written by the winners, and Civil War history is no exception, but sympathizers of the South have hardly been mute. During the first half of the twentieth century, historians sympathetic to the Confederate cause gained a substantial hearing, but later, especially as racial attitudes changed in the twenty years after World War II, these renditions of the story lost ground, eventually becoming so rare as to seem cranky. Among academic historians, even in the South, such views are now extremely rare.

Historical understanding varies greatly among people who know anything at all about the war. At the level of "what every schoolboy knows," the prevailing myth is pretty simple. The Southerners (the bad guys), in order to preserve slavery, attempted to secede from the United States; the Northerners (the good guys, led by the saintly Abraham Lincoln), provoked by the bombardment of Fort Sumter, rose up in righteous indignation to free the slaves, and, after much bloodshed, did free them; the victors then reconstructed the nation, amending the Constitution to ensure a level playing field for the blacks. (The wily Southerners soon reestablished white supremacy, but that's supposed to be another story.)

Even as we transcend this vulgar understanding, we find that the question of secession continues to be viewed as locked tightly to the question of slavery. Because nobody now wishes to defend the perpetuation of slavery, a defense of Southern secession labors under a heavy burden. Hummel, however, willingly takes up this burden.

Against Slavery, For Secession

At the outset, Hummel proposes that we can advance our understanding of why the war occurred by posing two questions: First, why did the Southerners want to secede? Second, why didn't the Northerners allow them to secede? Refusing to be tied in the usual knot, Hummel insists that "slavery and secession are separate issues" (p. 8). Like the abolitionist Lysander Spooner, whom he cites, Hummel will draw "no moral analogy between slaves violently rising up to secure their liberty and the central government violently crushing aspirations for self-determination on the part of white southerners" (p. 205). By simultaneously condemning slavery (along with all the social and political evils it fostered) *and* the Northern resort to violence to prevent Southern secession, Hummel stakes out a seldom-occupied territory among historians.

All serious historians appreciate that President Lincoln, whatever his personal attitudes toward slavery and blacks, did not resort to armed force to suppress the secession in order to destroy slavery. Indeed, during the interim between his election in 1860 and his inauguration in 1861, Lincoln supported a proposed unamendable constitutional amendment that would have prohibited interference with slavery in the states where it already existed.

Lincoln made his reasons for waging war against the Confederacy utterly clear in a letter to newspaperman Horace Greeley, dated August 22, 1862:

> My paramount object in this struggle *is* to save the Union, and is *not* either to save or to destroy slavery. If I could save the Union without freeing *any* slave I would do it, and if I could save it by freeing *all* the slaves I would do it; and if I could save it by freeing some and leaving others alone I would also do that. What I do about slavery, and the colored race, I do because I believe it helps to save the Union; and what I forbear, I forbear because I do *not* believe it would help save the Union. (pp. 207–8)

When prosecution of the war bogged down in 1862, Lincoln formulated the Emancipation Proclamation, largely to dissuade Britain and other powers from recognizing the Confederacy and partly to encourage blacks to join the Union army. When formally promulgated on January 1, 1863, the proclamation freed not a single slave, because it applied exclusively to territory then under rebel control. Noting that the proclamation left slavery intact in all areas under U.S. control, the *London Spectator* observed: "The principle is not that a human being cannot justly own another, but that he cannot own him unless he is loyal to the United States" (p. 210).

Later, as Union troops advanced, hundreds of thousands of slaves fled to the safety of army camps, finding freedom and a rather wretched existence, because supplies were often insufficient to feed the refugees as well as the soldiers, and commanders resorted to putting the runaways to work as laborers. Even where the rebels retained control, slavery began to break down as the presence of nearby Union troops encouraged the slaves to resist the impositions of their owners. Union victory, of course, finally did result in the complete destruction of slavery. In 1865, the victors forced the vanquished to ratify the Thirteenth Amendment. (How many Americans have ever considered that vital portions of the Constitution were ratified at gunpoint?)

Slavery's Achilles Heel

The decay of slavery within the Confederacy during the war illustrates a fact of supreme importance for Hummel's interpretation of antebellum political maneuvering and his assessment of whether the war was necessary to destroy slavery. Put simply, slaves preferred freedom to slavery, and, given a fair chance to escape, they would run away from their owners.

The fugitive slave issue, which Hummel characterizes as slavery's Achilles heel, was so important to the Southerners that it played a crucial part in the compromise that gave rise to the U.S. Constitution of 1787. Article IV, Section 2, states in part: "No person held to Service or Labour in one State, under the Laws thereof, escaping into another, shall, in Consequence of any Law or Regulation therein, be discharged from such Service or Labour, but shall be delivered up on Claim of the Party to whom such Service or Labour may be due." This provision, to the extent that it received effective enforcement, prevented the free states from serving as havens for runaway slaves and thereby placed a mighty prop under the slave system in the South.

Congress passed legislation to enforce the Constitution's fugitive slave clause in 1793. Under that law, national and state courts shared jurisdiction over the recovery of runaways. The number of slaves successfully escaping to the free states, almost all from the border states, probably never exceeded a thousand per year, but Hummel argues that "without a fugitive slave law, the number would have soared" (p. 55).

Besides enjoying the cooperation of the federal government and the free states in the apprehension and return of runaways, the slave states socialized the enforcement costs of the slave system by requiring virtually all able-bodied white men to serve in the local slave patrols. "Exemption usually required paying a fine or hiring a substitute," Hummel points out. "The slave patrols thereby affixed a tax that shifted enforcement costs to small slaveholders and poor whites who owned no slaves" (p. 48).

In the three decades before the war, the emergence and growth of the abolitionist movement heightened the Southerners' worries about runaway slaves. All slave states moved to suppress whatever fostered slave escape: they suppressed free speech, censored the mail, tightly restricted manumissions, and closely regulated the movement and activities of free blacks. As Hummel writes, "The South's siege mentality turned it into a closed society" (p. 25). This slavery-related repression contrasted starkly with the flowering of individual freedom in many other spheres of American life in the 1840s and 1850s.

Appreciating the vulnerability of the slave system to runaways, William Lloyd Garrison and some other abolitionists supported *Northern* secession. In their view, a separate free nation adjacent to the slave South would serve as an asylum for runaways far more effectively than would the free states of the

United States, which remained subject to the federal fugitive slave law.

In the 1830s and 1840s, radical abolitionists increased their efforts to evade the fugitive slave law and to challenge it in court. The "underground railroad" spirited a number of slaves to freedom in Canada. Seven Northern states passed personal-liberty laws, prohibiting state officials from assisting in capturing runaways or forbidding the use of state or local jails to confine fugitive slaves. These developments spurred Southerners to demand new protection of their property rights in slaves.

One upshot was the passage of a new federal fugitive slave act as part of the Compromise of 1850. This law, which Hummel calls "one of the harshest congressional measures ever" (p. 94), created federal commissioners to assist in capturing runaways, empowered these officers to conscript the aid of any private citizen, and paid them fees that created a financial incentive for them to identify blacks as escaped slaves.

As Hummel observes, free blacks in the North now "had no legal recourse if a Southerner claimed they were escaped slaves. Consequently the law fostered an unsavory class of professional slave catchers, who could make huge profits by legally kidnapping free blacks in the North and selling them into slavery in the South" (p. 94). Some previously hostile or indifferent Northerners came to support abolitionism after witnessing such horrifying abductions.

Was Slavery Efficient?

For more than thirty years, economic historians trained in neoclassical economics have tortured their data and pounded their word processors in a debate over the efficiency of slavery. Robert W. Fogel and Stanley L. Engerman, most notably in their 1973 book *Time on the Cross*,[2] argued that large slave plantations were much more efficient than Northern farms. Critics have disputed the claim, arguing that the apparent efficiency advantage reflected among other things such factors as the abnormally high price of cotton circa 1860 or the greater labor input coerced from the slaves. Though valuable facts have been unearthed along the way, several rounds of this debate have done little to close the gap between the disputants.

Unlike the neoclassical economists, Hummel never forgets that efficiency is a welfare concept that presupposes the existing property-rights regime. In this light, finding that slavery was efficient amounts to little more than finding that theft benefits thieves when legal conditions allow them to get away with it. Hummel does not lose sight of the crux, which is that the slaveowners were kidnappers and thieves, that slavery "involved a compulsory transfer from black slaves to white masters" (p. 40); hence, "the ability to coerce the slave is [the slave system's] only possible advantage over free labor" (p. 65).

Hummel faults Fogel for continuing to view "coercion and wages as *merely* two alternative ways to motivate workers" and for failing to "comprehend the fundamental economic distinction between a voluntary transaction, which because of its mutual gains moves the transactors toward greater efficiency and welfare (given the initial endowments), and a coercive transfer, which because of its nearly inevitable deadweight loss must reduce efficiency and welfare" (p. 70). Hummel's penetrating discussion of the efficiency debate, on pages 61–70, is by itself worth the price of the book.

Tyranny on Both Sides

Both sides fought under a flag of freedom: the North (eventually) to release the slaves from bondage, the South to gain political self-determination. Waging war, however, has its own logic independent of the belligerents' motives for fighting. In wartime, political authority dilates, and individual liberty shrinks. The Civil War was no exception.

When Lincoln took office as president, eight slave states remained in the Union. Lincoln's call for seventy-five thousand troops to suppress the "rebellion" prompted four of these states—Virginia, North Carolina, Tennessee, and Arkansas—to join the Confederacy. Virginia governor John Letcher wrote to Lincoln: "You have chosen to inaugurate civil war, and having done so, we will meet it in a spirit as determined as the Administration has exhibited toward the South" (p. 141).

Lincoln undertook to hold the remaining slave states in the Union at all cost. In Maryland, he suspended the writ of habeas corpus, imposed military occupation, and imprisoned leading secessionists without trial. Chief Justice Roger Taney wrote an outraged opinion declaring that the president had no constitutional authority to take these actions, whose effect would be that "the people of the United States are no longer living under a Government of laws, but every citizen holds life, liberty and property at the will and pleasure of the army officer in whose military district he may happen to be found" (p. 142). Lincoln ignored Taney's opinion and prepared standing orders (never served) for Taney's arrest. When Maryland held elections in the fall of 1861, federal provost marshals watched the polls and arrested secessionists who attempted to vote.

In Missouri, the administration took even more drastic actions. In an early confrontation with an angry crowd, army troops killed twenty-eight people, mostly innocent onlookers, thereby turning many Unionists into secessionists. Ostensibly loyal but clamped under martial law, Missouri became the scene of its own bitter civil war, featuring brutal guerrilla forays and scorched-earth tactics by the Union army for the duration of the war and beyond. These events left a "legacy of hatred" that would "continue to plague Kansas and Missouri long after the rest of the country attained peace" (p. 144). The outlaw Jesse

James was just one of the many involved in the Missouri conflict who continued to hold a grudge.

In Kentucky, where sympathies were similarly divided,

> Federal authorities declared martial law; required loyalty oaths before people could trade or engage in many other daily activities; censored books, journals, sermons, and sheet music; and crowded the jails with Rebel sympathizers. By 1862 the military was interfering with elections, preventing candidates from running, and dispersing the Democratic convention at bayonet point. The net result was that the people of Kentucky felt greater solidarity with the rest of the South at the war's end than at its beginning. (p. 146)

Unable to hold Virginia, the Lincoln administration finagled the creation of a new state, West Virginia, in 1863. By further political chicanery, the Republicans admitted Kansas and Nevada to the Union as states in 1861 and 1864, respectively. "And let us not ignore," writes Hummel, the "tampering with the soldiers' vote" at a time when ballots were not secret and "most of the army's junior officers and paymasters were members of the Republican Party" (p. 258). By such shenanigans, Lincoln managed to get himself reelected in 1864, though General George B. McClelland, the candidate of a Democratic Party whose platform called for an immediate cessation of hostilities, received 45 percent of the popular vote even on this sharply tilted political playing field.

Lincoln did not hesitate to act as a dictator when doing so served his purposes. A favorite tactic was to toss political dissidents or other troublesome persons into jail; at least fourteen thousand civilians met that fate at the hands of the Lincoln administration, not to speak of the many others similarly treated by state and local authorities. Union authorities monitored and censored the mails and telegraphs, and at one time or another closed more than three hundred newspapers. In promulgating his Emancipation Proclamation and in taking many other actions, Lincoln chose to ignore Congress.

Confederate authorities behaved similarly. President Jefferson Davis suspended the writ of habeas corpus in various areas. Confederate commanders sometimes instituted martial law, required loyalty oaths, and made mass arrests. "The courts viewed anyone not supporting the Confederacy as an enemy alien, outside any legal protections accorded to citizens." Private vigilance committees "imposed, to the point of lynching, their own versions of loyalty," and "the military's provost marshals required passports of travelers in nearly all Confederate-held territory" (p. 261). In the later stages of the war, Confederate army officers earned the hearty hostility of the Southern people by seizing property, especially foodstuffs and workstock, as the opportunity arose to resupply their units in this convenient way.

War Brought Big Government

When, to the surprise of most war hawks on both sides, the war turned out to be big, protracted, and gory rather than short and glorious, the warring governments faced the basic problem of going to war in a market economy: how to channel resources away from their current owners and into the war machine. Aside from receiving gifts, only two methods can serve. The government either buys the resources or just takes them. The former method can be facilitated by imposing new kinds of taxes, raising the rates of existing taxes, borrowing funds, or printing new money. Both sides in the war employed each of these means to get control of resources, though the mix of methods differed.

To make a complicated story as simple as possible, one might say that for the most part the North borrowed funds and bought resources, and for the most part the South printed paper money and bought resources. As a result, the paper dollar lost about half its value in the North during the war, and the purchasing power of paper money in the Confederacy fell by more than 95 percent, so that many Southerners abandoned the use of money and resorted to barter in 1864 and 1865. To stimulate purchases of its bonds, the Union government created the national banking system, in which federally chartered member banks had to buy U.S. bonds as backing for the national bank notes they might issue in making loans to customers. Like many other innovations of the Civil War, the national banking system remains a part of our economy today.

The war was tremendously expensive in dollars as well as in blood. In the four years of fighting, the federal government spent $3.4 billion, far more than it had spent in the entire preceding history of the United States ($1.8 billion). Although borrowing accounted for 77 percent of Union revenues, other receipts rose enormously: from $56 million in fiscal 1860, nearly all from customs, to $334 million in fiscal 1865, which included $209 million of internal revenue.

Republican politico James G. Blaine called the revenue act of 1862 "one of the most searching, thorough, comprehensive systems of taxation every devised by any Government" (p. 222). It included excises on a vast collection of goods, everything from liquor and tobacco to meat, carriages, and professional services, plus a stamp tax not unlike the one that had inflamed the American colonists in 1765. The wartime Congress also imposed taxes on incomes, inheritances, real estate, and nearly everything else that would stand still. Not surprisingly, many people attempted to evade the taxes—hence the creation of the Internal Revenue bureaucracy, another of the war's diabolical legacies to succeeding generations.

Still scrambling for funds, Congress authorized the issue of fiat paper money, the famous "greenbacks," and declared them to be a legal tender. Ultimately, $431 million was put into circulation by this means. When counterfeiters began to issue greenbacks of their own, the government established the Secret Service, another agency that refused to die after the war. While Congress was monkeying with the money, it banned private minting; thereafter the federal government would enjoy, as it never had before, a monopoly of the mintage.

In the financially less developed South, the Confederates had limited success in collecting taxes, which covered only 7 percent of their war expenses, or in borrowing money, which financed about one-fourth of their spending. Not that they didn't try. They imposed taxes on imports, exports, and excess profits; established a graduated income tax; and initiated license fees, excises, and taxes in kind. "A sequestration law, passed in response to the Union confiscation acts, expropriated all northern private property within Confederate jurisdiction" (p. 228).

In the main, however, the Confederacy just printed money—ultimately more than $1 billion. Individual Southern states added another $45 million, and local governments and private companies spewed out assorted "shinplasters," a kind of homemade small-denomination substitute for money. After injuring Southerners with hyperinflation, the outpouring of new fiat money insulted them at the conclusion of the war by becoming *totally* worthless. Hyperinflation and the economic collapse of the Southern economy it hastened may have done as much to ensure the rebels' defeat as their reversals on the battlefield.

The Republicans took advantage of their control of Congress: raising tariffs dramatically; authorizing subsidies to railroad companies and to states that established agricultural, mechanical, and military colleges; creating the Department of Agriculture; and serving its favored constituents in a variety of other ways—all of which Hummel lumps under the heading of Northern "neomercantilism."

The Confederate government, in contrast, did much more to involve itself directly in the ownership, control, and operation of productive enterprises, including arsenals, powder mills, smelters, mines, foundries, shipyards, textile mills, flour mills, salt works, and assorted other enterprises. Late in the war, it "took possession of all un-captured southern railroads, steamboats, and telegraph lines outright, incorporating their employees and officers into the military" (p. 236). Hummel calls these activities "State socialism." He concludes that despite the South's avowed loyalty to states' rights, "Confederate war socialism was more economically centralized than the Union's neo-mercantilism, which at least relied heavily on private initiative" (p. 238).

Ironically, the rebels' socialism, like so many other policies they adopted to wage war, also contributed to their defeat. "Rebel central planning, while adequately serving the single-minded goal of supplying conventional armies, otherwise misallocated resources and fostered inefficiencies" (p. 238). Moreover, "the despotic centralization of Jefferson Davis and his West Point cabal alienated the southern people from the cause of independence" (p. 289).

What both governments could not get in any other way, they just took. Hummel estimates that the South got "somewhere between one-fifth and one-third" of its soldiers by conscription and used draft exemptions as "the mechanism for manipulating the labor market" (p. 250). The North had better luck attracting volunteers, in part by paying large bonuses for enlistments, but in the latter half of the war the Union also resorted to conscription, and about 6 percent of those who served in its ranks were draftees.

In the land of the free, the people did not take kindly to conscription, and disturbances broke out in hundreds of places. Mayhem and murder ensued in draft riots, most notably in New York, where rampaging Irish immigrants and others vented their fury on local blacks. Draft evasion reached extreme levels in both the North and the South.

Aftermath

When the guns finally fell silent in the spring of 1865, the devil must have been smiling. Some 360,000 Northern and 260,000 Southern soldiers had died; some 400,000 combatants had been seriously wounded, many maimed for life. Even the survivors with bodies intact would have to live with the nightmares of the horror they had experienced. For countless relatives and friends of those who did not return home, the heartache would never end. Across the South, where more than 50,000 civilian casualties augmented the military losses, many towns and cities, railroads, farms, and mills lay in ruins, and frightening specters loomed over the region's economic, social, and political future. For sowing with slaves, Americans had reaped a whirlwind. Nor was the full price paid yet. Perhaps it never will be.

Twelve years later, Reconstruction had run its course; the damaged Southern economy had been repaired and reorganized with free labor; and the rebels had regained political control of their states. Northerners had grown tired of trying to secure justice for the Southern blacks, abandoning them to the tender mercies of their erstwhile masters. Although the freed people managed to continue improving their economic conditions, around the turn of the century the Southern whites created piecemeal the Jim Crow system of racial segregation and political disfranchisement that would inhibit and insult black people in the South until it was finally dismantled in the 1960s. So much blood, so little to show for it.

Nor was that disappointment all. Hummel argues that the war destroyed the best government the country ever had: "The national government that emerged victorious from the conflict dwarfed in power and size the minimal Jacksonian State that had commenced the war" (p. 328). With the old federation of sovereign states shattered forever, the national government began the long march that eventually transformed it into the monstrous police state we know today. Intellectuals, who once took seriously the ideals of state sovereignty and secession, became for the most part worshipers of central government power. Federal taxing and spending ratcheted up; federal involvement in economic life increased in important sectors, including banking and transportation. The national debt, almost negligible before the war, had reached $2.8 billion by the war's end. Tariffs, jacked up to finance the war, remained high for decades afterward.

No one can deny that the Civil War was a turning point in the long-run growth of government in the United States, but Hummel overstates the extent of government power in the late nineteenth century and the degree to which the growth of government that did occur during those decades sprang from war-related causes. A huge retrenchment did take place immediately after the war, and some war-spawned measures, such as the subsidization of railroad building, the income tax, and almost all of the federal excise taxes, were terminated within a few years.

Much of the growth of government in the late nineteenth century occurred at the municipal level, as cities undertook to impose public-health regulations and to build schools, paved streets, transport and water-supply systems, sewers, and other urban infrastructure, all of which probably would have occurred even if the war had never been fought.

At the federal level, such developments as passage of the Act to Regulate Commerce (1887), the Sherman Antitrust Act (1890), and the Food and Drugs Act (1906), as well as many other interventions also might have occurred in any event. Despite the political entrenchment of mildly statist Republicans, recurrently waving the bloody shirt, something approximating classical liberalism retained a strong hold on most Americans, even on many opinion leaders, prior to the Progressive Era. Still, although one may quarrel about the magnitudes, Hummel is surely correct to argue that the war had an enduring effect in augmenting the size and scope of government.

War Weighed in the Balance

Nowadays few Americans hesitate to conclude that, on balance, the war was a good thing. Yes, they will say, it was horrible in many ways, but it was the price that had to be paid to destroy slavery. Hummel does not dispute the war's great benefit: "the last, great coercive blight on the American landscape, black chattel slavery, was finally extirpated—a triumph that cannot be overrated" (p. 350). Moreover, "the fact that abolition was an unintended consequence in no way gainsays the accomplishment" (p. 352).

But a justification of the war on the grounds that it destroyed slavery holds only if the war alone could have destroyed slavery. Hummel denies that this horrible price—one dead soldier for every six freed slaves—had to be paid. Thus, for him, as for the abolitionist Moncure Conway, the war that radiates such grandeur in American mythology reduces to "mere manslaughter" (p. 355).

Although Hummel accepts the research of economic historians who have shown that slavery was flourishing and not at all on the brink of withering away, he argues that even without the war it would have petered out:

> Slavery was doomed *politically* even if Lincoln had permitted the small Gulf Coast Confederacy to depart in peace. The Republican-controlled Congress would have been able to work toward emancipation within the border states, where slavery was already declining. In due course the Radicals could have repealed the Fugitive Slave Law of 1850. With chattels fleeing across the border and raising slavery's enforcement costs, the peculiar institution's final destruction within an independent cotton South was inevitable. (p. 353)

Maybe. One still wonders, though, whether slavery could have been ended easily or quickly in the border states; whether the Gulf Confederacy might have been able to stem the flow of runaways; and whether, ultimately facing a serious threat to its slave system because of escapees fleeing to the North, it might have gone to war eventually anyway. In the last scenario, we have the worst of worlds—a prolongation of slavery *and* the horrors of war, perhaps an even more horrible war.

Of course, no one can know. Counterfactuals defy direct testing; we cannot rerun history to find out what would have occurred had some critical event not happened. Yet all causal thinking necessarily involves counterfactuals. Too often in historical analysis the counterfactuals lie quietly between the lines, frequently in the form of unquestioned assumptions. A great merit of Hummel's book is that it brings new counterfactuals to the surface, compelling a reconsideration of assumptions too long taken for granted, especially the assumption that the secession required that Lincoln wage a war to preserve the Union and the assumption that only a terrible civil war could end slavery.

It is worth recalling that the people of every slave society in the New World save two—Haiti and the United States—managed to terminate this vile institution without immersing themselves in blood. In Haiti, the slaves quite justifiably took matters into their own hands; the masters got no more than they deserved. In the United States, however, the termination of slavery occurred only in conjunction with a disastrous war and bitter reconstruction that left many issues unsettled and harmed a great many innocents. How tragic that the means by which men overthrew a wicked institution should also have been the means by which they arrested the progress of their own freedom—that emancipating slaves entailed enslaving free men.

Notes

1. Chicago and La Salle, Ill.: Open Court, 1996. Hereafter cited parenthetically by page number in the text.

2. Boston: Little Brown, 1973.

35

The Rise of Big Business in America

It would have been nice if we could have had industrialization without having to put up with the industrialists, or so it must seem to readers of college textbooks in U.S. history. For generations, we have been taught that the great entrepreneurs were greedy and rapacious at best and downright vicious at worst. They inflicted on the nation an "ordeal" of social and economic transformation so wrenching that it nearly tore the country apart. At the same time, they corrupted our democratic political institutions and created a de facto plutocracy. Fortunately, heroic and selfless Progressives, New Dealers, and other forward-looking defenders of the downtrodden masses eventually countervailed against the unmitigated perniciousness of the classic captains of industry and their undeserving scions.

This portrait is less a caricature than you might think. As Stanford University historian David M. Kennedy, coauthor of a best-selling textbook, has written, "Most American academic historians have thought of themselves as the political heirs of the Progressive tradition."[1] They have written their textbooks accordingly. For the Progressives, much of social, economic, and political life boiled down to a matter of the People versus the Trusts—little people versus big business. Good and evil divided along the same line. This perspective has become deeply embedded in the way historians usually tell the story of U.S. industrialization and economic growth during the late nineteenth and early twentieth centuries.

Now comes Burton W. Folsom Jr. with a book disputing the received wisdom, *Entrepreneurs vs. the State: A New Look at the Rise of Big Business in America, 1840–1920.*[2] The standard tale, he maintains, fails to distinguish two fundamentally different kinds of entrepreneurs. As a result, it goes wrong on many other aspects of the story.

Two Kinds of Entrepreneurs

Yes, the great entrepreneurs, almost by definition, had a keen desire to become rich. This elemental fact, however, does not justify the common description of them as greedy. Greed suggests, if it does not actually denote, selfishness. Many of the great entrepreneurs, however, are still remembered for the most part because of their philanthropy: their names have been familiar to generations who have benefited by virtue of the charitable foundations, universities, libraries, museums, even cities that the great entrepreneurs founded or fostered. Carnegie, Vanderbilt, Rockefeller, Scranton, Stanford, Ford, Duke, Johns Hopkins—nearly anyone can make a long list of examples. Before his death, John D. Rockefeller *gave away* more wealth to charities—some $550 million—than any American before him had *possessed.* So an inordinate desire to make money, far from indicating selfishness, might have been—and no doubt often was—consistent with extraordinary altruism.

What matters to Folsom, however, is neither the great capitalists' desire for wealth nor the raw fact that they acquired it. The crux is *how* they got rich. Two quite different avenues presented themselves. The entrepreneurs could earn their wealth in the market by offering consumers new or higher-quality products, cutting their costs of production and marketing, and devising new techniques of production. Or they could enrich themselves by grasping the helpful hand of government, thereby gaining subsidies, tariff protection, and restrictions on the entry of competitors into their markets. The first avenue Folsom calls *market entrepreneurship;* the second he calls *political entrepreneurship.*

Barring gifts, one can acquire more wealth either by creating it or by stealing it. When the power of government serves to redistribute wealth, the transfer is not legal theft, but it is substantive theft. What one person has created is taken from him under threat of violent coercion and made a benefit to another. Owing to deficiencies in their grasp of moral principles, more people are willing to steal with government as the go-between than are willing to steal on their own. This generalization applies to people in business as well as to welfare cheats and other notorious ne'er-do-wells.

With this basic distinction as a guide, Folsom reconsiders some of the most famous American entrepreneurs—Cornelius Vanderbilt, James J. Hill, Charles Schwab, and John D. Rockefeller, as well as Joseph, George W., and Selden T. Scranton. His purpose is not so much to describe their accomplishments, which other historians have already written about in great detail, but to use their histories as test cases to illustrate the usefulness of distinguishing market entrepreneurs and political entrepreneurs.

Commodore Vanderbilt

Robert Fulton is remembered as the innovator of practical steamboat transportation in America, but he was also a notable political entrepreneur. He obtained from the New York legislature a monopoly on carrying steamboat passengers in the state. Young Cornelius Vanderbilt, in contrast, began his career as what the *New York Evening Post* called "the greatest practical anti-monopolist in the country" in 1817, when Thomas Gibbons, a New Jersey capitalist, hired him to challenge Fulton's monopoly. Defying capture by the New York authorities, Vanderbilt transported passengers between Elizabeth, N.J., and New York City at reduced fares. His ship's flag proclaimed "New Jersey must be free." This competition later resulted in a landmark decision of the U.S. Supreme Court, *Gibbons v. Ogden* (1824), in which the Court struck down the Fulton monopoly, holding it to be a violation of the national government's exclusive power to regulate interstate commerce.

Vanderbilt went on to drive the Fulton interests into bankruptcy and to establish steamboat transportation throughout the Northeast. Hallmarks of his strategy were technical innovations—tubular boilers instead of the heavy, expensive copper ones and anthracite coal for fuel instead of the more costly cordwood—as well as reduced costs and fares. For a while in his rivalry with the Hudson River Steamboat Association, he carried passengers from New York to Albany without charge, depending on their purchases of food en route to cover his costs. Finally his competitors on this route bought him out, paying him $100,000 plus $5,000 per year for ten years just to stay away. (The payoff failed to secure their monopoly: other competitors came along who also had to be bought out.)

In 1838, the Cunard line, aided by a subsidy from the British Parliament, inaugurated scheduled trans-Atlantic steamboat transportation of mail and passengers. Political entrepreneurs in the United States, like their present-day counterparts, used the foreign subsidies as justification to plead for similar government aid to Americans. Edward K. Collins, successfully appealing to American nationalism, received a large subsidy from Congress to build and operate ships in competition with the Cunard line. Once the principle had been established, others rushed in. Congress then awarded mail subsidies to two companies, an Atlantic line and a Pacific line, to carry mail from the East to California via Panama. "All argued that a generous subsidy now would help them become more efficient and lead to no subsidy later" (p. 6). Of course, that outcome did not come about. The subsidized lines, having no compelling incentive to lower their costs, became even less efficient. Collins "went to Washington and lavishly dined and entertained President Fillmore, his cabinet, and influential Congressmen" (pp. 6–7), lobbying for even greater subsidies.

In 1855, Vanderbilt decided to challenge the Collins line. He declared his willingness to carry on the trans-Atlantic business at reduced cost. Collins, however, had Congress locked into his scheme. Hence, the legislators turned down Vanderbilt's offer and continued payments of $858,000 per year to Collins. Vanderbilt then decided to challenge Collins in the marketplace. He slashed charges for mail and passenger service and introduced a new service—third-class, or "steerage." He found ways to cut expenses and to increase the volume of traffic. He built a new steamship, the largest ever built up to that time, to facilitate a bigger business. Embarrassed by Collins's obvious mismanagement and by Vanderbilt's successful conduct of an unsubsidized business, Congress revoked the subsidies in 1858. Collins's enterprise quickly went bankrupt.

Meanwhile, similar events took place in the California business. The two subsidized lines began business in 1849 aided by $500,000 per year in mail subsidies from the Post Office—a privately arranged deal never opened for bidding. Vanderbilt developed a new route via Nicaragua, where he obtained the rights to build a canal and to improve navigation on the San Juan River. While his competitors charged $600, he cut the California fare to $400 and promised faster service. Later he cut the fare to $150 and offered to carry the mail without charge. Still he was making money. Panic-stricken, his competitors went back to Congress and secured an increase of their subsidy to $900,000 per year.

In 1854, when the Nicaraguan government revoked Vanderbilt's canal rights, he resorted to the Panama route, competing head to head with his subsidized rivals. He cut the fare to $100. Having no taste for market competition, the California lines bought him out. They agreed to pay him 75 percent of their $900,000 annual subsidy in exchange for his promise to leave them alone.

Congress could not hide from the scandal created by Vanderbilt's ability to extract most of the subsidy being given to "these small plunderers that come about the Capitol," in Senator Robert Toombs's words (p. 13). After having paid Collins and the California companies more than $11 million to build ships and to carry the mail between 1848 and 1858, Congress ended the subsidies. Privately financed innovation and rate cutting had triumphed over monopoly, privilege, and federal aid—to consumers' immense benefit and to taxpayers' great relief.

Vanderbilt went on to even greater achievements in the railroad industry, where he built the New York Central, one of the nation's largest enterprises. When he died in 1877, he was the richest man in America.

Railroad Subsidies

In the 1860s, Congress, encouraged by rampant bribery, gave subsidies in the form of land grants to a number of railroad companies, including several transcontinental lines. The Union Pacific and the Central Pacific, the lines that met to form the first transcontinental line in 1869, also received loans. The grants were given according to the mileage constructed, which created an incentive for the companies to construct as many miles of track as possible, regardless of grade, route, or quality. Shoddy construction resulted.

Enormous potential for the private appropriation of public wealth existed—ultimately Congress gave away more than 131 million acres of land—

and therefore many businessmen regarded large political payoffs as an excellent investment. Historian Richard Hofstadter reports that the Union Pacific spent $400,000 on bribes between 1866 and 1872, the Central Pacific as much as $500,000 per year between 1875 and 1885—fabulous sums at a time when a dollar had vastly greater purchasing power than it has now.[3] Nor were these companies the only ones playing the payoff game.

The scandal eventually became too malodorous to ignore, and Congress passed legislation to fix what it had broken in the first place. The Union Pacific, for example, was made subject to strict federal regulation. It was forbidden, among other things, to build spur lines that would have increased the volume of traffic and promoted greater profitability. From this experience, Folsom draws an insightful lesson. Government aid bred inefficiency, which raised costs and rates and angered consumers; the angry consumers demanded government regulation; the resulting regulation promoted even greater inefficiency and led to the Union Pacific's eventual bankruptcy.

Along the way, however, the political entrepreneurs who arrived first at the government trough became spectacularly wealthy and powerful. This crowd of predators included men such as the Big Four—Leland Stanford, Collis Huntington, Charles Crocker, and Mark Hopkins—who headed the Central Pacific (later the Southern Pacific), and Henry Villard, the chief promoter of the Northern Pacific, the largest recipient of federal land grants, whom Folsom describes as a sort of grotesque pioneer who "rushed into the wilderness to collect his subsidies" (p. 23).

Though critical of the corruption and waste that attended the building of the western railroads, historians have usually accepted the argument that these great enterprises would not have been undertaken in the absence of the subsidies. Economists have calculated that when all economic gains, not just those captured by the investors, are taken into account, the subsidized railroads were actually of great net benefit to the nation. Folsom disputes this argument in two ways.

One counterargument is that the economists' calculations of so-called social rates of return are incomplete: they ignore the harmful social and political consequences of the grants. The largess bestowed on the builders of the first transcontinental railroads established a precedent for further subsidies that diverted resources from uses that consumers valued more highly. The grants encouraged shady business ethics and political corruption. Moreover, they led to a "mass of lawmaking, much of it harmful, all of it time-consuming, that state legislatures, Congress, and the Supreme Court did after watching the UP, the CP and NP in action" (p. 32). A great deal of the subsequent regulation had harmful if unintended consequences. In short, the subsidies breathed life into a monster that indirectly as well as directly wreaked havoc on the U.S. economy and the polity for decades.

James J. Hill

The other counterargument is the story of James J. Hill. Between 1878, when he and a group of Canadian friends bought a small bankrupt railroad extending only a few miles west from St. Paul, Minnesota, and 1893, when the Great Northern Railroad reached Puget Sound, Hill methodically built a railroad and promoted the development of a region larger than France and Germany combined. He did so without subsidy. Realizing that his railroad would never prosper unless the region through which it passed were made to flourish, Hill encouraged immigration and promoted agricultural research and development. He steadily reduced the company's costs and improved its services. While other railroad men spent their time buttering up and buying politicians, Hill looked after business. "A railroad," he said, "is successful in the proportion that its affairs are vigilantly looked after" (p. 28).

When other railroads lobbied against Hill's attempt to gain congressional approval for a right-of-way through several Indian reservations in Montana and North Dakota—a right already granted to the competing Northern Pacific and a right for which Hill was prepared to pay fair market value—he complained: "It really seems hard, when we look back at what we have done in opening the country and carrying at the lowest rates, that we should be compelled to fight political adventurers who have never done anything but pose and draw a salary" (p. 29).

Other Creators

Folsom's chapters on Schwab, Rockefeller, and the Scrantons and their city are interesting but not very effective in making the central point of the book. These chapters lack the clear and compelling contrasts between market entrepreneurs and political entrepreneurs so strikingly developed in the chapters on Vanderbilt and Hill. Still, they are instructive in knocking down some hardy myths—for example, that Rockefeller succeeded only because of rebates and drawbacks from the railroads—and in setting forth some oft-neglected aspects of these great industrialists' histories. Folsom does a laudable job in showing how difficult it was for Standard Oil to compete with the Russians in the world market for refined oil products. Many people forget that Standard exported the bulk of its production, so its international competitiveness was critical. Present-day companies, who typically run crying to Washington for protection and subsidies when they cannot compete in the world market, might take useful lessons from Standard's "oil war" with the Russians during the thirty years before World War I.

Folsom emphasizes that market entrepreneurship is creative. All of these men, as he says of the Scrantons, "created something out of nothing. They created their assets and created opportunities for others when they successfully bore the risks.... Without them, almost everybody else in the region would have been poorer" (p. 52). In a free market, economic life is not a zero-sum game. Political entrepreneurship, by contrast, is worse than a zero-sum game. It is part of a negative-sum game, for not only do the people who receive their benefits from government privilege gain at the expense of others, but the whole scheme sets up perverse incentives that lead to the dissipation and misallocation of resources and thereby make the entire society poorer.

Historians Against Economic Freedom

In a concluding chapter entitled "Entrepreneurs vs. the Historians," Folsom considers how several leading college history textbooks treat the entrepreneurs and their accomplishments. He finds that virtually without exception they "lump the predators and political adventurers with the creators and builders" (p. 107). They offer a "morality play of 'greedy businessmen' fleecing the public until at last they are stopped by the actions of the state" (p. 114). They emphasize how seldom vertical mobility took place within the industrializing cities and how often wealth bred more wealth while the toiling masses remained lodged in poverty and subject to exploitation. They laud the actions of governments at all levels in opposition to the robber barons. Responsibility for the bribery of governmental officials and for their other venality they lay on the businessmen who gave the graft, rather than on the officials who extorted and received it.

Although Folsom bemoans the prevailing "misconceptions" (p. 108) expressed in the textbooks and points out several crucial technical flaws in historical studies of social mobility, he does not inquire into the sociology of knowledge in the historical profession. He urges his fellow historians to set the record straight along the lines made clear in his chapters on the great entrepreneurs and their work. Such exhortation will prove fruitless, however, if the prevailing historical interpretation is rooted in something more fundamental than mere ignorance of economic fact or misunderstanding of economic theory. The fundamental problem, I believe, is ideological.

The historians' view of the great entrepreneurs and their accomplishments is but a part of their overall view of economic freedom and the market society. Almost without exception, they look upon the market with jaundiced eyes. Ideologically, almost all academic historians in the United States stand to the left of center. Most are left liberals, the ideological descendants of the Progressives. A substantial minority consists of outright Marxists, quasi-Marxists, and assorted other left radicals. All hold the market society in contempt and take pleasure in ridiculing its most characteristic personalities, chief among whom are the classic entrepreneurs. One cannot expect such professors to accept

Folsom's lessons. So long as the historical profession's ideological center of gravity remains at its present left-of-center position, students of U.S. history will continue to receive confused, biased, and misleading instruction in economic history.

Notes

1. Introduction to David M. Kennedy, ed., *Progressivism: The Critical Issues* (Boston: Little, Brown, 1971), p. xiii.

2. Reston, Va.: Young America's Foundation, 1987. Hereafter cited parenthetically by page number in the text.

3. Richard Hofstadter, *The American Political Tradition, and the Men Who Made It* (New York: Vintage, 1974), p. 219.

36

Origins of the
Corporate Liberal State

Between Grover Cleveland's second term as president and Woodrow Wilson's first, the beliefs of American opinion leaders and political activists about the proper relationship between the government and the economy underwent a radical shift. As late as the mid-1890s, the dominant ideology could still be described as liberal in the sense that liberalism was understood in the nineteenth century. Twenty years later, classical liberalism was in full retreat, as evidenced by the triumph of the Wilsonian economic program—the enthusiastically received outpouring of federal enactments between 1913 and 1916 that taxed, subsidized, and regulated economic activities.

The Progressive Era, circa 1900–1916, bequeathed a legacy of economic institutions—federal income taxation, central banking by the Federal Reserve System, more detailed antitrust laws, tighter control over the railroads, regulation of ocean shipping, federal responsibility for food and drug purity, and agricultural credit institutions, to name only some of the more prominent ones—without which one can scarcely imagine the economic and political life of the United States during the past ninety years. In a mere decade and a half, the country moved from a policy regime not too distant from laissez faire to one immediately recognized as modern activist interventionism. Why?

To provide the answer, or at least a great deal of the answer, is Martin J. Sklar's task in his massive and important book *The Corporate Reconstruction of American Capitalism, 1890–1916: The Market, The Law, and Politics.*[1] Even scholars who do not accept Sklar's interpretation will recognize his volume as a major work. Sklar has dug deeply into the archives and emerged with interesting and valuable findings. He has thought long and hard about how to comprehend the changing relation of the government to the economy in the Progressive Era. He expresses his ideas in careful and discriminating—often painfully discriminating—prose. Yet although Sklar has built his interpretive structure on a solid foundation of facts and pertinent scholarship, he has produced a twisted and unsatisfactory edifice. My task in this essay is to explain why I have come to this conclusion.

The Rise of Big Business

Until the very end of the nineteenth century, Americans usually conducted their economic affairs either individually or within small firms organized as proprietorships or partnerships. Business corporations were not unknown, and indeed such enterprises as turnpikes, canals, railroads, and commercial banks usually took the corporate form, but in industry, commerce, and agriculture— that is, nearly everywhere except in transportation, banking, and public utilities—corporations were unusual. Before the 1890s, only a single manufacturing firm, the Pullman Palace Car Company, had shares traded on the New York Stock Exchange, where railroad and public-utility shares constituted the market.[2]

During the 1890s, more and more industrial firms adopted the corporate form. Then, around the turn of the century, a wave of corporate consolidation transformed manufacturing industry with a suddenness that shocked many contemporaries, whose only knowledge of huge industrial enterprises pertained to the infamous trusts formed in the 1880s. From that time forward, public policy for regulating the size and conduct of large corporations would be known as antitrust policy, even though large enterprises legally organized as trusts disappeared at the turn of the century. The "Trust Problem" was actually the problem of how to adjust in economic and political affairs to the presence of many large corporate enterprises.

Because large corporations enjoyed substantial shares of the markets in which they sold their goods, they faced, as economists say, downward-sloping demand curves; they could raise the prices at which they offered their wares without losing all their customers. In this respect, the big firms differed from, say, wheat or cotton farmers, *price takers* who faced virtually horizontal demand curves and were compelled to sell at no more than the going market price. In the terminology of mainstream economics, wheat farmers are *perfect competitors*, whereas big firms with hefty market shares have *monopoly power*. These terms, although well understood in the literature of economics, have always been misleading to noneconomists because they suggest that the "perfect competitor" *competes* in the layman's sense of engaging in rivalry with other sellers, but that sellers with "monopoly power" do not or need not do so.

In reality, the opposite is the case. Price takers do not engage in rivalry with other sellers. Because of the nature of the (homogenous) product and the market structure in which they operate (many sellers, complete information), they can do nothing to win a rivalry with "competing" sellers. What mainstream economists call perfect competition is actually the antithesis of economic rivalry. Conversely, firms with so-called monopoly power, which are better designated as *price searchers* because they have many price options and must search for the optimal price to charge, strive incessantly to ward off rival or potentially rival firms. By advertising, cutting costs and prices, establishing new markets, and developing new products and processes of production, they routinely compete in a variety of rivalrous ways unknown to the perfect competitor.[3]

Sklar, notwithstanding the radicalism of his neo-Marxist framework of analysis, accepts the standard economic model of market structures. Thus, he views the advent of large manufacturing corporations at the turn of the century as a transition from the "proprietary-competitive stage" to the "corporate-administered stage" of American capitalism—that is, from a market of powerless price-taking firms to a market of powerful price-searching firms organized as corporations with widely dispersed, publicly traded shares and therefore a presumptive separation of ownership from managerial control (his presumption, not mine). He asserts that the transformation of industrial market structures was pervasive and that it gave rise to corporate "dominance" of the overall U.S. political economy during the first decade of the twentieth century (pp. 4–5).

In this view, when huge, powerful firms come to dominate a political economy, the protection that the public previously has received from competitive market processes no longer exists. People must control the monster roaming loose in the marketplace, or it will devour them. The question becomes: Who will regulate the economy, and, therefore, who will control the country? Obviously, individuals are powerless. The choices reduce to just two, the big corporations and the government. More specifically, because the big firms operate nationwide, state governments lack the power to control them; only the federal government has the scope of authority needed to do the job. If the federal government does not act, if its officials insist on following laissez-faire precepts that restrict their involvement in the economy, then the managers of the big corporations are free to "regulate" or "administer" the market and thereby to control the country (p. 181).

Sklar proceeds to interpret in painstaking detail the legal and political history of antitrust in the Progressive Era, viewing the Trust Question as the crux of the multifaceted conflict over the nature of the modern political economy. His assumption is always that unless a market consists of nothing but price-taking firms, it will necessarily be "regulated" by either the corporations or the federal government (pp. 167–69, 251). He cannot conceive that price-searching firms might be subject to severe competitive constraints on their freedom of action.

Sklar's assumption does not fit the facts. As Joseph Schumpeter observed sixty years ago, "in capitalist reality as distinguished from its textbook picture, it is not [price] competition which counts but the competition from the new commodity, the new technology, the new source of supply, the new type of organization ... competition which commands a decisive cost or quality advantage and which strikes not at the margins of the profits and the outputs of the existing firms but at their foundations and their very lives."[4] The big firms routinely faced just such competition; and, notwithstanding what many economist have alleged, there was plenty of price competition, too.[5]

For example, the railroad companies, the nation's first big businesses, chronically failed to suppress competition, despite repeated efforts. Not only did they compete by adopting improved equipment and organizational innovations that allowed them to deliver improved service; they also regularly competed by offering lower rates than rival companies. Thus, the late nineteenth century witnessed "intense and persistent rate competition"—indeed, outright rate wars from time to time—notwithstanding the railroad companies' huge size and big market shares.[6]

Not even Standard Oil, the most notorious of the trusts, could control the market. After the turn of the century, Standard's competitors steadily gained market share in the petroleum-refining industry as they, unlike Standard, developed new sources of petroleum in Texas and Oklahoma and concentrated on supplying fuel oil and gasoline, for which the market was growing rapidly, rather than Standard's mainline product, kerosene. Even during the late nineteenth century, however, as Dominick Armentano observes, "Standard's price and output behavior [that is, its rapidly falling real price and rapidly rising output] is entirely consistent with what would have been expected under competitive conditions.... There was no restriction of supply, and monopoly prices were never realized.... Standard was a large, competitive firm in an open, competitive market."[7] Standard's suppression of competition is a myth.

In fact, except for one insignificant industry (castor oil), all the industries alleged to have been monopolized by the trusts in the 1880s had relatively rapidly rising outputs and relatively rapidly falling prices between 1880 and 1900—just the opposite of the behavior one expects from a monopoly. Thomas DiLorenzo has documented this pattern for salt, petroleum, zinc, steel, bituminous coal, steel rails, sugar, lead, liquor, twine, iron nuts and washers, jute, cottonseed oil, leather, and linseed oil.[8] Where's the evidence of monopoly power?

Sklar's central assumption that unless the government regulated the markets, the big firms would do so is simply not true in any important sense of the word *regulate*. What price-searching firms do is not accurately expressed by saying that they "regulate" or "administer" the market. Markets are not so easily controlled because competition can and does take place on many different margins.[9] But Sklar's confusion on this account is not the end of his misapprehension regarding regulation.

For Sklar, all regulation is alike. Whether it is done by big corporations or by the federal government affects only the identity of the actor, not the nature of the action. But equating "regulation" by private firms, however big they may be, with regulation by the federal government cannot be justified. Large firms, even if they hold monopoly positions in their own industries, always face either actual or potential competition. Apart from international competition, which is important in many industries, firms compete across industry lines. Even if U.S. Steel had become the only steel producer in America after it was formed in 1901 (as opposed to merely the largest among scores of competing firms), it would have faced competition in many markets from wood, masonry, concrete, glass, and so forth (and later from plastics, aluminum, and other metals), depending on the particular market considered. The telephone industry giant American Telephone and Telegraph faced competition from the telegraph industry giant Western Union in the long-distance communications market and from a host of messengers in local communications markets—not to mention competition from the post office. In the market for electrical transmission wires, the big copper companies faced competition from the aluminum monopoly Alcoa. And so it went, in one industry after another. Orthodox definitions of what constitutes an *industry* are more or less arbitrary and have little to do with the scope of actual rivalry within a particular market, which encompasses all products regarded as substitutes by demanders. Government regulation, in contrast, rests on the government's coercive power; its potential for shutting off avenues of escape is immensely greater.

Perhaps Sklar fails to perceive this difference because he believes that the political economy tends toward a tight internal coherence in which every part of the social system—technologies, property rights, political powers, ideology, and social classes—comes into compatible alignment. Business, he asserts, is also power. "Business, or capitalism . . . is not simply 'economics,' although it subsumes economics. It is property relations; it is class relations; it is a sociopolitical mode of control over economics and over a broad field of social behavior besides; it is a system of law and governance; it is ideology" (pp. 8–9). I am not sure whether Sklar regards this sweeping statement as a definition or as a hypothesis to be tested against the facts, although in view of his subsequent argument the former seems more likely.

Sklar overlooks the voluminous evidence that the great business consolidations formed at the turn of the century could not control competition and tended to lose market share as time passed (examples include U.S. Steel, American Sugar, Standard Oil, American Tobacco, United States Envelope, International Paper, American Hide and Leather, International Silver, Glucose Sugar Refining Company, International Harvester, Amalgamated Copper).[10] Many of the turn-of-the-century consolidations eventually went bankrupt and were reorganized (for example, United States Leather, National Cordage, American Malting, and the Distilling and Cattle Feeding Company).[11] Those that failed to reduce their costs fared especially badly.[12] After surveying the historical data, Nathan Rosenberg and L. E. Birdzell concluded that "the events of 1880 to 1914 did not restructure American industry into monopolies. . . . It is not likely that the events of 1880 to 1914, although they reduced the number of firms in some industries, left Western industry as a whole [including U.S. industry] any less competitive than it had been, once we allow for other trends that were, concurrently, increasing competition."[13]

Like virtually all writers on the left, Sklar loses perspective on the overall economy by focusing too heavily on manufacturing, overlooking other equally important sectors. From evidence about consolidations in the manufacturing sector, he concludes that big corporations dominated the entire U.S. economy.[14] The numbers don't support such a conclusion. During the Progressive Era, less than 20 percent of the national income originated in manufacturing, and much of that part came from small and medium-size firms. Nearly as much income originated in agriculture, where a much larger proportion of the labor force found employment. Almost two-thirds of all income originated in mining, construction, transportation, trade, services, and government.[15] In none of these sectors except transportation and public utilities did big firms loom very large. To speak of the manufacturing giants as dominating the economy is to make the tail wag the dog. Recognizing that the large firms did not "dominate" the economy helps us to understand the complexity of Progressive Era politics and why contemporary legislative reforms commonly struck some sort of compromise. As Stephen Skowronek concludes, "there were no unqualified triumphs in building the new American state."[16]

As evidence of the dominance of concentrated manufacturing, Sklar offers the estimate that between 1904 and 1939 the largest 18,423 plants produced more than 75 percent of the value of all U.S. manufactured products at each census date (p. 46). That's high concentration? Anyone who has ever tried to direct a meeting of 18,423 participants knows just how much trouble the bourgeoisie must have had getting organized in 1904. To be fair, one must recognize that Sklar's focus seems to be on the top 200 to 500 firms; but the point remains. As Morton Keller observes, "big business was not a homogenous, single-interest entity."[17] Eastern capitalists versus midwestern or southern capitalists; exporting capitalists versus importing capitalists; transportation-selling capitalists versus transportation-buying capitalists; lending capitalists versus borrowing capitalists—the list of divisions goes on and on. At one point (pp. 31–32), Sklar himself concedes the point, but the concession has no apparent effect on the thrust of his argument.

A Capitalist Class?

Sklar's failure to appreciate the heterogeneity of big-business interests may spring from his left-radical conception of class and class conflict. He asserts that "the capitalist class consists of associated people with goals, values, ideas, and principles, as well as interests. They are people with a way of life to develop, defend, and extend, based on a definite type of property ownership and labor exploitation" (pp. 2–3). If this description is correct, then members of the class need not consciously coordinate their political actions; as members of the same class, they share a common conception of the problems they face and a common aspiration to effect certain changes viewed as favorable to all members of that same class. There is some truth in such a depiction. Ideologies sometimes motivate individuals to act in the interest of a group to which they belong and with which they identify strongly.[18] Surely, for example, virtually all capitalists circa 1904 opposed the election of socialists to public office. (There remains a free-rider problem, however, which ideological solidarity does not always overcome.)[19] In any event, however, the mere fact—if it really is a fact—that all capitalists shared *certain* attributes and interests is insufficient to justify a class conception of how they acted politically and economically.

In many situations, the greatest threat to a capitalist is another capitalist. Especially striking is the extent to which the opposing political factions of the Progressive Era were segments *within* the capitalist "class." The results of this internecine conflict appear in many of the Progressive Era reform acts. Thus, eastern financial tycoons failed to get the monolithic central bank they wanted. Instead, the system created by the Federal Reserve Act contained twelve loosely coordinated regional reserve banks, reflecting the influence of country bankers as well as western and southern business interests in general. The Federal Trade Commission Act and the Clayton Act did not contain the federal incorporation provision favored by certain big eastern capitalists; nor did those acts provide for advisory decisions by the Federal Trade Commission, which the moguls wanted. Instead, those acts allowed for continued state incorporation and stipulated only "cease and desist" orders by the Federal Trade Commission subject to judicial review, again as favored by midwestern and smaller capitalists. The exemption of labor unions from all liability under the antitrust acts, which was favored by the establishment capitalists associated with the National Civic Federation, failed to gain enactment because of opposition from the rabidly antiunion small businessmen represented by the National Association of Manufacturers. Many other examples of such divisiveness within the business "class" appear in Robert Wiebe's *Businessmen and Reform,* published forty years ago. Although Sklar acknowledges the heterogeneity of the capitalist class (pp. 31–32), the acknowledgment does not deter him from proceeding with a thoroughgoing class analysis.

He portrays the capitalists as being engaged in a struggle to create, solidify, and maintain a social, economic, and political order favorable to their values and way of life (pp. 14, 34, 87, 252). Of course, one can find some evidence consistent with this way of viewing history, especially in the content of the law, the social background of judges, and the actual workings of political and judicial processes.[20] Sklar's account of the National Civic Federation, which provides perhaps the best illustration of this thesis, is instructive. However, like Wiebe, who concluded that "Progressive businessmen singularly lacked a grand social vision,"[21] I am struck far more by the frequency with which the politics of each policy question pivoted on much narrower concerns and objectives rather than on conflict regarding the grand politicoeconomic system. Where Sklar sees the big capitalists engaged in a multidimensional conflict to determine the nature of the political economy, I see them engaged in a multitude of particular conflicts, each of which concerned them for the most part because it affected more or less immediately the magnitude of their profits or the value of their wealth.

A case in point has to do with the institutional developments that emerged from the deep depression of the mid-1890s. Problems brought to the fore during that severe business slump gave rise to diverse efforts to repair the economic machine, efforts that eventually included both the creation of a central bank and the formation of hundreds of industrial consolidations. The major problem in the capitalists' minds, however, seems to have been the simple absence or insufficiency of returns on their investments during the depression. With demand abated, competition among sellers had grown fiercer.[22] Sklar illustrates the problem with a quotation from a contemporary commentator, Edward S. Meade, who observed in 1900 that the manufacturers wanted "to stop this worrisome struggle, whose benefits are nearly all of them gained by the consumer in low prices.... They want a larger profit without such a desperate struggle to get it" (p. 56). Producers in 1900, it seems, were no different from those described by Adam Smith in 1776.

In both cases, the capitalists' principal concern was their own individual wealth, and the greatest threat to each one's attainment of his goal was the competition offered by fellow capitalists. Of course, mergers into larger firms might have promised to stave off some of the competition temporarily, but the market contained no permanent safe havens. Thus, the big capitalists with business in many states turned to the federal government, seeking legal means by which they could bring to bear the government's coercive power to keep competitors at bay.[23]

As already noted, however, the big capitalists were scarcely the only interest group or class pounding on the government's door, and it was simply impossible for everybody to get inside at once. The large railroad companies and the opposing (much smaller but much more numerous) shippers could not simultaneously control the Interstate Commerce Commission's decisions during the Progressive Era, and the shippers prevailed.[24] Unionist Samuel Gompers, who rubbed shoulders with the sympathetic eastern business elite in the National Civic Federation, could not make organized labor's position prevail during the process of amending the ill-fated Hepburn bill of 1908; opposition from the small capitalists in the National Association of Manufacturers and allied organizations was too strong, as Sklar himself recognizes (pp. 254–59). On one issue after another, big business was one interest among many—often itself only a hodgepodge of more or less antagonistic interests. Despite its impressive strength, it certainly did not always get its way in the policy struggle. Robert Wiebe has gone so far as to conclude that the big eastern capitalists, whom Sklar portrays as seated firmly astride Progressivism, "despised the Wilsonian compromise [policies enacted during 1913–16] which they believed had in each case sacrificed their interests."[25]

The Twists and Turns of Antitrust

Nothing illustrates the absence of enduring big-business domination better than antitrust law. Ever since the passage of the Sherman Antitrust Act in 1890, antitrust law has fluctuated. The law has been amended by statute on several occasions. More important, the courts have rendered varying decisions on the exact meaning to be attached to the statutory language. Economists, historians, and others who have not closely studied this legal history usually fail to appreciate its actual twists and turns during the past century.

No period of antitrust history is more misunderstood than its first twenty years. In presenting a clear and compelling reinterpretation of the law during this period, Sklar is at his best. This part of the book—a chapter of ninety pages that might almost have stood by itself as a monograph—suffers less than the other parts of the book, especially the first and last chapters, from distortions associated with Sklar's analytical framework.

The key is to understand that the Sherman Act was not at all the vague statute it was later said to be. The law declared illegal "every contract, combination in the form of trust or otherwise, or conspiracy, in restraint of trade or commerce among the several States, or with foreign nations." Further, "every person who shall monopolize, or attempt to monopolize, or combine or conspire with any other person or persons, to monopolize any part of the trade or commerce among the several States, or with foreign nations, shall be deemed guilty." Many commentators have claimed that the root problems of these provisions are that they fail to spell out what it is about a contract, combination, or conspiracy that places it "in restraint of trade" and that they offer no guidance as to how to determine which businesses are "monopolies" and which are not. Thus, the framers of the legislation stand accused of enacting nothing more than an airy declaration against the "trusts," to which subsequent litigation necessarily had to give concrete meaning. Hence, the fluctuating interpretations of the judges, who lacked any firm statutory anchor. Although the judges' vagaries cannot be denied, Sklar shows convincingly that the framers of the Sherman Act are innocent of the subsequent charges against them. He demonstrates that a correct understanding of what the framers intended to do, in contrast to the literal understanding suggested by the statutory language and favored for a time by a majority of the Supreme Court, opens up a much fuller understanding of the politics of antitrust in the Progressive Era.

Sklar argues that the framers of the Sherman Act intended only to codify the common law that had emerged during the preceding sixty years, adding criminal sanctions to the remedies of the civil law and providing for treble damages to be paid to successful private plaintiffs. The terms *restraint of trade* and *monopolize* had well-established meanings among contemporary lawyers:

> The general rule at common law with respect to restraint of trade stipulated that voluntary restraints among parties, whether partial or general, to maintain prices at a profitable level and to protect their business interests, were to be held reasonable and therefore valid, provided their intent or effect did not exceed such purposes, were not considered to be detrimental to the public interest, and did not include the physical prevention of, or a conspiracy to prevent, others from entering or remaining in the line of business or trade concerned—that is, did not restrain the trade of outsiders, or did not prevent or seek to prevent competition. (p. 98)

In the language that came into use later, one could say that the common law already employed a "rule of reason" regarding restraint of trade long before the Supreme Court decisions of 1911 with which that rule is usually associated. As for the second key term, the common law held that firms *monopolized* when they acquired "the whole business for themselves by preventing outside competitors from pursuing trade or maintaining their independent existence" (p. 99).

Clearly the law did not hold bigness per se to be unlawful, nor did it regard sole occupancy of the market as unlawful unless active measures to prevent the entry of rivals had been undertaken. As Sklar puts it, the common law as it stood circa 1890 "may be described as the juristic hypostatization of the dogma of natural liberty" (p. 100). The common law "was not intended to protect weaker or inefficient competitors from stronger or more efficient competitors, not even to compel competition.... Rather, by the late nineteenth century it was intended to safeguard the right of individuals freely to enter the market and make contracts, and to let the operations of the market determine the outcome" (p. 104). The framers of the Sherman Act sought to proscribe as criminal offenses *restraint of trade* and *monopoly* in these and only these senses. Moreover, from 1890 to 1897 the federal courts, in their rulings on antitrust cases, applied just such an understanding of legislative intent.

Then, in the *Trans-Missouri* case of 1897, the U.S. Supreme Court effected what Sklar terms a "coup de jure." From that time until the "rule of reason" decisions of 1911, a majority of the Court, led by Justice John Marshall Harlan, took the position that the Sherman Act, rather than codifying the common law, had superseded or reversed it, thereby requiring that, with just two exceptions, monopolies and restraints of trade be found unlawful regardless of whether they were legally reasonable or not. The two aspects of the previous jurisprudence that persisted as the Court construed the Sherman Act were the lawfulness, first, of monopolies achieved through lawful competition or purchase of property and, second, of incidental restrictions of competition. In other respects, however, the Court's position from 1897 to 1911 represented a substantial departure from traditional legal doctrine.

> For the traditional judicial doctrine that reasonable restrictions of competition in interstate trade were legal, the Court's majority had substituted the doctrine that no direct restrictions of competition were legal; for the traditional doctrine upholding the right to compete and contractual liberty as distinguished from a compulsion to compete, the Court's majority had substituted a doctrine that set compulsory competition against contractual liberty. As against calculative attempts by capitalists to regulate the market in order to maintain the remunerative nature of pecuniary pursuits, the Court now asserted the natural, impersonal rule of the unfettered market, enforced where necessary by government regulation of capitalists' behavior. (p. 138)

During the fifteen years of this phase, in Sklar's view, the Court created a fundamental conflict between corporate impulses to control the market and strictures against even "reasonable" restraints of trade. At no time did the law proscribe bigness or "market power" as such, but it did condemn many forms of "restraint of trade" regarded as lawful either before 1897 or after 1911.

In the interim, the capitalists suffered from chronic anxiety, operating in "an incongruous legal order" (p. 166). Theodore Roosevelt's administration took advantage of the situation by consulting regularly with big businessmen and following a policy of selective prosecution. Corporations that pleased Roosevelt, which he called "good trusts," escaped prosecution and therefore never ran afoul of the courts' strict interpretation of the antitrust laws. Corporations that displeased him found out why he enjoyed some notoriety as a "trustbuster." By conducting his policy in this fashion, Roosevelt failed to perform his constitutional duty to execute the laws faithfully, but that never bothered the Rough Rider, who had an expansive view of presidential powers under the Constitution. Meanwhile, the objectives of the great corporate capitalists during those years were "to change the law and get the corporation question 'out of' politics" (p. 167), objectives they ultimately achieved with the Court's decisions of 1911 and, more decisively, with passage of the Federal Trade Commission Act and the Clayton Act in 1914.

Having told in considerable detail the story of the evolution of antitrust jurisprudence, Sklar then retells the story from the political side, devoting 261 pages to this narrative, paying special attention to the antitrust question as seen and dealt with by Presidents Roosevelt, Taft, and Wilson. This part of the book contains much of interest to specialists but packs less revisionist punch than the long chapter on the judiciary. I shall not attempt to summarize the arguments in detail, but the analytical style of this and other parts of the book deserves some comment.

Sklar's Conceptual Framework

Sklar does not present his explanatory framework as an explicit or formal model, but from his evident assumptions and his conceptual terms, some of which he pauses to clarify, one can make out fairly clearly what the framework is. Although it is not Marxism pure and simple, it can be described as a variant of the Marxist model. Morton Keller refers to it as an example of a "more moderate neo-Marxist line of interpretation" associated with the term *corporate liberalism,* which Sklar has helped to popularize (pp. 18, 174).[26]

Sklar views the political economy as passing though stages, but his stages are not just convenient descriptions of how the system tended to operate at various times. Rather, they seem to be historically necessary categories, waiting patiently for empirical reality to pass through them, as it must. Thus, "capitalism is the sociopolitical organization of economics, the larger social framework and relations of power within which input-output and allocative functions proceed at a certain stage of a society's history" (p. 6); "the passage of capitalism from its proprietary-competitive stage to its corporate-administered stage, which transpired during the period 1890–1916, was a part of capitalism's historical development in the United States" (p. 3); and "the national reform legislation of 1913–1916 represented the culmination of corporate liberalism in its emergent phase of ascendancy" (p. 422). Sklar sometimes speaks not of the U.S. economy at a certain time but of an economy *like* the U.S. economy at a certain time, as if he has in mind some eternal categories that the empirical case before him just happens to exemplify.

For Sklar, a political economy like that of the United States at the turn of the twentieth century acquires its dynamics from class struggle. "The process of change will be expressed in significant conflict in the spheres both of the market and the law, and hence in politics. The law becomes a major terrain of contest, as existing property and market relations come into conflict with emergent property and market relations (or relations of production)" (p. 89). The classic Marxian struggle between the capitalist class and the proletariat, however, gets only incidental mention. In its place, Sklar puts a broader conflict "within and between ascending and declining movements, corresponding with ascending and declining forms, or stages, of the capitalist property-production system" (p. 14). The declining movement included most prominently the petty bourgeoisie and the Populist farmers who wished to retain the old order of powerless, price-taking firms. Although they were declining in economic importance, these "strata" were well represented in Congress and in the state legislatures. The conflict between the old middle class and the ascending corporate class became inevitable around the turn of the century because "critical components of the extant governmental system of power, including the legal order, fell out of phase with the changing pattern of authority in the property-production system and its expression in trends of thought" (pp. 14–15).

Not surprisingly, Sklar views ideas as springing from technological and economic conditions. Thus, the changes in productive techniques and economic organization associated with the rise of big corporate business "generated new professional, technical, and managerial functions with their corresponding social strata and, in turn, their values, attitudes, and ideological dispositions" (p. 431). There is no room in this view for ideas as an independent variable; sooner or later the "mode of production" determines everything else in social and political life.

In many other respects as well, Sklar speaks the language of Marxism. Capitalists are said to be exploiting labor. The "modern capitalist market is," among other things, "a realm of law of class domination and its related arts of power, politics, and ideology" (p. 87). Big corporations are routinely assumed to "dominate" the economy. When any mention of businessmen's interest in foreign trade or investment occurs, Sklar labels it "imperialism."

Notwithstanding the blinders of his explanatory framework, Sklar strives for an interpretation with a degree of subtlety that matches the complexity of the evidence. He is not always so heavy-handed as I may have suggested in the foregoing remarks. Indeed, one may well wonder how, in light of the many caveats he makes, he can cling to his own interpretation. He acknowledges that corporate capitalism did not "'take over' society and simply vanquish or blot out everything else." Rather,

> market relations, forms of thought, political movements, and cultural patterns associated with small-producer and proprietary enterprise remained widespread, influential and strongly represented in party politics, Congress, and the judiciary, and at the state and local levels of politics and government. They continued to exert a large impact, moreover, in the national electoral arena and in national legislative forums. The large corporations and corporate-administered markets, for some time to come, lacked anything near full legitimacy in the minds of a considerable segment of the people and their political representatives. (p. 15)

One many well ask: Can this description be regarded as a portrait of corporate-capitalist dominance? So sweeping are the qualifications of the thesis that one may read them not as qualifying the thesis but as refuting it.

Thus, in describing differences "within and among the trade and civic associations," Sklar admits that conflicts "among variations of the corporate and proprietary outlook characterized the entire period" (p. 16). Further, "conflicting proposals for government regulation of the market derived from ... all manner of bourgeois sources within the market, as well as from intellectuals, social reformers, independent professions, trade unionists, and political leaders" (p. 17). Amid such multidimensional struggles, where are the clear-cut classes and the alleged class conflict?

Corporate liberalism, Sklar concedes, "emerged not as the ideology of any one class, let alone [of] the corporate sector of the capitalist class, but rather as a cross-class ideology expressing the interrelations of corporate capitalists, political leaders, intellectuals, proprietary capitalists, professionals and reformers, workers and trade-union leaders, populists, and socialists" (p. 35). Who's left out? Given the admission that the new order served the perceived interests of such a broad and diverse collection of social groups, how can Sklar conclude that the Progressive movement established "the dominant position in the market of the corporate sector of the capitalist class" (p. 35)?

After hundreds of pages documenting the multiplicity of interests that shaped the Progressive Era's economic and political accomplishments, Sklar concludes that "a broad proregulatory consensus defined the common ground of the great debate over the reorganization of the market. Upon this ground, disagreement proceeded" (p. 433). Such a bland and sensible conclusion is hardly news to anyone acquainted with the literature on Progressivism.[27] Nor does it provide a sufficient foundation for Sklar's more exacting interpretation.

Apart from the Marxist apparatus and the objections one may make regarding the adequacy of Sklar's evidence to sustain his argument in its particulars, one may object to the nature of his explanations in general. Sklar seems to believe that simply by naming an institution, event, or other phenomenon, one has thereby explained it. (He is hardly the only scholar guilty of this sin. In the higher reaches of sociological theory, the practice is common.) Throughout the book, his references to "the corporate reconstruction of capitalism" and "the corporate administration of the market" seem to serve this function. In general, things are either X or not X; or they are becoming X or are entering the X stage and leaving the Y stage. Movements for X contend with movements for Y. This argumentative style sets up a series of dichotomies in which everything stands in either-or relations. Lost is any sense of continuous variation wherein things are not either X or not X, but rather more or less X.

For example, Sklar argues that "resort to the corporate form of enterprise ... became increasingly more compelling in the United States.... The property form matched inducement and need with effective and available market instrumentalities" (p. 166). How then is one to understand the (unacknowledged) fact that many industrial firms did not adopt the corporate form and that in important sectors of the economy (agriculture, trade, services) corporations never became common until much later, after World War II?[28] (High postwar tax rates and provisions of the tax laws permitting the sheltering of some corporate income from taxation, rather than fundamental economic or technological imperatives, may account for the eventual adoption of the corporate form in these sectors.) For Sklar, the question of incorporation, like other questions he considers, elicits a nominal answer. In contrast, for social scientists who strive to "explain the variance" in empirical data, as many do nowadays, recognizing that some variables are continuous rather than categorical is built into the research strategy.

Politics and Statism

In analyzing the options for the future of the political economy under debate during the Progressive Era, Sklar settles on a trichotomy that mirrors the alternatives supported by the three major presidential contenders in the election of 1912, Theodore Roosevelt, William Howard Taft, and Woodrow Wilson. (He dismisses any possibility of a hands-off policy regime, on the grounds that no politically important segment of the public favored that option [pp. 10, 33, 35, 53–54] and that in any event laissez faire was impossible in an economy dominated by giant corporations. Nor did thoroughgoing socialism stand a chance under American conditions circa 1900–1916 [p. 77].)

Roosevelt's position was the most extreme. During his presidency, Roosevelt became more and more inclined to support sweeping executive-branch government controls over big business. During his last year in office, he presided over a series of machinations related to the so-called Hepburn bill to amend the Sherman Act. (The bill had virtually nothing to do with Representative William P. Hepburn of Iowa, the influential chairman of the Committee on Interstate and Foreign Commerce. After passing through more than a dozen revisions, it ended up as a bill supported by Roosevelt but almost no one else.) The bill never gained passage. Even those who had initially supported it concluded that "the direct participation of the government in marketplace decision-making, a participation centered in extraordinary executive powers . . . was more than they had bargained for," according to Sklar (p. 248).

Roosevelt could not have been surprised by the defeat and was not dismayed by it. He seems to have used the occasion to stake out a position with an eye to political campaigns farther down the road. His goal, which came into clearer focus during the campaign of 1910–12, was essentially to transform all big business into public utilities, subject to the same kind of exacting federal regulation already exercised over the railroad industry. "We must," he declared in 1911, "abandon definitely the *laissez-faire* theory of political economy, and fearlessly champion a system of increased Governmental control, paying no heed to the cries of the worthy people who denounce this as Socialistic" (quoted on p. 344).

During Roosevelt's presidency, William H. Taft had loyally supported Roosevelt's policies, but after Taft's own election to the presidency he moved to the right at the same time that Roosevelt moved to the left. Taft, always the jurist at heart, looked askance at proposals to create an executive-branch agency with extreme discretion to regulate the large corporations. He feared the "undermining of our Constitutional Government" (quoted on p. 349). Although the Taft administration in four years initiated more than twice as many antitrust prosecutions as the Roosevelt administration had in seven years, Taft heartily approved the Supreme Court's "rule of reason" decisions handed down in the *Standard Oil* and *American Tobacco* cases in 1911. He had favored the rule of reason all along, just as he had always favored the resolution of antitrust complaints by the courts, not by the executive branch or its agencies, such as the Bureau of Corporations (created in 1903). "To Taft, property rights constituted a basic human right and were not to be viewed as in conflict with, and hence subordinate to, human rights" (p. 365). He feared the consequences of having a federal bureau empowered to set aside the contracts, agreements, and arrangements of businessmen who were acting in ways that the common law had long regarded as reasonable and consonant with the public interest.

As Roosevelt and Taft headed in opposite directions, they opened up a space in the middle for Woodrow Wilson to step into in 1912. For a long time, Wilson and Roosevelt had been on good terms and had shared similar views. Wilson, however, moved only moderately toward the left, whereas Roosevelt went much further. By 1912, Wilson favored "regulating business methods through a mix of commission and judicial enforcement of a common-law based antitrust law, with ultimate judicial supremacy in the process as a whole" (p. 381). This position, of course, was the one destined to prevail legislatively in 1914 and afterward.

Sklar's account of these three presidential positions and the politics that accompanied them is immensely interesting and revealing, but the language he uses to state his conclusions is perplexing. For Sklar, the events of 1914 "effectively 'settled' the trust question" (p. 381); they "took the trust question ... 'out of politics'" (p. 425). The resolution effected in 1914 meant that the Roosevelt-championed "statist" option had been repudiated once and for all, as had Taft's conservative alternative that relied on judicial determinations and the rule of law. The winning option was then and remains to this day "Wilson's antistatist, regulatory corporate liberalism" (p. 382).

Sklar overstates the extent to which the corporation question was ultimately resolved in 1914. It is true, of course, that the Federal Trade Commission still exists and that the Clayton Act has not been repealed, but the antitrust laws were amended by major legislation in 1936, 1950, and 1976, not to mention the measures authorized by the ill-fated National Industrial Recovery Act, countless shifts of enforcement policy by the Federal Trade Commission and the Justice Department, and a plethora of antitrust efforts at the state level. It goes much too far to say that the question was "taken out of politics" after 1914, even if one means by "politics," as Sklar does, politics only in the sense of party platforms and electoral competition. The Trust Question never again loomed as large at it had during the Progressive Era, to be sure, but it did not disappear form the political arena. Like many other issues, it came more and more to be resolved by the indirect politics of enforcement (or the lack thereof) rather than by the direct politics of the ballot box.

As for Sklar's conception of what is and is not "statist," I must register a more fundamental disagreement. Sklar seems to consider government measures as statist only when they represent the exercise of effectively unbounded powers by government executives or their agents unchecked by judicial review of their actions and decisions. Thus, Roosevelt's proposals of 1910–12 qualify as statist because they called for an executive agency to regulate prices, investments, and other fundamental aspects of the conduct of (ostensibly) private enterprises. Sklar sees Wilson's alternative, in contrast, as eschewing statism because it did not call for quite such sweeping agency regulation and did provide for judicial review of agency decisions. Again, an either-or distinction will not do; instead, we need a sense of more or less. With some ninety years of hindsight, we can see quite plainly that Wilsonian political economy has abided the potential for the government's controls to expand virtually without limit, as occurred most conspicuously after the Supreme Court decisions of 1937 through 1942, in which the justices declared that any degree of federal economic regulation whatsoever would be regarded as constitutional.[29] Nor is purely judicial regulation apolitical: even the courts, which formed the core institution of Taft's "conservative" alternative, are branches of the government and are constantly embroiled in politics.

When Sklar writes that the Federal Trade Commission Act "maintained judicial supremacy over executive administration, and with it the supremacy of society in its market relations over the state" (p. 422), he is employing a conception of either "society" or "supremacy" that obfuscates our understanding in at least two senses. First, it embraces a long-discredited idealism about judicial independence from political give-and-take. Second, it diverts our attention from the massive entanglement of state and society characteristic of the twentieth century—an oversight that allows leftist analysts to continue to call the mixed economies of the West "capitalistic," linguistically justifying greater state intervention by implying that there is at present not much of it. Once more, an ill-chosen conceptual framework only muddles and detracts from Sklar's painstaking account of what actually happened in the years when the modern state was being created.

Notes

1. Cambridge: Cambridge University Press, 1988. Hereafter cited parenthetically by page number in the text.

2. Nathan Rosenberg and L. E. Birdzell, *How the West Grew Rich: The Economic Transformation of the Industrial World* (New York: Basic Books, 1986), p. 221.

3. Friedrich A. Hayek, "The Meaning of Competition," in *Individualism and Economic Order* (Chicago: University of Chicago Press, 1948), pp. 92–106; Thomas J. DiLorenzo and Jack C. High, "Antitrust and Competition, Historically Considered," *Economic Inquiry* 26 (July 1988), p. 425; Alfred D. Chandler Jr., *The Visible Hand: The Managerial Revolution in American Business* (Cambridge, Mass.: Belknap Press of Harvard University Press, 1977), p. 413.

4. Joseph A. Schumpeter, *Capitalism, Socialism, and Democracy*, 3rd ed. (New York: Harper Torchbooks, 1962), p. 84. Hayek observed that "competition is by its nature a dynamic process whose essential characteristics are assumed away by the assumptions underlying static analysis" ("The Meaning of Competition," p. 94).

5. Chandler, *The Visible Hand*, p. 317 and passim; Gabriel Kolko, *The Triumph of Conservatism: A Reinterpretation of American History, 1900–1916* (New York: Free Press, 1963), esp. pp. 26–56; Naomi R. Lamoreaux, *The Great Merger Movement in American Business, 1895–1904* (Cambridge, Eng.: Cambridge University Press, 1985), passim.

6. Dominick T. Armentano, *Antitrust and Monopoly: Anatomy of a Policy Failure*, 2d ed. (Oakland: The Independent Institute, 1990), p. 61. See also Paul W. MacAvoy, *The Economic Effects of Regulation: The Trunk-Line Railroad Cartels and the Interstate Commerce Commission Before 1900* (Cambridge, Mass.: MIT Press, 1965), and Gabriel Kolko, *Railroads and Regulation, 1877–1916* (Princeton, N.J.: Princeton University Press, 1965).

7. Armentano, *Antitrust and Monopoly*, p. 66. See also Chandler, *The Visible Hand*, p. 326 and passim, and Kolko, *The Triumph of Conservatism*, pp. 39–42.

8. Thomas J. DiLorenzo, "The Origins of Antitrust: An Interest-Group Perspective," *International Review of Law and Economics* 5 (1985): 78–80.

9. Hayek, "The Meaning of Competition," pp. 92–106; Chandler, *The Visible Hand*, p. 413 and passim; Israel M. Kirzner, *Competition and Entrepreneurship* (Chicago: University of Chicago Press, 1973); George J. Stigler, *The Organization of Industry* (Homewood, Ill.: Irwin, 1968).

10. Armentano, *Antitrust and Monopoly*, pp. 50–51, 66–67, 88, 98; Lamoreaux, *The Great Merger Movement*, pp. 141–42; Kolko, *Triumph of Conservatism*, pp. 27–29, 37, 46, 50. See also Stigler, *Organization of Industry*, pp. 100–104, and Chandler, *The Visible Hand*, pp. 315–44.

11. Lamoreaux, *The Great Merger Movement*, p. 141.

12. Ibid., pp. 189–90.

13. Rosenberg and Birdzell, *How the West Grew Rich*, p. 295.

14. Even within manufacturing, Sklar overstates the extent to which big business became dominant. Alfred Chandler, in his definitive work, found that big integrated firms became the norm where they could use "capital-intensive, energy-consuming, continuous or large-batch production technology to produce [standardized products] for mass markets" (*The Visible Hand*, p. 347). Where such technological and market conditions did not exist (for example, in textiles, apparel, leather goods, machine tools, and publishing and printing), big firms rarely appeared.

15. U.S. Bureau of the Census, *Historical Statistics of the United States: Colonial Times to 1970* (Washington, D.C.: U.S. Government Printing Office, 1975), pp. 238, 240.

16. Stephen Skowronek, *Building a New American State: The Expansion of National Administrative Capacities, 1877–1920* (Cambridge, Eng.: Cambridge University Press, 1982), p. 18. For detailed historical accounts that emphasize the great and growing diversity of contending interests during the Progressive Era, see Robert H. Wiebe, *Businessmen and Reform: A Study of the Progressive Movement* (Cambridge, Mass.: Harvard University Press, 1962), and Morton Keller, *Regulating a New Economy: Public Policy and Economic Change in America, 1900–1933* (Cambridge, Mass.: Harvard University Press, 1990).

17. Keller, *Regulating a New Economy*, pp. 2–3. See also Kolko, *The Triumph of Conservatism*, pp. 54–55.

18. Robert Higgs, *Crisis and Leviathan: Critical Episodes in the Growth of American Government* (New York: Oxford University Press, 1987), pp. 39–45.

19. Hansjorg Siegenthaler, "Organization, Ideology, and the Free Rider Problem," *Journal of Institutional and Theoretical Economics* 145 (March 1989): 215–31, and Robert Higgs, "Comment," *Journal of Institutional and Theoretical Economics* 145 (March 1989): pp. 231–37.

20. Along lines similar to Sklar's is James Livingston's *Origins of the Federal Reserve System: Money, Class, and Corporate Capitalism, 1890–1913* (Ithaca, N.Y.: Cornell University Press, 1986). For a broader view of the law in relation to economy and society, see Lawrence M. Friedman, *A History of American Law*, 2d ed. (New York: Simon and Schuster, 1985).

21. Wiebe, *Businessmen and Reform*, p. 217.

22. Lamoreaux, *The Great Merger Movement*, pp. 12, 46, 100, 116, 118, 188.

23. Profuse documentation of this claim appears throughout the works of Kolko, Wiebe, Lamoreaux, and Armentano already cited.

24. Albro Martin, *Enterprise Denied: Origins of the Decline of American Railroads, 1897–1917* (New York: Columbia University Press, 1971).

25. Wiebe, *Businessmen and Reform*, p. 156.

26. Keller, *Regulating a New Economy*, p. 4.

27. Higgs, *Crisis and Leviathan*, pp. 113–16.

28. Robert Hessen, *Do Business and Economic Historians Understand Corporations?* Working Paper in Economics no. E-89-14 (Stanford, Calif.: Hoover Institution, Stanford University, May 1989), p. 8.

29. Higgs, *Crisis and Leviathan*, pp. 180–95.

37

When Ideological Worlds Collide
Reflections on Kraditor's *Radical Persuasion*

Ideology ranks among the prime determinants of social action, especially where that action takes the form of mass political mobilization. Historians, sociologists, and political scientists have produced a vast literature on the nature, functions, and significance of ideology and on its causes and consequences. Lately even neoclassical economists, who have long disdained any appeal to such an ambiguous and nonquantitative concept, increasingly have resorted to it.[1] Notwithstanding all these scholarly efforts, the role of ideology in history remains an ill-developed subject much in need of fresh theoretical insights and careful empirical research.

Aileen S. Kraditor's *The Radical Persuasion, 1890–1917,* provides a felicitous combination of conceptual penetration and detailed documentation expressed in admirably lucid and forceful prose.[2] The book's meticulously descriptive subtitle tells us that it deals with "aspects of the intellectual history and the historiography of three American radical organizations." Though literally accurate, this characterization of the book's subject matter fails to alert the prospective reader that the work is much more than a monograph on three radical organizations near the turn of the twentieth century. Especially in its first four and last two chapters, it offers provocative ideas about the study of social history in general and of labor history in particular. Further, it deals extensively and revealingly with ideology.

It does so a bit reluctantly; the index contains no entry for "ideology." Yet the word appears scores of times in the text, and words such as *worldview, theory,* and *philosophy,* which Kraditor employs as synonyms, also recur frequently. So even though it may be incorrect to describe *The Radical Persuasion* as a book about ideology, because it is much more than that, it is unquestionably inter alia a book about ideology.

Moreover, it creates an especially enticing opportunity for an exploration of ideology because it deals, often simultaneously, with ideology on two distinct planes. On one level, it considers the ideologies of certain radicals—members of the Socialist Labor Party, the Socialist Party, and the Industrial Workers of the World—in relation to the ideologies of the workers whom they sought to enlist in their organizations and more generally in their movement to overthrow the existing political economy. On another level, it considers the ideologies of those who—usually with passionate sympathy—have studied and written about the radicals. Here one confronts the role of ideology in the work of historians who study the role of ideology in history. In many places, Kraditor, herself a former radical now become conservative, carries on a running battle with radical labor historians and, literally, with herself as expressed in earlier publications. (There must be a certain delight in debating with one's former self, emergence as a winner being assured.) In sum, the book exhibits a sophisticated self-consciousness and a richness of argumentation rarely encountered in historical work. It offers an excellent point of departure for a reassessment of the roles of ideology in history and in historians.

What Is Ideology?

In *The Radical Persuasion*, Kraditor, uncharacteristically, deals casually with the concept of ideology. Nowhere does she define it, and her propensity to substitute other terms for it suggests that she does not intend to employ the term in a rigorous sense. Elsewhere, however, she has expressed her conception of ideology more explicitly. Contrasting the ideologue and the scholar, she depicts the former as a species of dogmatist lacking intellectual curiosity, a system thinker obsessed by the "need to make all activities and interests serve the ideology's single goal."[3] On another occasion, she distinguishes between ideology and conservatism: the former possesses a "reality denying essence," whereas the latter is "the negative of ideology" so that its proponents "accept reality" and "feel no need, even unconsciously to distort what they find."[4] She has personally informed me that she retains "Marx's pejorative definition" of ideology.[5]

I am convinced that this definition, which has been called the "restrictive conception" of ideology, is not analytically the most fruitful one. Nor is this the conception that Kraditor consistently employs in *The Radical Persuasion*. To proceed, I indicate what I mean by *ideology* and how I understand its nature, functions, and significance. In doing so, I rely heavily on the work of Martin Seliger, whose treatises on this subject I find penetrating and persuasive.[6]

Ideology denotes a class of belief systems about social relations. To say that an ideology is a system implies that its components have some coherence; the elements hang together, though not necessarily in a way that would satisfy a logician. It is also a fairly comprehensive belief system, subsuming a wide variety of social categories and their interrelations. Notwithstanding its extensive scope, it tends to revolve about one or a few central values—for example, individual freedom, social equality, or national glory. An ideology serves four distinct but closely intertwined functions: cognitive, affective, programmatic, and solidaristic. Thus, it determines an individual's perceptions and understandings of the social world and expresses those cognitions in characteristic symbols; it tells him whether what he "sees" is good, bad, or morally neutral; and it propels him to act on his cognitions and evaluations as a committed member of a political-action group in pursuit of definite social objectives. Ideologies perform an essential service because in their absence individuals cannot possibly know, assess, and respond to much of what belongs to the vast world of social relations. An ideology simplifies a reality too huge and complicated to be comprehended, evaluated, and reacted to in any "scientific" or other disinterested way. In the sense in which I am characterizing ideology, which has been called the "inclusive conception," one can say that everyone—except perhaps those who are completely apathetic politically—has an ideology.

Although ideology as a concept has considerable breadth, it differs from several related concepts sometimes used synonymously with it. *Worldview* is closely related but differs in its greater vagueness and its lack of programmatic and solidaristic dimensions. *Social or political philosophy* is both broader and differently motivated; like worldview, it has no necessary impulse toward political action nor any implied community membership. *Science* or *theory* differs in its striving for moral neutrality; relative to ideology, it is more inclined toward pragmatism, empirical testing, and an aversion to political involvement. *Culture* denotes a much wider system of symbols and beliefs to which ideologies belong as subsystems.

Most hypotheses about the determinants of ideologies fall into two broad sets: interest theories, wherein people are supposed to pursue wealth or power, and ideas are weapons in the struggle for legitimacy; and strain theories, wherein people are supposed to flee from anxieties, and ideas can bring them comfort and fellowship.[7] The former set includes the classical Marxian formulation, which maintains that one's ideology reflects one's class situation, although this reflection expresses a "false consciousness" of true class destinies. (As Seliger puts it, "the [Marxian] assertion of bourgeois misapprehension boils down to the failure—or unwillingness—of the bourgeoisie to fall in with the forecast of its doom.")[8] Kraditor's theory of ideology belongs to the set of strain theories. Her radicals sought, again in the Marxist language paraphrased by Seliger, "to bridge the gap between the proletariat's imperfect consciousness of its historic destiny (and hence of its unwillingness to achieve it) and the postulated inevitability of its victory."[9] But they undertook this task in pursuit of a solidarity that their would-be comrades had already found elsewhere. Fleeing from anxieties that the masses for the most part did not share, they could recruit only a minuscule following of fellow refugees.

The System Model Versus the Society Model

Although members of the three radical organizations Kraditor studies differed in many respects, they—and afterward most of the radical historians who wrote about them—shared a common ideology in the cognitive and affective dimensions. Kraditor calls this the System paradigm. When they looked at the social world around them, they "saw" only the Capitalist System, a comprehensive abstraction that neatly divides all aspects of social reality into capitalists and proletarians, the exploiters and the exploited, and the relationships that tie all other actors and actions to the fundamental categories. The manifest ills of society—poverty, violence, ignorance, and degradation—all were intrinsic to the System. Hence, attempts to reform it were futile; only its utter destruction and its replacement by socialism held genuine promise of human progress. Although a small radical minority fervently maintained this ideology, the overwhelming majority of ordinary working people at the turn of the century did not accept it. Neither does Kraditor.

In its place, she proposes the Society paradigm. In this view, the Society had "'social space' that allowed a variety of institutions, lifestyles, values, aspirations, and beliefs to exist independently of the interests and needs of the rulers of the economy" (p. 3). Kraditor's Society model

> includes interdependent and mutually influencing institutions, communities, and ideological currents, with unequal power and influence. It acknowledges the existence of class and other conflicts within, as well as between, these components of the Society, some of those conflicts extending beyond the boundaries of the components within which they originated. But it also takes account of the partial autonomy of those institutions and communities and belief-systems, and of the limits of their influence. It implies a criticism of the System model for exaggerating the synchronic at the expense of the diachronic shapers of social formations. (p. 3)

Thus, the Society model affirms a good deal of slack, and even some gaps, in the interrelations of a society's component institutions and forms of behavior; it denies the close-bound tightness and universal connectedness of the interrelations postulated by the System model.

Intellectuals are notorious for craving tight and comprehensive explanations. Mainstream economists call such explanatory structures "general theories" and bestow their highest approbation on those who devise them—David Ricardo, Léon Walras, and John Maynard Keynes, for example. Sociologists likewise revere those who create far-reaching abstractions—Karl Marx, Emile Durkheim, Max Weber, and Talcott Parsons, for example. One is less puzzled by labor historians' affinity for the System model than by the devotion that a small group of workers gave to it. What accounts for the latter group's acceptance of the System paradigm? And why did the masses refuse to "see" the world as they did? For Kraditor, the same facts answer both questions.

Each person seeks a meaning for his life and for his relationships with others. We want to belong to a community, to find solidarity with others of "our kind." Most of us establish such connections close to home, among those who share our milieus and institutions of family, neighborhood, occupation, religion, and ethnicity. Inevitably, however, some fail to do so; they are the "marginal" or "alienated" ones. They are likely to become especially anxious and receptive to an ideology that promises the meaning and solidarity they have not found elsewhere.

Those who embraced the radical ideology at the turn of the twentieth century tended to project their own perceptions and values onto the working masses. Could the workers not "see" the System and its inherent iniquities? Could they not "arouse" themselves to throw off the yoke of oppression? Such questions scarcely provoked the average worker. John Q. Worker, as Kraditor calls him, "was not alienated, and hence [the radicals] offered him a solution to a problem he did not have; they had to make him feel alienated and *then* offer him their movement as the cure for his condition. But, not having the disease, he did not need the medicine" (p. 284, emphasis in original).

To a remarkable degree Kraditor's interpretation parallels that offered at the turn of the century by a leading Marxist revisionist, Eduard Bernstein. (No entry for Bernstein appears in Kraditor's index, nor can I find any mention of him in her text.) He recognized that most proletarians did not entertain the kind of class consciousness that Karl Marx and Friedrich Engels said they should exhibit. But this lack did not surprise Bernstein, who believed, as expressed in Seliger's paraphrase, that "it is wrong to assume in the first place that economic position alone determines consciousness."[10] Instead, the workers' ideologies were "formed also in spheres of life other than the working place," including such milieus as the home, the recreational group, the political party, and the religious community—in short, in all areas of their complex life situation and not merely in their (Marxian) class position.[11]

Why John Q. Worker Declined the Radical Invitation

Kraditor's explanation of why the radicals accepted while the masses rejected the System ideology has considerable plausibility, but, as she recognizes, compelling evidence in support of this explanation is difficult to adduce. To a large extent, this difficulty grows out of what Philip E. Converse has called the "'continental shelf' between elites and masses."[12] Kraditor's evidence comes mostly from the radicals' published speeches and writings. These pronouncements, produced mainly by radical leaders, are accepted as having "both influenced and reflected the thinking of members who belonged voluntarily and who could resign or demote the spokesmen if they disagreed" (p. 6). Perhaps, but still one wonders about how faithfully the leaders' views represent the followers' views, especially when it is admitted that "intellectuals of middle-class origin" constituted a highly disproportionate share of the radical organizations' "most effective writers, speakers, and functionaries" (p. 117). John Q. Worker's view of the radicals is even more problematic. That perception, according to Kraditor herself, "can only be guessed at on the basis of indirect evidence, and hypotheses must be offered tentatively" (p. 230). This situation leaves considerable room for disagreement with the specific descriptions and arguments that Kraditor offers.

One serious shortcoming is her incorrect belief that most industrial workers were immigrants. She alludes repeatedly to "John Q. Worker, who in most cases was a recent immigrant" (p. 16), to "the foreign-born majority of American industrial workers" (p. 84), to "the vast majority of industrial workers [who] were foreign-born" (p. 310), to "the industrial working class [that] was by then [1913] overwhelmingly foreign-born" (p. 76). It just was not so. In 1910, when foreign-born whites' relative importance in the labor force was at or near its zenith, they constituted only 37 percent of the manual laborers in nonfarm occupations, 30 percent of the nonfarm craftsmen and operatives, and 21 percent of private household workers.[13]

Kraditor argues that John Q. Worker ignored or resisted the radical ideology in large part because he already enjoyed meaningful solidarity in an ethnic community. His ethnicity "made it easier in the United States than it would have been in the Old Country for John Q. Worker to separate the work sphere and the private sphere in his value-system" (p. 313) and hence to live a satisfactory life within a Society rather than merely to suffer (or fight) oppression within a System. Also, "John Q. Worker's solution—the construction of his hyphenate community—lasted longer than the radicals' surrogate 'communities' because the former was an autochthonous adaptation of a traditional culture, with roots in the past and capable of creative response to changing conditions" (p. 320).

Obviously such arguments have no pertinence to the overwhelming majority of the working class, the native-born Americans whom the radicals also failed to convert. Other elements of Kraditor's argument, which relate to the workers' identities in connection with family, neighborhood, religion, or other immediate institutional milieus, apply to natives as well as to immigrants. It is unfortunate that she makes so much of the ethnicity argument, because it applies to only a minority of the workers, and emphasizing it leads her to slight other sources of solidarity.

Capitalist Brutalities a Raw Reality?

Kraditor's intellectual commitments have changed enormously since her days as a radical, but in some respects the former lights seem still to shine in this "alumna of the Old Left" (p. 4). For a self-proclaimed conservative, she often employs odd-sounding rhetoric. To some extent, this language serves merely to frame the ideas of the radicals in their own terms, enabling Kraditor to express herself with subtle irony. Yet there remains a residue of apparently sincere characterizations of actors and events that ring with radical-sounding denunciation.

Such stigmatization appears starkly in her characterization of businessmen, those "economic overlords" (p. 92) and "rulers of the economy" (p. 95) who commanded "private armies" (p. 92), perpetrated "economic cannibalism" (p. 73), and fed on "powerless prey" (p. 92). She refers to "those flesh-and-blood capitalists who were the worst exploiters ... [and who] presided over the barbarities of industrialization" (p. 137), and she appeals to "evidence that industrialists were taking too big a share of the new surplus and using technological innovations to create not only abundance but also unemployment and insecurity" (p. 75). Thus, Kraditor, who espouses a conservatism described as "the negation of ideology," clearly employs an ideologically loaded rhetoric, and it certainly sounds like old-fashioned left-radical rhetoric.

Kraditor may protest that all these characterizations are well-known "facts," that they have been "documented," and that a critic is therefore obliged to "furnish facts that disprove [her] characterizations."[14] A Cliometrician might respond, however, that such things have not been adequately documented, that no reliable quantitative evidence exists on *how many* businessmen wielded enormous power, *how representative* were those who possessed private armies, *how much* the exploiters extracted from their victims, and so forth. But the question of magnitudes, though important, is not the main point here. The most critical problem is that Kraditor's descriptions do not lend themselves to measurement in the first place because they are essentially metaphorical. One does not simply observe an "economic cannibal" or a "powerless prey" in the U.S. economy of the late nineteenth century. One imposes such characterizations on one's observations by means of a rhetorical style.

Metaphor is a powerful means of expression, and one must be careful how one uses it. As Chaim Perelman and L. Olbrechts-Tyteca note, "acceptance of an analogy ... is often equivalent to a judgment as to the importance of the characteristics that the analogy brings to the fore."[15] A writer who describes businessmen as rulers or predators invites the reader to view business relationships as power plays or predation—in contrast, for example, to voluntary exchange via free contracting in product or labor markets. As Clifford Geertz emphasizes, ideological expression invariably possesses a "highly figurative nature" and relies heavily on metaphor, analogy, irony, hyperbole, and other elements of a distinctive symbolic style. "It is," he concludes, "not truth that varies with social, psychological, and cultural [including ideological] contexts but the symbols we construct in our unequally effective attempts to grasp it."[16] Regardless of what Kraditor's intentions may be, her symbolic representation of businessmen encourages the reader to conceptualize business dealings in a decidedly radical way—that is, as intrinsically exploitative.

She frequently seems to assume that the typical worker was not only an immigrant but also someone who worked in a factory under "atrocious" (p. 79), "brutal" (pp. 308–9), "onerous and dangerous" (p. 78) conditions in an "alienating" job (p. 53) and who "joined unions when possible" (p. 16). In fact, only a small minority of the labor force ever worked in factories, and one is hardly justified in describing all or even most of those who did as having been brutalized and alienated. In 1910, when the nonfarm labor force numbered 25.8 million (just 26 percent of them foreign born), there were only slightly more than 6.3 million production workers in all manufacturing, and many of them worked in small shops and mills rather than in factories.[17] Moreover, the workers rejected unions almost as readily as they rejected radical organizations. In the Progressive Era, unionized workers never constituted as much as 10 percent of the total labor force, and unions had more success in signing up railroad workers, construction craftsmen, and coal miners than they had in enlisting manufacturing laborers.[18]

According to Kraditor, "It's a proven fact that union membership was a very risky business in those days and all workers knew that they could and probably would get fired ... if they joined unions."[19] Hence, she sees no inconsistency between her claim that most workers "joined unions when possible" and the low levels of actual membership. One may well doubt, however, that *all* workers believed what Kraditor thinks they believed about the likely consequences of their joining a union. Even in the late nineteenth century, hundreds of thousands of workers joined unions, and it seems extremely unlikely that all of them did so anticipating dismissal from their jobs. Clearly, whatever they believed before the act, many did join unions and were not subsequently fired. The most pertinent aspect of all this for present purposes, however, is that no one—not Kraditor, not I, not anyone—can possibly know what "all workers knew"; and statements of this sort, assessing the balance of fear and courage among the masses, necessarily derive more from ideology than from facts.

Kraditor's propensity to view the relationship between employers and employees as—at least in the feelings of the actors themselves—essentially conflict rather than mutually beneficial cooperation also may be a legacy from her left-radical past. References to the "arbitrary power of owners of mines and factories" (p. 82) and to "the foreign-born majority of American industrial workers ... often treated arbitrarily by foremen and subject to barely limited power by bosses" (p. 84) overlook the capacity of competition in the labor markets to protect even the most powerless workers from the excesses of brutal employers.[20] In my view, the labor markets of the period 1890–1917 did not produce "chaos . . . as a variant of the competition that every new social institution or community experiences before an accepted rank order has evolved" (p. 73). Rather, the labor markets were usually orderly. All parties to the employment contract were constrained by competitive forces—some more than others, of course—and the labor markets did not require the establishment of an "accepted rank order" to function in an orderly and (most of the time) peaceful way.

Is Ideology-Free Analysis Possible?

Kraditor's portrayal of businessmen, workers, and labor markets is of secondary importance in her overall effort in *The Radical Persuasion,* the bulk of which deals, as the subtitle indicates, with intellectual history and historiography. Still, my objections to her depiction are not mere carping. A judgment of whether an ideology—radical, conservative, or any other—leads its subscribers to "distorted perceptions of current and past reality" (p. 3) requires that one know what "reality" is and was. In my view, Kraditor herself suffers from distorted perceptions of some of the actors in and the conditions of the U.S. economy during the era she has studied. Her most significant misapprehensions appear to result either from her inability to cast off completely her former left-radical ideology or from her adoption of an alternative ideology whose rhetoric is difficult to distinguish from that of left radicalism in certain realms of discourse.

Of course, contemporary "conservatives," as they are called by most people, march under several banners: libertarianism, traditionalism, and (especially during the Cold War era) anticommunism.[21] Kraditor identifies herself most closely with the traditionalists,[22] and such conservatives often view industrialization with fully as much loathing as do the radicals of the extreme left—a perfect example of what Seliger calls "ideological pluralism."[23] So it may be incorrect to ascribe Kraditor's views to her former left radicalism and more correct to locate their sources at a genuinely conservative fountainhead. Such relocation, however, hardly washes away their ideological character. As Geertz notes, Edmund Burke, the outstanding exponent of traditionalist conservatism, was "perhaps his nation's greatest ideologue."[24] Whatever their true source or proper name, the ideological "distortions" in Kraditor's writing remain.

I do not mean to suggest, however, that whereas Kraditor has misperceived certain aspects of "reality," I or someone else can delineate that reality with cosmic assurance. No one can. As Robert Berkhofer Jr. has aptly said, "Historians do not recapture or reconstruct the past when they analyze history; they interpret it according to surviving evidence and conceptual frameworks."[25] Such being the case, one wonders what to make of Kraditor's contrasting of "three things: the mode in which reality is perceived, the resulting picture of reality, and the objective reality" (p. 3). *Objective* reality?

At another point, Kraditor recognizes the elusiveness of this conception, remarking that "anthropologists and social psychologists are right when they insist that there is no such thing as a perception of raw reality unmediated and unorganized by culture" (p. 54). (Recall that ideology, in my view, is a subset of culture.) She then proposes a "way of getting closer to reality" that "requires us to see how each party to the encounter [between ordinary workers and the radicals] did in fact judge the other to be wrong, and to understand the grounds for both parties' judgments—in other words, that both be viewed with empathy and detachment" (p. 54). No honest scholar can object to this prescription, which is reminiscent of Karl Mannheim's hope for a "general form of the total conception of ideology" in which "the object of thought becomes progressively clearer with [an] accumulation of different perspectives on it."[26]

Kraditor, however, seems to believe that one who follows such advice will become ipso facto "a historian with no ideological axe to grind" (p. 102). If by this statement she means that the historian thereby becomes cleansed of all ideological contamination, I must demur. Intellectual honesty and a sincere attempt to empathize with one's subjects—virtues that shine brightly in Kraditor's own research—certainly can enhance the veracity of one's historical scholarship, but they cannot purge all ideological elements from it. Almost inevitably, historians filter their perceptions through ideological as well as theoretical and cultural lenses. For all her scholarly excellence, Kraditor is no exception to this rule.

Withal, a Splendid Book

I hope that no one will be dissuaded from reading *The Radical Persuasion* by any of the foregoing criticism. Kraditor's book is multidimensional, and I have not mentioned many of its salient themes. I have drawn from it selectively in my pursuit of what is but one of its many lines of inquiry. It is a book to read first for pure pleasure; seldom does one encounter such a virtuoso scholarly performance—the strong and precise prose alone is worth the price of the book. Then one will want to read it again, for study and reflection. It is one of the most provocative books I have read in years. And among its intellectual treasures are important insights into the role of ideology in history and in historians.

Notes

1. Douglass C. North, *Structure and Change in Economic History* (New York: W. W. Norton, 1981), pp. 45–58; James B. Kau and Paul H. Rubin, *Congressmen, Constituents, and Contributors: Determinants of Roll Call Voting in the House of Representatives* (Boston:

Nijhoff, 1982); and Joseph P. Kalt and M. A. Zupan, "Capture and Ideology in the Economic Theory of Politics," *American Economic Review* 74 (June 1984): 279–300. From these beginnings, a large and increasingly irrelevant literature soon emerged, focused almost exclusively on the econometric analysis of whether legislative roll-call-voting data display evidence of "shirking." As this literature grew ever more technically "sophisticated," it had ever less to do with ideology, although the authors themselves were nearly all blissfully unaware of their having lost touch with the true topic. For illustrations of this development, see Empirical Studies of Ideology and Representation in American Politics, special issue edited by Kevin B. Grier, *Public Choice* 76, nos. 1–2 (1993).

2. Aileen S. Kraditor, *The Radical Persuasion, 1890–1917: Aspects of the Intellectual History and the Historiography of Three American Radical Organizations* (Baton Rouge and London: Louisiana State University Press, 1981). Hereafter cited parenthetically by page number in the text.

3. Aileen S. Kraditor, "On Curiosity: Or, the Difference Between an Ideologue and a Scholar," *Intercollegiate Review* 15 (1980): 95–99.

4. Aileen S. Kraditor, "Introduction" [to a special issue on conservatism and history], *Continuity* 4–5 (1982): 1–9.

5. Kraditor to Higgs, October 22, 1982. She emphasizes, however, that her retention of the Marxian definition is "minus Marx's connection of ideology with class interests" (Kraditor to Higgs, April 20, 1983).

6. Martin Seliger, *Ideology and Politics* (New York: Free Press, 1976), and Martin Seliger, *The Marxist Conception of Ideology: A Critical Essay* (Cambridge, Eng.: Cambridge University Press, 1977).

7. Clifford Geertz, "Ideology as a Cultural System," in *Ideology and Discontent*, edited by David E. Apter (New York: Free Press, 1964), pp. 52–64.

8. Seliger, *The Marxist Conception of Ideology*, p. 56.

9. Ibid., p. 57.

10. Ibid., p. 104.

11. Ibid., p. 103. For a penetrating general discussion of "class interests, ideology, and reality," see Seliger, *Ideology and Politics*, pp. 149–69.

12. Philip E. Converse, "The Nature of Belief Systems in Mass Publics," in *Ideology and Discontent*, ed. Apter, p. 255.

13. Richard A. Easterlin, "Economic and Social Characteristics of the Immigrants," in Richard A. Easterlin, David Ward, William S. Bernard, and Reed Ueda, *Immigration* (Cambridge, Mass.: Belknap Press of Harvard University Press, 1982), p. 25.

14. Kraditor to Higgs, April 20, 1983.

15. Chaim Perelman and L. Olbrechts-Tyteca, *The New Rhetoric: A Treatise on Argumentation* (Notre Dame, Ind.: University of Notre Dame Press, 1971), as quoted in Donald N. McCloskey, "The Rhetoric of Economics," *Journal of Economic Literature* 21 (June 1983), p. 508.

16. Geertz, "Ideology as a Cultural System," pp. 59, 64.

17. Easterlin, "Economic and Social Characteristics of the Immigrants," p. 25, and U.S. Bureau of the Census, *Historical Statistics of the United States: Colonial Times to 1970* (Washington, D.C.: U.S. Government Printing Office, 1975), p. 666.

18. U.S. Bureau of the Census, *Historical Statistics,* p. 178.

19. Kraditor to Higgs, April 20, 1983.

20. Robert Higgs, *Competition and Coercion: Blacks in the American Economy, 1865–1914* (New York: Cambridge University Press, 1977).

21. George H. Nash, *The Conservative Intellectual Movement in America, since 1945* (New York: Basic Books, 1976).

22. Kraditor to Higgs, April 20, 1983.

23. "The sharing of ideas between contemporaneous ideologies is evinced in the fact that ideologies of the Right, Centre, and Left are not divided, for instance, over what brought the market economy about, its mechanism and its general social consequences, although they hold different opinions concerning the degree to which the market economy can ensure optimal production and/or a morally defensible distribution of benefits" (Seliger, *Ideology and Politics,* p. 162).

24. Geertz, "Ideology as a Cultural System," p. 63.

25. Robert F. Berkhofer Jr., *A Behavioral Approach to Historical Analysis* (New York: Free Press, 1969) , p. 23.

26. Karl Mannheim, *Ideology and Utopia: An Introduction to the Sociology of Knowledge,* translated by Louis Wirth and Edward Shils (New York: Harcourt Brace Jovanovich, n.d. [first published 1936]), p. 77. The second quotation in the sentence is from Peter L. Berger and Thomas Luckmann, *The Social Construction of Reality: A Treatise in the Sociology of Knowledge* (New York: Doubleday, 1966), p. 10.

38

On Ackerman's Justification
of Irregular Constitutional Change
Is Any Vice You Get Away With a Virtue?

What kind of argument do we find in Bruce Ackerman's book *We the People: 2. Transformations?*[1] Although the author presents a great deal of historical evidence and narrative, his primary objective is not to give an account of certain past events. The historical inquiry is merely a means to an end. Moreover, although the author pays considerable attention to questions of cause and effect, his primary objective is not to give us to a keener understanding of "how the world works." The social scientific analysis also is merely a means to an end.

We appreciate Ackerman's purpose best if we view his book as a contribution to jurisprudence or, more specifically, to the moral philosophy of constitutional law. Ackerman refers to his "central claim" that "officials have an *obligation* to follow the People" (p. 92, emphasis in original). The "entire point of this book," he declares, "is to reject [a] dichotomy between legalistic perfection and lawless force" (p. 116). He asks whether the Roosevelt revolution "should be viewed as a constitutive act of popular sovereignty that *legitimately* changed the preceding Republican Constitution" (p. 280, emphasis in original). And he plainly states, "I mean to raise a question of legitimacy" (p. 344). Thus, when the author describes his purpose, the rhetoric is unmistakably normative.

Moreover, Ackerman seeks not merely to justify a particular conception of constitutional law; he aims to instruct lawyers and judges to act in accordance with that conception. "Modern lawyers," he asserts, "are wrong.... They should follow instead ..." (p. 232). "It is about time," he writes, "for lawyers to move beyond their myopic focus on the work of the courts" (p. 252). As he proceeds, he pauses from time to time to knock down an opponent (seldom identified in person) labeled the *hypertextualist,* a lawyer or judge so unimaginative that he "treats the Founding text as the exclusive source of law" (p. 72). Ackerman aims his critical arrows especially at the hypertextualist's insistence on playing by the Article V rules for amending the U.S. Constitution. Striving to move "beyond formalism" in constitutional jurisprudence, he describes his "interdisciplinary excursions" as "in the service of a fundamentally legal enterprise.... I am focusing on a single question: If Americans of the 1990s wish to revise their Constitution, what are the *legal* alternatives they may legitimately pursue?" (p. 28, emphasis in original). Clearly, the book is intended to persuade its readers, in particular those who are constitutional lawyers and judges, to accept an unorthodox conception of what should be regarded as *legal* in changing the Constitution.

The historical inquiry plays such an expansive role in the book because Ackerman uses it to support his argument that on three previous occasions Americans broke the established rules for changing the Constitution and changed it radically, but that those de facto revolutionary changes have as much legitimacy as the amendments adopted by the formally prescribed methods. Indeed, he argues, the constitutional revolutions of the Reconstruction and New Deal eras—"paradigm cases of popular sovereignty" (p. 70)—ought to be accepted as models for "future constitutional revolutions" (p. 277).

The Proof Is in the Process?

Ackerman does not argue that any aberrant constitutional change whatsoever ought to be accepted as legitimate; only those that emerge from a certain *process*.[2] In that process, political elites interact with unusually aroused masses, especially by means of a series of campaigns for and elections to political office, long enough to justify the conclusion that ultimately the citizenry has embraced the change. "Popular sovereignty," Ackerman argues, "cannot be won in a single moment. . . . [A] rising reform movement must engage in a temporally extended process—in which it is obliged to defend its claims to speak for the People time and again in a series of escalating institutional contests for popular support" (p. 93). A new order demonstrates its constitutional legitimacy by "repeatedly winning this cycle of popular election and institutional confrontation" (p. 125). Thus, for Ackerman, constitutional legitimacy arises from a process sometimes described in other contexts as survival of the fittest.

This argument raises many questions. The most fundamental one is whether the mere political survival of irregular constitutional changes has any bearing one way or the other on their legitimacy. Ackerman appears to be arguing from an *is* to an *ought*. Therefore, his argument may amount to little more than a naturalistic fallacy written down at great length. No doubt he would deny that suggestion, maintaining that the legitimacy he affirms actually arises from a species of consent of the governed. Even if we accepted such an argument in the abstract, however, serious questions would remain.

What Do Electoral Outcomes Mean?

By appealing to electoral victories as the major feature of popular validation of irregular constitutional changes, Ackerman places more weight on ordinary political elections than they can bear. The first question, raised far too rarely by scholars, is whether the ostensible electoral outcomes are genuine in the most elementary sense. Hardly anything is more American than ballot-box stuffing. For centuries, votes have been freely added and subtracted in back rooms across the land, not least during the crisis periods that loom so large in Ackerman's story. Ackerman himself occasionally takes note of such hanky-panky, mentioning, for example, the North Carolina Federalists who had "run off with some ballot boxes" (p. 58) in 1788 and the South Carolina Federalists whose victory "was owed entirely to a gerrymander" (p. 60). He asserts that the electoral triumphs of the Reconstruction Republicans and the New Deal Democrats rest on firmer ground, but the victors in those elections also resorted to tilting the playing field.[3]

Consider, for example, how the Radical Republicans gained the "validation" of their reconstruction program after the Civil War. Most important, they placed the defeated South under military administration, even going so far as to put the army in charge of voter registration and the supervision of elections. Faced with a boycott by Southern white voters, Congress changed its own rules, passing the Fourth Reconstruction Act to repeal its earlier requirement that at least half of all registered voters cast ballots: "so long as the Republicans got a majority of the voters who braved the boycott, the Fourth Act professed itself satisfied with the new constitution's legitimacy" (p. 230). In addition, the Republicans manipulated the size of the U.S. Supreme Court, first allowing it to shrink, then enlarging it, in order to gain judicial approval of the Fourteenth Amendment and the legal tender laws.

Yet, for Ackerman, those scenes of political trickery, manipulation, intimidation, and threats of violent force inspire exhilaration: "whereas before, We the People consisted of a union of states that defined their own citizenship criteria, it now consisted of a union in which the People of the Nation imposed fundamental criteria of citizenship on the people of each state" (p. 236). His own statement of the facts, however, seems better characterized as a description of how, by hook or crook, the winners of the War of Secession imposed their desired changes on the losers. Adapting one of Al Capone's maxims, we might declare: you can accomplish more with a proposed constitutional amendment and an army than you can with just a proposed constitutional amendment. Ackerman himself observes, "Only one thing was clear: the Army's sustained support would be crucial in pushing the process despite the resistance of the established [state] governments" (p. 208). The mere fact that the bigger battalions triumphed in no way establishes the *legitimacy* of the constitutional conditions their commanders imposed. The idea that we ought to embrace the history of Reconstruction as a model for future constitutional reform boggles the mind in more than one way.

Likewise, when Ackerman considers the constitutional revolution wrought by the New Dealers, he loads too much weight on their capacity to keep winning congressional and presidential elections. "New Deal Democrats," he emphasizes, "gained the sustained consent of majorities in *all* regions of the country" (p. 269). Although he takes note of an alleged "power of 'economic royalists' to buy their way to victory in thirteen states" (p. 341), thereby foiling the ratification of a formal amendment, he seems oblivious to the operation of the New Deal itself as a vast vote-buying scheme. Whereas the "economic royalists" used their own money to buy votes, the New Dealers, true to their democratic pretensions, used the public's money. Can anyone doubt that handing out doles from the federal treasury on a wholly unprecedented scale, not to speak of the other forms of benefits dispensed, made a material contribution to the electoral success of the Democrats from 1934 through 1940? Obviously, millions of voters repaid their political benefactors at the polls time after time.[4] Does a series of electoral victories purchased in such fashion betoken constitutional *legitimacy?*

For Ackerman, federal elections present an opportunity for the voters to give or to withhold their blessing of clearly understood *constitutional* changes, regardless of the irregularities involved in effecting those changes. Elections can have this "clear meaning" (p. 289). Having cast their ballots "with such [constitutional] questions ringing in their ears" (p. 310), the voters should be seen as having given the electoral victors a "mandate" to continue to conduct the nation's governmental affairs in the new way. Ackerman speaks of "national elections to win popular mandates for fundamental change" (p. 280).

This interpretation of the nature of ordinary elections strikes me as ill founded. People cast their ballots as they do for all sorts of reasons, and sometimes for no reason whatsoever—after all, where else are individuals so utterly free of personal responsibility for their choices as they are in marking their ballots? In 1936, one man cast his vote for Roosevelt because he was grateful for his job with the Works Progress Administration; another because he liked those friendly "fireside chats"; still another because he received a check from the Treasury for—mirabile dictu—*not* growing wheat; and so on. One woman liked the president's looks; another his jovial sense of humor and the jaunty tilt of his cigarette holder; still another judged him to be more compassionate than Alf Landon; and so on. Is the aggregation of all these reasons to be understood as "validating constitutional change"?

A Metaphor Run Amok

A book about constitutional jurisprudence is aptly titled *We the People,* after the words at the beginning of the U.S. Constitution. Those words remind us that this constitution rests on the idea of popular sovereignty, the notion that the consent of those ruled constitutes the ultimate justification of the powers wielded by their rulers. So far, so good.

Unfortunately, however, Ackerman tries to make the words *We the People* serve a more critical rhetorical purpose. By using them as the subject of sentences that, in order to make empirical sense, require a more definite term, he lapses into mystification, obscuring the reality of who was doing what to whom for what purpose. Seemingly by design, he glosses over the many political differences that invariably set Americans apart from each other. Reliance on the term *We the People* leads the author toward fallacies of reification and toward the false supposition that something he calls "the national purpose" (p. 4), "the national will" (p. 348), or "the will of We the People" (p. 258) actually exists and can be revealed by political rituals such as elections and court proceedings.

Of the two major historical transformations Ackerman analyzes, we are told that during the Reconstruction Era the Radical Republicans "sought to coordinate legalistic and extralegal elements in a distinctive dynamic that ultimately allowed them to *earn* constitutional authority to speak in the name of We the People" (p. 121, emphasis in original) and that after the elections of 1940 "it was clear to ordinary Americans that the folks in Washington had finally gotten the message: We the People had endorsed the New Deal vision of activist government" (p. 359).

Does this style of writing add anything to what we know from an honest description of the raw political realities? We all agree, for example, that the Union army defeated the secessionists on the battlefield and that the postbellum Republicans managed by various means, some fair and some foul, to gain apparent approval of their formally proposed amendments to the Constitution. We all know that the Democrats won by wide margins in the congressional elections of 1932 through 1940, that FDR was elected president four times in succession, and that from 1937 onward the Supreme Court upheld the federal government's authority to engage in pervasive economic regulation previously condemned as in conflict with substantive due process. We know such facts, but what else do we learn from the declaration that these events represented the will of We the People?

Well, nothing. Worse yet, not only does the rhetorical ploy—the recurrent reference to We the People, to "earning" the authority to speak on behalf of the People, to the "constitutional creativity" of Radical Republicans and New Dealers—fail to add anything of value, but it also actually detracts from our understanding because it sanctifies the actions of those who successfully violated the established rules, which many of the violators themselves had sworn to uphold, and it pushes offstage all those who concurrently or subsequently dissented from the new constitutional regime, as if their objection deserved no notice.

To appreciate the knots in which Ackerman ties himself with his rhetoric, consider his elucidation of the Second Reconstruction Act:

the Nation was now telling the People of the Southern states how their constitutional will might validly be expressed, but it was still up to the

People in each state to make their own judgment. Reconstruction would still culminate with a writing that *took the appearance of an Article Five* "amendment," though the reality would have horrified the Federalists, who never imagined that nonconsenting states could be barred from the Congress so long as they ignored the expression of the Nation's constitutional will. (p. 204, emphasis in original)

Here is my own account. The congressional Republicans controlled the Congress and the U.S. Army, which occupied the defeated Southern states. Those Republicans required the Southern states to ratify the Fourteenth Amendment as a condition of escaping from military rule and regaining political representation in Congress. In consideration of the Republicans' military might, most of the Southern states complied, although large majorities of the Southern white people despised the necessity of doing so. That compliance signified the utility of one group's superior military power in compelling the political submission of another group. Period.

Ackerman looks back at the episode quite differently, as if it were much more than a coerced jumping through hoops. "We the People of the United States," he declares, "had somehow managed to reconstruct itself—whereas before, We the People consisted of a union of states that defined their own citizenship criteria, it now consisted of a union in which the People of the Nation imposed fundamental criteria of citizenship on the people of each state" (p. 236). He is correct to use the word *imposed* but wholly misleading to write that "the People of the Nation" did the imposing. As he later notes, "The new Republican governments of the South were now dominated by interracial coalitions that left many whites out in the cold" (p. 244). The people out in the cold evidently did not belong to We the People.

Similarly, in writing about the New Deal, Ackerman allows that 17 million people voted for Alfred Landon in 1936, yet, notwithstanding the magnitude of that dissenting group, he concludes in the same paragraph that "the People were indeed supporting a change in their governing philosophy" (p. 311). Such argumentation suggests that for Ackerman "We the People" means little more than electoral majorities, regardless of how the elections were conducted or how the majorities were elicited. In 1936, according to Ackerman, "Americans were more impressed with the urgent need for revolutionary reform" (p. 311) than with Republican condemnations of FDR and the New Deal or with Landon's defense of the old Constitution. Ackerman makes no mention, as noted, of the de facto vote buying by means of the various New Deal giveaways. Again, are we to accept that marshaling three or four successive electoral majorities gives *legitimacy* to the circumvention of long-established constitutional limitations of government? If so, why even have a constitution? Why not just decide everything by ordinary elections, inasmuch as in the end we are doing so anyhow?

Appoint Your Own High Priests, Receive Absolution

"The Constitution," many have remarked, "is what the Supreme Court says it is." Ackerman, of course, would not accept that declaration, and in a sense he actively disputes it, but if the Court's opinions are not everything, neither are they nothing. The Court's "validation" of an irregular constitutional transformation plays an important role in Ackerman's account of the process by which the new order gains consolidation and hence ultimate legitimacy. Ackerman recognizes that because so many Americans respect the Court's pronouncements on the constitutionality of statutes, any would-be constitutional revolutionaries who decide to circumvent the Article V methods will seek the Court's blessing.

In the two major episodes analyzed, the revolutionaries did indeed gain the Court's blessing in what Ackerman calls "transformative judicial opinions." Thus, in the second *Legal Tender* case and in the *Slaughterhouse* case, the Court validated important parts of the Radical Republican revolution;[5] and in the late 1930s and early 1940s, the Court's opinions "transformed *Lochner* into a symbol of an entire constitutional order that had been thoroughly repudiated by the American people." Thus, "these New Deal opinions have operated as the functional equivalent of formal constitutional amendments, providing a solid foundation for activist intervention in national social and economic life for the past sixty years" (p. 26). Certainly, practicing lawyers and judges have had to accept the new rulings and to frame their subsequent arguments and decisions in accordance with them.

With regard to the *legitimacy* of the great irregular changes of the Constitution, however, one wonders what the Supreme Court's "transformative opinions" add to the weight of the argument. For me, they add nothing. In view of the political plotting and orchestration that preceded and elicited those opinions, they merely reflect rather than magnify the legitimacy, if any exists, of the political programs they uphold. As Ackerman notes, in 1868 "Republicans in the White House and Capitol Hill took aggressive steps to pack the Supreme Court with men who would vindicate their new vision of the Union" (p. 211). For Ackerman, that "vindication" constituted the final stage of a legitimate constitutional transformation. Likewise, later, did the Court's famous 1937 "switch in time." In both cases, however, the reigning administration did everything it could to stuff the Court with justices favorably disposed toward its "transformative" vision of the Constitution. Lincoln nominated Salmon P. Chase because "we wish for a Chief Justice who will sustain what has been done" (p. 274). For exactly the same reason, FDR "restricted his nominations to public adherents of the New Deal philosophy of activist government" (p. 353).[6] Constitutional revolutionaries gain no additional legitimacy by appointing to the Court men who are committed to blessing their revolution. Such appointments represent nothing but still another attempt to "fool some of the people all of the time, all of the people some of the time." It is good politics, but, Ackerman's argument notwithstanding, the splendid cloth of constitutional legitimacy cannot be woven from such shabby political threads.

Seize and Defend the Commanding Heights

The Constitution declares itself to be and is understood by virtually all Americans to be "the supreme Law of the Land." Moreover, "the judges in every State ... [the U.S.] Senators and Representatives ... and the Members of the several State Legislatures, and all executive and judicial Officers, both of the United States and of the several States, shall be bound by Oath or Affirmation, to support this Constitution" (Article VI). No doubt Landon had this passage in mind when he spoke at the 1936 Republican convention: "Our Constitution is not a lifeless piece of paper. It is the underlying law of the land and the charter of liberties of our people. The people, and they alone, have the right to amend or destroy it. Until the people in their combined wisdom decide to make the change, it is the plain duty of the people's servants to keep within the Constitution. It is the plain meaning of the oath of office that they shall keep within the Constitution" (quoted by Ackerman, p. 307). Of those five sentences, Ackerman's argument, taken as a whole, conforms with the first three. With the fourth and fifth sentences, however, Ackerman disagrees. Moreover, he endorses a process that involves in a central way the violation of their oath of office by many public officials, most notably by the president of the United States.

For Ackerman, it has been, and it remains, legitimate for the president and other public officials, not excluding the judges, to violate their oath to support the Constitution: "For Americans, law-breaking does not necessarily imply lawlessness.... By breaking the law we will find higher law" (p. 14). Indeed, relishing presidential leadership for constitutional change à la FDR in the 1930s, Ackerman yearns for a Law Breaker in Chief. Better, he argues, to fight out the issues at the polls than to plod through the cumbersome and demanding Article V procedure every time one feels a need to amend the Constitution. "My model of modern constitutional change," he avows, "recognizes the rise of the Presidency to a plebiscitarian role, but roots this development in a larger process mediated by Congress, the Supreme Court, and ordinary Americans at the polls" (p. 381).

Arguing for such "unconventional" constitutional change, Ackerman expresses no fear that the people may stumble into an unwanted transformation of their fundamental law. He imagines that in past revolutionary episodes and again in future episodes, "the broader public was [and will be] actively engaged" (p. 324); that they endorse de facto constitutional revolutions at the polls "with their eyes open" (p. 381); that they give the revolutionaries a "decisive and sustained majority after years of mobilized debate penetrating deeply into the consciousness of ordinary citizens" (p. 29). To reiterate, this view of ordinary political elections cannot withstand critical scrutiny. If nothing else, most voters' colossal ignorance discredits it.

Perhaps the most important unacknowledged weakness of Ackerman's argument is its failure to deal with a critically important reality: those in positions of political power, however those positions are gained, possess major advantages over their opponents in elections, Supreme Court proceedings, and other political encounters. Frequently, the incumbents have gained their positions by misrepresenting themselves. When Abraham Lincoln campaigned in 1860, he did not promise to mount a military invasion of the slave states.[7] Nor in 1932 did Roosevelt give notice of the New Deal that lay in store.[8] Once in office, however, those men resorted to powerful means of achieving their political ends, most notably the U.S. Army in Lincoln's case and the U.S. Treasury in Roosevelt's.[9] Having seized the commanding heights, the Republicans of the 1860s and the New Deal Democrats of the 1930s used their powers to reshape the contours of the political landscape, greatly diminishing their opponents' ability to depose them. Ackerman appreciates how they did so, but he remains unruffled. All is well, he seems to assume, so long as elections continue to be held and the revolutionaries continue to garner the greater number of votes. If they stuff the Supreme Court with their friends, well, so much the better. After all, if We the People didn't favor the whole course of events, we would stop electing the revolutionaries.

As a depiction of how a political program gains, or ought to gain, constitutional legitimacy, this account has little to recommend it. It is hard enough for the general public to appreciate what is at stake even when the Article V procedure for amending the Constitution is followed. But in that case, at least, anyone who cares to pay attention understands that something fundamental is at issue. In contrast, the course of workaday politics, spread over a multitude of diverse matters, sends no comparable signal that a radical transformation may be occurring. Candidates make deceitful promises and befog the issues. Voters carry different models in their minds as they cast their ballots, and many vote so carelessly that their voting deserves to be characterized as sheer capriciousness. To suppose that out of the inevitable political and electoral jumble a legitimate constitutional consensus will emerge is to surrender to wishful thinking.

In sum, despite what some people might have believed in the nineteenth century, "survival of the fittest" has no moral implications. Especially in politics, an inherently nasty business, passing the test of time does not necessarily validate a claim to legitimacy. Just getting away with a vice does not make it a virtue.

Notes

1. Cambridge, Mass.: Belknap Press of Harvard University Press, 1998. Hereafter cited parenthetically by page number in the text.

2. The clearest succinct description of that process appears on pp. 187–88.

3. According to Jeffrey Rogers Hummel, if Mississippi, Texas, and Virginia had not been excluded from participation in the election, and if the other Southern states "had not been under military domination, then Grant would undoubtedly have lost the very close election" of 1868. See *Emancipating Slaves, Enslaving Free Men: A History of the American Civil War* (Chicago and La Salle, Ill.: Open Court, 1996), p. 305.

4. In the words of John T. Flynn, "Roosevelt's billions, adroitly used, had broken down every political machine in America. The patronage they once lived on and the local money they once had to disburse to help the poor was trivial compared to the vast floods of money Roosevelt controlled. And no political boss could compete with him in any county in America in the distribution of money and jobs." See *The Roosevelt Myth* (Garden City, N.Y.: Garden City Books, 1948), p. 65. Moreover, "It was always easy to interest him [FDR] in a plan which would confer some special benefit upon some special class in the population in exchange for their votes" (p. 127).

5. In *Slaughterhouse,* the validation occurred not because of *how* the Court decided the case or justified its decision, but because of the Court's mere acceptance of the Fourteenth Amendment as a valid part of the Constitution.

6. Contra Ackerman, I am not convinced that FDR's appointment of James Byrnes was an anomaly in this respect.

7. Hummel, *Emancipating Slaves;* Thomas J. DiLorenzo, "The Great Centralizer: Abraham Lincoln and the War Between the States," *The Independent Review* 3 (fall 1998): 243–71.

8. As Ackerman notes (p. 283), the Democratic platform of 1932 promised an immediate reduction in government spending of at least 25 percent, annually balanced budgets, and maintenance of a sound currency—the very antithesis of what was done once FDR became president.

9. "When Alf Landon talked about Roosevelt's invasions of the Constitution, the man on relief and the farmer fingering his subsidy check replied 'You can't eat the Constitution'" (Flynn, *The Roosevelt Myth,* p. 89).

39

The So-Called Third Way

Anthony Giddens has seen the future that doesn't work, and he recommends it.

Giddens, a distinguished sociologist and director of the London School of Economics and Political Science, is described nowadays as Tony Blair's guru or favorite intellectual. In *The Third Way: The Renewal of Social Democracy*,[1] he offers a recipe for "social democratic renewal." In so doing, he exemplifies the desperate efforts of leftish intellectuals throughout the Western world during the past decade to vindicate far-reaching interventionism, to "reinvent" the imperious managerial state, and to defend it against its Thatcherite, Reaganite, and libertarian enemies.

Get the Golden Eggs; Redistribute Them

The post–World War II interventionist state ultimately provoked strong political challenge because it could not deliver the goods. By the 1970s, the economies of the interventionist states were floundering. Runaway regulation, high taxes, monetary inflation, and, in some countries, inefficient government-owned industry were sapping economic dynamism. At the same time, the notion that centrally planned economies could outperform market-oriented economies—the "convergence hypothesis" widely accepted in the West during the 1950s and 1960s—no longer seemed compelling, despite the reluctance of many authorities, from Nobel laureate economist Paul Samuelson to the Central Intelligence Agency, to abandon it. No matter how much the intellectuals might abhor the capitalist goose, they finally had no admit that no other kind could lay golden eggs at the same high rate. As large elements of the public arrived at the same conclusion, the political success of Thatcher, Reagan, and a number of lesser pro-market politicos in the West ensued. Ultimately, even the communists in China and the Soviet Bloc gave up on central planning and moved, ever so clumsily, in search of the miracle of the market.

"No one," Giddens recognizes, "any longer has any alternatives to capitalism—the arguments that remain concern how far, and in what ways, capitalism should be governed and regulated" (pp. 43–44). He never seems to doubt, though, that however much the social democrats might govern and regulate the market economy, it will remain "capitalism," and the goose will go on laying the golden eggs without pause.

At the very beginning of his tract, Giddens expresses the characteristic melancholy and sense of loss with which the Old Leftists have reluctantly accepted the market: "Socialism and communism have passed away, yet they remain to haunt us. We cannot just put aside the values and ideals that drove them, for some remain intrinsic to the good life that it is the point of social and economic development to create. The challenge is to make these values count where the economic programme of socialism has become discredited" (pp. 1–2).

Central among those revered values, it would appear, is envy. Throughout his discussion (for example, pp. 40–42, 78, 100, 106, 108, 147), Giddens repeatedly denounces the evil of inequality and endorses the continuation of the government's redistribution of income and wealth (pp. 100–103), which he views as an essential means of arresting the "widespread disaffection and conflict" that would spring from "large-scale inequality" (p. 42). He uses the term *social justice* without placing it in quotation marks (for instance, pp. 41, 45, 65), as if it signified something coherent. Despite a reference to F. A. Hayek as "the leading advocate of free markets" and a thinker whose ideas "became a force to be reckoned with" (p. 5), Giddens seems unaware of Hayek's demolition of the concept of social justice.[2]

"We Have to Manage"

If socialism "as a system of economic management" is indisputably kaput (p. 3), why not just rely on free markets? Giddens rejects that option because neoliberalism (his name for Thatcherism/Reaganism, which he views as the only live alternative to the Third Way) "creates new risks and uncertainties which it asks citizens simply to ignore" and "neglects the social basis of markets themselves" (p. 15). "Free trade," he admits, "can be an engine of economic development, but given the socially and culturally destructive power of markets, its wider consequences need always to be scrutinized" (p. 65). For commentators endowed with the Third Way mentality, it is never acceptable simply to allow citizens to adapt their economic and social affairs to suit themselves. As Tony Blair has declared, "We have to manage that change to produce social solidarity and prosperity" (p. 1). The conceit may be fatal, but it is obviously not dead.[3] In a most anti-Hayekian declaration, Giddens asserts that "civil society is not, as some fondly imagine, a source of spontaneous order and harmony" (p. 85). Why, what if unanimous agreement failed to arise spontaneously at the local level? "Government must adjudicate" (p. 85).

Giddens affirms, correctly, that "the nation-state is not disappearing, and the scope of government, taken overall, expands rather than diminishes as globalization proceeds" (p. 32). Indeed, for those intent on presiding over a New World Order, globalization presents not so much an obstacle as an opportunity, as government must now become "more wide-ranging" (p. 32). "Globalizing processes have transferred powers away from nations and into depoliticized global space," and, sure enough, "this new space needs regulation" (p. 141). "We can't leave such [global] problems to the erratic swirl of global markets and relatively powerless international bodies" (p. 153).

For Giddens, contemporary government's agenda remains vast. He writes that "government exists to"

- provide means for the representation of diverse interests;

- offer a forum for reconciling the competing claims of these interests;

- create and protect an open public sphere, in which unconstrained debate about policy issues can be carried on;

- provide a diversity of public goods, including forms of collective security and welfare;

- regulate markets in the public interest and foster market competition where monopoly threatens;

- foster social peace through control of the means of violence and through the provision of policing;

- promote the active development of human capital through its core role in the education system;

- sustain an effective system of law;

- have a directly economic role, as a prime employer, in macro- and micro-economic intervention, plus [in] the provision of infrastructure;

- more controversially, have a civilizing aim—government reflects widely held norms and values but can also help shape them, in the education system and elsewhere;

- foster regional and transnational alliances and pursue global goals. (pp. 47–48)

Giddens aptly remarks that "the list is so formidable that to suppose that the state and government have become irrelevant makes no sense" (p. 48). Certainly that conclusion would be persuasive if one were to agree that the listed actions fit within the scope of proper government activity.

Only Government Can Do the Job

In Giddens's eyes, one has no choice: "Markets cannot replace government in any of these areas," he declares, "but neither can social movements or other kinds of non-governmental organization" (p. 48). The claim is so wildly out of touch with actuality, not to speak of potentiality, that one scarcely knows where to begin a rebuttal. Can only government provide education? Then what are all the private schools and home-schooling parents doing? Can only government provide public goods? Then what are all the private producers of, for example, scientific knowledge doing?

One chokes hardest, however, on the notion that only government can foster social peace; the idea is nearly the opposite of the truth. Aside from the scores of millions killed in wars among various governments in the past century alone, *some 169 million persons were killed by their own governments* between 1900 and 1987,[4] and since 1987 the toll has continued to mount. In the wake of this almost inconceivable carnage comes Anthony Giddens to assure us that only government can foster social peace and have a civilizing aim. In consideration of the laudatory blurbs printed on the dust jacket of his book, I cannot help recalling Robinson Jeffers's lines:

Political men pour from the barrel
New lies on the old,
And are praised for kindly wisdom.[5]

If only government can foster social peace and promote civilization, may God have mercy on our souls. Giddens remarks that "far right parties and movements would be dangerous if they did become anything more than minority concerns" (p. 52). Obviously, the socialists of various stripes—Bolsheviks, Nazis, New Dealers, Labourites, and all the rest—who have ruled the world during the past century have done a dandy job of keeping us safe and civilized. Giddens shudders to contemplate radical devolution: "a world of a thousand city-states, which some have predicted, would be unstable and dangerous" (p. 129). Compared to what? Is it conceivable that a world of piddling principalities could produce anything even remotely approaching the death and destruction wrought by the megastates of the twentieth century?

Among the many areas in which Giddens feels the need for government to provide essential protection, the environment ranks high. In this area, reliance on "market fundamentalism" would be a "highly dangerous strategy" (p. 55). Therefore, we must hasten toward "engaging with the ideas of sustainable development and ecological modernization" (pp. 55–56). On the concept of sustainable development, Giddens could profit from reading a recent essay by Jacqueline R. Kasun in which she yokes sustainable development and tyranny.[6] Although "the notion of sustainable development doesn't admit of precision" and has been defined in at least forty different ways, Giddens nevertheless recommends it as "a guiding principle" (p. 56).

A New Mixed Economy?

"While government intervention is necessary to promote sound environmental principles" (p. 57), it should be sought by means of "'a partnership in which governments, businesses, moderate environmentalists, and scientists cooperate in the restructuring of the capitalist political economy along more environmentally defensible lines'" (p. 57, quoting John Dryzek, *The Politics of the Earth*).[7] Such fascistic arrangements, which Giddens recommends in other policy areas as well (pp. 69, 79, 88, 100, 126,), usually give rise to the kind of "partnership" entered into by Little Red Riding Hood's grandmother and the wolf, but maybe Giddens already knows that they do, and he isn't worried. After all, in his view, "There are no permanent boundaries between government and civil society" (pp. 79–80). I would be remiss, however, to leave the impression that he is totally wild-eyed with regard to environmental policy. He does observe that "there is presumably a limit to the number of scares that can or should be publicly promoted" (p. 62). Perhaps some clever mainstream economist can specify a formal model from which to derive the optimal number of times that the government should cry wolf.

"Third way politics," Giddens affirms, "advocates a *new mixed economy*" (p. 99, emphasis in original). In the "old" mixed economies, markets were subordinated to the state. "The new mixed economy looks instead for a synergy between public and private sectors, utilizing the dynamism of markets but with the public interest in mind" (pp. 99–100). We have here a distinction without a difference. Rock 'n' roll aficionados, recalling The Who's song "Won't Get Fooled Again," might translate Giddens's pitch: "meet the new boss, same as the old boss." Giddens recognizes that the welfare state has run into a few problems, such as the sacrifice of liberty, but "third way politics sees these problems not as a signal to dismantle the welfare state, but as part of the reason to reconstruct it" (p. 113). In short, if hitting your thumb with a hammer has not proved satisfying, you should change hammers and continue hitting it.

The age-old dream of politicians is to starve and pluck the goose while making off with an ever larger gathering of golden eggs. As for the fluff about government's promoting the public interest, Giddens needs to take a course in public choice, or at least to review Adam Smith's *Wealth of Nations*. Governments are good at many things—for example, the surveillance of unoffending citizens at home and the bombing of hapless men, women, and children abroad—but promoting the public interest is not one of those things.

In certain respects, Giddens's modestly revamped interventionist state would be an even greater nuisance than its predecessor because the new model not only retains all the old coercive presumptuousness but links it to a politically correct insistence on butting into the most personal realms of life. "The overall aim of third way politics," writes Giddens, "should be to help citizens pilot their way through the major revolutions of our time: *globalization, transformation in personal life* and our *relationship to nature*" (p. 64, emphasis in original). "Welfare institutions must be concerned with fostering psychological as well as economic benefits.... [C]ounseling, for example, might sometimes be more helpful than direct economic support" (p. 117). Naturally, this approach promises to head off further degeneration of people's "self-esteem" (p. 120). Heaven help us. If people need a priest, they should get a priest.

The Simple Truth

Notwithstanding Anthony Giddens's best efforts to put an appealing spin on the Third Way, it remains what it has always been, an ill-disguised Second Way, a species of sugar-coated despotism that recommends itself to those who fancy that slaves can be jived into loving their masters. There can be no Third Way. Either our rulers remove their spurs from our ribs, or they don't.

Notes

1. Cambridge, Eng.: Polity Press, 1998. Hereafter cited parenthetically by page number in the text.

2. See F. A. Hayek, *Law, Legislation, and Liberty,* vol. 2, *The Mirage of Social Justice* (Chicago: University of Chicago Press, 1976).

3. My allusion is to F. A. Hayek, *The Fatal Conceit: The Errors of Socialism,* edited by W. W. Bartley III (Chicago: University of Chicago Press, 1988).

4. R. J. Rummel, *Death by Government* (New Brunswick, N.J.: Transaction, 1994), p. 4.

5. From *Cassandra* (1948), with apologies for my rearrangement of lines and capitalization.

6. Jacqueline R. Kasun, "Doomsday Every Day: Sustainable Economics, Sustainable Tyranny," *The Independent Review* 4 (summer 1999): 91–106.

7. New York: Oxford University Press, 1997.

40

Thank God for the Nation State?

Basically decent people will go along with indecent schemes if these
seem to be inevitable features of their world. To many, questioning
the need for the state seems as daft as arguing with gravity.

—Gene Callahan, "The State and Illusion"
(LewRockwell.com, July 26, 2001)

Mancur Olson, one of the most influential economists of the late twentieth
century, died suddenly in 1998, leaving behind an almost completed manu-
script of his third major work, subsequently published as *Power and Prosperity*.[1]
In that book, Olson raises important issues about the relationship between the
nation state and economic progress, but, I maintain, his treatment of those issues leaves much to be desired.

Throughout his career, Olson focused his research on the analysis of collective action, a field to which his book *The Logic of Collective Action* made a
seminal contribution.[2] In that work, he argued that individuals have no economic incentive to participate in seeking large-group collective goods unless
coerced or presented with other "selective incentives." Therefore, small groups
have an advantage in organizing and lobbying for the provision of specific collective goods, and they gain that provision at the expense of larger, unorganized
groups such as taxpayers or consumers. Successful politicking corresponds with
the now-familiar shibboleth of public-choice theory, "concentrated benefits,
dispersed costs."

In his second major work, *The Rise and Decline of Nations*, Olson argued
that with the passage of time a stable regime suffers increasingly from "sclerosis" as more and more small groups organize and lobby successfully for government actions that serve their narrow interests but diminish the efficiency and
dynamism of the overall economy.[3] Only a crisis that destroys the political
efficacy of the previously entrenched lobbies and clears the political decks can
restore the economy's vitality.

In *Power and Prosperity*, Olson concentrates his analysis on that most venerable of economic topics, the wealth of nations. He takes an emphatically

"political economy" stance, insisting that "theories of markets that leave out government—or conceptions of politics in which the economy is exogenous—are inherently limited and unbalanced. They do not tell us much about the relationships between the form of government and the fortunes of the economy or adequately explain why some societies are rich and others are poor" (pp. xxv–xxvi). As the book's subtitle indicates, Olson seeks especially to shed light on the so-called transition economies of the 1990s, but he claims that his argument, "if correct, has important implications for economic policy in advanced democracies of Europe, North America, and Japan, as well as in the countries that are or have lately been under dictatorships" (p. xxvi).

Bandits, Government, and Economic Growth

To understand the relation between government and the economy, Olson declares, "we need to find out what those in power have an incentive to do and why they obtained power" (p. 2). Thus, chapter 1 deals with "the logic of power." Eschewing the standard public-choice assumption, he insists that "the logic of power cannot be adequately explained through voluntary transactions" because power "involves compelling authority and the capacity to coerce" (pp. 2–3). Abandonment of the standard exchange-theoretic assumption yields an important explanatory payoff: "When we pass beyond the voluntary trade and its transactions costs and include the gains from the exercise of coercive power in our analyses, there is no longer any bar to explaining the bad as well as the good things that governments do" (p. 61).

Government, in Olson's view, is best understood if we begin by likening it to a protection racket, a "stationary bandit." Such a predator has a direct interest in the well-being of those on whom he preys: "other things being equal, the better the community is as an environment for business and for living, the more the protection racket will bring in" (p. 5). Hence, up to a point, the stationary bandit will protect his prey from outside aggression, invest in public goods that enhance their productivity, and restrict his takings to a fairly predictable, tolerable tax. If governing power is not concentrated in a single bandit but dispersed among persons or groups, then those with the more encompassing interest in the economy's well-being will have a greater incentive to refrain from the kind of predation carried out by the "roving bandit," who snatches and runs without a thought for the morrow.

Expectations about future predation play a critical part in Olson's analysis because they determine whether people will choose to accumulate capital and thereby bring about economic growth. Obviously, if a government's promise to protect capital and its returns is not credible, then no one will forgo current consumption in order to invest. Notably, "the promises of an autocrat are never completely credible" (p. 27), as demonstrated by countless confiscations, repudiated loans, debased currencies, and other autocratic outrages over the centuries, but even if a particular autocrat were trusted to keep his promises, his successors might not be so reliable. In autocratic regimes, crises attend the succession of power, and "capital often flees from countries with continuing or episodic dictatorships" (p. 42). Thus, Olson argues, autocracy and economic progress tend to be incompatible. Historically, sustained economic growth had to await the emergence of a system of government he calls "democracy" (an unfortunate choice of words: better to have called it limited, representative government).

That emergence required the simultaneous satisfaction of three conditions: a dispersion and balance of power among various leaders, groups, or families; a geographical mingling of those powerful parties so that the formation of segregated "miniautocracies" was infeasible; and an absence of conquest by outsiders while democracy was developing within a given society. Under these conditions, the various powerful domestic parties, each incapable of overcoming the others, had an incentive to develop formal power-sharing institutions for the maintenance of peace and the provision of public goods, including a legal system to define and protect property rights, enforce contracts, and resolve disputes impartially. A society that currently lacks such conditions, however, cannot look to Olson for a recipe to create them because in his view the previous realizations of the requisite conditions were simply fortunate "accidents of history" (p. 31).

"Voluntary Collective Action Must Fail in Large Groups"

The middle part of *Power and Prosperity* contains a discussion of transaction costs, bargaining, and anarchy (to which I return later) and a reprise of subjects treated at greater length in Olson's previous books and now familiar to all who have dipped their toes into the literature on collective action. Here, as elsewhere in his writings, Olson adopts a model of purely instrumental action to explain the choice between participating (cost bearing) in collective action and free riding. Relying on this model, he concludes in a section headed "Voluntary Collective Action *Must* Fail in Large Groups": "Since many groups are large and have no opportunity to obtain selective incentives, they can *never* act in their collective interests" (pp. 77, 88, emphasis added).

This deduction stands only as long as one clings to the representation of the action in question as purely instrumental; it collapses once one admits that individuals may act in pursuit of expressive interests, such as the identity-related goals inherent in ideologically impelled action.[4] Aside from such theoretical problems, one might also note that Olson serenely disregards the many instances of large-group collective action that have occurred even in the absence of Olsonian selective incentives—for example, the mass demonstrations against the communist regimes of eastern Europe in 1989. (Olson's understanding of ideology was always blunt edged—see, for example, his remarks on pages 112 and 130. For the most part, he simply ignored the issue.)

Olson also includes a short chapter on law enforcement and corruption, in which he reaches the stock conclusion that "legislation or regulation that is *market contrary* must leave all or almost all parties with the incentive to evade the law, and it is likely to promote criminality and corruption in government" (p. 107, emphasis in original). He appears to believe that in peaceful, orderly, rights-respecting societies, it is the government that creates those auspicious conditions (p. 106)—a largely erroneous belief, in my judgment.

Why Centrally Planned Economies Fail

Whereas Olson's midvolume discussions merely lack freshness, his chapters "The Theory of Soviet-Type Autocracies" and "The Evolution of Communism and Its Legacy" are astonishingly ill informed. Though dealing with a topic to which members of the Austrian School have made all the fundamental contributions, Olson never mentions Ludwig von Mises, F. A. Hayek, or any other Austrian economist. He treats almost as a news flash the fact that the Soviet government commanded resources not so much by explicit taxation of individual incomes as by setting the prices of inputs and outputs so that state-owned firms would generate "profits." He views with similar wonder both the well-known devices by which the Soviets made workers' marginal efforts more remunerative than the inframarginal efforts—bonuses, selective access to housing, better consumer goods, and so forth—and the similar setup in agriculture, where cooperatives had to deliver fixed quotas to the state but farmers could devote their marginal efforts to tiny individually controlled plots.

Olson treats the Soviet-type economies as if they succeeded in the short term and hence the puzzle is to explain why they "gradually deteriorated and ultimately collapsed" (p. 134). His explanation runs along the same lines laid out in his book *The Rise and Decline of Nations*. As time passes, "the difficulties of covert collective action are bound to be overcome in more and more enterprises, industries, localities, and ethnic or linguistic groups" (p. 153). "More and more small groups explicitly or tacitly agree that they will do less work, allocate more of the resources under their control to their own purposes, and share more of the state property among themselves" (p. 151). Hence, the "modicum of rationality" (p. 148) previously characteristic of the planning and administrative system breaks down, the rulers at the center lose their control over resource allocation, and eventually the state itself goes broke and is reduced to inflationary finance of its projects.

Olson's account of the deterioration of the centrally planned economy is not so much wrong as Procrustean. It adds a perspective, though hardly a new one, to one's understanding of the breakdown, but it wholly neglects more fundamental matters. In truth, the centrally planned economies were *never* economically successful, notwithstanding the fevered fears and hopes of various external commentators and propagandists. For a few decades, by forgoing almost everything else, the USSR managed to maintain a formidable military apparatus. Credit for that accomplishment belongs at least in part to the Russian people's patriotic efforts and sacrifices during the era of World War II. Information about the prices prevailing on world markets also gave the planners some guidance, allowing them to avoid setting their own prices completely at random. Nonetheless, as Olson fails to appreciate, the centrally planned economies were doomed from the start, *even if the bureaucratic and interest-group sclerosis he emphasizes had never occurred.* He does not understand that not even a perfect administration could maintain the production of genuine consumer-validated wealth, much less generate genuine economic growth, in a system lacking private-property rights and free markets. Centrally planned economies, because of their arbitrarily set prices, necessarily give rise to nothing more than what Mises called "planned chaos."

Olson claims that "economists, operations researchers, and systems analysts have long understood theoretically what would be needed for a fully efficient planned economy" (p. 136). This statement betrays a complete ignorance of the many pertinent issues Austrian economists have written about during the past eighty years. As Mises remarked, "The paradox of 'planning' is that it cannot plan, because of the absence of economic calculation [that arises from the absence of market-generated prices for the means of production]. What is called a planned economy is no economy at all. It is just a system of groping about in the dark. There is no question of a rational choice of means for the best possible attainment of the ultimate ends sought."[5]

Olson admits that "a bureaucracy cannot obtain or process all of the information needed to calculate an optimal allocation or put it into practice," but he has no appreciation that a planned economy cannot possibly *generate* the requisite information in the first place. The problem is not a practical one, it is a logical one. It is not, as Olson supposes, a matter of administrative processing of information and mutual monitoring by the bureaucrats. A centrally planned economy, by its very nature, suppresses the only means—free transactions in private-property rights—by which a movement toward an "optimal" allocation of resources might be set in motion. Olson recognizes that "firms with losses were about as likely to obtain resources as firms with profits" (p. 147), but he fails to appreciate that those so-called profits were themselves necessarily meaningless given their derivation from arbitrarily set prices of inputs and outputs. His reference to "a rational planned economy" (p. 164) speaks volumes about his ignorance of the fundamental aspects of this subject.

In his discussion of the transition from central planning, Olson makes cogent, if not very newsworthy points. Many enterprises and resources in the transition economies remain state owned. Those that have been privatized often continue to receive subsidies to keep them afloat, and influential klepto-crats preside over—and not infrequently loot—huge operations snatched dur-ing more-or-less fraudulent privatizations. In Olson's words, "the problem is the depressingly large percentage of organizations for collective action in the re-cently communist countries that have inherently inconsistent interests with economic efficiency" (p. 165). Yes, that problem exists, but it is far from the only one. Olson avers that China has performed better in making the transi-tion because during the Cultural Revolution it got rid of entrenched opponents of change. I have considerable doubts about the adequacy, and even the accu-racy, of that explanation.

Ancient Wisdom Reaffirmed

In the beginning and again in the conclusion of the book, Olson makes much of the ubiquity of markets. Even the USSR and other centrally planned econ-omies had markets in abundance—black, gray, off-white, and so on. Certain kinds of markets, however, especially those in which hard-to-hide or long-lived property is at stake, require more protective property-rights institutions for their operation. "Without such institutions, a society will not be able to reap the full benefits of a market in insurance, to produce complex goods efficiently that require the cooperation of many people over an extended period of time, or to achieve the gains from other multiparty or multiperiod arrangements. Without the right institutional environment, a country will be restricted to trades that are self-enforcing" (p. 185). And therefore the country will be poor. As Olson concludes, "Incomes are low in most of the countries of the world ... because the people in those countries do not have secure individual rights" (p. 194).

Thus, after some two hundred pages, Olson finds his way to the conclusion Adam Smith reached 228 years ago in *The Wealth of Nations* (book 5, chap. 3):

> Commerce and manufactures can seldom flourish long in any state which does not enjoy a regular administration of justice, in which the people do not feel themselves secure in the possession of their property, in which the faith of contracts is not supported by law, and in which the authority of the state is not supposed to be regularly employed in enforcing the payment of debts from all those who are able to pay. Commerce and manufactures, in short, can seldom flourish in any state in which there is not a certain degree of confidence in the justice of gov-ernment.

Or, in Olson's statement, "If a society has clear and secure individual rights, there are strong incentives to produce, invest, and engage in mutually advantageous trade, and therefore at least some economic advance" (p. 196). Even a casual inquiry into the course of events in the transition economies of eastern Europe reveals its correspondence with this ancient wisdom. In Russia, according to Roland Nash, chief economist for the Renaissance Capital investment house, "businessmen have found that there is a very large gray area of interpretation in Russian law, and that has caused a lot of problems."[6] In Romania, the worst-performing transition state, bribery of government officials has become the rule, and money-losing, state-owned firms continue to compose the bulk of the economy. Declining to seek reelection in 2000, President Emil Constantinescu said, "If we continue to break laws and if theft, crime and lies continue to proliferate, then any investments or support through international programs are in vain."[7] Where private-property rights have been more clearly established and better protected, as in Poland and the Czech Republic, the transition has proceeded more successfully.

Olson's Denseness with Respect to Anarchy

Mancur Olson was in many respects an admirable scholar. He concentrated his efforts on the analysis of important issues. He usually avoided the sort of exhibitionist pyrotechnics prized by the mainstream economics establishment. He ventured into adjacent intellectual domains and profited from what he discovered there. He wrote clear, straightforward prose, and he lectured in an instructive and delightful style. Yet, notwithstanding his scholarly virtues and contributions, there is something sad about his having arrived, after a long period of scholarship, at a set of conclusions so banal and, in certain respects, so ill-informed.

I have hinted at such deficiencies in my prior comments about Olson's views on centrally planned economies, views formulated in apparent ignorance of the most fundamental analyses of such systems. Another instance of such inadequacy appears in his comments on anarchy, which are scattered throughout *Power and Prosperity* but concentrated in chapter 3, "Coaseian Bargains, Transactions Costs, and Anarchy." This subject deserves more careful attention than it receives from Olson.

For Olson, any form of government—in his scheme, it is either "autocracy" or "democracy"—is vastly preferable to anarchy because to him anarchy is synonymous with chaos and rampant violence, a situation in which life is nasty, brutish, and otherwise "horrible" (p. 66). Anarchy, he maintains, is an "obviously inefficient outcome" (p. 60) because it "not only involves loss of life but also increases the incentives to steal and to defend against theft, and thereby reduces the incentive to produce" (p. 64). In contrast, a society under the rule of a government Olson characterizes as "a peaceful order." Of course, "governments are inherently compulsory" (p. 61), levying taxes, prescribing behavior, and waging wars, among other things. Nonetheless, "if a population acts to serve its common interest, it will never choose anarchy" (p. 65). "The gains from eliminating anarchy are so great that everyone can become better off" (pp. 89–90).

If these statements had issued from a lay person, they would be unremarkable, but coming as they do from a distinguished political economist, they strike me as facile and ill considered. Note, for example, that the world's several hundred nation states are usually at peace with one another. Moreover, the citizens of most nations routinely cooperate with the citizens of other nations, engaging in massive and complex transactions for the exchange of goods and services and for the sending and receiving of loans and investment funds. Yet the nations and their citizens who engage in these vast undertakings do so completely without the aid of what Olson declares to be the sine qua non of such transactions, "a third party with coercive power" (p. 62). If anarchy is bound to produce the horrors alleged by Hobbes, why does *international* anarchy work so successfully most of the time? Nor is this question the only one that springs to mind.

For most of the 1990s, Somalia, a country of some 7 million inhabitants, had no national government. According to a United Nations report of August 1999, "the functions that states perform, such as providing social services, regulating the movement of goods and people, controlling the environment, air space and coasts, and representing the Somali people in international bodies, are all absent."[8] Although some violence has occurred, "where it is not simple banditry, [it] is mainly defensive in nature." Notably, "approximately half of Somali territory is peaceful.... While struggles continue over control of some key southern towns, much of the day-to-day violence in Somalia is now criminal rather than political in origin,"[9] a statement that applies equally to, say, Mexico, a country blessed with plenty of government. Whatever else one might conclude about the Somali example, no one can dispute that Somalia compares favorably with many other African countries in which governments continue to exercise their power.[10]

According to the careful estimates R. J. Rummel compiles in *Death by Government*, some 169 million persons perished between 1900 and 1987 *at the hands of their own governments*, not counting the tens of millions who died in the wars their governments conducted against other states.[11] Can this ghastly experience be what Olson has in mind by a "peaceful order"? I submit that the Turkish Armenians in the mid-1910s, the peasants of the Ukraine in the early 1930s or of China in the late 1950s or of Cambodia in the late 1970s, or, needless to say, the German Jews in the early 1940s would have greeted anarchy as a godsend. The claim that the elimination of anarchy promises gains for everyone seems, if nothing else, empirically dubious. Olson never squarely faces the colossal demonstrated capacity of national governments for murder and mayhem.

Nor, Olson's assumption notwithstanding, does the operation of government relieve citizens of the need to protect their own persons and property. Even in the United States, the private provision of security ranks as a major economic activity, employing millions of persons and costing, in all its forms, countless billions of dollars annually. Why all this private effort? Because the governments with which the country is all too lavishly endowed are *not* accomplishing what Olson presumes to be their very raison d'etre. What then are they doing? Dare I suggest that they are busy plundering and menacing the very population whose rights they pretend to protect? The governments of the United States undoubtedly seize more wealth in a day than all the sneak thieves, pickpockets, con artists, and muggers in all the world have taken since the dawn of recorded time. If government is a blessing, as Olson insists, it is a manifestly mixed one.

Yet, as Adam Smith remarked, "the uniform, constant, and uninterrupted effort of every man to better his condition, the principle from which public and national, as well as private opulence is originally derived, is frequently powerful enough to maintain the natural progress of things toward improvement, in spite both of the extravagance of government, and of the greatest errors of administration" (*The Wealth of Nations,* book 2, chap. 3). What rich countries can tolerate from their governments, however, poorer countries cannot, and therefore Olson is correct to observe that "whatever the optimal role of government may be in developed nations, it is smaller in developing countries" (p. xvii). I would simply add that whatever the role of government is currently in any developed nation, its optimal role there is a much smaller one.

Notes

1. Mancur Olson, *Power and Prosperity: Outgrowing Communist and Capitalist Dictatorships* (New York: Basic Books, 2000). Hereafter cited parenthetically by page number in the text.

2. Mancur Olson, *The Logic of Collective Action: Public Goods and the Theory of Groups* (Cambridge, Mass.: Harvard University Press, 1965).

3. Mancur Olson, *The Rise and Decline of Nations: Economic Growth, Stagflation, and Social Rigidities* (New Haven, Conn.: Yale University Press, 1982).

4. On identity and ideologically motivated collective action, see Robert Higgs, *Crisis and Leviathan: Critical Episodes in the Growth of American Government* (New York: Oxford University Press, 1987), pp. 35–56.

5. Ludwig von Mises, *Human Action,* 3d rev. ed. (Chicago: Henry Regnery, 1966), pp. 700–701.

6. Jon Boyle, "Pope Case Highlights Business Risk in Russia," *Seattle Times,* December 7, 2000.

7. Quoted in Donald G. McNeil Jr., "Long-Suffering Romanians to Vote for a Leader Today," *New York Times,* November 26, 2000. See also Matthew Katnitschnig, "Romanian Vote Signals Return to the Past," *Wall Street Journal,* November 28, 2000.

8. Anthony Goodman, "'Black Hole' of Anarchy Swallows Somalia; National Government Simply Doesn't Exist," *Seattle Times,* August 19, 1999.

9. Ibid.

10. On the fascinating and much misunderstood case of Somalia, see also Peter Maass, "Ayn Rand Comes to Somalia," *Atlantic Monthly* (May 2001), at http://www.theatlantic.com/ issues/2001/05/maass.htm; Graham Green, "Somalia Customary Law," at http://economic .net/somalia/xeer.html; Abdishakur Sh. Ali Jowhar, "Aid Lords, Warlords, and the Rise of Philanocracy," *Somaliland Forum,* August 22, 2001, at http://www.somalilandforum .com/Opinions26-AidLords.htm; Michael van Notten, "From Nation-State to Stateless Nation: The Somali Experience," at http://www.liberalia.com/htm/mvn_stateless _somalis.htm; and Frank Douglas Heath, "Whither Somaliland?" at http://www.liberalia.com/ htm/mvn_whither_somali.htm.

11. New Brunswick, N.J.: Transaction, 1994, p. 4.

Index

"Bush Should Tone Down National Missile Defense" (Rose), 267n63(259)
"Bush's Budget Balance" *(Wall Street Journal),* 264n3(247)
"Bush's Grandiose Missile Defense Scheme" (Eland), 267n64(259)
Business, Government, and the Public (Weidenbaum), 193, 199n37, 200n44(195)
business interests, **311–18**; and antitrust laws, 187–88, 279, 319–35; Big Business, 311–18; and Eximbank, 118, 145–52; government skewering of, 202–3; international nature of, 272; labor and, 326–27; price-searching firms, 320–21, 322; price-taking firms, 320–21, 330; rise of, 311–18, 320–24; F. D. Roosevelt and, 185–90; T. Roosevelt and, 329, 333–34; Sherman Antitrust Act (1890), 75–76, 309, 327–29, 333; Sherman Antitrust Act vs., 327–30. *See also* industry
businessmen, 345
Businessmen and Reform (Wiebe), 325–26, 327, 337n21, 337n25
"By Prescription Only ... Or Occasionally?" (Peltzman), 73n46(67)
Byrnes, James, 360n6(357)

CAB (Conformity Assessment Body), 79
Cabinet Office, Government of Japan, 159n7(158)
Cabrera, Sigfredo A., 51n8(50)
Calfee, John E., 69n3(60)
Campbell, Colin, 7n2(3), 8n6(5)
Campbell, Noel D., 72n41(67), 82n15(78)
"Can Bill Clinton Save America" *(Seattle Times),* 56
Canada, Geoffrey, 96
Cannon, Michael F., 70n6(61)
Capital in the American Economy (Kuznets), 119, 121n16
capitalism, defining, 330, 342
Capitalism, Socialism, and Democracy (Schumpeter), 321, 336n4
capitalist class, 324–27
"Capture and Ideology in the Economic Theory of Politics" (Kalt and Zupan), 348n1(339)
Carrington, Tim, 244n17(242)
cartelization, 80, 167, 181–82, 254, 285
Carter, Jimmy, 191–92, 205
"Carter's Wage-Price Guidelines" (Higgs), 199n28(191)
Cassandra (Jeffers), 364, 366n5(364)

Catledge, Turner, 38
Cato Institute, 268n82(262)
CBS News, 266n31(252)
CE Mark, 67–68
CEA (U.S. Council of Economic Advisers): fudge factor, 121nn9–10(117); governmental expansion, 119–20; real output statistics, 222; Social Security system, 28n1(21); state and local government spending, 294n2(290); Stiglitz working at, 49–50; taxation statistics, 143nn3–4; unemployment statistics, 129n1(123), 129n3(123), 129nn4–5(124), 129n9(126). *See also* Census, U.S. Bureau of the; Management and Budget, U.S. Office of
censorship, 60, 166, 169–70, 302, 305
Censorship, Office of, 169
Census, U.S. Bureau of the: crime statistics, 88n5(85), 105n8(103); GDP, 159n6(158); incarceration statistics, 100n1(95); IRS enforcement statistics, 143nn1–2(137); labor force, 159n11(159), 350n18(346); military conscription statistics, 216n30(208); payroll taxes, 130n11(126); Progressive Era income statistics, 337n15(324); regulations, 81n2(75); statistics on inequality, 4–5, 8n5
Center for Defense Information, 265nn18–20(249–250), 266n36(253), 266n38(253), 266n42(253)
Central Pacific Railroad, 314–15
central planning, 61, 63–64
"Certificates for Europe" (TÜV Product Service), 67, 73n43
Cessna, 241
Chambers, John Whiteclay, 174n3(165), 174n16(168)
Chandler, Arthur D., Jr., 336n3(321), 336n5(322), 336n9(322), 336n10(323), 336n14(324)
Chandler, Lester V., 17n12(12), 18n16(14)
"Changing Conceptions of Constitutionalism" (Belz), 215n24(207)
charitable acts and institutions, demise of, 24–25, 28
Charles, Searle F., 17n9(12)
Charles Evans Hughes and the Supreme Court (Hendel), 216n34(209), 217n57(212), 217n61(213)
Charles Evans Hughes (Pusey), 216n37(209)
Chase, Salmon P., 357
childcare business, 279

About the Author

ROBERT HIGGS is Senior Fellow in Political Economy at The Independent Institute and Editor of the Institute's quarterly journal, *The Independent Review: A Journal of Political Economy.* He received his Ph.D. in economics from the Johns Hopkins University, and he has taught at the University of Washington, Lafayette College, and Seattle University. He has been a visiting scholar at Oxford University and Stanford University.

Dr. Higgs is the editor of three Independent Institute books, *Arms, Politics, and the Economy: Historical and Contemporary Perspectives* (1990), *Hazardous to Our Health? FDA Regulation of Health Care Products* (1995), and *Re-Thinking Green: Alternatives to Environmental Bureaucracy* (2004) and of the volume *Emergence of the Modern Political Economy* (1985). His authored books include *The Transformation of the American Economy 1865–1914: An Essay in Interpretation* (1971), *Competition and Coercion: Blacks in the American Economy, 1865–1914* (1977), and *Crisis and Leviathan: Critical Episodes in the Growth of American Government* (1987). A contributor to numerous scholarly volumes, he is the author of more than 100 articles and reviews in academic journals of economics, demography, history, and public policy.

His popular articles have appeared in the *Wall Street Journal, Los Angeles Times, Providence Journal, Chicago Tribune, San Francisco Examiner, San Francisco Chronicle, Society, Reason,* AlterNet, and many other newspapers, magazines, and Web sites, and he has appeared on NPR, NBC, ABC, C-SPAN, CBN, CNBC, PBS, America's Talking Television, Radio America Network, Radio Free Europe, Talk Radio Network, Voice of America, Newstalk TV, the Organization of American Historians' public radio program, and scores of local radio and television stations. He has also been interviewed for articles in the *New York Times, Washington Post, Al-Ahram Weekly, Terra Libera, Investor's Business Daily,* UPI, *Congressional Quarterly, Orlando Sentinel, Seattle Times, Chicago Tribune, National Journal, Reason, Washington Times,* WorldNetDaily, *Folha de São Paulo,* Newsmax, *Financial Times,* Creators Syndicate, *Insight, Christian Science Monitor,* and many other news media.

Dr. Higgs has spoken at more than 100 colleges and universities and to such professional organizations as the Economic History Association, Western Economic Association, Population Association of America, Southern Economic Association, International Economic History Congress, Public Choice Society, International Studies Association, Cliometric Society, Allied Social Sciences Association, American Political Science Association, American Historical Association, and many others.

INDEPENDENT STUDIES IN POLITICAL ECONOMY

For further information and a catalog of publications, please contact:

THE INDEPENDENT INSTITUTE

100 Swan Way, Oakland, California 94621-1428, U.S.A.

510-632-1366 • Fax 510-568-6040 • info@independent.org • www.independent.org